Deed Abstracts
Belmont County
Ohio

Volumes A, B and C
(1800-1811)

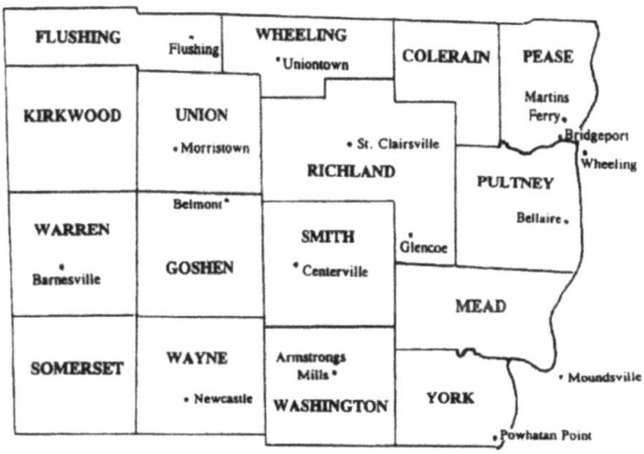

Compiled by

Lorraine Indermill Quillon

HERITAGE BOOKS
2008

HERITAGE BOOKS
AN IMPRINT OF HERITAGE BOOKS, INC.

Books, CDs, and more—Worldwide

For our listing of thousands of titles see our website
at
www.HeritageBooks.com

Published 2008 by
HERITAGE BOOKS, INC.
Publishing Division
100 Railroad Ave. #104
Westminster, Maryland 21157

Other books by the author:

Deed Abstracts, Belmont County, Ohio: Volumes D, E, and F (1811-1817)
Deed Abstracts, Belmont County, Ohio: Volume G (1817-1820)
Will Abstracts, Belmont County, Ohio: Volumes A, B, and C (1810-1827)
Will Abstracts, Belmont County, Ohio: Volumes D, E, and F (1827-1839)

International Standard Book Numbers
Paperbound: 978-1-58549-623-5
Clothbound: 978-0-7884-7161-2

TABLE OF CONTENTS

DEDICATION

To my parents,
Roy C. Indermill and Kathryn B. Kauffman Indermill,
who gave me a healthy start in life,
quietly taught me about honor,
and unwittingly provided me
a most intriguing pedigree to pursue.

❧

INTRODUCTION

This volume contains deeds recorded officially between 1801 and 1809; however, the execution dates frequently fall outside that range, especially toward the beginning of Volume A. In addition, there is an interesting smattering of other records such as marriages and wills which occasionally surprise us in these pages.

The information is given in the following general order: volume and page of the deed book on which the document appears, date of execution, grantor (and wife) and residence; grantee and residence. Amount of consideration offered, land description, history of land, neighbors, if conveyed in fee simple, date by which payments should be completed if done in installments, amount of land involved; the way the grantor(s) signed the document; names of witnesses; name of interviewer (and his office) who conducted the acknowledgment interview (and date of interview if date of document and its approximate recording date are separated by a substantial period of time [a purely subjective evaluation on the compiler's part]); recording data. Some of these elements may be missing in some deeds.

Surnames are placed in all capitals to make them easier to find on the page. Variations in recording of names within the documents are indicated with square brackets. The most frequently used spelling within the document is the one which was indexed, unless there was an unusually divergent variation. The only names omitted in the index are those of the U.S. presidents involved with the patenting of land. Please be sure to scan the entire abstract page indicated in the index in order to find any names repeated in subsequent entries on that page.

Dates are entered in standard genealogical order (day, 3-letter month, year). However, if in the original text a month was numbered rather than named (i.e., "the fourth day of the sixth month"), the entry would read as follows: "4 d 6 m" before the year. This will allow for any possibility that the archaic Quaker system of month identification might have been used. Dates recorded subsequently in the affected records may clarify the dating system used.

Belmont County is indicated by "BCO"; Jefferson County, by "JCO." Because some of the records included in these volumes were executed prior to the actual formation of the state, "NWT" will refer to North West Territory.

The letters "S T R" refer to Section, Township, and Range and will be listed with their given numbers. Although "rood" is often used in the original, it was replaced by the more conventional "rod." Although the name of the city of Steubenville was consistently spelled "Stubenville" in these volumes, it was corrected to the modern spelling.

Introduction

J.P. refers to Justice of the Peace. Court of Common Pleas is sometimes reduced to CCP.

An honest attempt has been made to report this information exactly as it appears in the original document. However, it is hoped that the reader will make allowances for human frailties on the part both of the original recorders and the compiler. Square brackets indicate uncertainty of interpretation or alternate spellings of the entry in the text as well as any additional comments or observations by the compiler. A seeming discrepancy in dates or unusual names will be underlined or marked by "[sic]" to show that these items have been rechecked and the entry appeared as recorded in the abstract.

If a researcher wishes to check the abstract against the original (an action which is highly recommended), please remember that the page number given is the page on which the record commences. Some documents are multiple pages long, so a search should be made of those subsequent pages as well in order to find the indexed names.

Incidentally, the reader will notice that Deed Book A officially lists its dates as 1801-1806. However, because some of the documents were recorded in 1800, the book title was changed to reflect these earlier documents.

Special appreciation must be mentioned here to two gentlemen who made outstanding contributions to this volume. Mr. Walter E. Kinsey (to whom I am proud to be related by blood) procured the direct copies of the plats which were so plentiful in these first three volumes. And Mr. O. John Quillon (to whom I am happily related by marriage) assisted me with the excruciatingly tedious rechecking of the index. To both of these individuals, reader and compiler alike are obliged to offer tremendous thanks.

It is earnestly hoped that researchers will find this series a useful tool for locating individuals in the Belmont County area during this time period.

Lorraine Indermill Quillon
Charlottesville, Virginia
December 2000

Deed Abstracts, Belmont County, Ohio

Volume A (Oct 1800 - Sep 1806)

p. 1 - Indenture, 20 Oct 1800, Henry LINGO (wife Rebecca, Rebekah), JCT; Robert BELL [BELE], same. $500, 100 acres, part of S 24 T 6 R 3, surveyed pursuant of an ordinance of Congress passed on 20 Mar 1785, granted to Robert JOHNSTON by patent dated 17 Apr 1780, registered in Patent Book 52, conveyed to Obediah HARDESTY on 31 Jan 17_4, conveyed by HARDESTY to LINGO by deed dated 7 Mar 1796, recorded in JCO, Book A, folio 119; both mark; WIT: David VANCE, Robert VANCE; ack. JCO, 13 Oct 1800, David VANCE, Judge, CCP.

p. 2 - Articles of agreement, 27 Oct 1801, Nelly LEMMONS, widow of George LEMMONS, dec'd, David VULGAMONT [WALGAMOTT], Isaac DEWITT [DUETT], Andrew CLARK, Thomas LEMMONS, Elizabeth LEMMONS, Susannah LEMMONS, Jude LEMMONS, John LEMMONS, Jacob LEMMONS. Nelly gives her 1/3 part of estate (50 £ Penn currency) in the hands of VULGAMONT in return for keeping her and family sustained until 3 boys reach 21 and the 2 girls reach 18, Susannah, Jude, John, and Jacob to receive 10 £ each as well as Isaac, Andrew, Thomas, and Elizabeth; all seal except for Elizabeth and Hannah who mark; WIT: Mathias NICHOLS, Moses MILLIGAN, James DALLAS; [no ack.].

p. 3 - Indenture, 29 Oct 1800, David NEWELL (wife Sally) and Benjamine NEWELL (wife Jane), JCT; James CALDWELL [COLDWELL], Ohio County, Virginia. $32, lots #28 and #53 in St. Clairsville, each 1/4 acre, fee simple; all seal; [no witnesses given]; ack. JCT, James NEWELL, J.P.

p. 4 - Indenture, 21 Jan 1801, David NEWELL (wife Sally) and Benjamine NEWELL (wife Jane), JCT; David RUSSELL [RUSSEL], Winchester, Frederick County, Virginia. $21, lot #97 in St. Clairsville, 1/4 acre, fee simple; all seal; [no witnesses given]; ack. JCT, James E. NEWELL.

p. 4 - Indenture, 21 Nov 1801, David NEWELL (wife Sally), BCT; Enoch RUSH [RUCH], Brook County, Virginia. $12, lot #157 in St. Clairsville, 1/4 acre, fee simple; both seal; WIT: Sterling JOHNSTON, Jno. ISRAEL; ack. James E. NEWELL.

p. 5 - Indenture, 24 Nov 1801, David NEWELL (wife Sally), BCT; Enoch RUSH, Brook County, Virginia. $12, lot #156 in St. Clairsville, 1/4 acre, fee simple; both seal; WIT: Sterling JOHNSTON, Jo. ISRAEL; ack. James E. NEWELL, Judge CCP.

p. 6 - Marriage of Samuel PRIER and Sarah STEPHENS, 3 Aug 1801, by David LOCKWOOD, J.P.

p. 6 - Marriage of William DANFORD and Elizabeth MORE on 19 Nov 1801, by David LOCKWOOD, J.C.P.

p. 7 - Indenture, 21 Dec 1801, David NEWELL (wife Sally); John FRANCIS, all BCT. "Dollars," lot #40 in St. Clairsville, 1/4 acre, fee simple; both seal; WIT: J. E. NEWELL, John THOMPSON; ack. J. E. NEWELL, Justice, CCP.

p. 7 - Indenture, 22 Dec 1801, David NEWELL (wife Sally), BCT; John WOODBURN, Washington County, Pennsylvania. $10, lot #85 in St. Clairsville, 1/4 acre, fee simple; both seal; WIT: J. E. NEWELL, Jeremiah MARTIN; ack. J. E. NEWELL, Judge, CCP.

p. 8 - Indenture, 28 Nov 1801, David NEWELL (wife Sally), BCT; Jacob HOLTZ, St. Clairsville, BCT. $20, lot #37 in St. Clairsville, 1/4 acre, fee simple; both seal; WIT: Philip WENDLE, Jeremiah MARTIN; ack. J. E. NEWELL, Judge, CCP.

p. 9 - Indenture, 28 Nov 1801, David NEWELL (wife Sally), BCT; Jacob HOLTS [HOLTZ, HOULTS], St. Clairsville, BCT. $28, lot #12 in St. Clairsville, 1/4 acre, fee simple; both seal; WIT: Philip WINDLE, Jeremiah MARTIN; ack. J. E. NEWELL, Judge, CCP.

p. 10 - Indenture, 28 Nov 1801, David NEWELL (wife Sally), BCT; Jacob HOULTS [HOLTZ], St. Clairsville, BCT. $32, lots #3 and #11, 1/2 acre, fee simple; both seal; WIT: Philip WENDLE, Jeremiah MARTAIN [MARTIN]; ack. J. E. NEWELL, Judge, CCP.

p. 11 - Indenture, 22 Dec 1801, David NEWELL (wife Sally), BCT; Phillip WENDLE, St. Clairsville, BCT. $15, lot #92 in St. Clairsville, 1/4 acre, fee simple; both seal; WIT: J. E. NEWELL, Jeremiah MARTIN; ack. J. E. NEWELL, Judge, CCP.

p. 12 - Indenture, 22 Dec 1801, David NEWELL (wife Sally), BCT; Phillip WINDLE, St. Clairsville, BCT. $12, lot #91 in St. Clairsville, 1/4 acre, fee simple; both seal; WIT: J. E. NEWELL, Jeremiah MARTIN; ack. J. E. NEWELL, Judge, CCP.

p. 13 - Indenture, 22 Dec 1801, David NEWELL (wife Sally), BCT; Philip WINDLE, St. Clairsville, BCT. $10, lot #99 in St. Clairsville, 1/4 acre, fee simple; both seal; WIT: J. E. NEWELL, Jeremiah MARTIN; ack. J. E. NEWELL, Judge, CCP.

p. 14 - Indenture, 22 Dec 1801, David NEWELL (wife Sally), BCT; Phillip WINDLE, St. Clairsville, BCT. $15, lot #100 in St. Clairsville, 1/4 acre, fee simple; both seal; WIT: J. E. NEWELL, Jeremiah MARTIN; WIT: J. E. NEWELL, Jeremiah MARTIN; ack. J. E. NEWELL, Judge, CCP.

p. 15 - Indenture, 19 Dec 1801, David NEWELL (wife Sally), BCT; Michael GROVE, St. Clairsville, BCT. $217, 11 acres 26 perches, NBR: Valentine [Volentine] AULT and others, fee simple; both seal; WIT: Sterling JOHNSTON, James E. NEWELL; ack. J. E. NEWELL, Judge, CCP.

p. 16 - "Know all men," Jacob LEWIS, Wheeling, Virginia, for $360 paid by John ANDREAS, same, conveys six lots in Pultney, BCT, as follows: #4 in square #9, #16 in square #30, #4 in square #16, #16 in square #31, #4 in square #34, #16 in square #34, conveyed on 16 Jun 1797 from Robert TROUT, Esqr. to LEWIS, signed 15 Oct 1801; his seal; WIT: James EVANS, John LANE, Noah LINSLY; ack. Jacob RUPSHUR, Justice, CCP.

p. 17 - Indenture, 28 Dec 1801, David NEWELL (wife Sally), BCT; Samuel HARBERT, Green County, Pennsylvania. $20, lot #113 in St. Clairsville, fee simple; both seal; WIT: Sterling JOHNSTON, Robert JOHNSTON; ack. J. E. NEWELL, Judge, CCP; lot bound for $10.50 payable by 1 Jan 1805 with interest, which was paid Jan 1805.

p. 18 - Indenture, 28 Dec 1801, David NEWELL (wife Sally), BCT; Samuel HARBERT [HERBERT], Green County, Pennsylvania. $10, lot #19 in St. Clairsville, 1/4 acre, fee simple; both seal; WIT: Sterling JOHNSTON, Robert JOHNSTON; ack. J. E. NEWELL, Judge, CCP.

p. 19 - Indenture, 3 Dec 1801, David NEWELL (wife Sally), BCT; David RUSSEL, Winchester, Frederick County, Virginia. $50, 5 acres, NBR: Peter SUNDELAND [SUNDERLAND], Michael GROVE, and others, fee simple; both seal; WIT: Sterling JOHNSTON, John THOMPSON; ack. William VANCE, Judge, CCP.

p. 20 - Indenture, 8 Jan 1802, David NEWELL (wife Sally), BCT; Nicholas STONER [STENER], St. Clairsville, BCT. $16, lot #128 in St. Clairsville, 1/4 acre, fee simple; both seal; WIT: Sterling JOHNSTON, John THOMPSON; ack. William VANCE, Judge, CCP.

p. 21 - Indenture, 8 Jan 1802, David NEWELL (wife Sally), BCT; Christian ROSE, St. Clairsville, BCT. $10, lot #143 in St. Clairsville, fee simple; both seal; WIT: Sterling JOHNSTON, John THOMPSON; ack. William VANCE, Judge, CCP.

p. 23 - Indenture, 8 Jan 1802, David NEWELL (wife Sally), BCT; Christian ROSE, St. Clairsville, BCT. $30, lot #144 in St. Clairsville, 1/4 acre, fee simple; both seal; WIT: Sterling JOHNSTON, John THOMPSON; ack. William VANCE, Judge, CCP.

p. 24 - Indenture, 8 Jan 1802, David NEWELL (wife Sally), BCT; John CLOUSE, St. Clairsville, BCT. $10, lot #122 in St. Clairsville, 1/4 acre, fee simple; both seal; WIT: Sterling JOHNSTON, John THOMPSON; ack. William VANCE, Judge, CCP.

p. 25 - Indenture, 8 Jan 1802, David NEWELL (wife Sally), BCT; John CLOUSE, St. Clairsville, BCT. $20, lot #121 in St. Clairsville, 1/4 acre, fee simple; both seal; WIT: Sterling JOHNSTON, John THOMPSON; ack. William VANCE, Judge, CCP.

p. 26 - Indenture, 8 Jan 1802, David NEWELL (wife Sally), BCT; Abraham LASH, BCT. $15, lot #153 in St. Clairsville, 1/4 acre, fee simple; both seal; WIT: Sterling JOHNSTON, John THOMPSON; ack. William VANCE, Judge, CCP.

p. 27 [p. 31 of old book] - Plat of St. Clairsville, BCT, S 4 T 7 R 4, by David NEWELL, surveyed by J. ISRAEL; ack. William VANCE, Judge, CCP; entered 8 Jan 1802. (See Appendix.)

p. 28 - Indenture, 8 Jan 1802, David NEWELL (wife Sally), BCT; Phillip WINDLE, St. Clairsville, BCT. $36, lot #67, #75, and #83 in St. Clairsville, 3/4 acre, fee simple; both sign; WIT: Sterling JOHNSTON, John THOMPSON; ack. William VANCE, Judge, CCP.

p. 29 - Indenture, 19 Jan 1802, David NEWELL (wife Sally), BCT; Michael GROVES, St. Clairsville, BCT. $46, lots #70, #78, and #86 in St. Clairsville, fee simple; both sign; WIT: Sterling JOHNSTON, J. E. NEWELL; ack. J. E. NEWELL, Judge, CCP.

p. 30 - Indenture, 17 Mar 1801, John JOHNSTON, Washington County, Pennsylvania; Andrew ANDERSON, same. $345.00 specie, beginning at SE corner of S 14 T 7 R 4, JCT, part of S granted to William DUER by patent dated 3 Mar 1789, Treasury folio #88, DUER conveyed to Stephen TILLIHOST, TILLIHOST conveyed to Nathaniel ALLCOTT, and ALLCOTT to JOHNSTON, 160 acres; his seal; WIT: John [McCAMANT], Samuel HEDGE; ack. JCT, Hugh GRIFFITH, J.P.

p. 31 - Indenture, 17 Apr 1801, David NEWELL (wife Sally), [JCT], and Benjamine NEWELL (wife Jane), JCT; Andrew MARSHALL, same. $10, lot

p. 31 - Indenture, 17 Apr 1801, David NEWELL (wife Sally), [JCT], and Benjamine NEWELL (wife Jane), JCT; Andrew MARSHALL, same. $10, lot #65 in St. Clairsville, 1/4 acre, fee simple; all seal; [no witnesses given]; ack. JCT, James E. NEWELL, J.P.

p. 32 - Indenture, 17 Apr 1801, David NEWELL (wife Sally), JCT, and Benjamine NEWELL (wife Jane), JCT; Andrew MARSHALL, same. $28, lot #36 in St. Clairsville, 1/4 acre, fee simple; all seal; WIT: J. E. NEWELL, Joseph McCONALD; ack. JCT, James E. NEWELL, J.P.

p. 32 - Indenture, 29 Jan 1801, David NEWELL (wife Sally), JCT, and Benjamine NEWELL (wife Jane), JCT; John THOMPSON, JCT. $192, lots #4 in St. Clairsville (1/4 acre) and one out lot of 10 acres N of the commons, fee simple; all seal; WIT: J. E. NEWELL; ack. JCT, James E. NEWELL, J.P.

p. 33 - Indenture, 14 May 1801, Bezeleel [Bazaleel] WELLS (wife Sally), JCT; Joseph PARRISH [PERISH], JCT. $240, land in Jefferson County on McMahan's Creek, part of S 9 T 7 R 4, NBR: Thomas TIPTON, BRYAN, James WOODS, 160 acres, originally granted to William DUER of New York City by patent dated 3 Mar 1789, recorded in Patent Book Folio 87, transferred from DUER to WELLS by deed of Indenture dated 8 Aug 1796, recorded in records of Washington County in the Territory aforesaid, Vol. 4, p. 86; both seal; [no witnesses given]; ack. Jacob MARTIN, Judge, CCP.

p. 35 - Indenture, 13 Dec 1801, John JOHNSTON, Washington County, Pennsylvania; Charles CAMPBELL, same. $1,330, S 28 T 7 R 4, S granted to John HOPKINS by patent dated 3 Mar 1789, conveyed by HOPKINS to William DUER by deed dated 5 Jun 1792, by DUER conveyed to Henry ABORN by deed dated 1 Dec 1796, by ABORN to Stephen TILLINGHOST by deed dated 10 Apr 1798, by TILLINGHOST to Nathaniel OLCOTT by deed dated 9 Dec 1799, by OLCOTT (wife Ann) to JOHNSTON by deed dated 25 Jan 1800, 640 acres; his seal; WIT: John GOODING, D. McELHERON [McELHERAN]; ack. BCT, 22 Jan 1802, D. McELHERON, Justice, BCT, certified 4 Feb 1802 by Sterling JOHNSTON, Recorder.

p. 36 - Indenture, 17 Apr 1801, David NEWELL (wife Sally), JCT, and Benjamine NEWELL (wife Jane), JCT; Joseph McCONALD, Westmoreland County, Pennsylvania. $11, lot #13 in St. Clairsville, 1/4 acre, fee simple; all seal; [no witnesses given]; ack. JCT, J. E. NEWELL, J.P., certified 12 Feb 1802 by Sterling JOHNSTON, Recorder.

p. 37 - Indenture, 1 Aug 1801, Archebald [Archibald] WOODS (wife Ann), Ohio County, Virginia; Robert WOODS, same. $2.00 per acre, S 33 T 4 R 4, JCT,

640 acres; [no witnesses given]; ack. JCT, James McMILLEN, J.P., certified 12 Feb 1802 by Sterling JOHNSTON, Recorder.

p. 38 - Indenture, 16 Feb 1801, David NEWELL (wife Sally), JCT, and Benjamine NEWELL (wife Jane), JCT; Valentine AULT, JCT. $40, lot #37 in St. Clairsville, 1/4 acre, fee simple; all seal; [no witnesses given]; ack. JCT, James E. NEWELL, Justice, certified 12 Feb 1802 by Sterling JOHNSTON, Recorder.

p. 39 - "Know all men," Robert THOUP [THROUP], Justice of U.S. in district of New York, for $14.50 paid by Anthony McCONOUGHEY, now of Ohio County, Virginia, lot #13 in square #33 in Pultney (T 2 R 2), signed 1 Nov 1799, by D. McELHERON his attorney; WIT: John GOODING, Jos. CALDWELL; ack. BCT, 9 Feb 1802, by Daniel McELHERON, Thomas THOMPSON, Esqr., Justice CCP, certified 24 Feb 1802 by Sterling JOHNSTON, Recorder.

p. 40 - "Know all men," Anthony McCONOUGHEY (wife Rebecca), Ohio County, Virginia; John LEE, now of Ohio County, Virginia. [Unspecified dollars], lot #13 in square #33 in Pultney as surveyed by Jacob LEWIS, signed 20 Feb 1802; both mark; WIT: Richd. FREEMAN, Thos. THOMPSON; ack. BCT, Thos. THOMPSON, J.P., certified 24 Feb 1802 by Sterling JOHNSTON, Recorder.

p. 41 - Marriages
Joseph FINLEY and Phebe LEWIS on 12 Jan 1802 by John FARRES, Esqr.
James WHITAKER and Elenor _____ [no surname given] on 16 Feb 1802, by John FERRES.
Asa GRIFFEY and Rebecca DILLEY on 31 Dec 1801 by David LOCKWOOD, J.C.P.
Aaron WARD and Janes KIRKBRIDGE on 20 Dec 1801 by David LOCKWOOD, J.C.P.
Peter SUNDERLAND and Mary ELY on 2 Mar 1802 by Sterling JOHNSTON.
John JAY and Mary WILLIAMS on 9 Mar 1802 by Sterling JOHNSTON.

p. 41 - Marriages (continued)
William RYAN and Sally LINGO on __ of J__ 1802 [probably January as the records haven't gotten to June yet] by William VANCE, J.C.P.

p. 41 - Condition of sale of lots in Pultney. To highest bidder, purchasers to receive certificate, payment of half purchase price in thirty days, remainder at end of year, etc.; ack. 22 Aug 1799, by Daniel McELHERON, Esqr., Sterling JOHNSTON, J.P., certified by JOHNSTON on 24 Feb 1802.

by Daniel McELHERON, sole proprietor; ack. Jacob RUPSHER, Esqr., J.P.; recorded 24 Feb 1802 by Sterling JOHNSTON.

p. 43 - Plat of Pultney. (See Appendix)

p. 44 - Plat of Pultney (continued). (See Appendix.)

p. 44 - Indenture, 20 Feb 1802, David NEWELL (wife Sally), BCT; Nicholas STENER [STENOR], St. Clairsville, BCT. $15, lot #127 in St. Clairsville, 1/2 acre, fee simple; both seal; WIT: William CONGLETON, Henry JOHNSTON; ack. 27 Feb 1802, Sterling JOHNSTON, J.P., certified 27 Feb 1802 by Sterling JOHNSTON, Recorder.

p. 45 - Indenture, 27 Feb 1802, David NEWELL (wife Sally), BCT; James BELL, Virginia. $18, lot #28 in St. Clairsville, 1/4 acre, fee simple; both seal; WIT: William CONGLETON, Henry JOHNSTON; ack. Sterling JOHNSTON, J.P., recorded 27 Feb 1802.

p. 46 - Indenture, 27 Feb 1802, David NEWELL (wife Sally), BCT; Lydia ALLES, wife of Jonathan ALLES, same. $12, lot #146 in St. Clairsville, 1/4 acre, fee simple; both seal; WIT: Wm. CONGLETON, Henry JOHNSTON; ack. Sterling JOHNSTON, J.P., recorded 27 Feb 1802.

p. 48 - Indenture, 29 Jan 1802, David NEWELL (wife Sally), BCT; Jacob HOLTS [HOLTZ], St. Clairsville, BCT. $9, lot #38 of St. Clairsville, 1/4 acre, fee simple; both seal; WIT: William CONGLETON, Henry JOHNSTON; ack. Sterling JOHNSTON, J.P.; recorded 27 Feb 1802.

p. 49 - Indenture, 19 Jan 1802, David NEWELL (wife Sally), BCT; James BRIAN, BCT. $18, lot #84 in St. Clairsville, 1/4 acre, fee simple; both seal; WIT: William CONGLETON, Henry JOHNSTON; ack. Sterling JOHNSTON, J.P.; recorded 27 Feb 1802.

p. 50 - Indenture, 28 Mar 1801, David NEWELL (wife Sally), JCT, and Benjamine NEWELL (wife Jane), JCT; Jacob DEVARER [DEVORER], BCT. $16, lot #129 in St. Clairsville, 1/4 acre, fee simple; both seal; all seal; [no witnesses given]; ack. JCT, 20 Jun 1801, James E. NEWELL, J.P.; recorded 8 Mar 1802.

p. 51 - Plat of Morristown, S 20 T 8 R 5, signed on 14 Apr 1802 by John LANE and William CHAPPLEN [CHAPLIN]. (See Appendix.)

p. 52 - Ack. 20 Apr 1802, Sterling JOHNSTON, J.P. [Here John LANE looks more like John ZANE.] Articles of agreement for purchase of lots in Morristown.

p. 53 - Indenture, 29 Apr 1802, David NEWELL (wife Sally), BCT; Christipher [Christopher] CLOUSE, Pennsylvania. $10, lot #135 in St. Clairsville, 1/4 acre, fee simple; both seal; WIT: William BROWN, Sterling JOHNSTON; ack. 20 Apr 1802, Sterling JOHNSTON, J.P.; recorded 30 Apr 1802.

p. 54 - Indenture, 1 May 1802, David NEWELL (wife Sally), Richland twp., BCT; Christopher CLOUSE, Senr., Washington County, Pennsylvania. $10, lot #136 in St. Clairsville, 1/4 acre, fee simple; both seal; WIT: Sterling JOHNSTON, Elizabeth NEWELL; ack. Sterling JOHNSTON, J.P.; recorded 1 Apr 1802.

p. 55 - Indenture, 30 Apr 1802, David NEWELL (wife Sally); James CALDWELL and Moses MOREHEAD, all BCT. $43.50, lot adjoining commons of St. Clairsville, 3 1/2 acres 25 poles, fee simple; both seal; WIT: Sterling JOHNSTON, William BROWN; ack. 13 Apr 1802, Sterling JOHNSTON, Justice CCP; recorded 30 Apr 1802.

p. 56 - Indenture, 11 Mar 1802, Stephen MILLER (by attorney George MILLER), New York City; Joseph IRWIN, BCT. $350, S 24 T 7 R 4, NBR: Hugh McCOY, George KELLER, Neal MAHON, Wm. DEBASTON, 100 acres, part of land conveyed to John HOPKINS by Samuel OSGOOD and Walter LEVINGSTON [LIVINGSTON], Commissioners of the Board of Treasury of the U.S. by instrument dated 3 Mar 1787; seal of Stephen MILLER by attorney George MILLER; WIT: Sterling JOHNSTON, Mary JOHNSTON; ack. Sterling JOHNSTON, Judge CCP; recorded 30 Apr 1802.

p. 57 - Indenture, 13 Apr 1802, David NEWELL (wife Sally), Richland twp., BCT; James WOODS, same. $12, lot #52 in St. Clairsville, 1/4 acre, fee simple; both seal; WIT: Wm. BROWN, Sterling JOHNSTON; ack. Sterling JOHNSTON, J.P.

p. 58 - Indenture, 13 Apr 1802, David NEWELL (wife Sally), Richland twp., BCT; Peggy WOODS (daughter of James WOODS), BCT. $10 paid by James for daughter Peggy, lot #5 in St. Clairsville, 1/4 acre, fee simple; WIT: Wm. BROWN, Sterling JOHNSTON; ack. Sterling JOHNSTON, J.P.; recorded 30 Apr 1802.

p. 59 - Indenture, 27 Apr 1802, David NEWELL (wife Sally), BCT; Mary NOWLS (wife of James NOWLS), BCT. $10, lot #101 in St. Clairsville, 1/4 acre, fee simple; both seal; WIT: Wm. BROWN, Sterling JOHNSTON; ack. Sterling JOHNSTON, J.P.; recorded 30 Apr 1802.

p. 60 - Indenture, 3 Mar 1802, David NEWELL (wife Sally), Richland twp., BCT; James FINLEY, St. Clairsville, BCT. $10, lot #148 in St. Clairsville, 1/4 acre, fee simple; both seal; WIT: Wm. BROWN, Sterling JOHNSTON; ack. Sterling JOHNSTON, J.P.; recorded 30 Apr 1802.

p. 61 - Indenture, 27 Apr 1802, David NEWELL (wife Sally), BCT; James FINLEY, St. Clairsville, BCT. $10, lot #147 in St. Clairsville, 1/4 acre, fee simple; both seal; WIT: Sterling JOHNSTON, Wm. BROWN; ack. Sterling JOHNSTON, J.P.; recorded 30 Apr 1802.

p. 62 - Indenture, 27 Apr 1802, David NEWELL (wife Sally), BCT; David KIRKPATRICK, St. Clairsville, BCT. $13, lot #71 in St. Clairsville, 1/4 acre, fee simple; both seal; WIT: Wm. BROWN, Sterling JOHNSTON; ack. Sterling JOHNSTON, J.P.; recorded 30 Apr 1802.

p. 63 - Indenture, 27 Apr 1802, David NEWELL (wife Sally), BCT; David KIRKPATRICK, St. Clairsville, BCT. $20, lot #72 in St. Clairsville, 1/4 acre, fee simple; both seal; WIT: Sterling JOHNSTON, Wm. BROWN; ack. Sterling JOHNSTON, J.P.; recorded 30 Apr 1802.

p. 64 - Indenture, 27 Apr 1802, David NEWELL (wife Sally), BCT; William BROWN, St. Clairsville, BCT. $20, lots #25 and #26 in St. Clairsville, each 1/4 acre, fee simple; both seal; WIT: Sterling JOHNSTON, Mary JOHNSTON; ack. Sterling JOHNSTON, J.P.; recorded 30 Apr 1802.

p. 65 - Indenture, 20 Apr 1802, David NEWELL (wife Sally), BCT; John BLY, Virginia. $16, lot #24 in St. Clairsville, 1/4 acre, fee simple; both seal; WIT: Wm. BROWN, Sterling JOHNSTON; ack. Sterling JOHNSTON, J.P.; recorded 30 Apr 1802.

p. 66 - Indenture, 27 Apr 1802, David NEWELL (wife Sally), BCT; Christopher CLOUSE, Pennsylvania. $12, lot #160 in St. Clairsville, 1/4 acre, fee simple; both seal; WIT: Wm. BROWN, Sterling JOHNSTON; ack. Sterling JOHNSTON, J.P.; recorded 30 Apr 1802.

p. 67 - Indenture, 27 Apr 1802, David NEWELL (wife Sally), BCT; Isaac IRWIN, St. Clairsville, BCT. $9, lot #107 in St. Clairsville, 1/4 acre, fee simple; both seal; WIT: Sterling JOHNSTON, Wm. BROWN; ack. Sterling JOHNSTON, J.P.; recorded 30 Apr 1802.

p. 68 - Indenture, 27 Apr 1802, David NEWELL (wife Sally), BCT; Isaac IRWIN, St. Clairsville, BCT. $10, lot #108 in St. Clairsville, 1/4 acre, fee simple; both seal; WIT: Wm. BROWN, Sterling JOHNSTON; ack. Sterling JOHNSTON, J.P.

p. 69 - Marriages

Ezekiel BOGGS and Mary TIPTON on 17 Dec 1801 by Elijah MARTIN, J.P. in Kirkwood twp.

John [NOWS] and Hetty VULGAMORE on 20 Apr 1802 by Elijah MARTIN, J.P. in Kirkwood twp.

Wm. DANFORD and Elizabeth MORE on 19 Nov 1801 by David L. WOOD, J.C.P., York twp.

Samuel [YOHS] and Elizabeth PREBBLE on 4 May 1802 by David L. WOOD, J.C.P., York twp.

Henry MORE and Susanna JULEN on 6 May 1802 by David L. WOOD, J.C.P.

Phillip WIGGINS and Pheby STEEDS on 11 Mar 1802 by David L. WOOD, J.C.P.

Isaac BATES and Catharine MORE on 17 May 1802 by David L. WOOD, J.C.P.

Isaac BAKER and Ruth PERKINS on 6 May 1802 by David L. WOOD, J.C.P.

Asa [ZANE] and Elizabeth WHITTAKER [but looks like might be WHITTAKEN] on 30 Mar 1802 by John FAIRES, Esqr., "and the two Securities taken by me in a certificate before Witness Present the Securities names to their seals." John BRYSON, Thomas MILLS.

p. 70 - Indenture, 16 Aug 1800, Absalom MARTIN of JCT; James ROBSON [ROBERTSON], JCT. $300, part of S 13 T 6 R 3, 107 acres, granted to Robert JOHNSTON by patent dated 1788 registered in Book A, Folio __ in the Treasury office, conveyed by JOHNSTON to MARTIN by deed in fee simple on 24 May 1799; his seal; WIT: David VANCE; ack. 16 Aug 1800, David VANCE, Judge, CCP; recorded 27 May 1802.

p. 71 - Indenture, 8 May 1802, David NEWELL (wife Sally), Richland twp., BCT; William IRWIN, Wheeling, Virginia. $16, lot #20 in St. Clairsville, 1/4 acre, fee simple; both seal; WIT: Sterling JOHNSTON; ack. Sterling JOHNSTON, J.P.; recorded 27 May 1802.

p. 72 - Indenture, 29 Jun 1802, David NEWELL (wife Sally), Richland twp., BCT; David TRENNEL, Cumberland County, Pennsylvania. $15, lot #133 in St. Clairsville, 1/4 acre, fee simple; both seal; WIT: Jacob NAGLE, Sterling JOHNSTON; ack. Sterling JOHNSTON, J.P.

p. 73 - Indenture, 29 Jun 1802, David NEWELL (wife Sally), Richland twp., BCT; David TRENNEL, Cumberland County, Pennsylvania. $10, lot #118 in

St. Clairsville, 1/4 acre, fee simple; both seal; WIT: Jacob NAGLE, Sterling JOHNSTON; ack. Sterling JOHNSTON, J.P.

p. 74 - [left blank by recorder Wm. FARIS]

p. 75 - Indenture, 29 Jun 1802, David NEWELL (wife Sally), Richland twp., BCT; David TRINNEL, Cumberland County, Pennsylvania. $20, lot #117 in St. Clairsville, 1/4 acre, fee simple; both seal; WIT: Jacob NAGLE, Sterling JOHNSTON; ack. Sterling JOHNSTON, J.P.

p. 76 - Indenture, 29 Apr 1802,David NEWELL (wife Sally), Richland twp., BCT; Nancy NEWELL, St. Clairsville, BCT. For divers good causes and considerations, gift lot #62 in St. Clairsville, fee simple; both seal; WIT: Jacob NAGLE, Sterling JOHNSTON; ack. Sterling JOHNSTON, J.P.

p. 77 - Indenture, 29 Jun 1802, David NEWELL (wife Sally), Richland twp., BCT; Daniel McPEEK, same. $12, lot #50 in St. Clairsville, 1/4 acre, fee simple; both seal; WIT: Jacob NAGLE, Sterling JOHNSTON; ack. Sterling JOHNSTON, J.P.

p. 78 - Indenture, 29 Jun 1802, David NEWELL (wife Sally), Richland twp., BCT; Daniel McPEEK, same. $8, lot #49 in St. Clairsville, 1/4 acre, fee simple; both seal; WIT: Jacob NAGLE, Sterling JOHNSTON; ack. Sterling JOHNSTON, J.P.

p. 79 - Indenture, 7 Jun 1802, David NEWELL (wife Sally), Richland twp., BCT; Isaac IRWIN, same. $24, lot #115 in St. Clairsville, 1/2 acre, fee simple; both seal; WIT: Jacob NAGLE, Sterling JOHNSTON; ack. Sterling JOHNSTON, J.P.

p. 80 - Indenture, 15 Dec 1801, David NEWELL (wife Sally) and Benjamine NEWELL (wife Jane), BCT; James CALDWELL, BCT. $42, lots #44, #51, and #53 in St. Clairsville, each 1/4 acre, fee simple; all seal; WIT: David KIRKPATRICK, James E. NEWELL, Sterling JOHNSTON, and Robert JOHNSTON; ack. J. E. NEWELL, Justice, CCP.

p. 81 - Indenture, 4 Mar 1802, Robert WOODS (wife Elizabeth), Ohio County, Virginia; Henry HARVY [HARVEY], Brook County, Virginia. $4 per acre, part of S 63 [probably 36] T 4 R 7, NBR: Rev. McANDERSON, 300 acres; both seal; [no witnesses given]; ack. Tho. THOMPSON, J.P.

p. 82 - 8 Jul 1801, "Know all men," Joseph ROBSON [ROBESON/ ROBISON], JCT, for $117 paid by Bazel PUMPHREY, Brook County, Virginia, sells land on NW side of St. Clairsville, 4 acres, NBR: Jacob HOLTS [HOLTZ], Robert

THOMPSON, William BOGGS, said Joseph ROBESON, void if $117 paid by 1 Jul 1802; his seal; WIT: David VANCE, William ROSS; ack. 20 Aug 1801, JCT, David VANCE, J.P.

p. 83 - Indenture, 23 Jul 1802, David NEWELL (wife Sally), Richland twp., BCT; William YOUNG, Allegheny County, Pennsylvania. $20, lot #26 in St. Clairsville, 1/4 acre, fee simple; both seal; WIT: Sterling JOHNSTON; ack. Sterling JOHNSTON, J.P.

p. 84 - Indenture, 31 Jul 1802, David NEWELL (wife Sally), Richland twp., BCT; William VANCE, Esqr., same. $15, lot #31 in St. Clairsville, 1/4 acre, fee simple; both seal; WIT: Sterling JOHNSTON, Jacob NAGLE; ack. Sterling JOHNSTON, J.P.

p. 85 - Indenture, 31 Jul 1802, David NEWELL (wife Sally), Richland twp., BCT; William VANCE, same. $16, lot #32 in St. Clairsville, 1/4 acre, fee simple; both seal; WIT: Sterling JOHNSTON, Jacob NAGLE; ack. Sterling JOHNSTON, J.P.

p. 86 - Indenture, 4 Aug 1802, David NEWELL (wife Sally), BCT; William MATHERS, same, merchant. $45, 3 adjoining lots #14, #22, and #30 in St. Clairsville, "as recorded in the office for recording deeds in and for the County of Belmont reference being thereto had will more fully and at large appear in Record Book No. 2 Range 31"; both seal; WIT: John THOMPSON, Robert JOHNSTON; ack. [not signed, but a J.P.].

p. 87 - Indenture, 31 Jul 1802, David NEWELL (wife Sally), Richland twp., BCT; John THOMPSON, same. $60, lot #81 in St. Clairsville, 1/4 acre, fee simple; both seal; WIT: Wm. MATHERS, Sterling JOHNSTON; ack. 4 Jul 1802 [probably 4 Aug], Sterling JOHNSTON, J.P.

p. 88 - Indenture, 13 Aug 1802, David NEWELL (wife Sally), Richland twp., BCT; Sally THOMPSON, wife of John THOMPSON of St. Clairsville, BCT. $10, lot #27 in St. Clairsville, 1/4 acre, fee simple; both seal; WIT: Sterling JOHNSTON, Mary JOHNSTON; ack. Sterling JOHNSTON, J.P.

p. 89 - Indenture, 13 Aug 1802, David NEWELL (wife Sally), Richland twp., BCT; Absalom MARTIN, same. $12, lot #124 in St. Clairsville, 1/4 acre, fee simple; both seal; WIT: Sterling JOHNSTON, John THOMPSON; ack. Sterling JOHNSTON, J.P.

p. 90 - Indenture, 16 Dec 1795, Henry SMITH, Ohio County, Virginia; Martin SHUEY [SHUES], Washington County, NWT. 40£ Penn's currency, part of S 35 T 1 R 2, 40 acres, NBR: Benjamine LOCKWOOD, part of 200 acres bought by SMITH of Absalom MARTIN of Washington County, NWT, remaining 160 acres sold to James SMITH (his brother) who has MARTIN's deed for the land; his seal; WIT: George STRICKER, And. WOODS, Nathan FRISH; ack. 15 Jul 1802, David LOCKWOOD, Justice, CCP.

p. 91 - "Know all men," Jacob REPSHER, Esqr., (wife Elizabeth), referees of Daniel McELHERON of Pultney, BCT, for $150 paid by Richard RILEY, BCT, lots #57 and #58 in Pultney, 5 acres each, T 2 R 2, signed 19 Aug 1802; both seal; WIT: Alex. WILLIAMSON, Isabella SMITH; ack. 19 Aug 1802, John FAIRES, J.P.

p. 92 - Indenture, 17 Aug 1802, David NEWELL (wife Sally), Richland twp., BCT; Robert GRIFFITH, St. Clairsville, BCT. $16, lot #139 in St. Clairsville, 1/2 acre, fee simple; both seal; WIT: Sterling JOHNSTON, Mary JOHNSTON; ack. Sterling JOHNSTON, J.P.

p. 93 - Indenture, 19 Aug 1802, David NEWELL (wife Sally), Richland twp., BCT; Robert GRIFFITH, St. Clairsville, BCT. $17, lots #132 and #140 in St. Clairsville, 1/2 acre, fee simple; both seal; WIT: Sterling JOHNSTON, Mary JOHNSTON; ack. Sterling JOHNSTON, J.P.

p. 94 - Indenture, 22 Aug 1802, David NEWELL (wife Sally), Richland twp., BCT; Thomas CONLEY, same. $60, 3 acres beginning at NE corner of William CONGLETON's line, fee simple; both seal; WIT: Sterling JOHNSTON, Mary JOHNSTON; ack. Sterling JOHNSTON, J.P.

p. 95 - Indenture, 23 Aug 1802, David NEWELL (wife Sally), Richland twp., BCT; Thomas THOMPSON, same. $19, lot #80 in St. Clairsville, 1/4 acre, fee simple; both seal; WIT: Sterling JOHNSTON, Mary JOHNSTON; ack. Sterling JOHNSTON, J.P.

p. 96 - Indenture, 2 Sep 1802, David NEWELL (wife Sally), Richland twp., BCT; Joseph IRWIN, same. $20, lot #57 in St. Clairsville, 1/4 acre, fee simple; both seal; WIT: Joseph POSEY, Sterling JOHNSTON; ack. Sterling JOHNSTON, J.P.; recorded 3 Sep 1802.

p. 97 - Indenture, 13 Aug 1802, John THOMPSON (wife Sally), St. Clairsville, BCT; William COGLETON [CONGLETON], same. $300, lot #81 in St. Clairsville, 1/4 acre, conveyed to THOMPSON from David NEWELL (wife Sally) on 31 Jun 1802, fee simple; both seal plus Sterling JOHNSTON; WIT: Sterling JOHNSTON, David NEWELL; ack. Sterling JOHNSTON, J.P.; recorded 3 Sep 1802.

p. 98 - Indenture, 23 Aug 1802, David NEWELL (wife Sally), Richland twp., BCT; Thomas THOMPSON, Esqr., same. $12, lot #79 in St. Clairsville, 1/4 acre, fee simple; both seal; WIT: Sterling JOHNSTON, Mary JOHNSTON; ack. Sterling JOHNSTON, J.P.; recorded 11 Sep 1802.

p. 99 - Indenture, 7 Aug 1802, David NEWELL (wife Sally), Richland twp., BCT; Elijah WOODS, Virginia. $12, lot #24 in St. Clairsville, 1/4 acre, fee simple; both seal; WIT: Sterling JOHNSTON, Mary JOHNSTON; ack. Sterling JOHNSTON, J.P.; recorded 11 Sep 1802.

p. 100 - Indenture, 17 Sep 1802, David NEWELL (wife Sally), Richland twp., BCT; Noah [LEAN] [probably ZANE], Virginia. $10, lot #68 in St. Clairsville, 1/4 acre; both seal; WIT: Sterling JOHNSTON, Mary JOHNSTON; ack. Sterling JOHNSTON, J.P.; recorded 21 Sep 1802.

p. 101 - Indenture, 11 Sep 1802, David NEWELL (wife Sally), Richland twp., BCT; Magdalin PIPER, same. $24, unspecified amount of land, NBR: James NEWELL; both seal; WIT: Sterling JOHNSTON, Mary JOHNSTON; ack. Sterling JOHNSTON, J.P.; recorded 11 Sep 1802.

p. 102 - Indenture, 16 Sep 1802, David NEWELL (wife Sally), St. Clairsville, BCT; William CONGLETON, same. $18, lot #113 in St. Clairsville; both seal; WIT: Jacob NAGLE, Sterling JOHNSTON; ack. Sterling JOHNSTON, J.P.; recorded 16 Sep 1802.

p. 103 - Indenture, 7 Aug 1802, David NEWELL (wife Sally), Richland twp., BCT; Joseph MARTIN, same. $8, lot #93 in St. Clairsville, 1/4 acre, fee simple; both seal; WIT: Sterling JOHNSTON, Robert JOHNSTON; ack. Sterling JOHNSTON, J.P.; recorded 24 Sep 1802.

p. 104 - Indenture, 7 Sep 1802, David NEWELL (wife Sally), Richland twp., BCT, and Benjamine NEWELL, Fairfield County, NWT; Joseph IRWIN, Richland twp., BCT. $12, lot #58 in St. Clairsville, 1/4 acre + 825 feet, fee simple; all seal; WIT: Robert JOHNSTON, Sterling JOHNSTON; ack. Sterling JOHNSTON, J.P.; recorded 24 Sep 1802.

p. 105 - Indenture, 23 Sep 1802, David NEWELL (wife Sally), Richland twp., BCT; William BELL, same. $18, lot #53 in St. Clairsville, 1/4 acre, fee simple; both seal; WIT: Sterling JOHNSTON, Robert JOHNSTON; ack. Sterling JOHNSTON, J.P.; recorded 24 Sep 1802.

p. 106 - Indenture, 23 Sep 1802, David NEWELL (wife Sally), Richland twp., BCT; William BELL, same. $10, lot #44 in St. Clairsville, 1/4 acre, fee simple;

both seal; WIT: Robert JOHNSTON, Sterling JOHNSTON; ack. Sterling JOHNSTON, J.P.; recorded 24 Sep 1802.

p. 107 - Indenture, 23 Sep 1802, David NEWELL (wife Sally), Richland twp., BCT; William BELL, same. $28, lot #8 in St. Clairsville, 1/4 acre, fee simple; both seal; WIT: Robert JOHNSTON, Sterling JOHNSTON; ack. [not signed]; recorded 24 Sep 1802.

p. 107 - Marriages:
Levy WILLIAMS and Hannah LEMONS on 15 Jul 1802 by Elijah MARTIN.
Joseph BARR and Elizabeth WALKER on 10 Aug 1802 by Elijah MARTIN.
Alexander [DALLAS or DALLAM] and Sarah HARDESTY on 7 Oct 1802 by Elijah MARTIN.

p. 108 - Indenture, 9 Oct 1802, David NEWELL (wife Sally), BCT; Samuel McELROY, same, hatter. $12, lot W of St. Clairsville, 1/4 acre; both seal; WIT: Sterling JOHNSTON, Mary JOHNSTON; ack. Sterling JOHNSTON, J.P.; recorded 8 Oct 1802.

p. 109 - Indenture, 6 Oct 1802, David NEWELL (wife Sally), Richland twp., BCT; William BELL, same. $10, lot #7 in St. Clairsville, 1/4 acre, fee simple; both seal; WIT: Sterling JOHNSTON, Mary JOHNSTON; ack. Sterling JOHNSTON, J.P.; recorded 9 Oct 1802.

p. 110 - Indenture, 5 Oct 1802, David NEWELL (wife Sally), Richland twp., BCT; William FROST, St. Clairsville, BCT. $15, lot #149 in St. Clairsville, 1/4 acre, fee simple; both seal; WIT: Sterling JOHNSTON, Mary JOHNSTON; ack. Sterling JOHNSTON, J.P.; recorded 9 Oct 1802.

p. 111 - Indenture, 9 Oct 1802, David NEWELL (wife Sally), Richland twp., BCT; John DUGAN, same. $30, lot on W of St. Clairsville, 1/2 acre, fee simple; both seal; WIT: Sterling JOHNSTON, Mary JOHNSTON; ack. Sterling JOHNSTON, J.P.; recorded 9 Oct 1802.

p. 112 - Indenture, 10 Oct 1802, David NEWELL (wife Sally), Richland twp., BCT; John DUGAN, same. $30, lot on W of St. Clairsville, 1/2 acre, fee simple; both seal; WIT: Sterling JOHNSTON, Mary JOHNSTON; ack. Sterling JOHNSTON, J.P.; recorded 9 Oct 1802.

p. 113 - "Know all men," John MARTIN of Baltimore revokes power of attorney previously granted to John LEE of Wheeling to sell land in S 10 T 7, signed 17 Sep 1802; his seal; WIT: Owen DORSEY; ack. Owen DORSEY, J.P., certified by Wm. GIBSON, Clerk, Baltimore County.

p. 113 - U.S. of America, for $640 conveying all but 1/3 mining rights of S 6 T 6 R 3 to Joseph HARDY, dated 3 Mar 1789, by Samuel OSGOOD and Walter LEVENGSTON [LIVINGSTON] (both seal); [no witnesses given]. Now for $640, HARDY sells to John JOHNSTON, Washington County, Pennsylvania, for $640; his seal; WIT: James M. HUGHES, A. H. VAN BOKKEIM; ack. New York, 25 Jun 1802, James M. HUGHES.

p. 114 - Indenture, 20 Aug 1802, John JOHNSTON, Washington County, Pennsylvania; Alexander LATTIMORE, BCT. $800, S 6 T 6 R 3, excepting 1/3 of all mining rights; his seal; WIT: James ALEXANDER, Elener SMITH [her mark]; ack. James ALEXANDER, J.P.; recorded 26 Oct 1802.

p. 115 - Indenture, 12 Nov 1801, Daniel McELHERON, JCT; James ROSS, Pittsburgh, Alleghany County, Pennsylvania. $800, S 14 T 2 R 3, originally granted to Richard PLATT [PLAT] by patent dated 3 Mar 1789, from PLAT to William DURR, from DURR to William BIRD, from BIRD to William HILL, from HILL to Robert TROUP, from TROUP to Daniel McELHERON; his seal; WIT: Baze WELLS, Thomas JOHNSTON; ack. JCT, 12 Nov 1801, Alexander EDIE, J.P.; recorded 29 Oct 1802.

p. 116 - Indenture, 4 Nov 1802, David NEWELL (wife Sally), St. Clairsville, BCT; William MATHERS, same. $50, lot #61 in St. Clairsville; both seal; WIT: John THOMPSON, Sterling JOHNSTON; ack. Sterling JOHNSTON, J.P.; recorded 8 Nov 1802.

p. 117 - Indenture, 29 Oct 1802, David NEWELL (wife Sally), BCT; John McCLAIN, Virginia. $26, lot on E of St. Clairsville, 1/4 acre, fee simple; both seal; WIT: John THOMPSON, Sterling JOHNSTON; ack. Sterling JOHNSTON, J.P.; recorded 8 Nov 1802.

p. 118 - Indenture, 29 Oct 1802, David NEWELL (wife Sally), Richland twp., BCT; Jacob HOULTS, same. $80, 4 1/4 acres near St. Clairsville, NBR: Joseph ROBENSON, Robert THOMPSON, Bazel ISRAEL, fee simple; both seal; WIT: John THOMPSON, Sterling JOHNSTON; ack. Sterling JOHNSTON, J.P.; recorded 8 Nov 1802.

p. 119 - Indenture, 27 Oct 1802, David NEWELL (wife Sally), Richland twp., BCT; Samuel BUCHANON, Washington County [no state mentioned, but see next entry]. $10, lot #87 in St. Clairsville, 1/4 acre; both seal; WIT: John THOMPSON, Sterling JOHNSTON; ack. Sterling JOHNSTON, J.P.; recorded 8 Nov 1802.

p. 120 - Indenture, 27 Oct 1802, David NEWELL (wife Sally), Richland twp., BCT; Samuel BUCHANON, Pennsylvania. $16, lot #88 in St. Clairsville, 1/4 acre, fee simple; both seal; WIT: John THOMPSON, Sterling JOHNSTON; ack. Sterling JOHNSTON, J.P.; recorded 8 Nov 1802.

p. 121 - Indenture, 29 Oct 1802, Josiah DILLING [DILLON] (wife Dorothy), Richland twp., BCT; Isaac HOGUE, same. $600, SE 1/4 of S 23 T 7 R 4, 160 acres, originally conveyed to John HOPKINS by patent dated 3 Mar 1789, sold by Labon BRANSON to DILLON on 7 Jan 1799, fee simple; both seal; WIT: Sterling JOHNSTON, Mary JOHNSTON; ack. Sterling JOHNSTON, J.P.; ["This ought to have been recorded sooner but it was mislaid and over look."]

p. 122 - Indenture, 28 Nov 1801, Daniel McELHERON, BCT; Alexander NELAN [NALON, NEALEN, NEALON], Fayette County, Pennsylvania. $800, S 5 T 6 R 3, granted to Richard PLATT by patent dated 3 Mar 1789, exceptions respecting mines; his seal; WIT: Noah LINSLEY, Nemeah HARRIS; ack. Thomas THOMPSON, J.P.

p. 123 - Indenture, 11 Oct 1802, David NEWELL (wife Sally), Richland twp., BCT; William GIBSON, same. $12, lot #152 in St. Clairsville, 1/4 acre, fee simple; both seal; WIT: John THOMPSON, Sterling JOHNSTON; ack. Sterling JOHNSTON, J.P.; recorded 8 Oct 1802.

p. 124 - Indenture, 27 Oct 1802, David NEWELL (wife Sally), Richland twp., BCT; William FROST, same. $30, lots #150 and 158 in St. Clairsville, 1/2 acre, fee simple; both seal; WIT: John THOMPSON, Sterling JOHNSTON; ack. Sterling JOHNSTON, J.P.; recorded 8 Nov 1802.

p. 125 - Indenture, 30 Oct 1802, David NEWELL (wife Sally), Richland twp., BCT; Robert GIFFEN, same. $30, lots #69 and #77 in St. Clairsville, 1/2 acre, fee simple; both seal; WIT: Josiah DILLON, Isaac HOGE; ack. Sterling JOHNSTON, J.P.; recorded 8 Nov 1802.

p. 126 - Indenture, 26 Aug 1794, Robert ALEXANDER and John HILLES, overseers of the poor for East Nottingham twp, Chester County; David WHERRY, same. With consent of Robert SMITH and Phillip SCOTT, J.P.'s for Chester County, bind a poor boy, Jesse MASSEY [MASSIE] for 7 years 6 months to David WHERRY (wife Ann) until Jesse is 21, "to furnish said apprentice suffi[ci]ent apparel meat drink washing & lodging during said term and likewise to teach or cause to be taught to read write and cypher and the end of said term to furnish him with two suits of apparel one whereof shall be new and a new Bible for the true performance of each part of the above covenants and engagements; seals of ALEXANDER and HILLES, mark in behalf of MASSIE; WIT: [Chester County] R. SMITH, Phillip SCOTT; ack. 28 Apr 1801, Washington County, Pennsylvania, William CLARK and Craig RITCHEE,

Esqrs. and J.P.'s, interviewed MASSEY who declared himself willing to go with WHERRY; recorded 18 Nov 1802.

p. 127 - Indenture, 6 Dec 1802, David NEWELL (wife Sally), Richland twp., BCT; Thomas HELLEMS, Washington County, Pennsylvania. $800, part of S 4 T 7 R 4, 39 acres 97 perches, fee simple; both seal; WIT: Sterling JOHNSTON, Debarah KINKED; ack. Sterling JOHNSTON, J.P.; recorded 6 Dec 1802.

p. 128 - Indenture, Indenture, 9 Dec 1802, David NEWELL (wife Sally), Richland twp., BCT; William GIBSON, same. $8, lot #151 in St. Clairsville, 1/4 acre, fee simple; both seal; WIT: Sterling JOHNSTON, William VANCE; ack. Sterling JOHNSTON, J.P.; recorded 8 Dec 1802.

p. 129 - Indenture, 20 Nov 1802, Stephen MILLER, New York City, merchant, by attorney George MILLER; Abraham ENGLE, Burlington County, New Jersey. $1,120, S 1/2 of S 27 T 7 R 4, NBR: Obediah HARDESTY, John HATCHER, 320 acres, conveyed to John HOPKINS by Samuel OSGOOD and Walter LIVINGSTON on 3 Mar 1789; his seal by attorney; WIT: Joseph VANLOW, John CARTER, Peter YARNALL; ack. Thomas THOMPSON, Justice, CCP.; recorded 17 Dec 1802.

p. 130 - Indenture, 1 Aug 1801, Absalom MARTIN (wife Catharine), JCT; William NORMAN, same. $7 per acre, part of Ss 15 and 21 (fractional) T 4 R 2, 80 acres, NBR: Joseph TILTON, John COLENS [COLLINS]; both seal [her name given as Caty]; [no witnesses given]; ack. 1 Aug 1801, JCT, James McMILLEN, J.P.; recorded 10 Dec 1802.

p. 131 - "Know all men," Jacob REPSHER (wife Elizabeth), Pultney, JCT, for $100 paid by Jacob LEWES [LEWIS], Wheeling, Virginia, conveyed lot #1 in donation square #4 in Pultney, conveyed by Daniel McELHERON on 25 Feb 1801, this instrument signed 7 Sep 1801; both seal; WIT: John CARPENTER, George MILLER; ack. 2 Feb 1802, John FAIRES, J.P.

p. 131 - "Know all men, Jacob REPSHER (wife Elizabeth), Pultney, BCT, for $65 paid by John ALEXANDER, Washington County, Pennsylvania, lot #16 in Square #33, same conveyed by Robert THROUP, New York, to Jacob LEWIS on 16 Jun 1797, signed 19 Aug 1802; both seal; WIT: David McKNIGHT, John BRYSON; ack. 25 Nov 1802, BCT, Daniel McELHERON, J.P.

p. 132 - "Know all men," Robert TROUP, Judge of the U.S. for the district of New York, for $13 paid by Jacob LEWIS of Pennsylvania, conveys lot #6, Square #32 in Pultney, signed 16 Jun 1797; his seal; WIT: Robt. MURRY, A.

WAUGHT; ack. New York, 22 Jun 1797, Johnston HOBERT, Justice, Supreme Court of Judicator of New York; recorded 12 Dec 1802.

p. 133 - "Know all men," Daniel McELHERON, Pultney, BCT, for $50 paid by Jacob LEWIS, same, conveys lot #1 in fractional Square #6 in Pultney, Wegee Bottom, signed 17 Mar 1802; his seal; WIT: Jacob REPSHER, George BARNET; ack. 7 Mar 1802, Jacob REPSHER, J.P.

p. 133 - Indenture, 28 Dec 1802, David NEWELL (wife Sally), BCT; William CONGLETON, St. Clairsville, BCT. $105, front lot #65 and back lots #98, #2, #74, and #66; both seal; [no witnesses given]; ack. Sterling JOHNSTON, J.P.; recorded 28 Dec 1802.

p. 134 - Indenture, 26 Nov 1802, John WILLIAMS (wife Elizabeth), Ohio County, Virginia; David [also Daniel?] PRIAN, Hamilton County, NWT. $500, lot 5 in first 1/4 of T 1 R 3 of tract appropriated for satisfying warrants for military service, 100 acres, bounded N lot #6, W lot #12, S lot #4, E township line, patented 9 Jun 1802; his seal, her mark; WIT: Thos. THOMPSON, Elijah WOODS; ack. Thomas THOMPSON, J.P.; recorded 11 Jan 1803.

p. 135 - Marriages

Christian CITTS and Mary YOHS on 6 Jul 1803 by David LOCKWOOD, J.C.P.

Isaac BEATS and Catharine MORE on 31 May 1802 by David LOCKWOOD, J.C.P.

BCT, York twp., David RUBLE, Esqr., advertised John HOPKINS and Sarah [FERREN] 26 Aug 1802 according to law, both of this county, and married them 10 Sep [1802]; signed by John HOPKINS and Sarah HOPKINS; WIT: William JALABY, William SPROUTS.

Richard DILLEY and Rebecca HAYWARD on 5 Oct 1802 by David LOCKWOOD, J.C.P.

Robert CANADY and Ester SUKKLES on 6 Jun 1802 by John FAIRES, Esqr.

Nicholas KITTS and Rebeckah [YAHS] on 9 Sep 1802 by David LOCKWOOD, J.C.P.

Hull and Easter PRICE on 22 Nov 1802 by Sterling JOHNSTON.

Robert WILLIS and Sarah SMITH on 21 Dec 1802, Joseph SHARP.

Jacob FISHER and Martha DILLY on 11 Dec 1803 [I suspect 1802] by David LOCKWOOD.

Seeman and Polly GODEN on __ day of __ 1803, Sterling JOHNSTON.

Johna BAILY and Sally [WOOK] on __ day of __ 1803 by Sterling JOHNSTON.

Henry JOHNSTON and Matty RUSSEL on __ day of __ 1803 by Sterling JOHNSTON.

York twp., George LEMBY and Catharine GATES, both of Belmont County, on 5 Apr 1803 by David RUBLE; WIT: Ruben PILLS, William DORTH, George BAKER.

Abraham ST. CLAIR and Margaret SHUE on 1 Mar 1803 by David LOCKWOOD, J.C.P.

p. 136 - Andrew RUSSELL, Judge, CCP, of Richland twp., BCO, deposes that on or about 2 Jul 1798 he was present and knows of Robert RUSSEL purchasing of John McROBERTS 100 acres of land, part of 339 1/2 acres in Donegall twp., Washington County, Pennsylvania at 20 shillings per acre (27.10£ in part payment, remainder payable Christmas or New Year's Day 1799), further terms of agreement given, signed 5 Feb 1803; WIT: David VANCE, J. E. NEWELL; ack. Sterling JOHNSTON, J.P.; recorded 5 Feb 1803.

p. 137 - Indenture, 3 Feb 1803, Joseph MARTIN (wife Nancy), Richland twp., BCO; George MIRES, same. $30, lot #1 in St. Clairsville, 1/4 acre, conveyed from David NEWELL (wife Sally) to MARTIN on 27 Aug 1802, fee simple; his seal, her mark; WIT: Sterling JOHNSTON, Wm. CONGLETON; ack. Sterling JOHNSTON, J.P.; recorded 5 Feb 1803.

p. 138 - Indenture, 3 Feb 1803, David NEWELL (wife Sally), Kirkwood twp., BCO; George MIRES, Richland twp., BCO. $16, lot #116 in St. Clairsville, 1/4 acre, fee simple; both seal; WIT: Sterling JOHNSTON, Joseph MARTIN; ack. Sterling JOHNSTON, J.P.

p. 139 - Indenture, 15 Oct 1802, Jacob RUPSHER, Pultney, BCT; Joseph CALDWELL, Wheeling, Ohio County, Virginia. 396£ 17 shillings and 8 pence farthing Pennsylvania currency, outlot to Pultney containing a brick yard upon which John JUIT now lives (7 acres), #59 (5 acres), lot #60 (5 acres), lots #2 and #3 in donation square #4, lot #1 in square #34-1, lot #16 in square #16, letter E (5 acres), 70 acres total; void if RUPSHER pays 400£ 8 shillings 10 pence farthing, Pennsylvania currency on or before 15 Apr 1803; his seal; WIT: Andrew WOODS, Senr., D. McELHERON; [no ack.]

p. 139 - Indenture, 14 Feb 1803, James CALDWELL, St. Clairsville, BCO; William BROWN, same. $30, lots #34 and #42 in St. Clairsville, each 1/4 acre, fee simple; his seal; WIT: William CONGLETON, Sterling JOHNSTON; ack. Sterling JOHNSTON, J.P.; recorded 14 Feb 1803.

p. 140 - Indenture, 7 Mar 1803, John CLOUSE (wife Christena), St. Clairsville, BCO; John FRYMAN, same. $20, lot #122 in St. Clairsville, 1/4 acre; his seal, her mark; WIT: Sterling JOHNSTON, Mary JOHNSTON; ack. Sterling JOHNSTON, J.P.; recorded 7 May 1803 [probably Mar].

p. 141 - Indenture, 14 Mar 1803, David NEWELL (wife Sally), BCO; James CALDWELL, BCO. $36, lots #34, #42 and #50 in St. Clairsville, each 1/4 acre, fee simple; both seal; WIT: Robert JOHNSTON, Sterling JOHNSTON; ack. Sterling JOHNSTON, J.P.; recorded 14 Mar 1803.

p. 142 - Indenture, 14 Mar 1803, David NEWELL (wife Sally), Richland twp., BCT; David KIRKPATRICK, same. $20, lots #55 and #63, 1/2 acre and 500 feet, fee simple; both seal; WIT: Sterling JOHNSTON; ack. Sterling JOHNSTON, J.P.; recorded 14 Mar 1803.

p. 143 - Indenture, 3 Feb 1803, David NEWELL (wife Sally), Richland twp., BCO; John LONG, Ohio County, Virginia. $85, lot #34 in St. Clairsville, 1/4 acre, fee simple; both seal; WIT: Sterling JOHNSTON, Joseph MARTIN; ack. of David on 3 Feb 1803, Sally on 14 Mar 1803, Sterling JOHNSTON, J.P.; recorded 15 Mar 1803.

p. 144 - Indenture, 3 Feb 1803, David NEWELL (wife Sally), Kirkwood twp., BCO; John LONG, Ohio County, Virginia. $85, lot #102 in St. Clairsville, 1/4 acre, fee simple; both seal; WIT: Sterling JOHNSTON, Joseph MARTIN; ack. of David on 3 Feb 1803, Sally on 14 Mar 1803, Sterling JOHNSTON, J.P.; recorded 14 Mar 1803.

p. 145 - Indenture, 5 Feb 1803, David NEWELL (wife Sally), Kirkwood twp., BCO; John McCLAIN, Virginia. $10, back lot E of St. Clairsville, 1/4 acre, fee simple; both seal; WIT: Jacob NAGLE, Sterling JOHNSTON; ack. Sterling JOHNSTON, J.P.; recorded 15 Mar 1803.

p. 146 - Indenture, 15 Feb 1803, David NEWELL (wife Sally), Kirkwood twp., BCO; John McCLAIN, Virginia. $12, second back lot E of St. Clairsville, 1/4 acre, fee simple; both seal; WIT: Jacob NAGLE, Sterling JOHNSTON; ack. Sterling JOHNSTON, J.P.; recorded 15 Mar 1803.

p. 147 - Indenture, 7 Jan 1803, David NEWELL (wife Sally), Kirkwood twp., BCT; Josiah HEDGE, St. Clairsville, BCT. $13, lot #45 in St. Clairsville, 1/4 acre, fee simple; both seal; WIT: Sterling JOHNSTON, John THOMPSON; ack. Sterling JOHNSTON, J.P.; recorded 15 Mar 1803.

p. 148 - Indenture, 14 Mar 1803, David NEWELL (wife Sally), BCO; Josiah HEDGE, same, merchant. $10, lot #46 in St. Clairsville, 1/4 acre; both seal; WIT: Sterling JOHNSTON; ack. Sterling JOHNSTON, J.P.; recorded 15 Mar 1803.

p. 149 - Indenture, 5 Feb 1803, Joseph FOULKE, Island of Curacoa, merchant, by his attorney Thomas STAAG [STAGG], New York City; John CLARK, State of Ohio, late Western Territory. Lease to farm land for 4 years in S 3 T 6 R 3, originally granted to Henry RUHL, $40 per year and clear and enclose 50 acres;

signed for FOULKE by Tho. STAGG and seal of CLARK; WIT: Tho. STAGG, Peter [CAUSIE], Thos. THOMPSON.

p. 150 - Indenture, 7 Sep 1802, James BELL, Ohio County, Virginia; John THOMPSON, St. Clairsville, Richland twp., BCT. $50, lot #28 in St. Clairsville, 1/4 acre, fee simple; his seal; WIT: Silas PAUL; ack. Thomas THOMPSON, J.P.; recorded 16 Mar 1803.

p. 151 - Indenture, 1 Apr 1803, Enoch RUSH (wife Marthew), Richland twp., BCO; William FROST, same. $22, lot #157 [in St. Clairsville], conveyed from David NEWELL (wife Sally) to RUSH on 4 Nov 1801, 1/4 acre, fee simple; his seal, her mark; WIT: Robert THOMPSON, Sterling JOHNSTON; ack. Sterling JOHNSTON, J.P.; recorded 1 Apr 1803.

p. 152 - Indenture, 4 Apr 1803, David NEWELL (wife Sally), BCO; Robert JOHNSTON, BCO. $200, lot near St. Clairsville, NBR: Jacob HOULTS, 5 acres, fee simple, his seal [no wife's signature]; WIT: Sterling JOHNSTON, Mary JOHNSTON; ack. Sterling JOHNSTON, J.P., recorded 4 Apr 1803.

p. 152 - Indenture, 12 Apr 1803, William YOUNG, Allegheny Co., Pennsylvania; John THOMPSON, Richland twp., BCO. $20, lot #6 in St. Clairsville, 1/4 acre, conveyed from David NEWELL (wife Sally) to YOUNG on 3 Jun 1802; his seal; WIT: Joseph SMITH, Sterling JOHNSTON; ack. Sterling JOHNSTON, J.P., recorded 12 Apr 1803.

p. 153 - Indenture, 18 Mar 1803, David KIRKPATRICK (wife Betsey), Richland twp., BCO; William COOK, same. $30, lots #55 and 63 in St. Clairsville, 1/2 acre, fee simple; his seal, her mark; WIT: Sterling JOHNSTON, Mary JOHNSTON; ack. Sterling JOHNSTON, J.P., recorded 18 Apr 1803.

p. 154 - Indenture, 18 Apr 1803, John JOHNSTON, Washington County, Pennsylvania; Rice and William BOGGS, BCO. $453, 160 acres, begin NE corner S 14 T 7 R 4, conveyed to William DUER by Samuel OSGOOD and Walter LIVINGSTON, DUER conveyed to Henry ABORN, ABORN conveyed to Stephen TILLINGHOST, TILLINGHOST to Nathaniel OLCOTT, OLCOTT (wife Ann) to John JOHNSTON, fee simple; his seal; WIT: Sterling JOHNSTON, Mary JOHNSTON; ack. Sterling JOHNSTON, J.P., recorded 18 Apr 1803.

p. 155 - Indenture, 18 Apr 1803, Absalom MARTIN (wife Emelia), Richland twp., BCO; Isaac IRWIN, same. $40, lot #124 in St. Clairsville, 1/4 acre, conveyed by David NEWELL (wife Sally) to MARTIN on 14 Aug 1802; both seal; WIT: Sterling JOHNSTON, Basil ISRAEL; ack. Sterling JOHNSTON, J.P., recorded 18 Apr 1803.

p. 157 - Indenture, 19 Apr 1803, John THOMPSON (wife Sally), St. Clairsville, BCO; Voluntine AULT, same. $40, lot #6 in St. Clairsville, conveyed from David NEWELL (wife Sally) to William YOUNG on 3 Jul 1802, YOUNG conveyed to THOMPSON on 12 Apr 1803; both seal; WIT: Sterling JOHNSTON, William BROWN; ack. Sterling JOHNSTON, J.P.; recorded 19 Apr 1803.

p. 158 - Indenture, 4 Jan 1800, David VANCE (wife Margaret), Jefferson County, NWT; James JOHNSTON, same. $330, 110 acres, part of S 5 T 7 R 4, patented to VANCE on 12 Feb 1798 as recorded in Philadelphia Patent Book A, p. 40; both seal; [no witnesses given]; ack. Jefferson County, NWT, 15 Jan 1800, James NEWELL, J.P., recorded 19 Apr 1803.

p. 158 - Indenture, 15 Apr 1803, David NEWELL (wife Sally), Kirkwood twp., BCO; Robert THOMPSON, Richland twp., BCO. $20 per acre, 29 acres, NBR: Basel ISRAEL, fee simple; his seal only; WIT: Sterling JOHNSTON, Mary JOHNSTON; ack. Sterling JOHNSTON, J.P., interviews Sally 6 May 1803, recorded 18 Apr 1803.

p. 159 - Indenture, 4 Feb 1803, David NEWELL (wife Sally), Kirkwood twp., BCO; William CONGLETON, St. Clairsville, BCO. $60, lots #104, #103, #114 and #123 (NBR: William VANCE, William BELL) in St. Clairsville, 1 acre; both seal; WIT: Sterling JOHNSTON, Josiah HEDGES; ack. Sterling JOHNSTON, J.P., recorded 30 Apr 1803.

p. 161 - Indenture, 6 May 1803, David NEWELL (wife Sally), Kirkwood twp., BCO; William COOK, Richland twp., BCO. $17, land adjoining St. Clairsville, 1 1/2 acre, 39 perches; both seal; WIT: William BROWN, William MATHERS; ack. Sterling JOHNSTON, J.P., recorded 6 May 1803.

p. 162 - Indenture, 6 May 1803, David NEWELL (wife Sally), Kirkwood twp., BCO; Mahlon SMITH, State of Virginia. $28.50, lot #29 in St. Clairsville, 1/4 acre, fee simple; both seal; WIT: William MATHERS, William COOK; ack. Sterling JOHNSTON, J.P., recorded 6 May 1803.

p. 163 - Indenture, 3 Feb 1803, David NEWELL (wife Sally), Kirkwood twp., BCO; William MATHERS, St. Clairsville, BCO. $12, lot in south side of St. Clairsville, 24 perches; both seal; WIT: Sterling JOHNSTON, Jacob NAZEL [NAGEL]; ack. 3 Feb 1803, Sterling JOHNSTON, J.P., recorded 6 May 1803.

p. 164 - Indenture, 3 Feb 1803, David NEWELL (wife Sally), Kirkwood twp., BCO; William MATHERS, St. Clairsville, BCO. $60, lot in south side of St. Clairsville, NBR: Enoch RUSH, 1 3/4 acre; both seal; WIT: Sterling

JOHNSTON, Jacob NAGLE; ack. 3 Feb 1803, Sterling JOHNSTON, J.P., recorded 6 May 1803.

p. 165 - Indenture, 3 Feb 1803, David NEWELL (wife Sally), Kirkwood twp., BCO; William MATHERS, St. Clairsville, BCO. $36, lots #126, #118, and #110, fee simple; both seal; WIT: Sterling JOHNSTON, Jacob NAZEL; ack. 3 Feb 1803, Sterling JOHNSTON, J.P., recorded 6 May 1803.

p. 166 - Indenture, 6 May 1803, David NEWELL (wife Sally), Kirkwood twp., BCO; Enoch RUSH, Richland twp., BCO. $18 per acre, 3 acres and 74 perches, NBR: William MATHERS, fee simple; both seal; WIT: William MATHERS, William COOK; ack. Sterling JOHNSTON, J.P.

p. 167 - Indenture, 5 May 1803, David NEWELL (wife Sally), Kirkwood twp., BCO; John THOMPSON, Richland twp., BCO. $20, lot #64 in St. Clairsville, 1/4 acre, fee simple; both seal; WIT: William MATHERS, William COOK; ack. Sterling JOHNSTON, J.P.

p. 168 - Indenture, 6 May 1803, David NEWELL (wife Sally), Kirkwood twp., BCO; Robert VANCE, Richland twp., BCO. $10, lot #141 in St. Clairsville, 1/4 acre, fee simple; both seal; WIT: William MATHERS, William COOK; ack. Sterling JOHNSTON, J.P., recorded 6 May 1803.

p. 169 - Indenture, 6 May 1802, David NEWELL (wife Sally), Kirkwood twp., BCO; Robert VANCE, Richland twp., BCO. $15, lot #142 in St. Clairsville, 1/4 acre, fee simple; both seal; WIT: Wm. MATHERS, William COOK; ack. 6 May 1803, Sterling JOHNSTON, J.P., recorded 6 May 1803.

p. 170 - Indenture, 6 May 1803, David NEWELL (wife Sally), Kirkwood twp., BCO; William BROWN, St. Clairsville, BCO. $25 per acre, lot near St. Clairsville, NBR: John McCLAIN, Michael GROVE, Peter SUNDERLAND, 6 1/2 acres and 16 perches, fee simple; both seal; WIT: Wm. MATHERS, William COOK; ack. Sterling JOHNSTON, J.P., recorded 6 May 1803.

p. 171 - Know all men, John LENT (wife Barbarah), town of Pultney, Belmont County, NWT; John BARNS [BARNES], same. $50, lot in Pultney, fractional square #3, lot #12 (a donation lot), signed 1 Nov 1802; his seal, her mark; WIT: Jacob LEWIS, George BARNET; ack. 26 Nov 1802, Daniel McELHERON, J.P.

p. 171 - Know all men, Phillip DOVER (wife Margaret), town of Pultney, Belmont County, NWT; Asa HEAD, State of Virginia. $50, lot in Pultney, fractional square #2, lot #20 (a donation lot), signed 1 Nov 1802; both seal; WIT: Patrick WHITE, James [HUSBARNS], ack. Daniel McELHERON.

p. 172 - Indenture, 14 May 1803, David NEWELL (wife Sally), Kirkwood twp., BCO; John WOODBURN, Washington County, Pennsylvania. $18, lot #109 in St. Clairsville, 1/4 acre, fee simple; both seal; WIT: Sterling JOHNSTON, Wm. CONGLETON; ack. Sterling JOHNSTON, J.P.; Sally's ack. 4 Sep 1803.

p. 173 - Indenture, 13 Dec 1802, Stephen MILLER, city, county and state of New York (by attorney George MILLER); Johnathon MILLER, Ohio County, Virginia. $240, S 23 T 7 R 4, NBR: George MILLER, 60 acres, part of land conveyed to John HOPKINS by Samuel OSGOOD and Walter LIVINGSTON on 3 Mar 1789; his seal by attorney; WIT: John GOODING, Phillip ROGERS; ack. Thomas THOMPSON, J.P., recorded 14 May 1803.

p. 174 - Indenture, 14 May 1803, John DUGAN (wife Hannah), Richland twp., BCO; Michael GROVE, St. Clairsville, BCO. $50, lot at west end of St. Clairsville, part of lot conveyed by David NEWELL (wife Sally) to DUGAN on 9 Oct 1802, recorded in Book A, p. 111, 1/4 acre, fee simple; both seal; WIT: Wn, CONGLETON, Bazel ISRAEL; ack. Sterling JOHNSTON, J.P.

p. 175 - Indenture, 12 May 1803, David WORLEY, BCO; Joseph WORLEY, same. $293.83 paid by Joseph for David's livestock and property [listed]; WIT: John DUNCAN and Andrew DICKSON as deposed to Sterling JOHNSTON, J.P., on 23 May 1803; relinquishment on p. 176.

p. 176 - Marriages:

Thomas HAYWOOD and Mary DILLE, 11 Oct 1802, by David LOCKWOOD, J.C.P.

James DAYLY and Delilah SMITH, 28 Dec 1802, by David RUBLE, Esq., given 29 Dec 1802.

John McVEY and Rachel ROSS, 24 Mar 1803, by David RUBLE; WIT: Jacob COLEMAN, David HART.

[partial entry] "This is to certify that Levy Ph–"

p. 176 - Joseph WORLEY returns goods purchased on p. 175, dated 26 Jan 1804, WIT: Sterling JOHNSTON, John CLARKSON, ack. Sterling JOHNSTON, J.P.

p. 176 - Indenture, 13 Oct 1802, Robert GIFFEN (wife Hetty), Richland twp., Belmont County, NWT; Michael GROVE, same. $100, lots #69 and #67 in St. Clairsville, 1/2 acre, same conveyed by David NEWELL (wife Sally) to GIFFEN recorded on p. 125 [date and lot number discrepancies double checked], fee simple; both seal; WIT: Sterling JOHNSTON; ack. Sterling JOHNSTON, J.P., ack. Hetty, 24 May 1803, recorded 24 May 1803.

p. 178 - Know all men, Daniel McELHERON, Town of Pultney, NWT; Nicholas ALLENDER, Washing [Washington?] County, Maryland. $60, lot #7 in square

#4, Town of Pultney and in the Wyee Bottom in T 2 R 2, signed 27 Oct 1802; WIT: John LEE, Andr. WOODS, Junr.; ack. 14 Jun 1803, Jacob RAPSHER.

p. 178 - Indenture, 10 Jun 1803, Daniel McELHERON, Pultney twp., BCO; Richard ALLENDER [ALENDER] and John ALLENDER [ALENDER], State of Maryland. $1,470, S 30 T 2 R 2, 245 acres, NBR: BUCHANON; his seal [D. McELHERON], WIT: James POTTS, Jacob REPSHER; ack. Jacob REPSHER, J.P., recorded 14 Jun 1803.

p. 180 - Indenture, 13 Apr 1803, James ALEXANDER, Senr., Richland twp., BCO; Thomas ALEXANDER, same. $300, 180 acres, NW corner S 31 T 4 R 2, NBR: George [BROOKLIN], Peter ALEXANDER, Robert ALEXANDER; his seal; WIT: Jacob NAGLE, James ALEXANDER; ack. 13 Apr 1803, James ALEXANDER, J.P., wife Margaret releases dower, recorded 14 Jun 1803.

p. 181 - Know all men, Daniel McELHERON, Town of Pultney, Jefferson County, NWT; Phillip DOVER, same. $16.50, lot #13 in square #32 in Pultney and Wegee bottom, T 2 R 2, signed 10 Oct 1800; WIT: Jacob REPSHER, Samuel DAY; ack. 28 Jun 1803, Sterling JOHNSTON, J.P., recorded 28 Jun 1803.

p. 181 - Know all men, John DILLE (wife Margaret), York twp., Belmont County, NWT; Phillip DOVER, Town of Pultney, Belmont County, NWT. $140, lot #14 in square #32 in Pultney, T 2 R 2, an instrument of writing to Samuel DAY, dated 9 Sep 1800, signed 9 Aug 1802; WIT: Joseph FORT, Samuel DILLE; ack. David LOCKWOOD, Assoc. Judge, recorded 28 Jun 1803.

p. 182 - Indenture, 10 Jun 1803, Richard ALENDER [ALLENDER] and John ALENDER [ALLENDER], State of Maryland; Daniel McELHERON, Pultney twp., BCO. For 5 shillings to secure payment to McELHERON of $540 with interest according to bond of same date, convey 245 acres in S 30 T 2 R 2, to be void if payment made within period of 17 months; WIT: James POTTS, Jacob REPSHER; ack. Jacob REPSHER; mortgage satisfied according to receipt signed by Daniel McELHERON and attested by Jacob DAVIS; ack. 15 Dec 1804, Sterling JOHNSTON, J.P.

p. 183 - Article of Agreement, made, canceled and agreed upon on 22 day of [month apparently omitted] 1801 between Stephen KIRKENDALL, Town of Pultney, Jefferson County, NWT; Jonas HARE, same county and territory. $55 paid in horse flesh, lot #12 in square #18 in Pultney, house 18x20 feet to be built with shingles and round logs before 1 Jun 1801; WIT: D. McELHERON, Henry CLARK; ack. McELHERON's witness of agreement, 2 Jul 1803, John FARRIS, J.P., recorded 2 Jul 1803.

p. 184 - Know all men, Daniel McELHERON, Pultney, Jefferson County, NWT; Stephen KUYKENDALL, same. $10, lot #12 in square #18 in Pultney and Wegee Bottom, T 2 R 2, signed 3 Oct 1800; his seal; WIT: Andw. WOODS, Senr.; 26 May 1801, Stephen KUYKENDALL (wife Rachel) assign rights to Thomas RICHARDS; his seal, her mark, 20 May 1803, Thomas RICHARDS assigns rights to Jonas HAIR, his seal; WIT: Sterling JOHNSTON, J. Clarence HAMILTON; ack. 2 Jul 1803, John FARRIS, J.P., recorded 2 Jul 1803.

p. 184 - Know all men, Phillip DOVER (wife Margaret), Pultney, Belmont County, NWT; Walter DENNY, State of Virginia. $140, lot #14 square #32 in Pultney and Wegge Bottom, T 2 R 2, signed 23 Feb 1803; both seal; WIT: David LOCKWOOD, John WINTER; ack. 23 Feb 1803, David LOCKWOOD, Justice of Common Peas, recorded 15 Jul 1803.

p. 185 - Know all men, Robert THROUP, Judge of U.S., District of New York; Job WRITE [WRIGHT], State of New York. $13, lot #2 square #17 in Pultney, T 2 R 2, according to map made by Jacob LEWIS on file in Secretary's office in State of New York, signed 16 Jun 1897 [1797?]; his seal [Rob THROUP]; WIT: Robt. MURRY, A. WAUGH; ack. State of New York, 27 Jun 1797, John Slon HOBERT [ROBERT], Justice of Supreme Court, State of New York. City of Philadelphia: Job WRIGHT conveys to Peter MULLS [MILLS], City of Philadelphia, for $13, signed 4 Aug 1797; WIT: Aaron RAWLING, Abel WILLY. Marietta, Washington County, Ohio: Peter MILLS conveys to Dennis COSSET and Noah ZANE of town of Wheeling for $10, deed supposed to have been lost, signed at Marietta 23 Jul 1803; WIT: [Elip[t]] FRAZER, Moses McFARLAND.

p. 186 - Know all men, Robert THROUP, Judge of U.S., District of New York; Job WRIGHT, State of New York. $13, lot #2 square #17 in Pultney, T 2 R 2, signed 16 Jun 1797; his seal; WIT: Robt. MURRY, A. WAUGH; ack. New York, 22 Jun 1797, John Slon HOBERT. City of Philadelphia: Job WRIGHT conveys to Peter MILLS, City of Philadelphia, for $13, signed 4 Aug 1797; his seal; WIT: U.S. [Avwil ROUBEY], Able WILEY. Marietta, Washington County, Ohio: Peter MILLS conveys to Dennis COSSET and Noah ZANE of town of Wheeling for $10, deed supposed to have been lost, signed at Marietta 23 Jul 1803; his seal; WIT: Elept FRAZER, Moses McFARLAND.

p. 187 - Indenture, 1 Mar 1803, Jacob DEVERER [DEVORE], BCO; Thomas IRELAND, same. $44, lot #129 in St. Clairsville, 1/4 acre, fee simple; his seal; WIT: Samuel GREGG, Junr., Sterling JOHNSTON; ack. 1 Mar 1803, Sterling JOHNSTON, J.P., recorded 1 Aug 1803.

p. 188 - Know all men, Robert THROUP, Judge of U.S., District of New York; Job WRIGHT, State of New York. $13, lot #16 square #46 in Pultney, T 2 R 2,

Supreme Court of Judicature. City of Philadelphia: Job WRIGHT conveys to Peter MILLER for "Thirtee Dollars" [probably $13], dated 7 Aug 1797; WIT: Able WILEY, [Jo.] EDWARDS. Marietta, Washington County, Ohio: MILLS conveys to Dennis COSSET and Noah ZANE of Wheeling for $10, deed lost, signed Marietta 23 Jul 1803; his seal [Peter MILLS]; WIT: Elept FRAZIER, Moses McFARLAND; recorded 1 Aug 1803.

p. 189 - Indenture, 26 Sep 1800, George DOUGLASS (wife Phebe), City of New York, by attorney in fact Abraham HUNT of Trenton, Hunderton, New Jersey; James ROSS, Esq., Pittsburgh, Pennsylvania. Deed of indenture dated 13 Jul 1790 set over to James [SAIDLER/SEIDLER], John TAYLOR, and Abraham HUNT as a trust, now selling to ROSS for $400, S 9 T 2 R 3, reserving 1/3 metals; his seal by attorney A. HUNT; WIT: Thomas BELLERJEAN, Wilson P. HUNT; ack. New Jersey, 19 Feb 1801, Isaac SMITH, J.P., recorded 12 Aug 1803.

p. 190 - Indenture, 13 Jul 1790, George DOUGLASS, merchant (wife Phebe); James SEADLER and John TAYLOR, same, merchants, Abraham HUNT, State of New Jersey. DOUGLASS in debt due to losses, conveying all his interests for "Five pounds lawful money" to be sold to pay debts; both seal; WIT: Joseph RIGG, Peter MARTERTON; Jacob BENJAMINE, Notary Public, ack. 12 Feb 1791, John RAY, one of masters in chancery, recorded in Office of Clerk of the City and County of New York in Lib. No. 48 of conveyances &c., p. 343, 6 Nov 1792, Robert BINSON, Clerk; further ack. of notarization, 20 Mar 1801, Jacob BENJAMINE. "To all to whom," sale of S 9 T 2 R 3 on 20 Mar 1788 to George DOUGLASS; signatures of Samuel OSGOOD, Walter LIVINGSTON, Arthur LEE; recorded in Book of Deeds A, Fols. 19, Wm. DUER, recorded [Belmont County?] 11 Aug 1803.

p. 194 - Indenture, 7 Aug 1801, Bazeleel WELLS (wife Sally), Jefferson County, NWT; James ROSS, Pittsburgh, Pennsylvania. WELLS received patent dated 15 Jan 1798 to S 15 T 2 R 3 in Washington County, NWT, 640 acres, deed to ROSS on 20 Nov 1799 for moiety of section, now sells for "one thousand" [no units specified, presumably dollars?] the remaining half; both seal; WIT: John MOODY, Silas PAUL; ack. Jefferson County, 7 Aug 1801, John MOODY, J.P.

p. 195 - Indenture, 13 Apr 1803, Cophas [Cephas] CAREY, Pultney twp., BCO; Andrew HITS [HITE], same. $44, donation lot #3 square #3; signed Stephas CARY; WIT: Danl. F. BARNEY, Arcd. SMITH; ack. Jacob REPSHER, J.P., recorded 15 Aug 1803.

p. 196 - Plat of annexation to St. Clairsville, submitted 17 Sep 1803 by William MATHERS; ack. Sterling JOHNSTON, J.P. (See Appendix.)

p. 196 - Plat of annexation to St. Clairsville, submitted 17 Sep 1803 by William MATHERS; ack. Sterling JOHNSTON, J.P.

p. 197 - Indenture, 1 Oct 1803, David NEWELL (wife Sally), Kirkwood twp., BCO; Sterling JOHNSTON, Richland twp., BCO. $18, lot #17 in St. Clairsville, 1/4 acre, fee simple; both seal; WIT: Wm. MATHERS, William COOK; ack. David VANCE, Associate Judge, recorded 1 Oct 1803.

p. 198 - Indenture, 9 Aug 1803, John D. MERCIER [MERCER], State of New York; Richard HARDESTY, BCO. $365.60, beginning at point on creek on 147 acres where he now lives, NBR: Richard HARDESTY, John LAMB , 162 1/4 acres, part of tract granted to Doctor Robert JOHNSTON by patent; John D. MERCIER by attorney Daniel McELHERON; WIT: John FARRIS, Danl. F. BARNEY; ack. 9 Aug 1803, John FAIRES, J.P., recorded 6 Dec 1803.

p. 199 - Indenture, 1 Nov 1802, Andrew ANDERSON [originally written ANNDERSON] (wife Jean), Jefferson County, NWT; John ANDERSON, Lancaster County, Pennsylvania. $345, SE 1/4 of S 14 T 7 R 4, 160 acres, granted to William DUER by patent dated 3 Mar 1789, DUER conveyed to Henry EBURN, EBURN to Stephen TILLINGHOST, TILLINGHOST to Nathaniel ELLECOTT, ELLECOTT to John JOHNSTON, JOHNSTON to ANDERSON; both seal; WIT: Thomas ELLIOTT; ack. Jefferson County, NWT, 2 Nov 1802, Thomas ELLIOTT, recorded 6 Dec 1803.

p. 200 - Indenture, 4 Oct 1802, Bazaleel WELLS (wife Sally), Jefferson County, NWT; Francis [originally written Frances, but referred to as "him"] COOPER, BCO. $560, on waters of Glens Run, SE 1/4 S 14 T 7 R 3, 160 acres; both seal; WIT: Archibale COLE, Alex EDIE; ack. Jefferson County, 4 Oct 1802, Alex. ELEOTT, recorded 7 Dec 1803.

p. 201 - Indenture, 5 Sep 1803, David NEWELL (wife Sally), Kirkwood twp., BCO; Sterling JOHNSON [probably JOHNSTON], Richland twp., BCO. $24, lots #2, #10, #18; both seal; WIT: Jacob NAGLE, Joseph MARTIN; ack. 1 Oct 1803, David VANCE, Associate Judge, recorded 7 Dec 1803.

p. 202 - Indenture, 20 Sep 1803, David NEWELL (wife Sally), Kirkwood twp., BCO; William NEWELL (son of James NEWELL), same. For "divers good causes and considerations," lot #26 in St. Clairsville, 1/4 acre, fee simple; both seal; WIT: Jacob NAGLE, Sterling JOHNSTON; ack. 9 Nov 1803, Sterling JOHNSTON, J.P., recorded 8 Dec 1803.

p. 203 - Indenture, 9 Nov 1803, David NEWELL (wife Sally), Kirkwood twp., BCO; Abraham and Simeon WOODROW, State of Virginia. $150, lot #89 in St.

Clairsville, 1/4 acre, fee simple; both seal; WIT: William CONGLETON, Sterling JOHNSTON; ack. Sterling JOHNSTON, J.P., recorded 8 Dec 1803.

p. 204 - Indenture, 26 Oct 1803, James CALDWELL, merchant, St. Clairsville, BCO; Moses MOREHEAD, same. David NEWELL (wife Sally) sold to CALDWELL and MOREHEAD 3 1/2 acres and 25 poles adjoining commons south of St. Clairsville, NBR: Michael GROVE, Abraham LASH, CALDWELL quit claims his interest to MOREHEAD for $300; his seal; WIT: Sterling JOHNSTON, Robert JOHNSTON; ack. Sterling JOHNSTON, J.P., recorded 8 Dec 1803.

p. 205 - Indenture, 18 Oct 1803, David NEWELL (wife Sally), Kirkwood twp., BCO; George MIRES, St. Clairsville, BCO. $40.60, 1 1/2 acre and [22?] rods, NBR: John DUGAN, fee simple; both seal; WIT: Sterling JOHNSTON, Alpheus FERRON; ack. (David) 18 Oct 1803, Sterling JOHNSTON, J.P., ack. (Sally) 9 Nov 1803, Sterling JOHNSTON, J.P., recorded 9 Dec 1803.

p. 206 - Indenture, 17 Sep 1803, David NEWELL (wife Sally), Kirkwood twp., BCO; John THOMPSON, St. Clairsville, BCO. $18 per acre, 6 acres, 2 rods, 13 poles near St. Clairsville, NBR: John THOMPSON, WELLS, CONGLETON, William VANCE, Robert THOMPSON; both seal; WIT: Sterling JOHNSTON, William CONGLETON; ack. 17 Sep 1803, Sterling JOHNSTON, J.P., recorded 9 Dec 1803.

p. 207 - Indenture, 26 Sep 1803, David NEWELL (wife Sally), Kirkwood twp., BCO; John THOMPSON, St. Clairsville, Richland twp., BCO. $50, lot #21 in St. Clairsville, 1/4 acre, NBR: "Meelon & Smith" [NOTE: there is a Mahlon SMITH in the area], John McCONOLD, fee simple; both seal; WIT: Sterling JOHNSTON, Wm. CONGLETON; ack. 26 Sep 1803, Sterling JOHNSTON, J.P., recorded 10 Dec 1803.

p. 208 - Indenture, 9 Nov 1803, David NEWELL (wife Sally), Kirkwood twp., BCO; Basil ISRAEL, BCO. $182, lots #59 and #60 in St. Clairsville, 10 acres; both seal; WIT: Sterling JOHNSTON, Samuel DILLIE; ack. Sterling JOHNSTON, J.P., recorded 10 Dec 1803.

p. 209 - Indenture, 28 Sep 1803, David NEWELL (wife Sally), Kirkwood twp., BCO; William CONGLETON, St. Clairsville, BCO. $150, lot in Kirkwood twp., part of town land, NBR: John THOMPSON, Thomas CONLEY, Thomas [HELLEMS?], William COOK, land formerly claimed by William VANCE, 10 acres 27 perches, fee simple; both seal; WIT: Jacob NAGLE, Sterling JOHNSTON; ack. 28 Sep 1803, Sterling JOHNSTON, J.P., recorded 10 Dec 1803.

p. 210 - Indenture, 28 Sep 1803, David NEWELL (wife Sally), Kirkwood twp., BCO; William CONGLETON, St. Clairsville, BCO. $22, lot #111 in St. Clairsville, 1/4 acre, fee simple; both seal; WIT: David VANCE, Sterling JOHNSTON; ack. 9 Nov 1803, Sterling JOHNSTON, J.P., recorded 11 Dec 1803.

p. 212 - Indenture, 28 Sep 1803, David NEWELL (wife Sally), Kirkwood twp., BCO; James CALDWELL, BCO. $32, lots #96 and #95 in St. Clairsville, 1/4 acre each, previously conveyed by David NEWELL (wife Sally) and Benjamine NEWELL (wife Jane) under original numbers 28 and 53, fee simple; both seal; WIT: Jacob NAGLE, Sterling JOHNSTON; ack. 28 Sep 1803, Sterling JOHNSTON, J.P., recorded 11 Dec 1803.

p. 213 - Know all men, Daniel McELHERON, Town of Pultney, Jefferson County, NWT; James SHANE, Jew, Jefferson County, NWT. $12, lot #11 square #32 in Pultney and Wegee Bottom, signed 14 Oct 1800; his seal; WIT: Samuel DAY, Isabella SMITH; ack., BCO, 24 Jun 1803, Jacob REPSHER, J.P., recorded 11 Dec 1803.

p. 213 - Indenture, 6 May 1803, David NEWELL (wife Sarah) and Benjamine NEWELL (wife Jane), BCO; Thomas IRELAND, BCO. $20, lot #130 in St. Clairsville, 1/4 acre, fee simple; signed only by David and Sally; WIT: Sterling JOHNSTON, Mary JOHNSTON; ack. 6 May 1803, Sterling JOHNSTON, J.P., recorded 12 Dec 1803.

p. 214 - Indenture, 9 Aug 1803, John D. MERCIER, State of New York; John LAMB, BCO. $221.61, 98 1/2 acres, NBR: Richard HARDESTY, part of tract originally patented to Doctor Robert JOHNSTON, parts of S 23 and 24, John D. MERCIER by attorney D. McELHERON; WIT: John FAIRES, Danl. F. BARNEY; ack. by McELHERON, 9 Aug 1803, John FAIRES, J.P., recorded 12 Dec 1803.

p. 215 - Indenture, 29 Oct 1803, Andrew MARSHALL (wife Margaret), BCO; James CALDWELL, BCO. $200, lots #36 and #35 in St. Clairsville, each 1/4 acre, fee simple; his seal, her mark; WIT: John THOMPSON, Charles W. SILBY; ack. 29 Oct 1803, John THOMPSON, J.P., recorded 12 Dec 1803.

p. 216 - Indenture, 29 Sep 1803, David NEWELL (wife Sally), BCO; James CALDWELL, BCO. $50, lot #33 in St. Clairsville, 1/4 acre, fee simple; both seal; WIT: Andrew MARSHALL, William COOK; ack. (David) 29 Sep 1803, Andrew MARSHALL, J.P., (David and Sally) 8 Nov 1803, Jacob REPSHER, J.P., recorded 13 Dec 1803.

p. 217 - Articles of Agreement, 3 Dec 1803, John THOMPSON and Jacob HOULTS, both of St. Clairsville, BCO. To dig for a well of water on lot #4 in St. Clairsville and share both expenses and access; THOMPSON's seal, HOULTS's mark; WIT: Sterling JOHNSTON, Robert JOHNSTON; ack. Sterling JOHNSTON, J.P., recorded 13 Dec 1803.

p. 218 - Indenture, 7 Feb 1803, John WOODBURN (wife Margaret), innkeeper in Washington County, Pennsylvania; William MATHERS, St. Clairsville, BCO. $120, lot #85 in St. Clairsville, 1/4 acre; his seal, her mark; WIT: Jos. ALEXANDER, Sally ALEXANDER; ack. Commonwealth of Pennsylvania, 7 Feb 1803, Jos. ALEXANDER, J.P., recorded 2 Jan 1804; William McKENNAN certifies ALEXANDER 7 Feb 1803.

p. 219 - Indenture, 25 Nov 1803, Noah ZANE, Ohio County, Virginia; William MATHERS, St. Clairsville, BCO. $50, lot #68 in St. Clairsville, fee simple; his seal; WIT: Andrew MARSHALL, John CALDWELL; ack. 25 Nov 1803, Andrew MARSHALL, J.P., recorded 2 Jan 1804.

p. 220 - Indenture, 6 Jan 1804, Thomas HELMS (wife Sarah), Washington County, Pennsylvania; James BARNES, BCO. $600, part of S 4 T 4 R 4 near St. Clairsville, 39 acres 97 poles, NBR: Peter SUNDERLAND, sold to HELMS by David NEWELL (wife Sally) on 6 Dec 1802, fee simple; his mark; WIT: Sterling JOHNSTON, Robert JOHNSTON; ack. Sterling JOHNSTON, J.P.

p. 221 - Indenture, 28 Jan 1804, William BELL (wife Sally), farmer, Richland twp., BCO; James BARNES, St. Clairsville, BCO. $50, lot #8 in St. Clairsville, 1/4 acre, same lot sold by David NEWELL (wife Sally) by deed dated 23 Sep 1802, recorded in Book A, p. 107 (p. 15 of abstracts), fee simple; his seal [Wm. BELL], her mark; [no witnesses]; ack. Sterling JOHNSTON, J.P., recorded 31 Jan 1804.

p. 222 - Indenture, 28 Jan 1804, William BELL (wife Sally), farmer, Richland twp., James BARNES, St. Clairsville, BCO. $50, lot #7 in St. Clairsville, 1/4 acre, sold to BELL by David NEWELL (wife Sally) on 6 Oct 1802 and recorded in Book A, p. 109 [p. 15 of abstracts], fee simple; his seal, her mark; WIT: Jacob NAGLE, Sterling JOHNSTON; ack. Sterling JOHNSTON, J.P., recorded 31 Jan 1804.

p. 223 - Indenture, 20 Jan 1804, William DEVELEN [DOVLON/ DEVELAN] and Neal MAHAN [MAHON] (wife Mary), BCO; Jonathan MILLER, BCO. $240, part of NE 1/4 S 24 T 7 R 4, NBR: George KELLER, Joseph IRWIN, 60 acres, part of land granted to John HOPKINS by Samuel OSGOOD and Walter LIVINGSTON dated 3 Mar 1789, sold by George MILLER attorney for Stephen MILLER to DEVELEN and MAHAN on 4 Sep 1800, fee simple; all seal; WIT:

George KELLER, Isaac HOGUER; ack. 13 Jan 1804 [probably 30], Sterling JOHNSTON, J.P.

p. 224 - Indenture, 4 Feb 1804, Valentine AULT (wife Catharine), BCO; Joseph MORRISON, St. Clairsville, BCO. $50, lots #48 and #47 in St. Clairsville, each 1/4 acre, fee simple; his seal, her mark; Andrew MARSHALL, Thomas BOONE; ack. Andrew MARSHALL, J.P., recorded 4 Feb 1804.

p. 225 - Indenture, 9 Jan 1804, David KIRKPATRICK (wife Elizabeth), Richland twp., BCO; James BARNES, St. Clairsville, BCO. $80, lot #71 in St. Clairsville, conveyed from David NEWELL (wife Sally) 9 Apr 1802, recorded Book A, p. 69 [p. 9 of abstracts], fee simple; his seal, her mark; WIT: Sterling JOHNSTON, Mary JOHNSTON; ack. 13 Feb 1804, Sterling JOHNSTON, J.P., recorded 14 Feb 1804.

p. 226 - Indenture, 9 Feb 1804, David KIRKPATRICK (wife Elizabeth), Richland twp., BCO; James BARNES, St. Clairsville, BCO. $120, lot #72 in St. Clairsville, conveyed from David NEWELL (wife Sally) on 27 Apr 1802, fee simple; his seal, her mark; WIT: Sterling JOHNSTON, Mary JOHNSTON; ack. Sterling JOHNSTON, J.P.

p. 227 - Indenture, 22 Oct 1803, William MATHERS (wife Anne), St. Clairsville, Richland twp., BCO; James KNOX, same. $300, lot #85 in St. Clairsville, 1/4 acre, sold by David NEWELL (wife Sally) on 22 Dec 1801, fee simple; both seal; WIT: Andrew MARSHALL, Jacob NAGLE; ack. Andrew MARSHALL, J.P.

p. 228 - Indenture, 7 Nov 1803, David NEWELL (wife Sally), Kirkwood twp., BCO; Abraham BARNHART, Washington County, Pennsylvania. $20, lot #137 in St. Clairsville, 1/4 acre, fee simple; both seal; WIT: Marthew JOHNSTON [her mark], Abraham LASH; ack. 17 Feb 1804, Sterling JOHNSTON, J.P.

p. 230 - Indenture, 8 Feb 1804, Abraham BARNHART (wife Catey), Washington County, Pennsylvania; James CALDWELL, St. Clairsville, BCO. $60, lot #137 in St. Clairsville, 1/4 acre, fee simple; both seal; WIT: Sterling JOHNSTON, John CLARKSON; ack. Sterling JOHNSTON, J.P.

p. 230 - Indenture, 7 Jan 1804, David NEWELL (wife Sally), Kirkwood twp., BCO; James BARNES, merchant, Richland twp., BCO. $20, 1 acre, NBR: John DUGAN, fee simple; David's seal only; WIT: Sterling JOHNSTON, Joseph HARRIS; ack. 17 Feb 1804, Sterling JOHNSTON, J.P.

p. 231 - Indenture, 17 Feb 1804, David NEWELL (wife Sally), Kirkwood twp., BCO; Robert VANCE, Richland twp., BCO. $30, lot #39 in St. Clairsville, 1/4 acre, fee simple; David's seal only; WIT: Sterling JOHNSTON, Jacob DEVORE; ack. Sterling JOHNSTON, J.P., recorded 22 Feb 1804.

p. 232 - Indenture, 9 Jul 1803, Archd. WOODS (wife Anne WOODS), Ohio County, Virginia; Richard McKIBBONS, BCO. $819, part of S 27 in fractional T 4 R 2, granted 15 Nov 1797, 181 1/2 acres, NBR: Joseph MOORE, John McCLURE, Joseph SCOTT, Andrew EAGLESON; both seal; [no witnesses given]; ack. 9 Jul 1803, James ALEXANDER, Associate Judge, recorded 24 Feb 1804.

p. 234 - Indenture, 9 Jul 1803, Archd WOODS (wife Ann), Ohio County, Virginia; Joseph SCOTT, BCO. $102, part of S 27 fractional T 4 R 2, granted 15 Nov 1797, 52 1/2 acres, NBR: MOORE, McCLURE, Richard McKIBBENS, Andrew EAGLESON; both seal; [no witnesses given]; ack. 9 Jul 1803, James ALEXANDER, Associate Judge, recorded 29 Feb 1804.

p. 235 - Indenture, 9 Jul 1803, Archd WOODS (wife Ann), Ohio County, Virginia; Andrew EAGLESON, BCO. $300, part of S 27 fractional T 4 R 2, granted 15 Nov 1797, 153 acres, NBR: Richard McKIBBENS, Joseph SCOTT; both seal; [no witnesses given]; ack. 9 Jul 1803, James ALEXANDER, Associate Judge, recorded 29 Feb 1804.

p. 236 - Know all men, Jacob COLEMAN, Sheriff, according to judgment recovered against Phillip WINDLE during August term 1803 exposed lot #92 (1/4 acre) in St. Clairsville to sale, Daniel CHURCH of St. Clairsville being the highest bidder at $100, signed 9 Jan 1804; his seal; WIT: Jacob NAGLE, David BARR; ack. 9 Jan 1804, John THOMPSON, J.P., recorded 29 Feb 1804.

p. 237 - Indenture, 25 Feb 1804, David NEWELL (wife Sally), Kirkwood twp., BCO; Moses MOREHEAD, St. Clairsville, BCO. $40, lot south of St. Clairsville, originally conveyed to NEWELL by Bazaleel WELLS, NBR: James NEWELL, 2 acres 1 rod 11 perches, fee simple; both seal; WIT: Jacob NAGLE, Sterling JOHNSTON; ack. Sterling JOHNSTON, J.P., recorded 1 Mar 1804.

p. 238 - Know all men, David NEWELL (wife Sally), BCO; Alphus FERRON, BCO. $12, lot #138 in St. Clairsville, 1/4 acre, signed 25 Feb 1804; both seal; WIT: Jacob NAGLE, Sterling JOHNSTON; ack. Sterling JOHNSTON, J.P., recorded 1 Mar 1804.

p. 238 - Indenture, 26 Feb 1804, David NEWELL (wife Sally), Kirkwood twp., BCO; John ISRAEL, same. $30, lot #125 in St. Clairsville, 1/4 acre, fee simple; both seal; WIT: Sterling JOHNSTON, Chas. SELBY; ack. Sterling JOHNSTON, J.P., recorded 26 Feb 1804.

p. 239 - Indenture, 25 Feb 1804, David NEWELL (wife Sally), Kirkwood twp., BCO; William GIBSON, St. Clairsville, BCO. $12, unspecified size lot of land at east end of St. Clairsville, fee simple; both seal; WIT: Sterling JOHNSTON, Robert JOHNSTON; ack. Sterling JOHNSTON, J.P., recorded 2 Mar 1804.

p. 240 - Indenture, 26 Feb 1804, David NEWELL (wife Sally), Kirkwood twp., BCO; William GIBSON, St. Clairsville, BCO. $12, unspecified size lot of land north of Main Street, St. Clairsville, fee simple; both seal; WIT: Sterling JOHNSTON, Robert JOHNSTON; ack. Sterling JOHNSTON, J.P., recorded 2 Mar 1804.

p. 241 - Indenture, 10 Feb 1804, Sterling JOHNSTON (wife Mary), St. Clairsville, BCO; Jacob LECE, same. $80, lot in Richland twp., NBR: Magdaline PIPER, 10 acres 2 rods, part of S 5 T 7 R 4, part of land conveyed by David VANCE, Esqr., to JOHNSTON on 9 Nov 1803; both seal; WIT: John CLARKSON, Robert JOHNSTON; ack. John THOMPSON, J.P., recorded 2 Mar 1804.

p. 242 - Indenture, 22 Oct 1803, James KNOX, Pultney town and twp., BCO; William MATHERS, St. Clairsville, BCO. $300, lot #85 in St. Clairsville, 1/4 acre, fee simple, to be void if KNOX pays MATHERS $300 by 22 Oct 1806; his seal; WIT: Jacob NAGLE, Andw. MARSHALL; ack. Andrew MARSHALL, J.P., recorded 5 Mar 1804.

p. 244 - Indenture, 25 Oct 1803, Abraham ENGLE (wife Patience), BCO; Caleb ENGLE, BCO. $560, S 1/4 of S 27 T 7 R 4, 160 acres, NBR: Joshua HATCHER, land conveyed to John HOPKINS by Samuel OSGOOD and Walter LIVINGSTON on 3 Mar 1797; both seal; WIT: William MORGAN, Grace BILLINGER, James STARR; ack. 25 Oct 1803, James STARR, J.P., recorded 5 Mar 1804.

p. 245 - Indenture, 1 Oct 1803, Thomas CONNELLY [CONLEY] (wife Rachel), St. Clairsville, BCO; "the Present" Joseph ANDERSON, same. $100, 3-acre lot in Richland twp. adjoining St. Clairsville, NBR: William CONGLETON, John THOMPSON, fee simple; both mark; WIT: Jacob NAGLE, Andw. MARSHALL; ack. Andw. MARSHALL, J.P., recorded 12 Mar 1804.

p. 246 - Indenture, 10 Mar 1804, Alexander LATIMORE (wife Rachel), Richland twp., BCO; William WILEY, same. $400, 363 acres 20 perches of S 6 T 6 R 3, part of land conveyed by John JOHNSTON of Washington County to LATIMORE on 20 Aug 1802, recorded in Book A, p. 114 [p. 16 of abstracts], fee simple; his seal, her mark; WIT: Thomas MITCHELL; ack. 10 Mar 1804, Thos. MITCHELL, J.P., recorded 12 Apr 1804.

p. 247 - Indenture, 9 Dec 1803, David VANCE, Esqr. (wife Margaret), Richland twp., BCO; Sterling JOHNSTON, same. $600, 110 acres, part of S 5 T 7 R 4, NBR: James JOHNSTON, William WOODS, William VANCE; his seal only; WIT: Jacob REPSHER, Wm. VANCE; ack. 9 Dec 1803, John THOMPSON, J.P., recorded 12 Apr 1804.

p. 248 - David BARR, Jefferson County, NWT; David VANCE. $73, S 31 T 7 R 3, signed 9 Aug 1800; his seal; WIT: Mathew THOMPSON, Isabel LAWSON; ack. Jefferson County, NWT, 9 Aug 1800, David L. WOOD, J.P.

p. 248 - Know all men, John GRANT, Richland twp., BCO; Isaac COWGILL [COGLE]. Two horses, void if $35 (a judgment against GRANT) repaid, signed 7 Apr 1804; his mark; WIT: Sterling JOHNSTON, John MOORE; ack. Sterling JOHNSTON, J.P.

p. 249 - Indenture, 8 Apr 1804, David NEWELL (wife Sally), Kirkwood twp., BCO; Robert JOHNSTON, BCO. $10, 1/4 acre, NBR: George MYERS [his out lot], fee simple; both seal; WIT: Sterling JOHNSTON, Nathan UPDEGRAPH; ack. Sterling JOHNSTON, J.P., recorded 15 Apr 1804.

p. 249 - Indenture, 12 Apr 1804, David NEWELL (wife Sally), Kirkwood twp., BCO; James BARNES, St. Clairsville, BCO. $20, 1 acre at west end of St. Clairsville, fee simple; both seal; WIT: Sterling JOHNSTON, Sally THOMPSON [her mark]; ack. Sterling JOHNSTON, J.P., recorded 16 Apr 1804.

p. 250 - Indenture, 13 Apr 1804, James CALDWELL (wife Nancy), St. Clairsville, BCO; Josiah DILLON, Richland twp., BCO. $40, lot #33 in St. Clairsville, 1/4 acre, fee simple; both seal; WIT: Nathan UPDEGRAFF, Sterling JOHNSTON; ack. Sterling JOHNSTON, J.P., recorded 16 Apr 1804.

p. 252 - Indenture, 13 Apr 1804, David NEWELL (wife Sally), Kirkwood twp., BCO; Nathan UPDEGRAFF, JCO. $20, lot #41 in St. Clairsville, 1/4 acre, fee simple; both seal; WIT: Josiah DILLON, James CALDWELL; ack. Sterling JOHNSTON, J.P., recorded 17 [Apr] 1804.

p. 253 - Indenture, 14 Apr 1804, David NEWELL (wife Sally), Kirkwood twp., BCO; William CONGLETON, same. $30, unspecified-size lot in Richland twp. on SW side of St. Clairsville, NBR: William FROST, John DUGAN, Robert JOHNSTON, George MYERS, John LONG, fee simple; his seal only; WIT: Sterling JOHNSTON, Robert GRIFFITH; ack. Sterling JOHNSTON, J.P. ("David only appeared and acknowledged.")

p. 254 - To all to whom, John WELSH, Junior, against Jacob REPSHER a certain writ of summons returnable May term1802, plea of trespass, WELSH awarded $200 plus interest from 14 Jul 1798 and costs of suit, property levied to cover damages, sold to Obediah JENNINGS lot #2 and #3 in Pultney, donation square #4, for $3.50 each, also lot #16 in square #16 in Pultney, also lot #1 in square #34 for $3.50 each, out lot "E" of 5 acres for $8.50, two other out lots #59 and #60 of 5 acres each for $8.50, out lot "A" of 7 acres for $59 (total $98.50), by Jacob COLEMAN, Sheriff, signed 18 Apr 1804; his seal; WIT: John CLARKSON, Sterling JOHNSTON; ack. Sterling JOHNSTON, J.P., recorded 20 Apr 1804.

p. 255 - Know all men, David NEWELL (wife Sally), BCO; Daniel CHURCH, BCO. $60, land near St. Clairsville, 3 acres 2 rods 4 rods [perches?], NBR: James BARNES, David NEWELL, Robert THOMPSON, William BOGGS, fee simple, signed 18 Apr 1804; both seal; WIT: John THOMPSON, James CALDWELL; ack. John THOMPSON, recorded 25 Apr 1804.

p. 256 - Indenture, 27 Apr 1804, Sterling JOHNSTON (wife Mary), St. Clairsville, BCO; Magdaline PIPER (widow), Richland twp., BCO. $60, 7 3/4 acres 38 rods in Richland twp., NBR: William WOODS, Jacob LECE, Sterling JOHNSTON, part of piece of land conveyed from David VANCE to JOHNSTON, fee simple; both seal; WIT: John THOMPSON, Robert JOHNSTON; ack. John THOMPSON, J.P., recorded 27 Apr 1804.

p. 257 - Indenture, 4 May 1804, Peter SUNDERLAND (wife Catharine), Richland twp., BCO; James BARNES, St. Clairsville, BCO. $1,800, land on which SUNDERLAND now lives, part of NE 1/4 S 4 T 7 R 4, 53 acres, part of land conveyed to SUNDERLAND by Bazaleel WELLS on 16 May 1797, recorded in Jefferson County Book A, p. 100, fee simple; both mark; WIT: Sterling JOHNSTON, John THOMPSON; ack. Sterling JOHNSTON, J.P.

p. 258 - Indenture, 4 May 1804, James BARNES, St. Clairsville, BCO; Peter SUNDERLAND, Richland twp., BCO. BARNES bound by above to SUNDERLAND in the penal sum of $1,600 to be paid by 4 May 1807, for securing debt of $800 conveying to SUNDERLAND 50 acres, part of land conveyed by SUNDERLANDs to BARNES, void if $800 paid; BARNES's seal; WIT: Sterling JOHNSTON, John THOMPSON; ack. Sterling JOHNSTON, J.P., recorded 9 May 1804. Satisfaction of mortgage on 16 May 1807; SUNDERLAND's mark; WIT: Sterling JOHNSTON, J.P.

p. 259 - Indenture, 4 May 1804, Francis SUNDERLAND (wife Ann), Richland twp., BCO; James BARNES, St. Clairsville, BCO. $423, 36 acres 30 rods of land in Richland twp., NBR: William BROWN, part of land conveyed by Peter SUNDERLAND to Francis SUNDERLAND on 29 Oct 1800, recorded in Jefferson County, State lib. A, p. 217, fee simple; both mark; WIT: Sterling

JOHNSTON, John THOMPSON; ack. Sterling JOHNSTON, J.P., recorded 9 May 1804.

p. 260 - Indenture, 5 May 1804, James BARNES, St. Clairsville, BCO; Francis SUNDERLAND, Richland twp., BCO. BARNES bound to SUNDERLAND in penal sum of $1,346, for payment of $673 due 4 May 1807 BARNES conveys to SUNDERLAND 36 acres conveyed to him on same date, fee simple, void if $673 paid to SUNDERLAND; BARNES's seal; WIT: Sterling JOHNSTON, Notley HAYS; ack. Sterling JOHNSTON, J.P. Mortgage satisfied 19 Oct 1807, WIT: Sterling JOHNSTON, Recorder.

p. 261 - Indenture, 7 May 1804, John THOMPSON, Esqr. (wife Sally), St. Clairsville, Richland twp., BCO; James BARNES, merchant, same. $800, lot #21 of St. Clairsville, 1/4 acre, fee simple; his seal, her mark; WIT: Notely HAYS, Sterling JOHNSTON; ack. Sterling JOHNSTON, J.P.

p. 262 - Indenture, 7 May 1804, John THOMPSON, Esqr. (wife Sally), St. Clairsville, Richland twp., BCO; James BARNES, same. $1,000, lot #4 in St. Clairsville, 1/4 acre, conveyed to THOMPSON by David NEWELL (wife Sally) on 29 Jan 1801, fee simple; his seal, her mark; WIT: Sterling JOHNSTON, Notely HAYS; ack. Sterling JOHNSTON, J.P., recorded 11 May 1804.

p. 263 - Indenture, 7 May 1804, John THOMPSON, Esqr. (wife Sally), St. Clairsville, Richland twp., BCO; James BARNES, same. $400, 10 acres north of St. Clairsville, conveyed from David NEWELL (wife Sally) to THOMPSON on 29 Jan 1801, part of S 4 T 7 R 4, fee simple; his seal, her mark; WIT: Sterling JOHNSTON, Notely HAYS; ack. Sterling JOHNSTON, J.P., recorded 12 May 1804.

p. 264 - Indenture, 7 May 1804, John THOMPSON, Esqr. (wife Sally), St. Clairsville, Richland twp., BCO; James BARNES, same. $200, 6 acres 2 rods 13 perches on north side of St. Clairsville, NBR: formerly John THOMPSON as sold lot this date, conveyed to THOMPSON by David NEWELL (wife Sally) on 17 Sep 1803, part of S 4 T 7 R 4, fee simple; his seal, her mark; WIT: Sterling JOHNSTON, Notely HAYS; ack. Sterling JOHNSTON, J.P., recorded 12 May 1804.

p. 265 - Indenture, 7 May 1804, James BARNES (wife Nancy), St. Clairsville, BCO; John THOMPSON, Esqr., St. Clairsville, BCO. 60 acres in Richland twp., land where Peter SUNDERLAND now lives also part of land conveyed by Bazaleel WELLS to SUNDERLAND, conveyed to BARNES on 4 May 1804, part of NE corner S 4 T 7 R 4, fee simple; his seal, her mark; WIT: Sterling JOHNSTON, Notely HAYS; ack. Sterling JOHNSTON, J.P. Satisfaction of mortgage on 19 Oct 1807, WIT: John THOMPSON.

p. 266 - Indenture, 7 May 1804, James BARNES, merchant, St. Clairsville, BCO; John THOMPSON, Esqr. [no location given here]. $3,000, house and lot #4 in St. Clairsville, another lot adjoining north Commons of 10 acres, another out lot of 6 acres 2 rods 13 perches (same lots sold to BARNES by THOMPSON on same date), fee simple, void if mortgages are paid by 4 May 1807; his seal; WIT: Sterling JOHNSTON, Notely HAYS; ack. Sterling JOHNSTON, J.P.

p. 267 - Know all men, Daniel CHURCH, St. Clairsville, BCO, Phillip WINDLE, same. $130, lot #92 in St. Clairsville, 1/4 acre, signed 8 May 1804; his seal; WIT: Sterling JOHNSTON, John CLARKSON; ack. Sterling JOHNSTON, J.P., recorded 14 May 1804.

p. 268 - Indenture, 11 May 1803, John CLOUSE (wife Christeena [Tena]), Washington County, Pennsylvania; Thomas IRELAND and Andrew MARSHALL, BCO. $48, lot #121 in St. Clairsville, 1/4 acre, fee simple; his seal, her mark; WIT: David WHERRY, John WHERRY; ack. Washington County, Pennsylvania, 11 May 1803, James WHERRY, J.P., WHERRY certified by William [McKENNON], recorded 15 May 1804.

p. 269 - Indenture, 28 Jan 1804, William BELL, Richland twp., BCO; James BARNES, St. Clairsville, same. BARNES bound to BELL in penal sum of $400, securing debt by conveying lots #8 and #7 in St. Clairsville, each 1/4 acre, void if $200 paid; his seal; WIT: Sterling JOHNSTON, Jacob NAGLE; ack. Sterling JOHNSTON, J.P., recorded 15 May 1804. Mortgage satisfied 19 Aug 1816, WIT: Wm. BELL.

p. 270 - Indenture, 28 Apr 1804, David NEWELL (wife Sallie), Kirkwood twp., BCO; Sterling JOHNSON [probably JOHNSTON], St. Clairsville, BCO. $20, lot #56 in St. Clairsville, fee simple; his seal only; WIT: John THOMPSON, Daniel CHURCH; ack. John THOMPSON, J.P., recorded 17 May 1804.

p. 271 - Indenture, 22 Oct 1803, Peter BOBB [BABB], Fredrick [sic] County, Virginia; Thomas SMITH, same. $320, 1/4 of S 27 T 7 R 3, fee simple; his seal; WIT: Charles McMANAS, Thos. MITCHELL; ack. 22 Oct 1803, BCO, Thos. MITCHELL, J.P.

p. 272 - Indenture, 22 Oct 1803, Peter BOBB [BABB], Senior, Fredrick [sic] County, Virginia; Peter BOBB [BABB], Junior, Richland twp., BCO. $640, 1/2 S side of S 27 T 7 R 3 [no size given]; his seal; WIT: Charles McMANAS, Thos. MITCHELL; ack. 22 Oct 1803, Thos. MITCHELL, J.P., recorded 23 May 1804.

p. 273 - Know all men, Jacob COLEMAN, BCO; Obediah HARDESTY, BCO. $100, livestock, household goods, farming implements, signed 1 Mar 1804; his seal; WIT: Elijah DYSON, Ralph HARDESTY [his mark]; ack. 8 May 1804 (statement of Ralph HARDESTY), Sterling JOHNSTON, J.P., recorded 29 May 1804.

p. 274 - Indenture, 13 May 1804, James BARNES (wife Nancy), St. Clairsville, BCO; Robert McCOMB [McCONALD] [no location]. $120, lot west of St. Clairsville, fee simple; his seal, her mark; WIT: Sterling JOHNSTON; ack. 31 May 1804, Sterling JOHNSTON, J.P., recorded 31 May 1804.

p. 274 - Indenture, 5 Jun 1804, John WINTERS, Richland twp., BCO; Joseph LYONS and John LYONS, same. $640, NE 1/4 S 25 T 8 R 4, fee simple, mortgage?, also refers to NW 1/4 S 19 T 8 R 4; John's seal; WIT: Sterling JOHNSTON, William LYON; ack. Sterling JOHNSTON, J.P., recorded 8 Jun 1804. Mortgage satisfied, 28 Mar 1806; WIT: Sterling JOHNSTON, Recorder.

p. 275 - Indenture, 16 Jun 1804, Phillip WINDLE (wife Barbara), St. Clairsville, BCO; William MATHERS, same. $50, lot #67 in St. Clairsville, 1/4 acre, fee simple; his seal, her mark; WIT: Sterling JOHNSTON, James KNOX; ack. Sterling JOHNSTON, J.P., recorded 17 Jun 1804.

p. 276 - Indenture, 16 Jun 1804, James KNOX (wife Ruth), St. Clairsville, Richland twp., BCO; William CONGLETON [no location given]. $150, lot #85 in St. Clairsville, 1/4 acre, fee simple; his seal; WIT: Sterling JOHNSTON, Joseph WORLEY; ack. Sterling JOHNSTON, J.P., recorded 17 Jun 1804.

p. 277 - Know all men, Daniel CHURCH, St. Clairsville, BCO; William WOODS, BCO. $60, land on NE corner of St. Clairsville, NBR: Robert JOHNSTON, 3 acres 37 rods, signed 19 Jun 1804; his seal; WIT: Sterling JOHNSTON, Joseph WORLEY; ack. Sterling JOHNSTON, J.P., recorded 20 Jun 1804.

p. 278 - Indenture, 9 Jul 1803, Archd. WOODS (wife Anne WOODS), Ohio County, Virginia; Joseph MOER [MOORE] and John McCLURE. $661, part of S 27 fractional T 4 R 2, NBR: Henry HARVEY, Richard McKIBBENS, Joseph SCOTT, 147 acres; both seal; [no witnesses given]; ack. James ALEXANDER, Associate Judge.

p. 279 - [will of Jacob STOKEY], 7 Jan 1804, son John STOKEY, dau Lida BROWN, dau Hannah GILLISPIE, dau Barbery BROWN, dau Rebeckah STOKEY, son Joseph STOKEY, daus [?] Elisabeth and Content, Stephen Jacob BROWN, executor, heirs of Jacob STOKEY [Junr.?]; his mark; WIT: Robert GILKISON, Thomas HARRISON [HARMASON]; ack. 22 Jun 1804, of GILKISON seeing HARMASON sign will, Sterling JOHNSTON, J.P.

p. 280 - Know all men, Daniel PERRY, Richland twp., BCO, appoints John PICKERING his attorney, signed 5 Jul 1804; his mark; WIT: George SMITH, John HARDESTY [his mark]; ack. Sterling JOHNSTON, J.P.

p. 281 - Indenture, 10 Nov 1803, Stephen MILLER (by attorney George MILLER), merchant, City, County, and State of New York; George KELLER, BCO. $350, part of S 23 T 7 R 4, NBR: Evan PHILIPS, Joseph IRWIN, Neal MAHON, Jonathan MILLER, 100 acres, part of land granted by Walter LIVINGSTON and Samuel OSGOOD dated 3 Mar 1789; Stephen MILLER by attorney Geo. MILLER; [no witnesses given]; ack. 23 Mar 1804, James ALEXANDER, Associate Judge, recorded 9 Aug 1804.

p. 282 - Know all men, Joseph LASHLEY, BCO; Joseph CALDWELL, Ohio County, Virginia. $170.50 for livestock and household goods, signed 21 Feb 1804; his seal; WIT: Danl. F. BARNEY, Joseph LASHLEY, Jew [sic, but I wonder if these entries were actually "Junr." misread?]; no ack.

p. 283 - Indenture, 14 Aug 1804, Joseph IRWIN (wife Mary), Richland twp., BCO; William WOODS, same. $150, lot #57 in St. Clairsville, 1/4 acre, fee simple; his seal, her mark; WIT: Sterling JOHNSTON, John WHERRY; ack. Sterling JOHNSTON, J.P.

p. 284 - Indenture, 14 Aug 1804, Joseph IRWIN (wife Mary), Richland twp., BCO; William WOODS, same. $50, lot #58 in St. Clairsville, 1/4 acre plus 825 feet, fee simple; his seal, her mark; WIT: Sterling JOHNSTON, John WHERRY; ack. Sterling JOHNSTON, J.P.

p. 285 - Indenture, 11 Aug 1804, Enoch RUSH (wife Martha), BCO; Robert LAUGHLIN, BCO. $50 in value received, lot #156 in St. Clairsville, 1/4 acre, fee simple; his seal, her mark; WIT: Andrew MARSHALL, Joseph MORRISON; ack. Andrew MARSHALL, J.P., recorded 8 Sep 1804.

p. 286 - Indenture, 27 Aug 1804, Obediah HARDESTY (wife Mary), Richland twp., BCO; Abraham ENGLE, same. $900, 1/4 S 21 T 6 R 4, 160 acres, laid of in SW corner of S, NBR: Daniel HARRIS, Elijah MARTIN, granted 24 Aug 1804 to HARDESTY by Orphan's Court through administrator of Absalom MARTIN, Esqr., Noah ZANE, fee simple; both mark; WIT: Sterling JOHNSTON, Robert JOHNSTON; ack. Sterling JOHNSTON, J.P.

p. 286 - Indenture, 7 Nov 1803, Bazeleel WELLS (wife Sally), JCO; John WHITE, BCO. $560, part of S 14 T 7 R 3, beginning at SW corner, 160 acres, granted to WELLS by patent dated 7 Aug 1802; both seal; WIT: Benjn. HOUGH; ack. JCO, Benjn. HOUGH, J.P.

p. 287 - Indenture, 9 Aug 1804, Daniel McELHERON (wife Amelia), BCO; John WORKMAN, same. $160, SE 1/4 S 2 T 6 R 3, 160 acres; both seal; WIT: Jacob DAVIS, James KELSEY; ack. Jacob DAVIS, J.P.

p. 288 - Indenture, 22 Sep 1804, David TRENNEL, Carlile, Cumberland County, Pennsylvania; Jacob ROLAND, West Liberty, Ohio County, Virginia. $30, lot #133 in St. Clairsville, 1/4 acre, conveyed from David NEWELL (wife Sally) to TRENNEL on 29 Jun 1802, fee simple; his seal; WIT: Sterling JOHNSTON, James BLACK; ack. Sterling JOHNSTON, J.P.

p. 289 - Indenture, 12 Mar 1804, Stephen MILLER, City, County, and State of New York by his attorney George MILLER; James PATTON, Ohio County, Virginia. $535, NE 1/4 S 24 T 7 R 4, 160 acres, NBR: Niel MAHON, William DEVLON, Hugh McCOY, William McWILLIAMS, part of tract granted to John HOPKINS by Samuel OSGOOD and Walter LIVINGSTON dated 3 Mar 1789; Stephen MILLER by his attorney George MILLER; WIT: Wm. [Erving?] PATTON, John MOFFETT, Fielding BELL; ack. 23 Mar 1804, James ALEXANDER, Associate Judge.

p. 290 - Indenture, 13 Sep 1804, James BARNES (wife Nancy), St. Clairsville, BCO; Doctor Luther SPENCER, same. $200, lots #8 and #7 in St. Clairsville, each 1/4 acre, conveyed by David NEWELL (wife Sally) to William BELL on 23 Sep 1802 and 6 Oct 1802, conveyed by BELL (wife Sally) to BARNES on 28 Jun 1804, fee simple; his seal, her mark; WIT: Sterling JOHNSTON, Robert JOHNSTON; ack. Sterling JOHNSTON, J.P., recorded 9 Oct 1804.

p. 292 - Indenture, 13 Sep 1804, Doctor Luther SPENCER, St. Clairsville, BCO; James BARNES, same. SPENCER bound to BARNES in penal sum of $520 for payment of $260, securing payment by conveying lots #7 and #8 in St. Clairsville, fee simple, void if paid by 15 Sep 1806; his seal; WIT: Sterling JOHNSTON, Robert JOHNSTON; ack. Sterling JOHNSTON, J.P.

p. 293 - Indenture, 28 Sep 1804, William VANCE (wife Mary), Richland twp., BCO; Thomas LAWSON, Fayette County, Pennsylvania. $20, lot #31 in St. Clairsville, 1/4 acre, conveyed by David NEWELL (wife Sally) on 1 Jul 1802, fee simple; both seal [his Wm. VANCE]; WIT: Sterling JOHNSTON, Andw. BYERS; ack. Sterling JOHNSTON, J.P.

p. 294 - Indenture, 28 Sep 1804, William VANCE (wife Mary), Richland twp., BCO; Thomas LAWSON, Fayette County, Pennsylvania. $60, lot #32 in St. Clairsville, 1/4 acre, conveyed by David NEWELL (wife Sally) on 1 Jul 1802, fee simple; both seal; WIT: Sterling JOHNSTON, Andw. BYERS; ack. Sterling JOHNSTON, J.P.

p. 295 - Know all men, Thomas MONTGOMERY, BCO; John FRANCIS, BCO. $100, wheat in S 17, livestock and household goods, signed 2 Jun 1804; his seal; WIT: Daniel CHURCH, David WORK [his mark], John GIBSON; ack. 28 Sep 1804, Sterling JOHNSTON, J.P.

p. 295 - Know all men, Thomas MONTGOMERY, BCO, John FRANCES, BCO. $60, additional livestock and household goods, signed 4 Sep 1804; his seal; WIT: James BARKLEY; ack. 28 Sep 1804, Sterling JOHNSTON, J.P., recorded 12 Oct 1804.

p. 295 - Indenture, 3Oct 1804, James BARNES (wife Nancy), St. Clairsville, BCO; Samuel SULLIVAN, same. $900, lot #21 in St. Clairsville, 1/4 acre, conveyed to John THOMPSON, Esqr., by David NEWELL (wife Sally) on 26 Sep 1803, from THOMPSON (wife Sally) to BARNES on 7 May 1804, fee simple; his seal, her mark; WIT: Sterling JOHNSTON, William JOHNSTON; ack. Sterling JOHNSTON, J.P., recorded 16 Oct 1804.

p. 297 - Indenture, 3 Oct 1804, Samuel SULLIVAN, St. Clairsville, BCO; James BARNES, same. SULLIVAN bound to BARNES in penal sum of $800, securing payment by conveying lot #21, fee simple, void if payment made by 3 Oct 1806; his seal [Saml. SULLIVAN]; WIT: William JOHNSTON, Sterling JOHNSTON; ack. Sterling JOHNSTON, J.P., recorded 16 Oct 1804. Mortgage satisfied 4 Oct 1806, James BARNES.

p. 298 - Indenture, 4 Apr 1804, Bazaleel WELLS (wife Sally), JCO; Joseph GENNEY, Washington County, Pennsylvania. $300, land on Glen's run and Steep run, NBR: Francis COOPER, EAGLESON, 75 3/4 acres; both seal; WIT: Benjn. HOUGH; ack. JCO, 4 Apr 1804, Benjn. HOUGH, J.P., HOUGH certified by John WARD, Clerk, recorded 16 Oct 1804.

p. 299 - Know all men, Noah ZANE, State of Virginia, administrator of Absalom MARTIN, Esqr., deceased, of BCO, by virtue of order from Orphan's Court April term 1804, convey to William WORKMAN, Pultney twp., BCO, which MARTIN had committed to on 5 Nov 1800 for $100, begin SW corner S 13 T 6 R 3, 50 acres, fee simple, signed 18 Aug 1804; his seal; [no witnesses given]; ack. 6 Oct 1804, Sterling JOHNSTON, J.P., recorded 22 Nov 1804.

p. 300 - Indenture, 11 Oct 1804, James FINLEY, Richland twp., BCO; Gabariel [sic] WILKINS, same. $80, two lots in St. Clairsville [#147 and #148], conveyed by David NEWELL (wife Sally) on 3 Mar 1802 and 27 Apr 1802, fee simple; his mark; WIT: Sterling JOHNSTON, Jacob NAGLE; ack. Sterling JOHNSTON, J.P.

p. 301 - Know all men, Timothy GREEN; Joseph POSEY [no locations]. $50, livestock and crops, signed 10 Oct 1804; his seal; WIT: David VANCE, Sterling JOHNSTON; ack. Sterling JOHNSTON, J.P.

p. 301 - Know all men, Noah ZANE, State of Virginia, administrator of Absalom MARTIN, Esqr., deceased, of BCO, by virtue of order from Orphan's Court August term 1804, convey to Obediah HARDESTY, Richland twp., BCO. $300, contracted during MARTIN's lifetime on 20 Jan 1800, 1/4 S 21 T 7 R 4, NBR: Daniel HARRIS, Elijah MARTIN, 160 acres, fee simple, signed 24 Aug 1804; his seal; WIT: Ebenezer ZANE, E. WOODS; ack. BCO, 16 Oct 1804, Sterling JOHNSTON, J.P., recorded 23 Nov 1804.

p. 302 - Indenture, 8 Nov 1804, John PERRY (wife Jennet), BCO; Andrew GILL, same. $200, part of SE 1/4 S 15 T 7 R 4, 60 acres, fee simple; both seal; WIT: Sterling JOHNSTON, William McWILLIAMS; ack. 8 Dec 1804, Sterling JOHNSTON, J.P.

p. 303 - Indenture, 12 Nov 1804, Andrew GILL (wife Susanna), Richland twp., BCO; Joseph PERISH [PERRISH], same. $450, part of SE 1/4 S 15 T 7 R 4, 60 acres, conveyed to GILL on 8 Nov 1804 by John PERRY (wife Jennett), fee simple; his seal, her mark; WIT: Alex BOGGS, Sterling JOHNSTON; ack. 12 Nov 1804, Sterling JOHNSTON, J.P.

p. 304 - Indenture, 22 Oct 1804, Bazaleel WELLS [no wife mentioned], JCO; James ROSS, Allegheny County, Pennsylvania. $82.71, fractional S 8 T 2 R 3, Marietta district, patented to WELLS on 29 Aug 1804; his seal; [no witnesses given]; ack. JCO, Benjamin HOUGH, J.P., HOUGH certified by Jno. WARD, Clk. J. Co.

p. 304 - Indenture, 15 Nov 1804, William IRWIN (wife Elizabeth), Wheeling, Virginia; Josiah DILLON, BCO. $150, lot #20 in St. Clairsville, 1/4 acre; his seal only; WIT: Sterling JOHNSTON, John DUGAN; ack. Sterling JOHNSTON, J.P. [no wife here either], recorded 1 Dec 1804.

p. 305 - Indenture, 13 Nov 1804, John WINTERS, BCO; Robert WINTERS, same. $400, SE 1/4 S 25 T 8 R 4, 160 acres, fee simple; his seal; [no witnesses given]; ack. Sterling JOHNSTON, J.P.

p. 306 - Indenture, 27 Oct 1804, David VANCE, Esqr. (wife Margaret), Richland twp., BCO; Robert HOPPER, same. $300, SE corner S 6 T 7 R 3, 100 acres, NBR: James JOHNSTON; both seal; WIT: John DUGAN, Sterling JOHNSTON; ack. 27 Oct 1804, Sterling JOHNSTON, J.P., recorded 3 Dec 1804.

p. 307 - Indenture, 20 Nov 1804, John WORKMAN (wife Alener), BCO; Isaac McCALISTER [McCALLESTER], same. $200, part of S 2 T 6 R 3, conveyed from Daniel McELHERON (wife Amelia) to WORKMAN on 9 Aug 1804, 83 acres 2 rods, fee simple; both mark; WIT: Sterling JOHNSTON, Benjamin WEEL [his mark]; ack. Sterling JOHNSTON, J.P., recorded 3 Dec 1804.

p. 308 - Indenture, James CAMPBELL (wife Mary), Loudoun County, Virginia; Andrew CAMPBELL [no location]. $339, 168 acres in NE corner S 12 T 9 R 6 by survey of John PLUMMER, signed 21 Sep 1804; both seal; WIT: William MOORE, Robert MOORE; 21 Nov 1804, Sterling JOHNSTON, J.P.

p. 309 - Indenture, 8 Sep 1804, John THOMPSON, merchant, St. Clairsville, BCO; William MATHERS, same. $1,000, lots #28 and #27 in St. Clairsville, each 1/4 acre, void if $1,000 paid by 1 Jun 1809; his seal; WIT: Wm. THOMPSON, Jacob NAGLE; ack. 8 Sep 1804, Andrew MARSHALL, J.P., recorded 4 Dec 1804. Mortgage satisfied by 16 Jan 1807; ack. R. JOHNSTON.

p. 310 - Indenture, 28 Sep 1804, Ebenezer ZANE (wife Elizabeth), Ohio County, Virginia; Andrew SCOTT, BCO. $300, NW 1/4 S 4 T 6 R 3; both seal; [no witnesses given]; ack. BCO, 28 Sep 1804, Jacob DAVIS, recorded 7 Jan 1805.

p. 311 - Indenture, 20 Aug 1804, Abraham PLUMMER, Kirkwood twp., BCO; Otho FRENCH, same. $200, begin NE 1/4 S 10 T 8 R 6, 100 acres, fee simple; his seal; St. Clairsville, John PLUMMER, John GREER, Junior; ack. 20 Aug 1804, John GREER, J.P.

p. 312 - Know all men, David NEWELL (wife Sally), BCO; William BROWN, BCO. $15, lot on SE corner of St. Clairsville, 1 acre 5 rods, signed 20 Aug 1804; his seal only; WIT: Daniel CHURCH, Jacob NAGLE; ack. (David only) 20 Aug 1804, Sterling JOHNSTON, J.P.

p. 312 - Indenture, 8 Dec 1804, Doctor Luther SPENCER, St. Clairsville, BCO; Enoch RUSH, same. $260, lots #8 and #7 in St. Clairsville, each 1/4 acre, conveyed from David NEWELL (wife Sally) to William BELL on 23 Nov 1802, from BELL to James BARNES on 28 Jan 1804, from BARNES (wife Nancy) to SPENCER on 13 Sep 1804, fee simple; his seal; WIT: James BARNES, Sterling JOHNSTON; ack. Sterling JOHNSTON, J.P.

p. 314 - [blank]

p. 315 - Indenture, 8 Dec 1804, Enoch RUSH, St. Clairsville, BCO; Doctor Luther SPENCER, same. RUSH bound to SPENCER in penal sum of $720 by bonds of even date, payment of $260, conveying lots #7 and #8 in St. Clairsville to secure payment, void if payment made by 15 Aug 1806; his seal; WIT: Sterling JOHNSTON, James [CLOYD?]; ack. Sterling JOHNSTON, J.P.

p. 316 - Know all men, John DOTY, York twp., BCO, power of attorney to "trusty friend, Joseph MARTIN, living on Middle Island Creek in State of Virginia, farmer, signed 17 Jan 1803; his seal; WIT: Isaac ETTKINSON, Jacob BROKE, Benj. McVAY; ack. [same day] David RUBLE, Esq., Levan OKEY, Esq., James HEUTHORN, Esq.

p. 316 - Indenture, 1 Aug 1804, James NOWELS [NOWLS] (wife Mary), BCO; Peter MOORE [MOOR], Loudoun [though is written like London] County, Virginia. $60, lot #101 in St. Clairsville, 1/4 acre, fee simple, conveyed to Mary NOWELS and James NOWELS on 27 Apr 1802 by David NEWELL (wife Sally), recorded in Book A, p. 59 [p. 9 of abstracts]; his seal, her mark; WIT: Isaac MOOR, Josiah BEAL; ack. 1 Aug 1804, John GREER, J.P.

p. 317 - Indenture, 19 Nov 1804, William WOODS (wife Jane), Richland twp., BCO; John SMITH, same. $400, lots #57 and #58 in St. Clairsville, conveyed by David NEWELL (wife Sally) to Joseph IRWIN on 2 Sep 1802, from IRWIN (wife Mary) to WOODS on 14 Aug 1804, fee simple; both mark; WIT: Sterling JOHNSTON, Mary JOHNSTON; ack. Sterling JOHNSTON, Recorder.

p. 319 - Indenture, 19 Nov 1804, John SMITH, St. Clairsville, BCO; William WOODS, BCO. SMITH bound to WOODS in penal sum of $250, securing payment by conveying lots #57 and #58 in St. Clairsville, fee simple, void if paid by 19 Nov 1807; his seal; WIT: Sterling JOHNSTON, Mary JOHNSTON; ack. Sterling JOHNSTON, J.P.

p. 320 - Indenture, 22 Dec 1804, Robert JOHNSTON, BCO; Josiah DILLON, same. $300, lot N of St. Clairsville commons, 7 acres, NBR: Jacob HOULTZ, fee simple; his seal; WIT: James CLOYD, Sterling JOHNSTON; ack. Sterling JOHNSTON, J.P.

p. 321 - Indenture, 1 Jan 1805, David NEWELL (wife Sally), Union twp., BCO; Robert GRIFFITH, same. $10, lot #155 in St. Clairsville, 1/4 acre, fee simple; both seal; WIT: Sterling JOHNSTON, John DUGAN; ack. John McDONALD, J.P.

p. 321 - 12 Jan 1805, Samuel HARBERT, Green County, Pennsylvania; John THOMPSON, Esq., St. Clairsville, BCO. $30, lot #19 in St. Clairsville, conveyed by David NEWELL (wife Sally) to HARBERT on 28 Dec 1801, fee simple; his seal; WIT: Wm. CONGLETON, William JOHNSTON; ack. Sterling JOHNSTON, J.P.

p. 322 - Indenture, 22 Jan 1805, Hugh McCOY (wife Martha), BCO; Archibald McELROY, same. $80, part of NW corner of S 1/2 of S 24 T 7 R 4, NBR: William McWILLIAMS "and others," [no size designation]; both seal; WIT: Sterling JOHNSTON, John THOMPSON; ack. Sterling JOHNSTON, J.P.

p. 323 - Indenture, 22 Jan 1805, Archibald McELROY (wife Sally), Richland twp., BCO; Phillip ROSEMAN, same. $160, part of NW corner of S 1/2 S 24 T 7 R 4, NBR: William McWILLIAMS, 40 acres, part of land conveyed from Laban BRANSON to Hugh McCOY on 6 Nov 1798, from McCOY to McELROY this date, fee simple; both seal; WIT: Sterling JOHNSTON, Merchant DEFORD; ack. Sterling JOHNSTON, J.P.

p. 324 - Indenture, 17 Aug 1804, Andrew MARSHALL (wife Margaret) and Thomas IRELAND (wife Sally) , St. Clairsville, BCO; Joseph MARSHALL, same. $64, lot #121 in St. Clairsville, 1/4 acre, fee simple; husbands seal, wives mark; WIT: Thomas MITCHELL, John McWILLIAMS; ack. Thos. MITCHELL, J.P.

p. 325 - Indenture, 7 Dec 1804, David NEWELL, Kirkwood twp., BCO; Sterling JOHNSTON, St. Clairsville, BCO. $13, lots at W end of St. Clairsville, fee simple; his seal; WIT: Jermiah [sic] MARTIN, Josiah HEDGES; ack. John THOMPSON, J.P.

p. 326 - Indenture, 31 Dec 1804, Sterling JOHNSTON, St. Clairsville, BCO; William McCONALD, BCO. $38, two lots at W end of St. Clairsville, conveyed to JOHNSTON by David NEWELL on 7 Dec 1804, fee simple; his seal; WIT: Alex GASTON, George SMITH; ack. John THOMPSON, J.P.

p. 327 - Indenture, 28 Sep 1804, Ebenezer ZANE (wife Elizabeth), [no location]; Elijah WOODS [no location]. $500, 1/2 S 29 T 3 R 2; both seal; [no witnesses given]; ack., BCO, 28 Sep 1804, Jacob DAVIS, J.P.

p. 328 - Indenture, 25 Mar 1805, William MATHERS (wife Anne), St. Clairsville, BCO; John G. HAMILTON, Esq., same. $100, lots #3 and #4 in St. Clairsville, fee simple; both seal [he Wm.]; WIT: A. MARSHALL, Edie ALEXANDER; ack. 25 Mar 1805, A. MARSHALL, J.P., recorded 17 Apr 1805.

p. 329 - Indenture, 25 Mar 1805, William MATHERS (wife Anne), St. Clairsville, BCO; William BROWN, same. $50, lot #29 S of St. Clairsville, 1/4 acre, fee simple; both seal; WIT: A. MARSHALL, Jacob NAGLE; ack. 25 Mar 1805, A. MARSHALL, J.P., recorded 17 Apr 1805.

p. 330 - Indenture, 25 Mar 1805, William MATHERS (wife Anne), St. Clairsville, BCO; John ALEXANDER, same. $100, lots #13 and #14 S of St. Clairsville, fee simple; both seal; WIT: A. MARSHALL, Edie ALEXANDER; ack. 25 Mar 1805, A. MARSHALL, J.P., recorded 17 Apr 1805.

p. 331 - Indenture, 25 Mar 1805, William MATHERS (wife Anne), St. Clairsville, BCO; Enoch RUSH, same. $40, lot in Richland twp. to S of St. Clairsville, formerly owned by David and James NEWELL, sold by James NEWELL to MATHERS, NBR: James CALDWELL, Moses MOOREHEAD, 2 acres, fee simple; both seal; WIT: A. MARSHALL, Edie ALEXANDER; ack. 25 Mar 1805, A. MARSHALL, J.P., recorded 17 Apr 1805.

p. 332 - 25 Mar 1805, William MATHERS (wife Anne), St. Clairsville, BCO; Enoch RUSH, same. $15, lot on S of St. Clairsville, NBR: William MATHERS commons, James NEWELL (formerly), conveyed by David NEWELL (wife Sally) to MATHERS on 3 Feb 1803, fee simple; both seal; WIT: William FARIS, John THOMPSON; ack. John THOMPSON, J.P., recorded 17 Apr 1805.

p. 333 - 13 Mar 1805, Caleb ENGLE (wife Mercy [Marsey]), BCO; Abraham ENGLE, BCO. $800, part of S 27 T 7 R 4, 160 acres, originally patented to John HOPKINS by Samuel OSGOOD and Walter LIVINGSTON on 3 Mar 1789 [written one thousand eight hundred but is relatively certain that this was a transcription error]; both seal; WIT: Hannah MOORE, James STARR; ack. 13 Mar 1805, James STARR, Esq., recorded 19 Apr 1805.

p. 334 - Indenture, 6 Apr 1805, 25 Mar 1805, William MATHERS (wife Anne), St. Clairsville, BCO; Allen STEWART and William IRWIN, administrators of Isaac IRWIN. $100, NBR: John LONG, A. STEWART, William MATHERS, 5 acres, fee simple; both seal; A. MARSHALL, Jacob NAGLE; ack. A. MARSHALL, J.P., recorded 19 Apr 1805.

p. 335 - Indenture, 22 Nov 1804, John CONNELL (wife Eleanor), Brooke County, Virginia; Joseph TILTON, JCO. $300, part of S 21 T 4 R 2, 120 acres, NBR: Archibald WOODS, James McMILLAN, granted to Archibald WOODS by patent dated 15 Nov 1799, conveyed by WOODS (wife Ann) to Absalom MARTIN by deed dated 1 Aug 1801, conveyed by MARTIN (wife Caty) to John CONNELL by deed dated 1 Aug 1801; both seal; WIT: Hezk. GRIFFITH, James KARR; ack. JCO, 22 Nov 1804, Hezk. GRIFFITH, J.P., recorded 19 Apr 1805.

p. 336 - Indenture, 25 Mar 1805, William MATHERS (wife Anne), St. Clairsville, BCO; Obediah JENNINGS, Steubenville, Jefferson County, Ohio. $100, lots #35 and #36 of land S of St. Clairsville, fee simple; both seal; WIT:

A. MARSHALL, Edie ALEXANDER; ack. A MARSHALL, J.P., recorded 20 Apr 1805.

p. 337 - Indenture, 22 Mar 1805, James E. NEWELL (wife Elizabeth), Union twp., BCO; William MATHERS, St. Clairsville, BCO. Bazaleel WELLS (wife Sally) in JCO execute deed dated 8 Jan 1805 granting James E. NEWELL land in Richland twp., part of S 4 T 7 R 4, 160 acres, then on 19 Jan 1804 NEWELL sold to James CALDWELL 23 acres 3 rods 7 poles of this land (NE corner), NBR: Moses MOREHEAD, Enoch RUSH, [another piece] Allen STEWART, selling to MATHERS for $2,470 ($8 per acre, 121 acres) all the land except for that sold to James CALDWELL and John LONG, fee simple, another exception for 1/2 acre for Moses MOREHEAD's tanyard; both seal; WIT: A. MARSHALL, Duncan MORRISON; ack. A. MARSHALL, J.P.

p. 339 - Indenture, 25 Sep 1804, Noah ZANE, administrator of Absalom MARTIN; John PURDY, BCO. $150, according to order from Court of Belmont County, April term 1804, conveys part of S 13 T 6 R 3, NBR: Andrew DIXEN, 60 acres; his seal; WIT: Jacob DAVIS; ack. 25 Sep 1804, Jacob DAVIS.

p. 340 - Indenture, 25 Sep 1804, John PURDY (wife Susan), BCO; Charles ECKLES, same. $150, part S 13 T 6 R 3, NBR: Andrew DICKSON, 60 acres; both mark; [no witnesses given]; ack. 25 Sep 1804, Jacob DAVIS, J.P., recorded 22 Apr 1805.

p. 341 - Indenture, 11 Apr 1805, David NEWELL, BCO; William VANCE [no location given]. $96, part of S 4 T 4 R 7 [probable switch of T and R here], NBR: Robert THOMPSON, William VANCE, 12 acres ($8 per acre), fee simple; his seal; WIT: Sterling JOHNSTON, James JOHNSTON; ack. Sterling JOHNSTON, J.P., recorded 22 Apr 1805.

p. 342 - Indenture, 10 Apr 1805, David NEWELL, BCO; William WOODS, same. $40, part of S 4 T 7 R 4, 5 acres ($8 per acre), fee simple; his seal; WIT: Lewis BRYAN, Sterling JOHNSTON; ack. Sterling JOHNSTON, J.P., recorded 22 Apr 1805.

p. 343 - Indenture, 13 Apr 1805, Josiah HEDGES, Sheriff, BCO; Joseph PATTON, same. $33.75, lots #110, #118, and #126 in St. Clairsville, by virtue of writ of fiere facias issued by Court of Common Pleas, BCO, dated 12 Mar 1805, property of William MATHERS, Joseph SHARP, and Andrew MARSHALL be sold to cover judgment of $1,025.31 awarded to James ROSS and James BOND, trading under firm of Ross and Bond, for use of Thomas FOULKE, recovered at August term 1804, plus $13.95 for cost of suit; his seal; WIT: Sterling JOHNSTON, Wm. CONGLETON; ack. Sterling JOHNSTON, J.P., recorded 24 Apr 1805.

p. 343 - Indenture, 13 Apr 1805, Josiah HEDGES, Sheriff, BCO; Bazaleel WELLS, JCO. [For background, see previous indenture.] $673.52, land in S 4 T 7 R 4, conveyed to MATHERS by James E. NEWELL (wife Elizabeth), dated 22 Mar 1805, other parcels sold to James BARNES and Moses MOREHEAD; his seal; WIT: C. HAMMOND, Sterling JOHNSTON; ack. Sterling JOHNSTON, J.P.

p. 345 - Indenture, 13 Apr 1805, Josiah HEDGES, Sheriff, BCO; James BARNES and Moses MOREHEAD, same. [For background, see first indenture on p. 343.] $112.01, land near St. Clairsville, NBR: John LONG, 3 acres, property of William MATHERS; his seal; WIT: Sterling JOHNSTON, William VANCE; ack. Sterling JOHNSTON, J.P.

p. 346 - Indenture, 13 Apr 1805, Josiah HEDGES, Sheriff, BCO; Bazaleel WELLS, JCO. [For background, see first indenture on p. 343.] $181.25, lots #27, #25, #26, #28, #39, #10, #11, #12, #17, #18, #19, #20, #15, #16, #21, #22, #23, #24, #31, #32, in part of St. Clairsville laid out by William MATHERS, called an addition to St. Clairsville; his seal; WIT: Sterling JOHNSTON, C. HAMMOND; ack. Sterling JOHNSTON, J.P.

p. 347 - Indenture, 25 Mar 1805, James JOHNSTON (wife Jane), Richland twp., BCO; Charles FRYMAN, BCO. $30, 3 acres of land with NBR: David VANCE, Esq., Robert HOPPER; both seal [her name Jenney]; WIT: Sterling JOHNSTON, Robt. GRIFFITH; ack. 5 Apr 1805, Sterling JOHNSTON, J.P., recorded 26 Apr 1805.

p. 348 - Indenture, 22 Mar 1805, James E. NEWELL (wife Elizabeth), Union twp., BCO; John LONG, St. Clairsville, BCO. $200, land in NW corner of land NEWELL sold to William MATHERS, NBR: Allen STEWART, 15 acres; both seal; WIT: A. MARSHALL, Wm. MATHERS; ack. 22 Mar 1805, A. MARSHALL, J.P., recorded 26 Apr 1805.

p. 349 - Indenture, 18 Apr 1805, 13 Apr 1805, Josiah HEDGES, Sheriff, BCO; John PATTERSON and Thomas McCALL, BCO. [For background, see first indenture on p. 343.] $22.80, lot #30 in St. Clairsville; his seal; WIT: Sterling JOHNSTON, Andrew BYERS; ack. Sterling JOHNSTON, J.P., recorded 29 Apr 1805.

p. 349 - Indenture, 9 Apr 1805, 13 Apr 1805, Josiah HEDGES, Sheriff, BCO; Samuel SULLIVAN, BCO. [For background, see first indenture on p. 343.] $24.05, lot #22 in St. Clairsville; his seal; WIT: Sterling JOHNSTON, Andrew BYERS; ack. Sterling JOHNSTON, J.P., recorded 29 Apr 1805.

p. 350 - Indenture, 15 Apr 1805, John FRANCIS (wife Easter), Richland twp., BCO; Thomas BARR, BCO. $100, lot #40 in St. Clairsville, 1/4 acre, conveyed by David NEWELL (wife Sally) to FRANCIS on 21 Dec 1801 as recorded in Book A, p. 7 [p. 2 of abstracts]; [no seal, no witnesses given, no signature on ack.].

p. 351 - Indenture, 8 Jan 1805, Bazaleel WELLS (wife Sally), JCO; James NEWELL, BCO. $560, part of S 4 T 7 R 4, 160 acres; both seal; WIT: Benj. HOUGH; ack. JCO, 8 Jan 1805, Benj. HOUGH, J.P., certification of HOUGH by Jno. WARD, Clerk.

p. 353 - Know all men, William HENDERSON, Richland twp., BCO; Richard COPELAND and Samuel MUCHMORE [MICHMORE], same. $30, roan mare, void if $30 judgment in favor of William FLETCHER on Sterling JOHNSTONE's docket is paid, signed 27 Apr 1805; his seal; WIT: Sterling JOHNSTON, J.P., Robt. GRIFFITH; ack. Sterling JOHNSTON, J.P., recorded 30 Apr 1805.

p. 353 - Indenture, 19 Apr 1805, John DUGAN (wife Hannah), Peas twp., BCO; Henry STONER [STENER], BCO. $50, begin at SW corner of lot belonging to Michael GROVE near St. Clairsville, 1/4 acre, fee simple; both seal; WIT: Sterling JOHNSTON, Andrew BYERS; ack. Sterling JOHNSTON, J.P.

p. 354 - Indenture, 19 Apr 1805, John DUGAN (wife Hannah), Peas twp., BCO; Henry STONER [STENER], BCO. $50, 1/2 acre near St. Clairsville, 1/2 acre, fee simple; both seal; WIT: Sterling JOHNSTON, Andw. BYERS; ack. Sterling JOHNSTON, J.P.

p. 355 - Indenture, 19 Apr 1805, Henry STONER, St. Clairsville, BCO; John DUGAN, BCO. $90 owed to DUGAN, two lots near St. Clairsville, 1/4 and 1/2 acre each [conveyed in two previous items], conveyed to DUGAN by David NEWELL (wife Sally) on 10 Oct 1802, recorded in Book A, pp. 111 and 112 [p. 16 of extracts], void if $90 paid by 25 Dec 1805; his seal; WIT: Sterling JOHNSTON, Andw. BYERS; ack. Sterling JOHNSTON, J.P.

p. 356 - Indenture, 19 Apr 1805, Henry STONER, St. Clairsville, BCO; James [BARGAU / BURGAU?], BCO. $50, lot at W end of St. Clairsville, fee simple; his seal; WIT: Sterling JOHNSTON, Thos. RICHARDS; ack. Sterling JOHNSTON, J.P., recorded 1 May 1805.

p. 357 - Indenture, 18 Feb 1805, John THOMPSON, Esq. (wife Sally), St. Clairsville, Richland twp., BCO; Samuel THOMPSON, Richland twp., BCO. $30, lot #64 in St. Clairsville, conveyed to J. THOMPSON from David NEWELL (wife Sally) on 5 May 1803, fee simple; his seal, her mark; WIT:

Sterling JOHNSTON, Samuel I. CRAWFORD; ack. 18 Feb 1805; Sterling JOHNSTON, J.P.

p. 358 - Indenture, 7 d 5 m 1805, Josiah DILLON, BCO; Thomas PHILLIPS, Loudoun County, Virginia. $466, S 24 T 5 R 3, Steubenville district, DILLON obtained by making first payment, PHILLIPS now has to make remaining payments; his seal; WIT: Horton HOWARD, Mahlon SMITH; ack. 7 May 1805, Sterling JOHNSTON, J.P.

p. 358 - Know all men, John BRANAN, Pease twp., BCO; Nancy BRANAN, same. Natural love and affection plus $.50, livestock and household goods, signed 14 Feb 1805; his mark; WIT: George LATTIMORE, John McWILLIAMS, Thos. THOMPSON; ack. 24 Apr 1805, Thos. THOMPSON.

p. 359 - Will of William BROWN, St. Clairsville, BCO. Son William to continue in service of Jacob HOULTS for one year according to contract, also to be under direction of his mother until 18, dau Mary to continue in service of Enoch RUSH for 12 months then under care of mother until 18, son John in care of mother until 18, son Fredrick in care of mother until 21, signed 11 May 1805; his seal; WIT: Robert GRIFFITH, Sterling JOHNSTON; ack. Sterling JOHNSTON, J.P.

p. 360 - Know all men, James McCONNALL (wife Rachel), Clumbina [sic] County, Ohio, signed in fee for 150 acres, part of patent for 1,000 acres conveyed to John SPOTTSWOOD, to Job SHARP for 500, Thomas SMITH, BCO, to get 350 acres, on waters of Paint Creek, Ross County, Thomas SMITH is attorney able to sell in fee simple, signed 29 d 9 m 1804; both seal; WIT: John CROZER, Thomas COWGILL; ack. Columbina [sic] County, Ohio, of power of attorney, John CROZER, J.P., CROZER certified 8 Oct 1804, Reasin BELL, Clerk, recorded 15 May 1805.

p. 361 - Plat of 15 lots joining to addition to St. Clairsville, 20 May 1805, by Bazaleel WELLS; ack. Sterling JOHNSTON, J.P. (See Appendix.)

p. 361 - Indenture, 23 May 1805, Michael GROVE, St. Clairsville, BCO; Moses MOREHEAD, same. $249, 10 acres adjacent to St. Clairsville, fee simple; his seal, her mark; WIT: Sterling JOHNSTON, Wm. FARIS, Junr.; ack. Sterling JOHNSTON, J.P., recorded 27 May 1805.

p. 362 - Know all men, Noah ZANE, State of Virginia, administrator of Absalom MARTIN, BCO, by order of Court of Common Pleas in April term 1804 convey to Elijah MARTIN, BCO, land sold to Elijah on 14 Jun 1800, for $480, 1/4 S 21 T 7 R 4, 160 acres, fee simple, signed 25 May 1805; his seal; WIT: Hetty WOODS, Jane WOODS; ack. Thos. THOMPSON, J.P., recorded 29 May 1805.

p. 363 - Indenture, 25 May 1805, Gabriel WILKINS, Richland twp., BCO; Henry DOUDNE [DOUDNA], BCO. $[1?]00 [number of hundreds omitted], lots #148 and #147 in St. Clairsville, each 1/4 acre, fee simple; his seal; WIT: Daniel WILKINS, Sterling JOHNSTON; ack. Sterling JOHNSTON, J.P., recorded 30 May 1805.

p. 364 - Indenture, 27 May 1805, Bazaleel WELLS (wife Sally), JCO; William BOGGS, BCO. $53.25, part of S 10 T 7 R 4, NBR: Ezekiel BOGGS, Allen STEWART, William BOGGS; both seal; WIT: Benj. HOUGH; ack. JCO, Benj. HOUGH, J.P., HOUGH certified by Jno. WARD, Clerk.

p. 365 - Know all men, Noah ZANE, State of Virginia, administrator of Absalom MARTIN, BCO, by order of Court of Common Pleas in April term 1804, convey to James KELSEY, BCO, land sold by MARTIN on 10 Oct 1800 for $130.50, part of S 13 T 6 R 3, 50 acres 3 rods, fee simple, signed 16 Feb 1805; his seal; [no witnesses given], ack. 16 Feb 1805, Jacob DAVIS, J.P., recorded 31 May 1805.

p. 366 -Indenture, 29 May 1805, Enoch RUSH (wife Martha), Richland twp., BCO; Joseph HARRIS, Richland twp., BCO. $600, lots #8 and #7 in St. Clairsville, each 1/4 acre, conveyed by David NEWELL (wife Sally) to William BELL, from BELL to James BARNES, from BARNES to Doctor Luther SPENCER, from SPENCER to RUSH; his seal, her mark; WIT: Sterling JOHNSTON; ack. Sterling JOHNSTON, J.P., recorded 4 Jun 1805.

p. 368 - Indenture, 31 May 1805, Enoch RUSH (wife Martha), BCO; James BARNES, BCO. $328, land S of St. Clairsville, 5 1/2 acres, fee simple; his seal, her mark; WIT: Joseph HARRIS, Sterling JOHNSTON; ack. Sterling JOHNSTON, J.P.

p. 369 - Indenture, 24 May 1805, Bazaleel WELLS (wife Sally), JCO; Ezekiel BOGGS, BCO. $1,158, part of S 9 and 10, T 7 R 4, NBR: James WOODS, David McWILLIAMS, William BOGGS, 329 1/2 acres; both seal; WIT: Benj. HOUGH; ack. JCO, Benj. HOUGH, J.P., HOUGH certified by Jno. WARD, Clerk.

p. 370 - Indenture, 19 May 1804, Frances [Francis] SUNDERLAND (wife Ann), Richland twp., BCO; William GIBSON, Ohio County, Virginia. $216, 13 acres 3 rods 10 perches, part of land conveyed to SUNDERLAND by Peter SUNDERLAND, Senr., on 29 Oct 1800, recorded in JCO Book A, p. 217, fee simple; both mark; WIT: Sterling JOHNSTON, Notely HAYS; ack. Sterling JOHNSTON, J.P., recorded 12 Jun 1805.

p. 371 - Indenture, 24 May 1805, Valentine AULT (wife Catharine), Richland twp., BCO; Notley HAYS, same. On 25 Oct 1798 AULT purchased 100 acres of land from Bazaleel WELLS, JCO, NBR: formerly Peter SUNDERLAND and now Notley HAYS, supposed to be within boundaries of S 4 T 7 R 4 but later surveying found that the line was further north, now for $71 AULT is selling to HAYS, 8 acres 3 rods 25 perches; his seal, her mark; WIT: John WHERRY, Robert JOHNSTON; ack. Sterling JOHNSTON, J.P., recorded 14 Jun 1805.

p. 372 - Indenture, 24 May 1805, Notely HAYS (wife Sarah), Richland twp., BCO; William WOODS, same. Peter SUNDERLAND purchased of Bazaleel WELLS of JCO 100 acres in S 4 T 7 R 4, for $71 conveying 9 1/2 acres to compensate for incorrect section line; his seal, her mark; WIT: Robert JOHNSTON, John WHERRY; ack. Sterling JOHNSTON, J.P., recorded 14 Jun 1805.

p. 374 - Indenture, 10 Jun 1805, David VANCE, Esq. (wife Margaret), Richland twp., BCO; Henry CLOSE, same. $1,650, 165 acres, part of S 5 T 7 R 4, granted to David VANCE by patent dated 12 Feb 1798, recorded in patent Book A, p. 40, NBR: James WILKINS, fee simple; his seal, her mark; WIT: John WHERRY, Sterling JOHNSTON; ack. 10 <u>May</u> 1805, Sterling JOHNSTON, J.P.

p. 375 - Indenture, 11 Jun 1805, Ezekiel BOGGS, BCO; Alexander BOGGS, same. $560, part S 10 T 7 R 4, NBR: William BOGGS, David WILLIAMS, 166 acres 2 rods, part of land granted [no dates] to Jacob BLACKWALL and transferred from him to John CRAWFORD, from CRAWFORD to Laban BRANSON, from BRANSON to Bazaleel WELLS, from WELLS to Ezekiel BOGGS, recorded in Washington and Jefferson Counties; his seal; WIT: Robert GRIFFITH, Robert JOHNSTON; ack. Sterling JOHNSTON, J.P., recorded 14 Jun 1805.

p. 376 - Indenture, 15 Jun 1805, Daniel McPEEK (wife Elizabeth), Richland twp., BCO; Job RIDGEWAY, BCO. $100, lot #49 in St. Clairsville, 1/4 acre, conveyed by David NEWELL (wife Sally) to McPEEK on 9 Jun 1802, fee simple; his mark [no wife]; WIT: Sterling JOHNSTON, John PICKERING; ack. Daniel only, Sterling JOHNSTON, J.P., recorded 1 Jul 1805.

p. 377 - Indenture, 15 Jun 1805, John WORKMAN (wife Eleanor), BCO; James KELSEY, BCO. $130, 50 acres in SW corner S 2 T 6 R 3, conveyed to WORKMAN by Daniel McELHERON on 9 Aug 1804, fee simple; both mark; WIT: Sterling JOHNSTON, Robert GRIFFITH; ack. Sterling JOHNSTON, J.P., recorded 1 Jul 1805.

p. 378 - Indenture, 15 Jun 1805, James KELSEY (wife Elizabeth), BCO; Abraham WORKMAN, same. $132, 58 acres 3 rods, part S 13 T 3 R 6, conveyed from Noah ZANE, administrator of Absalom MARTIN, to KELSEY on 16 Feb 1805, fee simple; both seal; WIT: Sterling JOHNSTON, Robt. GRIFFITH; ack. Sterling JOHNSTON, J.P., recorded 2 Jul 1805.

p. 379 - Indenture, 19 Jun 1805, John WINTERS, BCO; Benjamine PEARSON, same. $1,160, W 1/2 of S 25 T 8 R 4, 320 acres, patented by WINTERS, fee simple; his seal; WIT: Sterling JOHNSTON, Wm. CONGLETON, ack. Sterling JOHNSTON, J.P.

p. 380 - Indenture, 19 Feb 1801, David NEWELL (wife Sally) and Benjamine NEWELL (wife Jane), Jefferson County, NWT; Jonathan QUIGLEY, same. $12, lot #114 in St. Clairsville, 1/4 acre, fee simple; all seal; [no witnesses given]; ack. Jefferson County, 20 Feb 1801, James NEWELL, J.P., recorded 3 Jul 1805.

p. 380 - Indenture, 25 Mar 1805, William MATHERS (wife Anne), St. Clairsville, BCO; Henry JOHNSTON, same. $100, lots #1 and #2 in St. Clairsville, fee simple; both seal; WIT: A. MARSHALL, Jacob NAGLE; ack. 25 Mar 1805, A. MARSHALL, J.P., recorded 3 Jul 1805.

p. 381 -Indenture, 13 Apr 1805, Josiah DILLON [no location given]; Thomas VAN SWEARENGEN, Zanesville, Muskingum County, Ohio. $1,000, 7 acres in S 4 T 7 R 4, near St. Clairsville commons, void if DILLON pays $1,000 to VAN SWEARENGEN by 13 Apr 1807; both seal; WIT: [Milkman?], Richard ASHMAN, David HERRON; on 15 Apr 1805 VAN SWERINGEN transfers his title to James TAYLOR, WIT: Thomas STEEL; ack. 9 Jul 1805, Sterling JOHNSTON, J.P., entered 9 and recorded 12 Jul 1805.

p. 383 - Know all men, Joseph BALDWIN, Pultney, BCO; Daniel McELHERON, Esq. $166.67, livestock and household goods, signed 11 [?] 1805; his seal; WIT: Elizabeth SHOLER [her mark], Edward [FRUYD??] [his mark]; ack. 16 Jul 1805, Sterling JOHNSTON, J.P., recorded 19 Jul 1805.

p. 384 - Indenture, 18 Jun 1803, Daniel McELHERON, Pultney, BCO; Patrick WHITE, BCO. $200, 50 acres in S 32 T 2 R 2; his seal; WIT: Jacob REPSHER, Joseph LASHLEY; ack. [Daniel and wife Amelia], 17 Dec 1805, George HEAP, J.P.

p. 385 - Indenture, 13 Apr 1805, Josiah HEDGES, Sheriff, BCO; Andrew MOORE, BCO. [See p. 343 for details of order.] $27, lot #14 in St. Clairsville; his seal; WIT: C. HAMMOND, Sterling JOHNSTON; ack. 18 Jul 1805, Sterling JOHNSTON, J.P., recorded 22 Jul 1805.

p. 386 - Indenture, 8 Apr 1805, William MATHERS (wife Anne), St. Clairsville, BCO; David MATHERS, Washington County, Pennsylvania. $50, lot #67, fee simple; both seal; WIT: A. MARSHALL, Jacob NAGLE; ack. 8 Apr 1805, A. MARSHALL, J.P., recorded 23 Aug 1805.

p. 387 - Indenture, 8 Apr 1805, William MATHERS (wife Anne), St. Clairsville, BCO; David MATHERS, Washington County, Pennsylvania. $600, lot in St. Clairsville [no number given], 1/4 acre, fee simple; both seal; WIT: A. MARSHALL, Jacob NAGLE; ack. A. MARSHALL, J.P.

p. 388 - Indenture, 8 Apr 1805, William MATHERS (wife Anne), St. Clairsville, BCO; David MATHERS, Washington County, Pennsylvania. $500, lot in St. Clairsville [no number given], 1/4 acre, fee simple; both seal; WIT: A. MARSHALL, Jacob NAGLE; ack. 8 Apr 1805, A. MARSHALL, J.P.

p. 389 - Indenture, 11 May 1805, James BRYAN (wife Elizabeth), Richland twp., BCO; Isaac VORE, late of Fredrick County, Maryland, now of Ohio. $300, lot #84 in St. Clairsville, 1/4 acre, fee simple; his seal, her mark; WIT: Sterling JOHNSTON, Robert JOHNSTON; ack. 14 Aug 1805, Sterling JOHNSTON, J.P., recorded 24 Aug 1805.

p. 390 - Indenture, 16 Aug 1805, Andrew WILKINS, Richland twp., BCO; Joseph POSEY, same. POSEY bound to WILKINS for $19.01 payable to William MILLER by 10 Aug 1806, conveying cow bought of MILLER to secure payment, void if payment made; his seal; WIT: Sterling JOHNSTON, Wm. CONGLETON, ack. Sterling JOHNSTON, J.P.

p. 390 - Indenture, 27 Aug 1805, James WOODS (wife Jane), BCO; James CALDWELL, BCO. $200, lot #52 in St. Clairsville, 1/4 acre, fee simple; his seal, her mark; WIT: Sterling JOHNSTON, James CLOYD; ack. Sterling JOHNSTON, J.P.

p. 391 - Indenture, 5 Nov 1804, Thomas MITCHELL (wife Nancy), BCO; Robert T. FINNEY, BCO. $469, part of S 20 and 26 T 4 R 2, NBR: John HANNAH (sold by Bazaleel WELLS), 67 acres; both seal; WIT: James ALEXANDER; ack. 6 Nov 1804, James ALEXANDER, Judge, CCP, recorded 25 Aug 1805.

p. 392 - Indenture, 25 Mar 1805, William MATHERS (wife Anne), St. Clairsville, BCO; Joseph MARSHALL, BCO. $200, lots #5, 6, 7, 8, S of St. Clairsville commons, 1 acre total, fee simple; both seal; WIT: A. MARSHALL, Jacob NAGLE; ack. 25 Mar 1805, A. MARSHALL, J.P.

p. 393 - Indenture, 25 Mar 1805, William MATHERS (wife Anne), St. Clairsville, BCO; William B. HERRON, same. $100, lots #33 and #34, fee simple; both seal; WIT: A. MARSHALL, Edie MARSHALL; ack. 25 Mar 1805, A. MARSHALL, J.P.

p. 394 - Indenture, 28 Sep 1804, Bazaleel WELLS (wife Sally), JCO; Thomas MITCHELL, BCO. $245, part of S 20 and 26 T 4 R 2, NBR: John HANNAH, 67 acres; both seal; [no witnesses given], ack. JCO, 28 Sep 1804, Phillip CABLE, Judge, CCP, CABLE certified 29 Sep 1804, by Jno. WARD, Clerk.

p. 395 - Indenture, 7 Aug 1805, Robert RUSSEL (wife Hannah), Salem twp., Campagn [sic] County, Ohio; Caleb RUSSEL, Richland twp., BCO. $600, S 15 T 7 R 4, same conveyed by Labon BRANSON of City of New York to Robert and Caleb RUSSEL by deed dated 21 Jan 1799 as recorded in Jefferson County, 80 acres, NE 1/4 of land granted by Samuel OSGOOD and Walter LIVINGSTON to John HOPKINS on 3 Mar 1789; both seal; WIT: Thomas DAVIS, James STEPHENS; ack. Thos. DAVIS, Esqr., J.P.; ack. Champaign County, 8 Aug 1805, Joseph C. VANCE, J.P.

p. 397 - Indenture, 21 Oct 1805, Elijah MARTIN (wife Rebeckah), Adams County, Ohio; Abraham ENGLE, BCO. $1,280, begin NW corner S 21T 7 R 4, 160 acres, conveyed by Noah ZANE, administrator of Absalom MARTIN, to Elijah MARTIN on 25 May 1805 as recorded in Book A, p. 362 [p. 55 of abstracts], fee simple; his seal, her mark; WIT: Sterling JOHNSTON, Adam JOHNSTON; ack. BCO, Sterling JOHNSTON, J.P.

p. 398 - Indenture, 8 Nov 1805, Bazaleel WELLS (wife Sally), JCO; Matthew PATTON, BCO. $805, all of fractional S 14 and part of S 20 T 4 R 2, 254 1/4 acres; both seal; WIT: Benj. HOUGH; ack. JCO, Benj. HOUGH, J.P., HOUGH certified by Jno. WARD, Clerk.

p. 399 - Indenture, 12 Nov 1805, Josiah DILLON (wife Dorothy), St. Clairsville, BCO; Jesse McGEE, same. $200, lot #20 in St. Clairsville, 1/4 acre, conveyed from William IRWIN of State of Virginia to DILLON on 15 Nov 1804 as recorded in Book A, p. 304 [p. 47 of abstracts], fee simple; both seal; WIT: Henry ROBERTS, Sterling JOHNSTON, James CALDWELL; ack. Sterling JOHNSTON, J.P.

p. 400 - Indenture, 25 Jun 1805, Moses CHAPLIN (wife Mary) and Andrew WOODS (wife Mary), Ohio County, Virginia; Noah ZANE and John ZANE, same. $3,840, tract on Wheeling Creek granted to Moses CHAPLIN and Andrew WOODS by patent dated 15 Nov1797, S 33 T 3 R 2, 640 acres, common not joint tenants; all seal; WIT: Rebeckah KELLY, Josiah CHAPLIN, Henry

HOGAN; ack. Ohio County, Virginia, at court held on Tuesday, 8 Oct 1805, signed 11 Oct 1805, Moses CHAPLIN, Clerk of Court.

p. 401 - Indenture, 29 Oct 1805, Robert WINTER [WINTERS] (wife Sarah), Richland twp., BCO; John THOMPSON, St. Clairsville, BCO. $800, SE 1/4 of S 25 T 8 R 4 on which WINTERS now lives, 160 acres; his seal [wife not signing]; WIT: John WHERRY, John WINTER; ack. 29 Oct 1805 [both husband and wife], Sterling JOHNSTON, J.P.

p. 402 - Indenture, 28 Oct 1805, John WINTERS, St. Clairsville, BCO; John THOMPSON, Esqr., Richland twp., BCO. $1,400, land in Richland twp., NE 1/4 S 25 T 8 R 4, granted to WINTERS by patent dated 10 Apr 1804, fee simple; his seal; WIT: Sterling JOHNSTON, Robert JOHNSTON; ack. Sterling JOHNSTON, J.P.

p. 403 - Indenture, 12 Nov 1805, William McCONALD, Richland twp., BCO; John SOUTH, same. $39, at W end of St. Clairsville, NBR: Robert LAUGHLIN, sold by David NEWELL to Sterling JOHNSTON on 7 Dec 1804, from JOHNSTON to McCONALD on 31 Dec 1804, fee simple; his seal [McCONNALD]; WIT: James KNOX, Samuel MOORE; ack. Sterling JOHNSTON, J.P.

p. 404 - Indenture, 15 Oct 1805, Robert VANCE (wife Rebeckah), Richland twp., BCO; Robert CARNES, [no location given]. $50, lot #39 in St. Clairsville; both seal; WIT: Robert GRIFFITH, Sterling JOHNSTON; ack. 20 Dec 1805, John THOMPSON, J.P.

p. 405 - Indenture, 16 Nov 1805, Allen STEWART (wife Ann), BCO; David HERR [KERR], Bart twp., Lancaster County, Pennsylvania. $1,600, 79 acres on McMahon Creek, originally granted to Jacob BLACKWELL by patent dated 27 Jul 1789, from BLACKWELL to John CRAWFORD by deed dated 16 May 1796, from CRAWFORD to Labon BRANSON by deed dated 31 May 1796, from BRANSON to Bazaleel WELLS by deed dated 8 Aug 1796, from WELLS to STEWART by deed dated 18 Dec 1798, as recorded in Jefferson County, lot [section?] 10; his seal, her mark; WIT: A. MARSHALL, Richard BROWN, Jun.; ack. BCO, A. MARSHALL, Justice, CCP.

p. 406 - Indenture, 20 Nov 1805, James E. NEWELL (wife Elizabeth), BCO; Moses MOREHEAD, same. $200, NE corner of SW 1/4 of S 4 T 7 R4, purchased by NEWELL of Bazaleel WELLS, NBR: James CALDWELL, 3 1/2 acres; both seal; WIT: A. MARSHALL, Josiah HEDGES; ack. A. MARSHALL, J.P.

p. 407 - Indenture, 20 Nov 1805, James E. NEWELL (wife Elizabeth), BCO; James CALDWELL, same. $400, part of SW 1/4 of S 4 T 7 R 4, conveyed by NEWELL by Bazaleel WELLS, JCO, NBR: Moses MOREHEAD, 23 acres 3 rods and 7 perches, reservation made by NEWELL in deed to William MATHERS as recorded in Book A, p. 337 [p. 51 of abstracts]; both seal; WIT: Sterling JOHNSTON, Robert JOHNSTON; ack. Sterling JOHNSTON, J.P.

p. 408 - Indenture, 11 May 1805, James BARNES (wife Nancy), Richland twp., BCO; Joseph HARRIS, same. $1,000, land N of St. Clairsville, NBR: Notely HAYS, part of S 4 T 7 R 4, 28 acres, conveyed from David NEWELL (wife Sally) to Michael HELMS on 6 Dec 1802, from HELMS to BARNES on 6 Jan 1804, fee simple; his seal, her mark; WIT: Sterling JOHNSTON, Wm. FARQUHER; ack. 26 May 1805, Sterling JOHNSTON, J.P.

p. 409 - Indenture, 26 Nov 1805, James BARNES (wife Nancy), BCO; William FURQUHAR, late of Fredrick County, State of Maryland. $450, land on S of St. Clairsville, 5 1/2 acres, fee simple; his seal, her mark; WIT: Sterling JOHNSTON, Joseph HARRIS; ack. Sterling JOHNSTON, J.P.

p. 410 - Indenture, 19 Nov 1805, William VANCE (wife Mary), Richland twp., BCO; James WILKINS, same. $1,600, part of S 4 and 5 T 7 R 4, 160 acres, NBR: Henry CLOSE, part in S 4 conveyed by David NEWELL (wife Sally) on 11 Apr 1805 as recorded in Book A, p. 341 [p. 52 of abstracts], and part in S 5 granted to David VANCE by patent dated 12 Feb 1798, recorded in patent book A, p. 40, conveyed from David VANCE (wife Margaret) to William VANCE on 7 Dec 1798, recorded in Jefferson County, Book A, p. 89, fee simple; both seal; WIT: Sterling JOHNSTON, Wm. CONGLETON; ack. Sterling JOHNSTON, J.P.

p. 411 - Indenture, 28 Feb 1801, Jonathan BUCHANON, Washington County, Pennsylvania; Jacob DAVIS [no location given]. $800, land in Jefferson County, NWT, on McMahons Creek, 103 ("one hundred three three"...perhaps 133?] 1/3 acres; his seal; WIT: John GOODEN, Geo. [KNOX?], Josiah THORNBURY; ack. 4 Mar 1801, NWT, Hezk. GRIFFITH, Justice, Jefferson County.

p. 411 - [seems to be a repeat of the above] Indenture, 28 Feb 1801, John BUCHANAN [BUCHANON] (wife Ann), Washington County, Pennsylvania; Jacob DAVIS [no location given]. $800, reference to S 11 T 2 R 2, part of tract granted by William DUER to BUCHANAN in 1792; both seal; WIT: John GOOING [sic], Geo. KNOX, Josiah THORNBURGH; ack. NWT: 4 Mar 1801, Hezk. GRIFFITH, Justice, Jefferson County.

p. 412 - Territory NW of Ohio, Belmont County, Jacob COLEMAN, High Sheriff, BCO, Fiere faceas from Court of Common Pleas, returnable August term

1802, lot #6, square #31 in Pultney, sold to Alexander DAVIS, BCO, $29, signed 26 Aug 1802; his seal; WIT: Jacob COLEMAN, David LOCKWOOD; ack. 26 Aug 1802, David L. WOOD [sic – could this have been a misreading of LOCKWOOD?], J.P.

p. 413 - Know all men, Jacob REPSHER, Pultney, Belmont County, NWT; John BARNES, same. $50, lot #6 in square #31 in Pultney, by instrument dated 16 Jun 1797 from Robert THROUP, New York City, to Jacob LEWIS, by instrument dated 6 Sep 1801 from LEWIS to REPSHER; both seal (an Elizabeth signs also); WIT: Jacob LEWIS, Richard DILEY; ack. 1 Feb 1802, John FAIRES, J.P.

p. 413 - Indenture, 4 Sep 1805, Joseph McCONNEL (wife Sarah), Columbiana County, Ohio; John PATTERSON, St. Clairsville, BCO, and Thomas McCALL, Washington County, Pennsylvania. $200, lot #13 in St. Clairsville, 1/4 acre, conveyed by David NEWELL (wife Sally) and Benjamine NEWELL (wife Jane) to McCONNEL by deed dated 17 Apr 1801; both seal; WIT: Sterling JOHNSTON, William BOGGS; ack. BCO, 4 Sep 1805 for Joseph, Sterling JOHNSTON, J.P., 10 Dec 1805 for Sarah, Sterling JOHNSTON, J.P.

p. 414 - Indenture, 11 Oct 1805, Robert VANCE (wife Rebeckah), Richland twp., BCO; Sterling JOHNSTON, same. $30, lot #141 in St. Clairsville, 1/4 acre, conveyed by David NEWELL (wife Sally) on 6 May 1803, fee simple; both seal; WIT: Robert GRIFFITH, Jacob _____; ack. 20 Dec 1805, Sterling JOHNSTON, J.P.

p. 415 - To all people, Abijah HUNT, Natchez, Missippi [sic] Territory; Jeremiah HUNT, Indiana Territory. $4,800, S 2 and 8 T 4 R 3 near Captinah Creek, signed 10 May 1804; his seal; WIT: Wm. HOULEY, John MAYHARD; ack. Hamilton County, Ohio (Cincinnati), 15 Nov 1804, John MAHARD, J.P.

p. 416 - Indenture, 27 Dec 1805, Joseph PATTON (wife Letecia), St. Clairsville, BCO; John LONG, BCO. Josiah HEDGES, Esq., executed deed dated 10 Apr 1805 conveying to PATTON under fiere facias [see p. 343 for details], lot #110 in St. Clairsville, 1/4 acre, $50, fee simple; both seal; WIT: Sterling JOHNSTON, Lancelot ARMSTRONG; ack. Sterling JOHNSTON, J.P.

p. 417 - Indenture, 31 Dec 1805, Joseph HARRIS (wife Mary), Richland twp., BCO; John THOMPSON, Esq., same. $500, lots #8 and #7 in St. Clairsville, each 1/4 acre, conveyed from David NEWELL (wife Sally) to William BELL on 23 Sep 1802 and 26 Oct 1802, from BELL and wife to James BARNES, from BARNES (wife Nancy) to Luther SPENCER on 13 Sep 1804, from SPENCER to Enoch RUSH on 8 Dec 1804, from RUSH and wife to HARRIS on 29 May

1805; his seal, her mark; WIT: William THOMPSON, Robert JOHNSTON; ack. Sterling JOHNSTON, J.P.

p. 419 - Indenture, 6 Jan 1806, Henry STONER (wife Elizabeth), St. Clairsville, BCO; John YOUNG, same. $50, land near W end of St. Clairsville, 1/4 acre, conveyed from John DUGAN (wife Hannah) to STONER on 19 Apr 1805 as recorded in Book A, p. 354 [p. 54 of abstracts], fee simple; his seal, her mark; WIT: Sterling JOHNSTON, Mary JOHNSTON; ack. Sterling JOHNSTON, J.P.

p. 420 - Know all men, James McKIRK, BCO, Court of Common Pleas order in December term empowering him as a copartner with Andrew DIXON, deceased, in a contract during his lifetime on 22 May1797 which bound them to make a deed to Samuel WORLEY, BCO, for land in S 7 T 6 R 3, NBR: Andrew DIXON (deceased), James ROBERTSON, William JOHNSTON, 120 acres, fee simple [no money amount given], signed 6 Jan 1806; his seal; WIT: Sterling JOHNSTON, Joseph POSEY; ack. Sterling JOHNSTON, J.P.

p. 421 - Indenture, 24 Aug 1805, Bazaleel WELLS (wife Sally), JCO; Robert COCHRAN, Ohio County, Virginia. $150, part of S 20 T 4 R2, NBR: Mathew PATTON, 87 acres 16 perches; both seal; WIT: Thomas ELLET [probably ELLIOT?]; ack. JCO, 24 Aug 1805, Thomas ELLIOT, J.P., ELLIOT certified by John WARD, Clerk.

p. 422 - Indenture, 15 Jan 1806, Michael GROVE (wife Elizabeth), Richland twp., BCO; Samuel CRAWFORD, same. $80, land on W end of St. Clairsville, 1/4 acre, conveyed by David NEWELL (wife Sally) to John DUGAN on 9 Oct 1802, from DUGAN (wife Hannah) to GROVE on 14 May 1803, fee simple; his seal, her mark; WIT: Sterling JOHNSTON, John [COLOUR?]; ack. Sterling JOHNSTON, J.P.

p. 423 - Indenture, 4 Jan 1806, Samuel THOMPSON (wife Jane), Richland twp., BCO; William CONGLETON, same. $100, lot #60 in St. Clairsville, conveyed by David NEWELL (wife Sally) to John THOMPSON, Esqr., on 5 May 1803, from John (wife Sally) to Samuel on 18 Feb 1805, fee simple; his seal, her mark; WIT: Sterling JOHNSTON, John THOMPSON; ack. Sterling JOHNSTON, J.P.

p. 424 - Indenture, 21 Jan 1806, James BARNES (wife Nancy), BCO; Samuel POULTNEY [no location given]. $100, lot #3 in addition to St. Clairsville, 1/2 acre, fee simple; his seal, her mark; WIT: Sterling JOHNSTON, Henry ROBERTS; ack. Sterling JOHNSTON, J.P.

p. 425 - Indenture, 23 Jan 1806, John THOMPSON (wife Sally), merchant, St. Clairsville, BCO; Anthony KENNEDY and Benjamine C. CALHOON, merchants, Baltimore City. $600, lots #8 and #7 in St. Clairsville; his seal, her mark; WIT: David RUSK, Sterling JOHNSTON; ack. Sterling JOHNSTON, J.P.

p. 426 - Indenture, 16 Jan 1806, James BARNES (wife Nancy), BCO; Mahlon FARQUAR [no location given]. $100, lot #2 in addition to St. Clairsville; his seal, her mark; WIT: Sterling JOHNSTON, Henry ROBERTS; ack. Sterling JOHNSTON, J.P.

p. 427 - Indenture, 23 Jan 1806, John THOMPSON (wife Sally), merchant, St. Clairsville, BCO; Bolton, Jackson & Ross, City of Baltimore. $700, part of SE 1/4 S 25 T 8 R 4, Steubenville district, 100 acres; his seal, her mark; WIT: Sterling JOHNSTON, Nathan RICHARDSON; ack. Sterling JOHNSTON, J.P.

p. 429 - Indenture, 25 Jan 1806, George McNABB, Senr. (wife Martha), BCO; George McNABB, Junr., BCO. $200, 114 acres, part of S 14 T 7 R 4, conveyed to William DUER by Samuel OSGOOD and Walter LIVINGSTON on 3 Mar 1789, DUER to Henry ABORN, ABORN to Stephen TILLINGHOST, TILLINGHOST to Nathaniel OLCOTT, OLCOTT (wife Ann) to John JOHNSTON, JOHNSTON (half) to George McNABB, Senr., NBR: John McNABB, fee simple; both seal; WIT: Joseph POSEY, Sterling JOHNSTON; ack. Sterling JOHNSTON, J.P.

p. 430 - Indenture, 25 Jan 1806, George McNABB (wife Martha), BCO; John McNABB, BCO. $200, 120 acres, part of S 14 T 7 R 4, [see previous document for land history]; both seal; WIT: Joseph POSEY, Sterling JOHNSTON; ack. Sterling JOHNSTON, J.P.

p. 431 - Plat of land on E end of St. Clairsville, laid out by James BARNES, William BROWN, and Notely HAYS, part of S 4 T 7 R 4, signed 31 Aug 1805 [most of document is description of lots]; all seal; WIT: Robert GRIFFITH, Sterling JOHNSTON; ack. 13 Jan 1806, Sterling JOHNSTON, J.P. (See Appendix.)

p. 433 - Indenture, 16 Jan 1806, William McCONALD, BCO; Mathias CROY [no location given]. $30, lot at W end of St. Clairsville, NBR: William FROST, conveyed from David NEWELL to Sterling JOHNSTON, from JOHNSTON to McCONALD, fee simple; his seal; WIT: Sterling JOHNSTON, Connel [ABDIAL?]; ack. Sterling JOHNSTON, J.P.

p. 434 - Indenture, 7 Jun 1804, Alpheus FERRON (wife Nancy), BCO; Samuel KINKAID, BCO. $21.75, lot #138 in St. Clairsville, 1/4 acre, conveyed by David NEWELL (wife Sally) to FERRON by dee dated 25 Feb 1804; his seal, her mark; WIT: Sterling JOHNSTON, William B. HERRON, William LAPPIN; ack. 8 Jan 1806, Sterling JOHNSTON, J.P.

p. 435 - Indenture, 31 Dec 1804, Samuel KINKAID (wife Deborah), BCO; Joseph MARSHALL, BCO. $25, lot #138 in St. Clairsville, 1/4 acre; his mark, her seal; WIT: A. MARSHALL, William TILTON; ack. 31 Dec 1804, A. MARSHALL, J.P.

p. 436 - Indenture, 10 Jan 1806, John SOUTH, Richland twp., BCO; David WRIGHT, Pease twp., BCO. $60, land at W end of St. Clairsville, conveyed from David NEWELL to Sterling JOHNSTON on 7 Dec 1804, from JOHNSTON to William McCONNEL on 31 Dec 1804, from McCONNEL to John SOUTH on 12 Nov 1805, fee simple; his seal; WIT: Sterling JOHNSTON, Robert GRIFFITH; ack. 5 Feb 1806, Sterling JOHNSTON, J.P.

p. 437 - Know all men, William B. HERRON, BCO (Doct. of Physic), indebted to sundry persons, bailed by his lawful attorneys John G. HAMILTON and Alexander GASTON, for securing their risk and covering debt he is now conveying all his property including two lots of land at W side of Ann Street in St. Clairsville [#33 and #34?], signed 1 Aug 1805; his seal; WIT: John THOMPSON, William BOGGS; ack. 3 Feb 1806, Sterling JOHNSTON, J.P.

p. 438 - Indenture, 10 Jan 1806, John THOMPSON (wife Sally), St. Clairsville, BCO; John COPELAND, BCO. $360, part of S 25 T 8 R 4, Steubenville district, NBR: Bolton Jackson & Co., 60 acres; his seal, her mark; WIT: John WHERRY, Mary JOHNSTON; ack. 8 Feb 1806, Sterling JOHNSTON, J.P.

p. 439 - Indenture, 7 Feb 1806, John THOMPSON (wife Sally) [no location given here]; Charles HAMMOND [no location given here]. $2,500, NE 1/4 S 25 T 8 R 4, hold for use of Geo. Price & Co., Jenkins & Cochran, and Michael Terner & Co., all merchants of Baltimore; his seal, her mark; WIT: Sterling JOHNSTON, William THOMPSON; ack. Sterling JOHNSTON, J.P.

p. 440 - Indenture, 25 Jan 1806, James PATTON (wife Margaret), Ohio County, Virginia; Samuel PATTON, BCO. $535, NE 1/4 S 24 T 7 R 4, 160 acres, conveyed to PATTON by Stephen MILLER by his attorney George MILLER on 12 Mar 1804, recorded in Book A, p. 289 [p. 44 of abstracts], NBR: land conveyed from William DEVELON to Neal MAHAN, Hugh McCOY, William McWILLIAMS, land granted to John HOPKINS by Samuel OSGOOD and Walter LIVINGSTON on 3 Mar 1789, fee simple; both seal; WIT: Geo. MILLER, James McMACHAN, Prudence [HOLENS / HOLMS?]; ack. 8 Feb 1806, Thos. THOMPSON, J.P.

p. 441 - Indenture, 5 Feb 1806, Robert THOMPSON (wife Margaret), Richland twp., BCO; Josiah DILLON, same. $124, land on which THOMPSON now lives, 3 acres 18 perches, NBR: lot purchased from THOMPSON by DILLON;

his seal, her mark; WIT: Sterling JOHNSTON, Jas. CLOYD; ack. Sterling JOHNSTON, J.P.

p. 442 - Indenture, 10 Feb 1806, Robert THOMPSON (wife Margaret), Richland twp., BCO; Nicholas BOWERS, same. $90, lots #33 and #34 in addition on S of St. Clairsville, conveyed from William MATHERS (wife Ann) to William B. HERRON on 25 Mar 1805, from HERRON to John G. HAMILTON and Alexander GASTON, attorneys, on 1 Aug 1805, from HAMILTON and GASTON to THOMPSON on same date, fee simple; his seal, her mark; WIT: James CLOYD, Sterling JOHNSTON; ack. Sterling JOHNSTON, J.P.

p. 443 - Indenture, 1 Feb 1806, George MYERS [MAYERS] (wife Mary), BCO; Joseph MERRITT, same. $80, lot #116 in St. Clairsville, 1/4 acre, fee simple; his seal, her mark; WIT: Sterling JOHNSTON, James KNOX; ack. Sterling JOHNSTON, J.P.

p. 444 - Indenture, 14 Feb 1806, Nicholas BOWERS (wife Catharine), St. Clairsville, BCO; Thomas IRELAND, same. $250, lots #33 and #34 in addition on S of St. Clairsville, NBR: William MATHERS, conveyed from MATHERS (wife Anne) to William B. HERRON on 25 Mar1805, from HERRON to John G. HAMILTON and Alexander GASTON on 1 Aug 1805, from HAMILTON and GASTON to Robert THOMPSON on 10 Feb 1806, from THOMPSON (wife Margaret) to BOWERS, fee simple; his seal, her mark; WIT: Sterling JOHNSTON, James BRYAN; ack. Sterling JOHNSTON, J.P.

p. 445 - Indenture, 14 Feb 1806, Thomas IRELAND (wife Sally), St. Clairsville, BCO; Nicholas BOWERS, same. $250, lot #129 in St. Clairsville, 1/4 acre, conveyed by Jacob DEVORE to IRELAND by deed dated 1 Mar 1803, and lot #130 in St. Clairsville, 1/4 acre, conveyed by David NEWELL (wife Sally) to IRELAND by deed dated 6 May 1803, fee simple; his seal, her mark; WIT: Sterling JOHNSTON, James MILLER; ack. Sterling JOHNSTON, J.P.

p. 446 - Indenture, 15 Feb 1806, John FRYMAN (wife Peggy), St. Clairsville, BCO; Nicholas BOWERS, same. $100, lot #122 in St. Clairsville, 1/4 acre, fee simple; both mark; WIT: Jacob NAGLE, Sterling JOHNSTON; ack. Sterling JOHNSTON, J.P.

p. 447 - Indenture, 16 Oct 1805, Andrew MARSHALL, St. Clairsville, BCO; John THOMPSON, same. $600, lot #28 in St. Clairsville, 1/4 acre, fee simple, void if MARSHALL pays $600 by 16 Oct 1807, his seal; WIT: Jesse MAGEE; ack. Sterling JOHNSTON, J.P.

p. 448 - Indenture, 10 Feb 1806, John G. HAMILTON and Alexander GASTON, Richland twp., BCO, attorneys in fact for William B. HERRON of same place;

Robert THOMPSON, same. $76, lots #33 and #34 in addition on S side of St. Clairsville, conveyed by William MATHERS (wife Ann) to HERRON on 25 Mar 1805, from HERRON to HAMILTON and GASTON on 1 Aug 1805, fee simple; both seal; WIT: Sterling JOHNSTON, Josiah HEDGES; ack. Sterling JOHNSTON, J.P.

p. 449 - Indenture, 8 Nov 1805, Caleb RUSSELL (wife Lydia), BCO; Allen STEWART, BCO. $1,800, part of S 15 T 7 R 4, adjoining S 9 and 10, part of land conveyed by Laban BRANSON of City of New York to Robert and Caleb RUSSELL by deed dated 21 Jan 1797 as recorded in Jefferson County, 160 acres, NE 1/4 of land granted to John HOPKINS by Samuel OSGOOD and Walter LIVINGSTON on 3 Mar 1789; his seal, her mark; WIT: A. MARSHALL, Jacob NAGLE; ack. 8 Nov 1805, A. MARSHALL, J.P.

p. 450 - Indenture, 27 Feb 1806, John LAMB (wife Susanna), BCO; Robert THOMAS, Dorley, Delaware County, Pennsylvania. $770, 98 1/2 acres, NBR: Richard HARDESTY, same land conveyed by John D. MERCIER by attorney Daniel McELHERON on 9 Aug 1803, recorded in Book A, p. 214 [p. 33 of abstracts], parts of S 23 and 24; both mark; WIT: Sterling JOHNSTON, Robert JOHNSTON; ack. Sterling JOHNSTON, J.P.

p. 452 - Indenture, 6 Mar 1806, John WINTER, St. Clairsville, BCO; William LYONS, BCO. $30, 20 acres in NW corner of NE 1/4 of S 19 T 8 R 4, granted to WINTER by patent dated 11 Feb 1806, fee simple; his seal; [WINTERS]; WIT: Sterling JOHNSTON, Benjamin MERIDITH; ack. Sterling JOHNSTON, J.P.

p. 453 - Indenture, 6 Mar 1806, John WINTER, St. Clairsville, BCO; Joseph RALSTON, BCO. $130, 40 acres on which RALSTON now lives, begin in S 19 T 8 R 4; his seal [WINTER]; WIT: Sterling JOHNSTON, Joseph LYON; ack. Sterling JOHNSTON, J.P.

p. 454 - Indenture, 8 Mar 1806, John WINTER, St. Clairsville, BCO; James WRIGHT, BCO. $120, land in S 19 T 8 R 4, Steubenville district, 40 acres, part of patent to WINTER dated 11 Feb 1806; his seal; WIT: Sterling JOHNSTON, Mary JOHNSTON; ack. Sterling JOHNSTON, J.P.

p. 455 - Indenture, 7 Mar 1806, John WINTER, St. Clairsville, BCO; Andrew NIXON, BCO. $80, part of S 19 T 8 R 4, Steubenville district, part of patent to WINTER dated 11 Feb 1806, NBR: William LYON [sic], fee simple; his seal; WIT: Sterling JOHNSTON, Elisha BROWN; ack. Sterling JOHNSTON, J.P.

p. 456 - Indenture, 8 Mar 1806, John WINTER, St. Clairsville, BCO; John NIXON, BCO. $150, part of S 19 T 8 R 4, Steubenville district, part of patent to WINTER dated 11 Feb 1806, NBR: William LYONS, fee simple; his seal; WIT: Sterling JOHNSTON, Clark FULLANTON; ack. Sterling JOHNSTON, J.P.

p. 457 - Indenture, 8 Mar 1806, John WINTER, St. Clairsville, BCO; Benjamine MERREDITH, BCO. $240, part of S 19 T 8 R 4, Steubenville district, 80 acres, part of S granted to WINTER on 11 Feb 1806, fee simple; his seal; WIT: Sterling JOHNSTON, Elisha BROWN; ack. Sterling JOHNSTON, J.P.

p. 458 - Indenture [crossed out], 8 Mar 1806, Benjamine MERRIDETH, BCO; Isaac HILL, BCO. $200, 80 acres in S 19 T 8 R 4, part of patent to John WINTER dated 11 Feb 1806, conveyed by WINTER to MERRIDETH, fee simple, void if MERREDITH pays total of $230.00 by 1 Jun 1807; his seal; WIT: Sterling JOHNSTON, John NIXON; ack. Sterling JOHNSTON, J.P. 29 Jul 1806, HILL received $115, mortgage satisfied, ack. Sterling JOHNSTON, Recorder.

p. 459 - Indenture, 12 Mar 1806, John WINTER, St. Clairsville, BCO; Samuel GURLEY, BCO. $350, part of S 19 T 4 R 8 [think these should be switched?], Steubenville district, part of patent to WINTER on 11 Feb 1806, NBR: Joseph RALSTON, Andrew NIXON, 100 acres, fee simple; his seal; WIT: Sterling JOHNSTON, James KNOX; ack. Sterling JOHNSTON, J.P.

p. 460 - Ack., Sally NEWELL, wife of David NEWELL, relinquished right of dower in land given 11 Dec 1805, her seal; ack. Sterling JOHNSTON, Recorder [refer to p. 408 in old book–suspect this was a different year?].

p. 460 - Indenture, 11 Feb 1806, Sterling JOHNSTON (wife Mary), St. Clairsville, BCO; Joseph PATTON, BCO. $70, lots #141 and #142 in St. Clairsville, each 1/4 acre, conveyed by David NEWELL (wife Sally) to Robert VANCE, from VANCE (wife Rebeckah) to JOHNSTON on same date, fee simple; both seal; WIT: Robert VANCE, Robt. GRIFFITH; ack.20 Feb 1806, John THOMPSON, J.P.

p. 461 - Indenture, 10 Mar 1806, John WINTER, St. Clairsville, BCO; Samuel PATTON, BCO. $160, part of S 19 T 8 R 4, Steubenville district, part of patent to WINTER dated 6 Feb 1806, NBR: James WRIGHT, 40 acres, fee simple; his seal; WIT: Robert GRIFFITH, Sterling JOHNSTON; ack. Sterling JOHNSTON, J.P.

p. 462 - Indenture, 28 Feb 1806, Daniel McPEEK, BCO; William BROWN, St. Clairsville, BCO. $38, lot #50 in St. Clairsville, 1/4 acre, conveyed to McPEEK by David NEWELL (wife Sally) on 29 Jun 1802, fee simple; his mark; WIT:

Sterling JOHNSTON, Jas. CLOYD; ack. 12 Mar 1806, Sterling JOHNSTON, J.P.

p. 463 - Indenture, 25 Jun 1805, Samuel DILLE, York twp., BCO, Collector of the County Levies; William HARKINS, Ohio County, Virginia. $4.81, lot #16 square #16 in Pultney and Wegee Bottom, T 2 R 2; his seal; WIT: Rukey DILLE, Robert BROWN [his mark]; ack. Tho. THOMPSON, J.P.

p. 464 - Indenture, 22 Mar 1806, Jesse McGEE, BCO; John MARTIN, BCO. $800, lot #20 in St. Clairsville, conveyed from Josiah DILLON and wife to McGEE ON 12 Nov 1805; his seal; WIT: Sterling JOHNSTON, Thomas LOVE; ack. Sterling JOHNSTON, J.P.

p. 464 - Indenture, 12 Aug 1805, Bazaleel WELLS (wife Sally), JCO; Allen STEWART, BCO. Part of S 10 T 7 R 4 conveyed from WELLS to STEWART, supposed at the time to contain 80 acres but contains only 78 1/2 acres, now conveying 1 1/2 acres at NE corner of S 10 to make up for deficiency, $5.75; both seal; [no witnesses given]; ack. JCO, 12 Aug 1805, Philip CABLE, Associate Judge, CABLE certified by Jno. WARD, Clerk.

p. 465 - Indenture, 27 Mar 1806, John MARTIN (wife Elizabeth), St. Clairsville, BCO; Jesse McGEE, same. $800, 160 acres, part of S 20 T 7 R 4, part of land granted to MARTIN by Samuel OSGOOD and Walter LIVINGSTON and Arthur LEE by patent dated 4 Mar 1788, fee simple; both seal; WIT: Sterling JOHNSTON, Wm. SINCLAIR; ack. Sterling JOHNSTON, J.P.

p. 467 - Indenture, 28 Mar 1806, John WINTER, St. Clairsville, BCO; Joseph LYON, BCO. $640, NW corner S 19 T 8 R 4, Steubenville district, granted to WINTER by patent dated 11 Feb 1806, fee simple; his seal; WIT: Sterling JOHNSTON, Wm. LYON; ack. Sterling JOHNSTON, J.P.

p. 467 - Indenture, 26 Mar 1806, Moses CONGLETON, Brook County, Virginia; Robert JOHNSTON and James CLOYD, BCO. CONGLETON (wife Mary) for $160, lot #16 in St. Clairsville; his seal [only], WIT: Sterling JOHNSTON, Robert GRIFFITH; ack. BCO, Sterling JOHNSTON, J.P.

p. 469 - Indenture, 21 Aug 1805, William WILEY (wife Martha WILEY), Pease twp., BCO; George GIVEN, same. $128, part of S 6 T 6 R 3, NBR: William WILEY, Charles IRWIN, 32 acres 12 perches, conveyed from Alexander LATIMORE to WILEY on 4 Mar 1804 as recorded in Book A, p. 246 [p. 37 of abstracts], entire S conveyed from John JOHNSTON, Washington County, to LATIMORE on 20 Aug 1802 as recorded in Jefferson County Book A, p. 121; both seal; WIT: Thos. THOMPSON, Charles IRWIN; ack. 3 Mar 1806, Tho. THOMPSON, J.P.

p. 470 - Indenture, 31 Mar 1806, Nicholas BOWERS (wife Catharine), BCO; John MARTIN, BCO. $600, lots #129, #130, and #122 ["Twenty too"] in St. Clairsville, fee simple; his seal, her mark; WIT: Sterling JOHNSTON, Josiah HEDGES; ack. Sterling JOHNSTON, J.P.

p. 471 - Indenture, 31 Mar 1806, John MARTIN (wife Elizabeth), BCO; Nicholas BOWERS. $800, part of S 20 T 7 R 4, NBR: Jesse McGEE, 160 acres, part of land granted to MARTIN by Samuel OSGOOD, Walter LIVINGSTON, and Arthur LEE by patent dated 4 Mar 1788, fee simple; both seal; WIT: Josiah HEDGES, Sterling JOHNSTON; ack. Sterling JOHNSTON, J.P.

p. 472 - Indenture, 1 Apr 1805, William CONGLETON, Richland twp., BCO; Ezer DILLON, Loudoun County, Virginia. $300, lot #85 in St. Clairsville, 1/4 acre, conveyed to CONGLETON by James KNOX on 16 Jun 1804, fee simple; his seal; WIT: Sterling JOHNSTON, Josiah DILLON; ack. Sterling JOHNSTON, J.P.

p. 473 - Whereas land granted to Frances [sic] BOWEN, Jefferson County, NWT, at Steubenville on 17 Mar 1801, BOWEN entitled to patent for S 31 T 7 R 4, for $150 paid by George SNIDER, BCO, BOWEN transfers certificate to SNIDER, signed 7 Apr 1806; his seal; WIT: Sterling JOHNSTON, William CRAIG; ack. Sterling JOHNSTON, J.P.

p. 473 - Indenture, 25 Mar 1806, George HEAP (wife Elizabeth), Pultney, BCO; John BOLTON [no location given]. $100, lots #57 and #58 in Pultney, 5 acres each, also outlot C containing 7 acres; both seal [she "Eliz."]; WIT: Jacob DAVIS, Stephen FROST; ack. Sterling JOHNSTON, J.P.

p. 474 - Know all men, Isaac BATES, York twp., BCO; Ephriam [sic] BATES, same. $96, bay mare and colt, plus interest for three years, two notes (one $60 and one $36), signed 27 Nov 1805; his seal; WIT: Aaron HEADLEY, Isaac MOORE; ack. "February Levin Oken"[?].

p. 475 - Indenture, 16 Apr 1806, Joseph HARRIS (wife Polly), BCO; Robert DENT [no location given]. $75, outlot near St. Clairsville, 2 1/2 acres, NBR: Notely HAYS, fee simple; his seal, her mark; WIT: Sterling JOHNSTON, Andw. BYERS; ack. Sterling JOHNSTON, J.P.

p. 475 - Indenture, 21 Apr 1806, Robert JOHNSTON, BCO; Henry STENER [STONER], BCO. $20, 1/4 acre, NBR: George MYERS, conveyed by David NEWELL (wife Sally) to JOHNSTON [no date nor page number given], fee simple; his seal; WIT: Sterling JOHNSTON, James KNOX; ack. Sterling JOHNSTON, J.P.

p. 476 - Indenture, 5 May 1806, Valentine AULT (wife Catharine), Richland twp., BCO; David NEISWANGER, same. $65, lot #6 in St. Clairsville, conveyed by David NEWELL (wife Sally) to William YOUNG on 3 Jul 1802, from YOUNG to John THOMPSON on 12 Apr 1803, from THOMPSON to AULT on 10 Apr 1803, fee simple; his seal, her mark; WIT: A. MARSHALL, William MATHERS; ack. A. MARSHALL, J.P.

p. 477 - Indenture, 17 Mar 1806, John CLARK (wife Rebeckah), BCO; George NEFF, same. $216, part of S 13 T 6 R 3, NBR: Andrew DIXON, James KELSEY, 45 acres; both seal; WIT: Ezra WILLIAMS; ack. Thos. THOMPSON, J.P.

p. 478 - Indenture, 9 May 1806, Sterling JOHNSTON (wife Mary), BCO; Jacob LEASE, same. $100, lot #56 in St. Clairsville, conveyed from David NEWELL to Sterling JOHNSTON on 28 Apr 1804, as recorded in Book A, p. 270 [p. 41 in abstracts]; both seal; WIT: John THOMPSON, William McCONALD; ack. John THOMPSON, J.P.

p. 479 - Indenture, 9 May 1806, Jacob LEASE (wife Joanna), BCO; Sterling JOHNSTON, BCO. $100, part of S 5 T 7 R 4, 10 acres 2 rods, NBR: Magdaline PIPER, conveyed to LEASE by JOHNSTON (wife Mary) on 10 Feb 1804, as recorded in Book A, p. 231 [p. 46 in abstracts], fee simple; his mark, her seal; WIT: William McCONALD, John THOMPSON, ack. John THOMPSON, J.P.

p. 480 - Indenture, 25 Apr 1806, John CLARK (wife Rebecca), BCO; Charles ECKLES, BCO. $152.25, part of S 13 T 6 R 3, NBR: Charles ECKLES, James ROBENSON, 101 1/2 acres; both seal; WIT: Thos. THOMPSON; ack. Thos. THOMPSON.

p. 481 - Indenture, 9 May 1806, John CLARK (wife Rebecca), BCO; Abraham WORKMAN, BCO. [No monetary amount given], part of S 13 T 6 R 3, 4 acres; both seal; WIT: Thos. THOMPSON, George GIVEN; ack. Thos. THOMPSON, J.P.

p. 482 - Indenture, 5 May 1806, Josiah HEDGES, Esq., High Sheriff, BCO; William CONGLETON, St. Clairsville, BCO. Whereas Bazel ISRAEL on 15 Aug 1805 in Court of Common Pleas obtained a judgment against William B. HERRON for $38.31 debt and $.95 damage and $9.55 costs, a writ of fieri facias was issued dated 6 Mar 1806 directing Sheriff to sell some of HERRON's property, proceeds to be available to ISRAEL next court, therefore on 6 Mar 1806 HEDGES levied on house and two lots (#33 and #34) in addition to St. Clairsville, sold to William CONGLETON on 10 Apr 1806 for $60, fee simple; his seal; WIT: Sterling JOHNSTON, Jas. CLOYD; ack. Sterling JOHNSTON, J.P.

p. 484 - Indenture, 15 May 1806, Josiah HEDGES, Esq., High Sheriff, BCO; William CONGLETON, BCO. [See p. 482 for background; actually, this seems to be a duplicate of the one on p. 482.]

p. 485 - Indenture, 15 Mar 1806, Josiah DILLON (wife Dorothy), St. Clairsville, BCO; Thomas LOVE, same. $135, lot #33 in St. Clairsville, 1/4 acre, fee simple; both seal; WIT: John THOMPSON, Jesse McGEE; ack. John THOMPSON, J.P.

p. 486 - Indenture, 28 May 1806, John EDWARDS, Sen. (wife Eleanor), Richland twp., BCO; Thomas LAWSON, Richland twp., BCO. $500, 112 acres 40 perches, part S 36 T 7 R 4, granted to John EDWARDS, Sen., by patent dated 7 Apr 1806, NBR: Joseph BELL; his seal, her mark; WIT: Moses MERRIT, Thomas EDWARDS; ack. Moses MERRIT, J.P.

p. 488 - Indenture, 28 May 1806, John EDWARDS, [Sen.] (wife Eleanor), Kirkwood twp., BCO; John PRICE, Richland twp., BCO. $20, 61 acres 20 perches, part of S 36 T 7 R 4, granted to John EDWARDS, Sen., by patent dated 7 Apr 1806; his seal, her mark; WIT: Moses MERRIT, Wm. STEVENSON; ack. Moses MERRIT, J.P.

p. 489 - Indenture, 9 Jun 1806, William GIBSON, Senr. (wife [Evash?]), Richland twp., BCO; William GIBSON, Jun., same. $40, 2 acres, part of S 4 T 7 R 4, Steubenville district, NBR: Notely HAYS, part of land William, Senr., bought of Frances SUNDERLAND on 19 May 1804; both mark; WIT: Sterling JOHNSTON, Wm. VANCE; ack. Sterling JOHNSTON, J.P.

p. 490 - Indenture, 10 Jun 1806, John WINTER, St. Clairsville, BCO; John ALEXANDER, Richland twp., BCO. $210, part of S 19 T 8 R 4, 60 acres, part of land granted to WINTER by patent dated 11 Feb 1806, fee simple; his seal; WIT: Jas. CLOYD, Sterling JOHNSTON; ack. Sterling JOHNSTON, J.P.

p. 491 - Indenture, 13 Jun 1806, John WOODBURN (wife Sally), Westmoreland County, Pennsylvania; Ralph HEATH, Union twp., State of Ohio. $70, lot #109 in St. Clairsville, 1/4 acre, fee simple; both seal; WIT: Sterling JOHNSTON, Robt. DAVISON; ack. Sterling JOHNSTON, J.P.

p. 492 - Know all men, Jonah HOUGH [HUGH], Loudoun County, Virginia; power of attorney to Samuel GREGG living near 480 acres still remaining to him from 640 granted to him, Steubenville district, signed 18 Sep 1804; his seal [HOUGH]; [no witnesses given]; ack. Loudoun County, 10 Sep 1804, Samuel MURRY, J.P., MURRY certified by Charles BINNS, Clerk.

p. 492 - Indenture, 2 Apr 1806, Bazaleel WELLS (wife Sally), JCO; John NIXON, BCO. $400, on waters of Glens run, part of S 20 and 26 T 4 R 2, 99 acres 94 perches; both seal; WIT: Nicholas MURRY, Phillip CABLE; ack. JCO, Phillip CABLE, Associate Judge, CCP, CABLE certified by John WARD, Clerk.

p. 493 -Indenture, 28 Jan 1806, Richard McKIBBON (wife Sarah McKIBBON), BCO; Andrew EAGLESON [ENGLESON], BCO. $61.12 1/2, part of a tract purchased by McKIBBON of Archibald WOODS, part of S 27 fractional T 4 R 4, grant for this S issued 15 Nov 1797, 6 acres 18 perches, NBR: Andrew ENGLESON, Richard McKIBBON; both seal; [no witnesses given]; ack. 28 Jan 1806, James ALEXANDER, Associate Judge, CCP.

p. 495 - Indenture, 8 Jul 1806, James CAMPBELL, Loudoun County, Virginia; Thomas MOOR, same. $400, 168 acres, part of S 12 T 8 R 6, part of land granted to CAMPBELL; fee simple; his seal; WIT: Sterling JOHNSTON, John MOORE; ack. Sterling JOHNSTON, J.P.

p. 496 - Indenture, 14 Jul 1806, Joseph KIRKWOOD (wife Margaret), BCO; Ebenezer ZANE, Ohio County, Virginia. $50 and other good considerations, begin NW corner S 27 T 3 R 2, along Indian Wheeling creek, 50 acres; both seal; WIT: E. WOODS, Ezra WILLIAMS; ack. BCO, Thomas THOMAS, J.P.

p. 496 - Indenture, 14 Jul 1806, Ebenezer ZANE (wife Elizabeth), Ohio County, Virginia; Joseph KIRKWOOD, BCO. $50, along Wheeling creek, fractional S 20 T 8 [or 3?] R 2, 20 acres; both seal; WIT: Ezra WILLIAMS; ack. BCO, Thomas THOMPSON, J.P.

p. 497 - Indenture, 17 Mar 1806, John CLARK (wife Rebeckah), BCO; John PURDY, same. $200, part of S 4 T 6 R 3, 40 acres; both seal; WIT: Ezra WILLIAMS; ack. 17 Mar 1806, Thos. THOMPSON, J.P.

p. 498 - Indenture, 2 Apr 1806, George MAYERS (wife Mary), BCO; and John WINTER, BCO. $270, lot #93 in St. Clairsville, 1/4 acre, conveyed to MAYERS by Joseph MARTIN (wife Nancy) on 3 Feb 1803, fee simple; his seal, her mark; WIT: Sterling JOHNSTON, Phillip WINDLE; ack. 30 Jul 1806, Sterling JOHNSTON, J.P.

p. 499 - Indenture, 28 Jan 1806, John McCLURE, BCO; John MOORE, BCO. $83.53, NE 1/4 S 32 T 3 R 2, McCLURE has paid first installment in Steubenville, MOORE now responsible for further payments, patent to be issued in MOORE's name; his seal; WIT: John MITCHELL, Thomas MITCHELL; ack. Thos. MITCHELL, J.P.

p. 500 - Indenture, 28 May 1806, John EDWARDS, Sen. (wife Elenor), Kirkwood twp., BCO; Thomas EDWARDS, Richland twp., BCO. $20, 90 1/4 acres 17 perches, part of S 36 T 7 R 4, granted to John EDWARDS by patent dated 7 Apr 1806; his seal, her mark; WIT: Moses MERRIT, Wm. STEPHENS; ack. 28 May 1806, Moses MERRIT, J.P.

p. 501 - Indenture, 7 Aug 1806, David VANCE, Esq., BCO; William WOODS, BCO. $300, SE 1/4 S 5 T 7 R 4, 80 1/2 acres, fee simple; his seal; WIT: Sterling JOHNSTON, Robert JOHNSTON; ack. Sterling JOHNSTON, J.P.

p. 502 - Indenture, 9 Aug 1806, Sterling JOHNSTON, BCO; William WOODS, BCO. $20, part of S 5 T 7 R 4, 9 acres 3 rods 20 perches; both seal [Mary included here but not in first line]; WIT: John THOMPSON, Battle HARRISON; ack. Sterling JOHNSTON, J.P.

p. 503 - Indenture, 11 Aug 1806, John ISREAL (wife Rachael), BCO; John SIMESON, Washington County, Pennsylvania. $60, lot #125 in St. Clairsville, 1/4 acre; his seal, her mark; WIT: John THOMPSON; ack. John THOMPSON, J.P.

p. 504 - Indenture, 15 Aug 1806, Josiah HEDGES, Sheriff, BCO; Bazaleel WELLS [no location given here]. By deed dated 13 Apr 1805 "for divers consideration and causes" gave WELLS right to land owned by William MATHERS in S 4 T 7 R 4, conveyed to MATHERS by James E. NEWELL (wife Elizabeth) on 22 Mar 1805, now doubt has arisen as to what estate WELLS took by this deed, court empowered HEDGES to make another more specific deed, for $.01 with reservations from 13 Apr 1805 deed; his seal; WIT: C. HAMMOND, Jas. CLOYD; ack. Sterling JOHNSTON, J.P.

p. 505 - Indenture, 15 Aug 1806, Josiah HEDGES, Sheriff, BCO; Bazaleel WELLS [no location given here]. ". . . for divers considerations" lots #27, #25, #26, #28, #39, #10, #11, #12, #18, #19, #20, #15, #16, #21, #22, #23, #24, #31, #32, and #17 in addition to St. Clairsville, new deed conveying above property as there was some question about what estate WELLS had taken under a previous deed [see p. 504]; his seal; WIT: C. HAMMOND, Jas. CLOYD; ack. Sterling JOHNSTON, J.P.

p. 505 - Indenture, 27 Aug 1806, John MARTIN (wife Elizabeth), St. Clairsville, BCO; John B. MARTIN, City of Baltimore, State of Maryland. $500, lot #20 in St. Clairsville, 1/4 acre, conveyed from John McGEE to MARTIN on 22 Mar 1806, as recorded in Book A, p. 464 [p. 71 of abstracts], fee simple; both seal; WIT: Sterling JOHNSTON, John CARTER; ack. 28 Mar 1806, Sterling JOHNSTON, J.P.

p. 507 - Plat of Town of Canton, BCO; submitted by Ebenezer ZANE, Proprietor; ack. 9 May 1806, Thos. THOMPSON. (See Appendix.)

p. 508 - Indenture, 10 Jan 1806, William NORMAN (wife Mary), Pease twp., BCO; James McMILLON [McMILLEN], Warren twp., JCO. $1,000, part of S 15 and 21 T 4 R 2, NBR: Joseph TILTON, John CONNALD, 80 acres; his seal, her mark; WIT: Robert McCLEARY, Drusey CLARK [her mark]; ack. JCO, 10 Jan 1806, Robert McCLEARY, J.P.

p. 509 - Indenture, 23 Jun 1806, Joseph GUINEA (wife Margaret), Washington County, Pennsylvania; Andrew McMACHAN, BCO. $500, land in S 26 T 4 R 2, Glens run, NBR: Francis COOPER, 75 3/4 acres; both seal; WIT: James ALLISON, Jane SHEARER; ack. Washington County, James ALLISON, [Associate] Judge, CCP.

p. 510 - Indenture, 26 Aug 1806, Bazaleel WELLS (wife Sally), JCO; Obediah JENNINGS, same. $2,000, land in S 4 T 7 R 4, conveyed to William MATHERS by James E. NEWELL (wife Elizabeth) dated 22 Mar 1805, excepting tract conveyed to WELLS by Josiah HEDGES, Sheriff, dated 13 Apr 1805, also excepting tract conveyed to James BARNES and Moses MOREHEAD on date last mentioned, lots #27, #25, #26, #28, #39, #10, #11, #12, #17, #18, #19, #20, #15, #16, #21, #22, #23, #24, #31, #32 in addition to St. Clairsville, now conveying to JENNINGS; both seal; WIT: James WILSON, Zachs BIGGS; ack. Samuel HUNTINGTON, one of Supreme Judges of State of Ohio.

p. 511 - Indenture, 12 Aug 1806, Joshua HATCHER (wife Jane), BCO; Edward MILNER, BCO. $600, E 1/2 of S 9 T 8 R 5, Steubenville district, part of S granted to HATCHER by patent dated 8 Oct 1805, fee simple; his seal, her mark; WIT: Sterling JOHNSTON, Richard HARDESTY; ack. Sterling JOHNSTON, J.P.

P. 512 - Indenture, 12 Aug 1806, Joshua HATCHER (wife Jane), BCO; Levi PITMAN, BCO. $105, land in SW corner S 9 T 8 R 5, Steubenville district, patented to HATCHER on 8 Oct 1805, 30 acres, fee simple; his seal, her mark; WIT: Sterling JOHNSTON, Richard HARDESTY; ack. Sterling JOHNSTON, J.P.

p. 513 - Indenture, 3 Sep 1806, Obediah JENNINGS, JCO; Sterling JOHNSTON, BCO. $100, lots #15 and #16 in addition to St. Clairsville as laid out by William MATHERS; his seal; WIT: C. HAMMOND, Saml. SPRIGG; ack. John PATTERSON, J.P.

p. 513 - Indenture, 3 Sep 1806, Obediah JENNINGS, JCO; Robert JOHNSTON, BCO. $120, outlot #9, 6 acres 9 perches in plan of 15 outlots laid out by

Bazaleel WELLS adjoining addition to St. Clairsville; his seal; WIT: C. HAMMOND, Saml. SPRIGG; ack. BCO, Sterling JOHNSTON, J.P.

p. 514 - Indenture, 1 Sep 1806, Obediah JENNINGS, BCO; William CONGLETON, BCO. $50, lots #23, #28, #32, in addition to St. Clairsville as laid out by William MATHERS; his seal; WIT: James CLOYD, Andrew MOORE; ack. John PATTERSON, J.P.

p. 515 - Indenture, 1 Sep 1806, Obediah JENNINGS, JCO; Robert GRIFFITH, BCO. $26.65, outlot #4 adjoining addition to St. Clairsville, laid out by Bazaleel WELLS; his seal; WIT: Andrew MOORE, John G. HAMILTON; ack. BCO, John PATTERSON, J.P.

p. 515 - Indenture, 1 Sep 1806, Obediah JENNINGS, JCO; James CLOYD, BCO. $20, lot #24 in addition to St. Clairsville as laid out by William MATHERS; his seal; WIT: William CONGLETON, James JOHNSTON; ack. BCO, John PATTERSON, J.P.

End of Vol. A (copy certified by William FARIS, Recorder, ordered at March term 1842, sealed 17 Sep 1842.

A. S. TAYLOR, Recorder, made copy from that of William FARIS, sealed 14 Nov 1896.

Deed Abstracts, Belmont County, Ohio

Volume B (Sep 1806 - Feb 1809)

p. 1 - Indenture, 2 Sep 1806, Abadiah [Obediah] JENNINGS, JCO; William BROWN, BCO. $103, out lot #14 adjacent to addition to St. Clairsville, as laid out by Bazaleel WELLS, 5 acres 3 rods 30 perches; his seal; WIT: Andrew MOORE, Isaac VORE; ack. Saml. SULLIVAN, J.P.; entered 14 Sep 1806, recorded 29 Sep 1806.

p. 2 - "Know all men," David NEWELL (wife Sally) and Benjamin NEWELL (wife Jane), all then of JCO, conveyed about 1801 to Jonathan QUIGLEY, Westmoreland County, Pennsylvania, lot #114 in St. Clairsville, conveyance has been lost, for $.01 they are now confirming the sale, fee simple; David's seal only; WIT: Sterling JOHNSTON; ack. Sterling JOHNSTON, J.P.; entered 12 Sep 1806, recorded 29 Sep 1806.

p. 3 - Indenture, 12 Sep 1806, Jonathan QUIGLEY, Westmoreland County, Pennsylvania; Robert JOHNSTON, BCO. $30, lot #114 in St. Clairsville, fee simple; his seal; WIT: Josiah HEDGES, Jas. CLOYD; ack. Sterling JOHNSTON, J.P.; entered 13 Sep 1806, recorded 6 Oct 1806.

p. 4 - Indenture, 15 Sep 1806, Robert JOHNSTON, BCO; Jacob HOULTZ, BCO. $120, out lot #9 adjacent to addition to St. Clairsville, laid out by Bazaleel WELLS, 6 acres 9 perches; his seal; WIT: James CLOYD, Sterling JOHNSTON; ack. Sterling JOHNSTON, J.P.; entered 15 Sep 1806, recorded 7 Oct 1806.

p. 5 - Indenture, 28 Aug 1806, Charles FRYMAN (wife Mary), BCO; Jacob [CLAY-----], BCO. $42, part S 5 T 7 R 4, Steubenville district, NBR: David VANCE, Esqr., Robert HOPPER, conveyed to FRYMAN from James JOHNSTON on 25 Mar 1805, fee simple; both mark; WIT: Adam JOHNSTON, Sterling JOHNSTON; ack. Sterling JOHNSTON, J.P.; entered 18 Sep 1806, recorded 7 Oct 1806.

p. 6 - Indenture, 26 Sep 1806, Samuel BUCHANON (wife Mary), Ohio County, Virginia; James CALDWELL, BCO. $60, lots #88 and #87 in St. Clairsville, each 1/4 acre, fee simple; both seal; WIT: Sterling JOHNSTON, James CLOYD; ack. Sterling JOHNSTON, J.P.; entered 26 Sep 1806, recorded 7 Oct 1806.

p. 7 - Indenture, 29 Sep 1806, William CONGLETON (wife Nancy), Richland twp., BCO; Jacob LEASE, same. $100, lot #64 in St. Clairsville, conveyed from Samuel THOMPSON (wife Jane) to CONGLETON on 4 Jan 1806, recorded Book A, p. 496 (p. 423 in new book [p. 67 of abstracts]); both seal; WIT: Jacob

NAGLE, Sterling JOHNSTON; ack. Sterling JOHNSTON, J.P.; entered 29 Sep 1806, recorded 7 Oct 1806.

p. 8 - Indenture, 6 Oct 1806, Josiah DILLON (wife Dorothy), BCO; Alexander BOGGS [BOGG], George IRELAND, Alexander GASTON, David RUSK [RUSH], trustees for Rev. Joseph ANDERSON's congregation. $.25, begin at SW corner of out lot sold by Robert JOHNSTON to DILLON to be used for building a house of public worship for ANDERSON's congregation or congregation of any other Presbyterian minister; both seal; WIT: Sterling JOHNSTON, Wm. PHILPOT; ack. Sterling JOHNSTON, J.P.; entered 6 Oct 1806, recorded 7 Oct 1806.

p. 9 - Indenture, 13 Sep 1806, Casper SEEVERS, St. Clairsville, BCO; Phillip WINDLE, same. $270, lots #92, #91, #83, #75 in St. Clairsville, fee simple; his seal; WIT: Saml. SULLIVAN, Wm. FARIS, Junr.; ack. Saml. SULLIVAN, J.P.; entered 13 Oct 1806, recorded 21 Oct 1806.

p. 10 - Indenture, 13 Oct 1806, James RATIKEN, Loudoun County, Virginia; John TIMBERLAKE, Campbell County, Virginia. $480, SE corner of S 25 T 7 R 5, Steubenville district, 160 acres, fee simple; his seal; WIT: Charles PIDGEON, Sterling JOHNSTON; ack. Sterling JOHNSTON, J.P.; entered 14 Oct 1806, recorded 22 Oct 1806.

p. 11 - Indenture, 7 Aug 1806, Notley HAYS (wife Sally), Richland twp., BCO; James WILKINS, same. $160, part S 34 T 6 R 3, NBR: William HOUTH, 10 acres, granted to HAYS by patent dated 18 Feb 1806, fee simple; his seal, her mark; WIT: Sterling JOHNSTON, John COLOUR; ack. Sterling JOHNSTON, J.P.; entered 15 Oct 1806, recorded 22 Oct 1806.

p. 12 - Indenture, 17 May 1806, Daniel McPEEK (wife Elizabeth), BCO; Samuel POTTS, same. $1,125, plantation, part S 24 T 6 R 3, NBR: Obediah HARDESTY, 100 acres, granted to Robert JOHNSTON by patent dated 17 Apr 1788, recorded Book A, Folio 52 in Treasury Office of U.S., JOHNSTON conveyed to William SMITH of Ohio County, Virginia, SMITH conveyed to McPEEK on 25 Feb 1796; both mark; WIT: Thos. MITCHELL, J.P.; McPEEK ack. receipt of $825 on 14 May 1806, WIT: Sarah [PRICE] [her mark]; entered 16 Oct 1806, recorded 22 Oct 1806.

p. 13 - Indenture, 16 Oct 1806, Samuel POTTS (wife Mary), BCO; Robert THOMAS, Darby, Delaware County, Pennsylvania. $1,150, part S 24 T 6 R 3, NBR: Obediah HARDESTY (formerly), 100 acres, granted to Robert JOHNSTON by patent dated 17 Apr 1788, recorded Book A, Folio 52 in Treasury Office of U.S., conveyed by JOHNSTON to William SMITH, Ohio

County, Virginia, SMITH conveyed by deed to Daniel McPEEK, McPEEK (wife Elizabeth) conveyed by deed dated 17 May 1806 to POTTS; both seal; WIT: Sterling JOHNSTON, Mary JOHNSTON; ack. Sterling JOHNSTON, J.P.; POTTS ack. receipt of $1,150 on date of indenture; entered 16 Oct 1806, recorded 22 Oct 1806.

p. 14 - "Whereas" patent dated 3 Oct 1805 granted to Francis TOWNSEND, assignee of Joseph TOWNSEND for S 17 T 6 R 3, Steubenville district. $220, Francis TOWNSEND (wife Marrah [Marah]), Washington County, Pennsylvania sells part of S 17 T 6 R 3 to John BELL, BCO, NBR: Isaac HILL, Francis TOWNSEND, Jacob LASH, 100 acres, signed 2 Oct 1806; both seal; WIT: Saml. SHARPLESS, Preston SHARPLESS; ack. Thos. THOMPSON, J.P.; entered 16 Oct 1806, recorded 28 Oct 1806.

p. 15 - Indenture, 28 May 1806, John EDWARDS (wife Elener), Kirkwood twp., BCO; Joseph BELL, Richland twp., BCO. $238, part S 36 T 7 R 4, 68 acres, granted to EDWARDS by patent dated 7 Apr 1806; his seal, her mark; WIT: Moses MERRIT, Thomas LAWSON; ack. Moses MERRIT, J.P.; entered 16 Oct 1806, recorded 28 Oct 1806.

p. 16 - Indenture, 6 Oct 1806, Mordicai YARNELL (wife Phebe); Notley HAYS [no locations]. $2 per acre, part S 28 T 6 R 3, NBR: Valentine SHEARER, 46 acres, patented to YARNELL, both seal; WIT: Robt. WOODS, John CLARK; ack. Thos. THOMPSON, J.P.; entered 20 Oct 1806, recorded 31 Oct 1806.

p. 17 - Indenture, 13 Jun 1806, David BARR, BCO; John CONNELL, Charlestown, Brook County, Virginia. $2,000, S 31 T 7 R 3, 728 acres, patented by BARR 8 May 1806 is assigned to CONNELL; his seal; WIT: A. MARSHALL, John THOMPSON, ack. A. MARSHALL, J.P.; entered 22 Oct 1806, recorded 31 Oct 1806.

p. 18 - Indenture, 28 May 1806, John EDWARDS, Senr. (wife Elener), Kirkwood twp., BCO; John EDWARDS, Junr., Richland twp., BCO. $70, part S 36 T 7 R 4, granted to EDWARDS Senr. by patent dated 7 Apr 1806, 65 acres 80 perches, NBR: (Wheeling Creek); his seal, her mark; WIT: Moses MERRIT, Joseph BELL; ack. Moses MERRIT, J.P.; 23 Oct 1806, recorded 1 Nov 1806.

p. 19 - Indenture, 1 Nov 1806, Obediah JENNINGS, JCO; Josiah HEDGES, BCO. $36.--, lots #25 and #26, addition to St. Clairsville as laid out by William MATHERS; his seal; WIT: Andrew MOORE, James CLOYD; ack. John PATTERSON, J.P.; entered 23 Oct 1806, recorded 14 Nov 1806.

p. 20 - Indenture, 13 Dec 1806, Jonathan TAYLOR (wife Ann), JCO; Daniel BALLANGER [BALANGER/BALLENGER], BCO. $320, farm now occupied by Robert VERNON, W 1/2 of NE 1/4 S 9 T 8 R 6, patented to TAYLOR on 18 Mar 1805; both seal; WIT: John M. WILLIAMS, James ALEXANDER, ack. James ALEXANDER, Assoc. Judge.

p. 21 - Indenture, 14 Oct 1806, John MARTIN, St. Clairsville, BCO; John THOMPSON, same. $700, SE 1/4 S 20 T 7 R 4, void if $700 paid to THOMPSON by 1 Mar 1807; both seal; WIT: Saml. SULLIVAN, Jacob NAGLE; ack. Saml. SULLIVAN, J.P.; entered 8 Dec 1806 and recorded 19 Dec 1806; released 12 Dec 1807, WIT: Sterling JOHNSTON. [Actually should have been preceded by documents on pp. 22 and 23, but clerk turned two pages at once and thus got them out of order.]

p. 22 - Indenture, 6 Nov 1806, John THOMPSON (wife Sally), St. Clairsville, BCO; John BROWN, William ROBERTSON [ROBESON], Daniel McCURDY. $2,700, lots #28, #27, #19 (NBR: Jacob HOLTZ) in St. Clairsville, each 1/4 acre, also a lot of ground W of St. Clairsville, 4 1/4 acres 9 poles, NBR: Josiah DILLON, Bezel ISRAEL, Robert THOMPSON; his seal, her mark; WIT: Saml. SULLIVAN, Moses MOREHEAD; ack. Saml. SULLIVAN, J.P.

p. 24 - Indenture, 25 Aug 1806, George BROKAW (wife Jane), JCO; Robert FINNEY, BCO. $320, S 31 T 4 R 2, 61 1/2 acres; his seal, her mark; WIT: Adam DUNLAP, Richard McKIBBEN; ack. Thos. MITCHELL, J.P.; entered 11 Dec 1806, recorded 19 Dec 1806.

p. 25 - Indenture, 3 Sep 1806, Obediah JENNINGS, JCO; William MOSELEY, BCO. $200, out lots #1 (2 acres 1 rod 1 perch), #2 (2 acres 6 perches), #6 (4 acres 3 rods 37 perches), laid out by Bazaleel WELLS adjoining addition to St. Clairsville; his seal; WIT: C. HAMMON, Saml. SPRIGG, ack. Sterling JOHNSTON, J.P., entered 18 Dec 1806, recorded 20 Dec 1806.

p. 26 - Indenture, 17 Dec 1806, William MOSELEY, BCO; Sterling JOHNSTON, BCO. $411, out lots #1, #2, #6 [see above entry for sizes], fee simple, lots granted to MOSELEY from Obadiah JENNINGS on 3 Sep 1806, void if MOSELEY provides 80,220 bricks within 1/2 mile of St. Clairsville on or before 1 Jun next or $411; his seal; WIT: Saml. SULLIVAN, Robt. GRIFFITH; ack. Saml. SULLIVAN, J.P.

p. 27 - Indenture, 6 Dec 1806, Bazaleel WELLS (wife Sally), JCO; James COCHRAN [COUGHRAN], BCO. $28, part S 26 T 4 R 2, 45 1/2 acres; both seal; WIT: Alex. SNODGRASS, Archibald COLE; ack. JCO, Alex. SNODGRASS, J.P., SNODGRASS certified by Jno. WARD, Clerk, J.C.

p. 28 - Indenture, 18 Dec 1806, Thomas BARR, Richland twp., BCO; William GIFFIN, same. $100, lot #40 in St. Clairsville, 1/4 acre, conveyed by David and Sally NEWELL to John FRANCIS on 21 Dec 1801, FRANCIS to BARR on 15 Apr 1805, fee simple; his seal; WIT: James CLOYD, Sterling JOHNSTON; ack. Sterling JOHNSTON, J.P.

p. 29 - Indenture, 18 Dec 1806, William GIFFIN (wife Elizabeth), Richland twp., BCO; Rees BRANSON, Frederick County, Virginia. $300, lot #40 in St. Clairsville, 1/4 acre, [see previous entry for history]; his seal, her mark; WIT: Thomas BARR, Sterling JOHNSTON; ack. Sterling JOHNSTON, J.P.

p. 30 - Indenture, 18 Dec 1806, Rees BRANSON, Frederick County, Virginia; William GIFFIN, BCO. $150, lot #40 in St. Clairsville, void if BRANSON pays $150 to GIFFIN before 25 May "first ensuing"; his seal; WIT: Sterling JOHNSTON, Thomas BARR; ack. Sterling JOHNSTON, J.P.; entered 26 Dec 1806, recorded 27 Dec 1806; release 25 Jul 1807, WIT: Wm. FARIS, Junr., Recorder.

p. 31 - Indenture, 3 Nov 1806, Robert [H.] JOHNSTON (wife Rosannah), St. Clairsville, BCO; William MOSELEY, same. $100, lots #17, #18, #19, #20 in addition to St. Clairsville, conveyed from Obadiah JENNINGS to Robert H. JOHNSTON on 1 Sep 1806, fee simple; his seal, her mark; James CLOYD, John PATTERSON; ack. John PATTERSON, J.P.

p. 32 - Indenture, 6 Nov 1806, John BROWN, William ROBERTSON [ROBINSON], Daniel McCURDY, partners, St. Clairsville, BCO; John THOMPSON, same. $2,700, lots #28, #27, #19, in St. Clairsville, all 1/4 acre, plus 4 1/4 acres 9 poles (NBR: Josiah DILLON, Bazel ISRAEL, Robert THOMPSON, and commons), void if payments to be made 1807-1810; all seal; WIT: Saml. SULLIVAN, Moses MOREHEAD; ack. Saml. SULLIVAN, J.P.; released 15 Aug 1807, WIT: Sterling JOHNSTON.

p. 34 - Indenture, 27 Nov 1806, Campbell LEFEVER (wife Jane), Ohio County, Virginia; Thomas THOMPSON, BCO. $333, begin NW corner S 14 T 6 R 3, 100 acres, part of lot granted to LEFEVER by patent dated 4 Sep 1806, fee simple; his seal, her mark; WIT: Sterling JOHNSTON, Saml. KINKAID [his mark]; ack. Sterling JOHNSTON, J.P.; entered 26 Dec 1806, recorded 28 Dec 1806.

p. 35 - Indenture, 20 Dec 1806, James BARNES (wife Nancy), St. Clairsville, Richland twp., BCO; John THOMPSON, same. $2,000, lot #4 in St. Clairsville, 1/4 acre, conveyed from David and Sally NEWELL to THOMPSON on 29 Jan 1801, conveyed from THOMPSON to BARNES on 7 May 1804, fee simple; his seal, her mark; WIT: Saml. SULLIVAN, John BROWN; ack. Saml. SULLIVAN, J.P.; entered 26 Dec 1806, recorded 29 Dec 1806.

p. 36 - "Whereas," patent issued to Francis TOWNSEND, assignee of Joseph TOWNSEND, on 3 Oct 1805 for S 17 T 6 R 3, for $335 paid to Francis TOWNSEND (wife Marrah), Washington County, Pennsylvania, by Isaac HILL, BCO, part of S 17 T 6 R 3, NBR: Francis TOWNSEND, John BELL, 164 acres, allowances to be made if TOWNSEND decides to build a mill, signed 2 Oct 1806; both seal; WIT: Saml. SHARPLESS, Preston SHARPLESS; ack. Thos. THOMPSON, J.P.

p. 37 - Indenture, 25 Dec 1806, Andrew MOORE (wife Elizabeth), St. Clairsville, BCO; David NESWANGER, BCO. $50, lot #14 in St. Clairsville, conveyed from Josiah HEDGES, high Sheriff, to MOORE on 13 Apr 1805, recorded in Book A, p. 454 (p. 385 of new book [p. 61 of abstracts]), fee simple; both seal; WIT: Sterling JOHNSTON; ack. Sterling JOHNSTON, J.P.; entered 26 Dec 1806, recorded 29 Dec 1806.

p. 38 - Indenture, 25 Dec 1806, William BOGGS (wife Elizabeth), Richland twp., BCO; David NESWANGER, same. $22, lot on west end of St. Clairsville, 1 rod 35 perches; both seal; WIT: Sterling JOHNSTON; ack. Sterling JOHNSTON, J.P.; entered 26 Dec 1806, recorded 30 Dec 1806.

p. 39 - "Whereas," patent issued to Francis TOWNSEND, assignee of Joseph TOWNSEND, on 3 Oct 1805, for S 17 T 6 R 3, Steubenville district, Francis TOWNSEND (wife Marrah), Washington County, Pennsylvania, for $670 paid by Jacob LASH, BCO, convey NE 1/4 S 17 T 6 R 3 as well as 12 acres off the NW 1/4 S 17 T 6 R 3, NBR: John BELL, Isaac HILL, Francis TOWNSEND, signed 2 Oct 1806; both seal; WIT: Saml. SHARPLESS, Preston SHARPLESS; ack. Thos. THOMPSON, J.P.

p. 40 - Indenture, 29 Oct 1806, Mordicai YARNELL (wife Phebe) [no location]; Joseph FLORY [no location]. $3 per acre, part S 23 T 6 R 3, NBR: Job DILLON, John MAXFIELD, Moses WOLFORD, Joseph UPDEGRAFF, 2 acres 3 rods 39 perches, surveyed by Robert JOHNSTON; both seal; WIT: Jacob BURKILL, Lanc^{lt}. ARMSTRONG; ack. Sterling JOHNSTON, J.P.

p. 41 - Indenture, 13 Sep 1806, Phillip [Phellep] WINDLE (wife Barbara), St. Clairsville, BCO; Moses NIEL, same. $70, lot #99 in St. Clairsville; his seal, her mark; WIT: Wm. MATHERS, Wm. FARIS, Junr.; ack. Saml. SULLIVAN, J.P.; entered 27 Dec 1806, recorded 19 Jan 1807.

p. 42 - Indenture, 13 Sep 1806, Phillip [Phellep] WINDLE (wife Barbara), St. Clairsville, BCO; Moses NIEL, same. $220, lot #100 in St. Clairsville; his seal, her mark; WIT: Wm. MATHERS, Wm. FARIS, Junr.; ack. Saml. SULLIVAN, J.P.; entered 27 Dec 1806, recorded 19 Jan 1807.

p. 43 - Indenture, 23 Oct 1806, Jacob HOULTS (wife Margaret), St. Clairsville, BCO; John THOMPSON, same. $180, lot adjoining north commons of St. Clairsville, 4 1/4 acres 9 perches, conveyed from David and Sally NEWELL to HOULTS on 29 Oct 1802, recorded Book A, p. 125 (p. 118 of new book [p. 18 of abstracts]), fee simple; both mark; WIT: Sterling JOHNSTON, Moses MERRITT; ack. Sterling JOHNSTON, J.P.; entered 29 Dec 1806, recorded 22 Jan 1807.

p. 44 - Indenture, 8 Dec 1806, John MARTIN (wife Elizabeth), St. Clairsville, BCO; Joseph POSEY, BCO. $1,850, S 1/2 of S 20 T 7 R 4, 320 acres, granted to MARTIN by Samuel OSGOOD, Walter LIVINGSTON, and Arthur LEE on 4 Mar 1788, fee simple; both seal; WIT: Sterling JOHNSTON, Jacob GRUBB; ack. Sterling JOHNSTON, J.P.; entered 29 Dec 1806, recorded 22 Jan 1807.

p. 45 - Indenture, 31 Dec 1806, James CALDWELL, St. Clairsville, BCO; John MARTIN, ____, Virginia. $100, lot #137 in St. Clairsville, fee simple; his seal; WIT: Sterling JOHNSTON, Nath[n]. CUNNINGHAM; ack. Sterling JOHNSTON, J.P.; entered 31 Dec 1806, recorded 22 Jan 1807.

p. 46 - Indenture, 7 Nov 1806, Joseph IRWIN, yeoman (wife Mary), BCO; Samuel MITCHELL, innkeeper, BCO. $137, part of S 27 T 7 R 4, 30 acres; his seal, her mark; WIT: Saml. SULLIVAN, Joseph MERRITT; ack. Saml. SULLIVAN, J.P.; entered 5 Jan 1807, recorded 22 Jan 1807.

p. 47 - Indenture, 13 Jun 1806, David WRIGHT (wife Rebeckah), BCO; James SMITH, BCO. $40, lot at W end of St. Clairsville, conveyed from David and Sally NEWELL to Sterling JOHNSTON on 7 Dec 1804, from JOHNSTON to William McCONALD [McCONAL] on 31 Dec 1804, from McCONAL to John SOUTH on 12 Nov 1805; his seal, her mark; WIT: Sterling JOHNSTON, James CLOYD; ack. 6 Jan 1807, Sterling JOHNSTON, J.P.; entered 6 Jan 1807, recorded 24 Jan 1807.

p. 48 - Indenture, 3 Jan 1807, John G. HAMILTON, BCO; John PATTERSON, BCO. $45, lots #3 and #4 in St. Clairsville, laid out by Wm. MATHERS, void if HAMILTON pays PATTERSON $45 plus interest by 31 Aug 1807; his seal; WIT: Saml. SULLIVAN, Mahlon SMITH; ack. Saml. SULLIVAN; entered 9 Jan 1807, recorded 23 Jan 1807.

p. 49 - Indenture, 1 Sep 1806, Obadiah JENNINGS, JCO; John PATTERSON and Thomas McCALL, BCO. $250, lot #10 of 15 out lots to St. Clairsville, laid out by Bazaleel WELLS, 11 acres 1 rod 20 perches; his seal; WIT: Josiah HEDGES, Saml. SULLIVAN; ack. Saml. SULLIVAN; entered 9 Jan 1807, recorded 27 Jan 1807.

p. 50 - Indenture, 9 Jan 1807, William CONGLETON (wife Nancy), St. Clairsville, BCO; John PATTERSON and Thomas McCALL, partners known as Patterson and McCall. $100, lots #15 and #23 in St. Clairsville, conveyed to CONGLETON by David and Sally NEWELL on 4 Jan 1803, recorded Book A, p. 210 (p. 159 in new book [p. 26 of abstracts] but dated 4 Feb 1804), fee simple; both seal; WIT: Sterling JOHNSTON, James WRIGHT; ack. Sterling JOHNSTON, J.P.; entered 9 Jan 1807, recorded 28 Jan 1807.

p. 51 - Indenture, 10 Jan 1807, John MARTIN (wife Elizabeth), St. Clairsville, BCO; John THOMPSON, BCO. $500, lots #129, #130, #122 in St. Clairsville, same conveyed from Nicholas BOWERS and wife to MARTIN on 31 Mar 1806, recorded in Book A, p. 646 (p. 470 in the new book [p. 74 in abstracts]), fee simple; both seal; WIT: Sterling JOHNSTON, Jacob GRUBB; ack. Sterling JOHNSTON, J.P.; entered 18 Jan 1807, recorded 28 Jan 1807.

p. 52 - Indenture, 10 Jan 1807, Lewis BRYAN, BCO; John DULLY [DILLY], Wheeling, Virginia. $100 owed by BRYAN to DULLY, to be paid before 1 May first ensuing, secures loan by transfer of two copper stills containing 120 and 58 gallons, previously bought from DULLY, void if debt paid; his seal; WIT: Sterling JOHNSTON; ack. BCO, Sterling JOHNSTON, J.P.; entered 10 Jan 1807, recorded 28 Jan 1807.

p. 53 - Indenture, Nicholas BOWERS (wife Catharine), BCO; John DENT, BCO. $800, part of S 20 T 7 R 4, NBR: Jesse McGEE, 160 acres, part of land granted to BOWERS by John MARTIN dated 4 Mar 1806, fee simple; both seal; WIT: Saml. SULLIVAN, John THOMPSON; ack. Saml. SULLIVAN; entered 10 Jan 1807, recorded 28 Jan 1807.

p. 54 - Indenture, 6 Oct 1806, Mordicai YARNELL (wife Phebe), State of Virginia; John WOLFORD [WILFORD], State of Ohio. $3 per acre, part of S 28 T 6 R 3, NBR: Frederick AMERINE, 219 acres more or less, "agreeable to the patent granted by the United States"; both seal [he signs "M."]; WIT: Robt. WOODS, John CLARK; ack. Thos. THOMPSON, J.P.; entered 12 Jan 1807, recorded 31 Jan 1807.

p. 54 - Indenture, 17 Jan 1807, Alexander McCONALD (wife Jane), BCO; David RUSK, BCO. $322, SW 1/4 of S 7 T 8 R 4, 161 acres, granted to McCONALD by patent dated 21 Oct 1805, fee simple; his seal, her mark; WIT: Sterling JOHNSTON, William ROBISON; ack. Sterling JOHNSTON, J.P.; entered 17 Jan 1807, recorded 4 Feb 1807.

p. 56 - Indenture, 17 Jan 1807, Alexander McCONALD (wife Jane), BCO; James McCONALD, BCO. $323, NE 1/4 of S 7 T 8 R 4, 161 acres, granted to Alexander McCONALD by patent dated 21 Oct 1805, fee simple; his seal, her mark; WIT: Sterling JOHNSTON, William ROBISON; ack. Sterling JOHNSTON, J.P.; entered 17 Jan 1807, recorded 4 Feb 1807.

p. 57 - Indenture, 17 Jan 1807, Alexander McCONALD (wife Jane), BCO; William RAMAGE, BCO. $323, SE 1/4 of S 7 T 8 R 4, part of land granted to McCONALD by patent dated 21 Oct 1805; his seal, her mark [name written as Jain]; WIT: Sterling JOHNSTON, William ROBISON; ack. Sterling JOHNSTON, J.P.; entered 17 Jan 1807, recorded 4 Feb 1807.

p. 58 - "Know all men," Noah ZANE, Virginia, administrator of Absalom MARTIN, dec'd, late of BCO, by virtue of an order of the Court of Common Pleas at April term 1804 at St. Clairsville empowering him to convey to Charles ECKLES, BCO, which MARTIN had [tancet?] on 26 Feb 1801 for $163, part S 13 T 6 R 3, NBR: Andrew DICKSON, John PURDAY, 81 1/2 acres, fee simple, signed 25 Sep 1806; his seal; [no witnesses mentioned]; ack. 25 Sep 1806, BCO, Jacob DAVIS, J.P.; entered 17 Jan 1807, recorded 4 Feb 1807.

p. 59 - Indenture, 8 Jul 1806, Horton HOWARD [HOWART], BCO; Moses GIVEN, BCO. $460, tract of land "with the appurtenances situated in Belmont County formerly part of Jefferson county north western territory, NE 1/4 of S10 T 6 R 3, entered by HOWARD in land office at Stubanville [sic] and afterwards granted by U.S. to HOWARD by patent dated 22 Jan 1806; his seal; WIT: Moses PACKER, John PIGGOTT, Levinah HALL; ack. 23 Jan 1807, BCO, Sterling JOHNSTON, J.P.; entered 23 Jan 1807, recorded 6 Feb 1807.

p. 60 - Indenture, 6 Aug 1806, William HUGAN [HODGIN/HEUGIN], Kirkwood twp., BCO; William CHILDERS, same. $215, S 8 T 8 R 6, 100 acres, fee simple; his seal and mark of Agness HEUGIN [wife, but not mentioned previously]; WIT: Nathan SIDWELL, John GREER [GRIER]; ack. 6 Aug 1806, John GREER, J.P.; entered 26 Jan 1807, recorded 6 Feb 1807.

p. 61 - Indenture, 4 Sep 1806, William CONGLETON, BCO; Samuel HAWKINS, BCO. $50.--, lot #23 in addition to St. Clairsville; his seal; WIT: Sterling JOHNSTON, William JOHNSTON; ack. 4 Sep 1806, Sterling JOHNSTON, J.P.; entered 26 Jan 1807, recorded 12 Feb 1807.

p. 62 - Indenture, 6 Oct 1806, Mordicai YARNELL (wife Phebe); Valentine SHEARER [no locations given]. $4 per acre, land in S 28 T 6 R 3, NBR: Notley HAYS, John NEAWELLS, Frederick AMERINE, 125 acres 31 perches, surveyed by Robert JOHNSTON, mentions agreement with SHEARER and his wife but does not name her, land patented by YARNELL; both seal; WIT: Robt. WOODS, John CLARK; ack. Tho. THOMPSON, J.P.; entered 27 Jan 1807, recorded 10 Feb 1807.

p. 62 - Indenture, 28 Jan 1807, Obadiah JENNINGS, Stubanville, JCO; John THOMPSON, St. Clairsville. $50.--, lot #3 in plan of 15 out lots close to St. Clairsville, laid out by Bazaleel WELLS, 2 acres 6 perches; his seal; WIT: John PATTERSON, John G. HAMILTON; ack.John PATTERSON, J.P.; entered 27 Jan 1807, recorded 12 Feb 1807.

p. 63 - "Know all men," Peter MOORE of Loudoun County, Virginia, appoints Isaac MOORE, BCO, as attorney, signed 13 Jun 1806; his seal; ack. 13 Jun 1806, Loudoun County, Obadiah CLIFFORD, Ths. FOUCH, certified by Charles BINNS, Clerk; entered 5 Feb 1807; recorded 12 Feb 1807.

p. 64 - Indenture, 26 Nov 1806, John HENDERSON (wife Martha), BCO; James PARR, BCO. $300, [paid by said Thomas PARR, though all other references are to James], SW 1/4 of S 27 T 8 R 4, 100 acres, granted to John HENDERSON by patent dated 6 Jun 1806; his seal, her mark; WIT: Moses MERRITT [MERRIT], Thomas LAWSON; ack. Moses MERRITT, J.P.; entered 10 Feb 1807, recorded 12 Feb 1807.

p. 65 - Indenture, 4 Dec 1805, Magdaline PIPER, Richland twp., BCO; Jeremiah FAIRHURST, same. $100, 7 3/4 acres 38 rods, NBR: William WOODS, Jacob LEASE, fee simple, conveyed from David VANCE (wife Margaret) to Sterling JOHNSTON, from JOHNSTON (wife Mary) to PIPER on 7 Apr 1804, as recorded in Book A, p. 314 (p. 256 in new book [p. 41 of abstracts]); her mark; WIT: Sterling JOHNSTON, Wm. CONGLETON; ack. 4 Dec 1805, Sterling JOHNSTON, J.P.; entered 13 Feb 1807; recorded 17 Feb 1807.

p. 66 - "Know all men," Daniel McELHERON, Newark twp., Essex County, New Jersey, appoints Bazlee [Bazaleel] WELLS of Stubanville, JCO, as his attorney to act for him except monies due on promissory notes which was already given to Jacob DAVIS, Esqr., dated 13 Oct 1806; his seal; WIT: Elisha VAN ARSDALE, William S. PENNINGSTON; ack. New Jersey, 13 Oct 1806, William S. PENNINGTON, Justice of Supreme Court of Indenture; recorded JCO, Book B, p. 84, by John GILBREATH, Recorder; entered 14 Feb 1807, recorded 18 Feb 1807.

p. 67 - Indenture, 4 Feb 1807, James BARNES (wife Nancy), BCO; William BROWN, BCO. $15, lot in town laid out by James BARNES, William BROWN, and Notley HAYS, fee simple; his seal, her mark; WIT: Benjamine PEARSON, Robert DENT; ack. Saml. SULLIVAN, J.P.; entered 14 Feb 1807, recorded 18 Feb 1807.

p. 68 - Indenture, 20 Feb 1807, Job RIDGWAY (wife Rebeckah), BCO; Josiah DILLON, St. Clairsville, BCO. $100, lot #49 in St. Clairsville, 1/4 acre, conveyed from David and Sally NEWELL to Daniel McPEEK on 9 Jun 1802, from McPEEK to RIDGWAY on 15 Jun 1805, fee simple; both seal; WIT: Sterling JOHNSTON, Josiah HEDGES; ack. Sterling JOHNSTON, J.P.; entered 20 Feb 1807, recorded 25 Feb 1807.

p. 69 - Indenture, 8 Jul 1806, Horton HOWARD, BCO; John PICKERING, BCO. $480, NW 1/4 of S 10 T 6 R 3 (formerly in JCO, NWT), Steubenville district, granted to HOWARD by patent dated 22 Jan 1806; his seal; WIT: Moses PARKER, John PIGGOTT, Levinah HALL; ack. 23 Jan 1807, Sterling JOHNSTON, J.P.; entered 23 Feb 1807, recorded 25 Feb 1807.

p. 70 - Indenture, 20 Feb 1807, John PICKERING (wife Mary), BCO; Hugh PARKS, BCO. $484, part NW 1/4 of S 10 T 6 R 3, 107 acres, [see previous entry for history]; his seal, her mark; WIT: Charles McMANAS, Tho. THOMPSON; ack. 13 Feb 1807, Tho. THOMPSON, J.P.

p. 72 - Indenture, 23 Feb 1807, Robert JOHNSTON, BCO; Sterling JOHNSTON, BCO. $80, lot #16 in St. Clairsville, conveyed to Robert JOHNSTON and James CLOYD by Moses CONGLETON on 26 Mar 1806, fee simple; his seal; WIT: John PATTERSON, James WRIGHT; ack. John PATTERSON, J.P.; entered 23 Feb 1807, recorded 26 Feb 1807.

p. 73 - Indenture, 6 Feb 1807, Isaac MOORE, attorney in fact for Peter MORE; John FRETCH [no locations given]. $100, lot #101 in St. Clairsville, 1/4 acre, fee simple, conveyed by David and Sally NEWELL to Mary (wife of James NOWLS) by deed dated 27 Apr 1802 as recorded in Book A, p. 66 (p. 59 of new book [p. 9 of abstracts]; seal of Isaac MOORE for Peter MOORE; WIT: Sterling JOHNSTON, John G. HAMILTON; ack. Sterling JOHNSTON, J.P.; entered 28 Feb 1807, recorded 2 Mar 1807.

p. 74 - Indenture, 10 Mar 1807, John G. HAMILTON (wife Nancy), St. Clairsville, BCO; John PATTERSON [and Thomas McCALL], same. $110, lots #3 and #4 on S side of St. Clairsville, fee simple; both seal; WIT: Sterling JOHNSTON, Saml. SPRIGG; ack. Sterling JOHNSTON, J.P.; entered 10 Mar 1807, recorded 17 Mar 1807.

p. 75 - Indenture, 11 Mar 1807, John THOMPSON (wife Sally), St. Clairsville, BCO; William SMITH, same. $360, lots #129 and #130 in St. Clairsville, each 1/4 acre, both lots conveyed from John and Elizabeth MARTIN to THOMPSON on 10 Jan 1807, fee simple; his seal, her mark; Sterling JOHNSTON, Josiah DILLON; ack. Sterling JOHNSTON, J.P.; entered 11 Mar 1807, recorded 17 Mar 1807.

p. 76 - Indenture, 14 Mar 1807, Nicholas STONER (wife Mary), Richland twp., BCO; William CONGLETON, St. Clairsville, BCO. $200, lots #128 and #119 in St. Clairsville, 1/4 acre; his seal, her mark; WIT: Sterling JOHNSTON, James CLOYD; ack. Sterling JOHNSTON, J.P.; entered 14 Mar 1807, recorded 18 Mar 1807.

p. 77 - Indenture, 30 Sep 1806, Phillip WINDLE (wife Barbara), St. Clairsville, BCO; Casper SEEVERS, same. $250, lot #92 in St. Clairsville, fee simple; his seal, her mark; WIT: Wm. MATHERS, Wm. FARIS, Junr.; ack. 30 Sep 1806, Saml. SULLIVAN, J.P.; entered 16 Mar 1807, recorded 18 Mar 1807.

p. 78 - Indenture, 30 Sep 1806, Phillip WINDLE (wife Barbara), St. Clairsville, BCO; Casper SEEVERS, same. $200, lots #91, #83, and #75 (adjoining) in St. Clairsville, fee simple; his seal, her mark; WIT: William FARIS, Senr., Wm. FARIS, Junr.; ack. 30 Sep 1806, Saml. SULLIVAN, J.P.; entered 16 Mar 1807, recorded 18 Mar 1807.

p. 79 - Indenture, 30 Sep 1806, Moses NIEL, St. Clairsville, BCO; Casper SEEVERS, same. $120, lots #100 and #99 in St. Clairsville, fee simple, payments to be made periodically ending 1 Apr 1808; his seal; WIT: Saml. SULLIVAN, Wm. FARIS, Junr.; ack. 30 Sep 1806, Saml. SULLIVAN, J.P.; entered 16 Mar 1807, recorded 20 Mar 1807.

p. 80 - Indenture, 16 Mar 1807, William MOSELY, BCO; Samuel SULLIVAN, BCO. MOSELY bound to SULLIVAN for $150 for conveyance of out lot #6 to St. Clairsville as laid out by Bazaleel WELLS, secured by conveying two lots (#19 and #20) in the addition to St. Clairsville as laid out by William MATHERS, fee simple, void if deed to out lot #6 is made; his seal; WIT: Sterling JOHNSTON, James CALDWELL; ack. Sterling JOHNSTON, J.P.; entered 18 Mar 1807, recorded 20 Mar 1807; released 23 Jul 1807.

p. 81 - Indenture, 30 Jan 1807, Bazaleel WELLS, JCO, attorney for Daniel McELHERON of State of New Jersey; Christian HINKLE, BCO. $80, NW corner of S 2 T 6 R 3, Steubenville district, 40 acres; seal of Daniel McELHERON by attorney Bazaleel WELLS; WIT: Alex SNODGRASS, Butler

WELLS; ack. JCO, Alex SNODGRASS, J.P., certified by Jno. WARD, Clerk, JCO; entered 17 Mar 1807, recorded 20 Mar 1807.

p. 82 - "Whereas," patent dated 3 Oct 1805 granted to Francis TOWNSEND, assignee of Joseph TOWNSEND, for S 17 T 6 R 3; furthermore, Burdon STANTON (wife Charlotte), by their Indenture dated 27 Aug 1806 conveyed to Francis TOWNSEND the SW 1/4 of S 11 T 6 R 3; now Francis TOWNSEND (wife Marrah), for $1,600 paid by Aaron NEWPORT, BCO, convey SW 1/4 of S 11 and part of SW 1/4 of S 17 T 6 R 3, NBR: Jacob LASH, Jonathan TAYLOR, Preston SHARPLESS, 160 acres, signed 2 Oct 1806; both seal [her name given as Marah]; WIT: Saml. SHARPLESS, Preston SHARPLESS; ack. 3 Oct 1805, Thos. THOMPSON, J.P.

p. 84 - "Whereas" Bardon STANTON (wife Charlotte), BCO, by Indenture dated 27 Aug 1806 granted to Francis TOWNSEND of Washington County, Pennsylvania, the SW 1/4 of S 11 T 6 R 3, now TOWNSEND (wife Marrah), BCO, for $750 paid by Preston SHARPLESS, BCO, grant part S 11, NBR: Aaron NEWPORT, Moses GIVEN, Jonathan TAYLOR, 114 1/2 acres, signed 2 Oct 1806; both seall; WIT: Saml. SHARPLESS, Moses [SHERWOOD???--the transcriber seems to have had problems as well; ack. 2 Oct 1806, Thos. THOMPSON, J.P.

p. 85 - Indenture, 22 Dec 1806, Joseph W. SATTERTHWAITE, BCO; Horton HOWARD, BCO. $260, part of S 13 T 7 R 3, 30 acres, conveyed by lw&t of William SATTERTHWAITE [SATERTHWAITE], deceased, father of Joseph W., granted to William SATTERTHWAITE by patent dated 9 Mar 1803; his seal; WIT: Saml. POTTS, Joseph GIBBONS; ack. 4 Apr 1807, Sterling JOHNSTON, J.P.; entered 4 Apr 1807, recorded 9 Apr 1807.

p. 86 - Indenture, 6 Oct 1806, Mordicai YARNELL (wife Phebe); John MAXWELL [no locations given for either]. $5, 88 acres 29 perches agreeable to survey of Robert __, in S 28 T 6 R 3, NBR: V. SHEARERS, Notley HAYS; both seal; WIT: Robt. WOODS, John CLARK; ack. 6 Oct 1806, Thos. THOMPSON; entered 4 Apr 1807; recorded 22 Apr 1807.

p. 87 - Indenture, 4 Apr 1807, Josiah DILLON (wife Dorothy [Dorithy]), St. Clairsville, BCO; John BERRY, BCO. $160, part of S 35 T 3 R 3, 40 acres 3 rods 7 perches, granted to DILLON by patent dated 14 Jul 1806, fee simple; both seal; WIT: Sterling JOHNSTON, Jeremiah FAIRHURST; ack. Sterling JOHNSTON, J.P.

p. 88 - Indenture, 4 Apr 1807, Josiah DILLON (wife Dorothy [Dorithy], St. Clairsville, BCO; Joseph GILL, JCO. $2,711, part of S 35 T 6 R 3, Steubenville district, NBR: Notley HAYS, George IRELAND, John BERRY, Hugh LYONS, 403 acres, granted to DILLON by patent dated 14 Jul 1806, fee simple; both seal; WIT: Sterling JOHNSTON, Jeremiah FAIRHURST; ack. Sterling JOHNSTON, J.P.; entered 4 Apr 1807, recorded 22 Apr 1807.

p. 90 - Indenture, 4 Apr 1807, Josiah DILLON (wife Dorothy [Dorothe], St. Clairsville, BCO; Jeremiah FAIRHURST, same. $125, lot #49 in St. Clairsville, 1/4 acre, conveyed by David and Sally NEWELL to Daniel McPEEK on 9 Jun 1802, from McPEEK to Job RIDGWAY on 15 Jun 1805, from RIDGWAY to Josiah DILLON on 20 Feb 1807, fee simple; both seal; WIT: Sterling JOHNSTON, William FROST; ack. Sterling JOHNSTON, J.P.

p. 91 - Indenture, 8 Apr 1807, James BRYAN (wife Elizabeth), Richland twp., BCO; Thomas PLUMMER, same. $1,360, NE 1/4 of S 9 T 7 R 4, 160 acres, conveyed from Bazaleel and Sally WELLS to BRYAN on 5 Oct 1798 [actually written as "fifty day of October"], recorded in recording office in Jefferson County, Lib. A, p. 90, fee simple; his seal, her mark; WIT: Sterling JOHNSTON, Mahlon SMITH, George PAUL; ack. Sterling JOHNSTON, J.P.

p. 92 - Indenture, 25 Mar 1807, Andrew EAGLESON (wife Jean), JCO; Henry WEST, JCO. $249.99, part of S 27 T 4 R 2, 31 acres 2 rods 8 13/100 perches; both seal; WIT: Th^{s}. MITCHELL, Rich^{d}. McKIBBENS; ack. Thos. MITCHELL, J.P.

p. 93 - Indenture, 31 Mar 1807, Andrew EAGLESON (wife Jean), JCO; James McCLURE, BCO. $450.50, part of S 27 T 4 R 2, NBR: (formerly) Joseph SCOTT, Richard McKIBBENS, Henry WEST, 57 acres 2 rods 14 perches; both seal; WIT: Thos. MITCHELL, Rich^{d}. McKIBBENS; ack. Thos. MITCHELL.

p. 95 - Indenture, 3 Feb 1807, Daniel McELHERON, Newark, New Jersey (by attorney Bazaleel WELLS); Jane ALEXANDER (late Jane DICKSON) [no location given]. $320, part S 2 T 6 R 3, 160 acres; his seal by attorney; WIT: Alex SNODGRASS, Joseph [HEEUTON]; ack. JCO, Alex. SNODGRASS, J.P., certified by Jno. WARD, Clerk, JCO.

p. 96 - Indenture, 20 Feb 1807, James ALEXANDER (wife Margaret), Peas twp., BCO; George BROKAW, JCO. $430.50, land on Glens run, part of S 31 T 4 R 2, 123 acres, fee simple; his seal, her mark; WIT: Thos. MITCHELL, Robert FINNEY; ack. Thos. MITCHELL, J.P.; entered 14 Apr 1807, recorded 23 Apr 1807.

p. 97 - Indenture, 14 Apr 1807, Josiah DILLON (wife Dorothy [Dorithy]), St. Clairsville, Richland twp., BCO; Notley HAY [HAYS], Richland twp., BCO.

$60, part S 35 T 6 R 3, Steubenville district, 30 acres 1 rod 30 perches, part of S granted to DILLON by patent dated 14 Jul 1806, fee simple; both seal; WIT: Sterling JOHNSTON, William HULSE; ack. Sterling JOHNSTON, J.P.

p. 98 - Indenture, 15 Apr 1807, Joshua HATCHER (wife Jane), Richland twp., BCO; David WHERRY, BCO. $440, part of S 18 T 9 R 7, 160 acres, granted to HATCHER by patent dated 6 Mar 1806, fee simple; his seal, her mark; WIT: Sterling JOHNSTON, Samuel SMITH; ack. Sterling JOHNSTON, J.P.

p. 99 - Indenture, 11 Feb 1807, Bazaleel WELLS (wife Sally), JCO; Francis HARDESTY, BCO. $348, part S 26 T 4 R 2, 116 acres; both seal; WIT: Butler WELLS, Alex^r. SNODGRASS; ack. JCO, Alex^r. SNODGRASS, certified by Jno. WARD, Clerk, JCO.

p. 100 - Indenture, 1 Sep 1806, Obadiah JENNINGS, JCO; Michael GROVE, BCO. $200.--, out lot #7 laid out by Bazaleel WELLS adjoining addition to St. Clairsville, 5 acres 3 rods 3 perches; his seal; WIT: Saml. SPREGG, Josiah HEDGES; ack. BCO John PATTERSON, J.P.

p. 101 - Indenture, 14 Mar 1807, Obadiah [Obadia] JENNINGS (wife Ann), Steubenville, JCO; Joseph PATTON [no location given]. $50, out lot #5 adjoining addition to St. Clairsville, 3 1/2 acres 29 perches; both seal; WIT: Jonathan JENNINGS, John McELROY; ack. Alex^r. SNODGRASS, J.P.; entered 16 Apr 1807, recorded 24 Apr 1807.

p. 102 - Indenture, 20 Feb 1807, George BROKAW (wife Jane), JCO; Robert FINNEY, BCO. $246, NBR: Thomas CAVEN "and others," S 31 T 4 R 2, 61 1/2 acres; his seal, her mark; WIT: Thos. MITCHELL, Thos. ALEXANDER, ack. Thos. MITCHELL, J.P.; entered 16 Apr 1807, recorded 25 Apr 1807.

p. 103 - Indenture, 14 Mar 1807, Obadiah JENNINGS (wife Ann), JCO; Josiah DILLON, BCO. $300, lot #15 of out lots adjoining addition to St. Clairsville, 10 acres 97 perches; both seal; WIT: Jonathan JENNINGS, John McELROY; ack. JCO, Alex^r. SNODGRASS, J.P.; entered 16 Apr 1807, recorded 30 Apr 1807.

p. 103 - Indenture, 20 Feb 1807, George BROKAW (wife Jane), JCO; Thomas CAVEN, BCO. [Dollar amount seems to have been omitted], tract bounded by [NBR:] Robert FINNEY and others, S 31 T 4 R 2, 61 1/2 acres; his seal, her mark; WIT: Thos. MITCHELL, Thos. ALEXANDER; ack. Thos. MITCHELL, J.P.; entered 16 Apr 1807, recorded 1 May 1807.

p. 104 - Indenture, 18 Apr 1807, Notley HAYS (wife Sally), Richland twp., BCO; Joseph ROBERTS, same. $582, part S 35 and 34, T 6 R 3, Steubenville district, portion in S 34 granted to HAYS by patent from U.S., portion in S 35 granted by Josiah and Dorothy [Dorithy] DILLON, NBR: William HEUTH, Merchant DEFORD, William HOULTS, 97 acres 1 rod 32 perches, fee simple; his seal, her mark; WIT: Sterling JOHNSTON, Merchant DEFORD; ack. Sterling JOHNSTON, J.P.

p. 106 - Indenture, 18 Apr 1807, Notley HAYS (wife Sally), Richland twp., BCO; Merchant DEFORD, BCO. $425, part of S 34 and 28, T 6 R 3, Steubenville district, 100 acres 2 rods 20 perches, portion in S 34 granted to HAYS by patent, portion in S 35 from Josiah and Dorothy [Dorithy] DILLON, portion in S 28 from Mordicai and Phebe YARNELL, fee simple; his seal, her mark; [no witnesses given]; ack. Sterling JOHNSTON, J.P.; entered 20 Apr 1807, recorded 5 May 1807.

p. 107 - Indenture, 21 Apr 1807, John THOMPSON (wife Sally), St. Clairsville, BCO; Magdaline PIPER, same. $100, lot #122 in St. Clairsville, conveyed from Nicholas BOWERS and wife to John MARTIN on 31 Mar [1806], from MARTIN (wife Elizabeth) to THOMPSON on 10 Jan 1807, fee simple; his seal, her mark; WIT: Sterling JOHNSTON, James BRYAN; ack. Sterling JOHNSTON, J.P.; entered 21 Apr 1807, recorded 5 May 1807.

p. 108 - Indenture, 17 Apr 1807, Josiah HEDGES, Sheriff, BCO; Mahlon SMITH and Isaac VORE, BCO. By virtue of a writ of execution issued by Court of Common Pleas on 11 Mar 1807, whereas John [MECKLE?] at August term 1805 recovered of William MATHERS a judgment for $1,221.39, and whereas John MECKLE to chancery at December term 1805 complained that MATHERS had fradulently conveyed to David MATHERS 3 lots in St. Clairsville (#61, #67, #68) with a view to defraud him, at December term 1806 judges determined (after hearing testimony of the three parties) that the lots should be siezed and the MATHERS should pay costs of petition ($25.26), proceeds of property to be submitted to court on second Tuesday of April next, to render to MECKLE for an in consideration of $231 paid for lot #68 by SMITH and VORE; his seal; WIT: John PATTERSON, Sterling JOHNSTON; ack. Sterling JOHNSTON, J.P.; entered 22 Apr 1807, recorded 5 May 1807.

p. 109 - Indenture, 16 Apr 1807, Josiah HEDGES, Sheriff, BCO; John PATTERSON, BCO. By virtue of a writ of execution from CCP in chancery on 11 Mar 1807 [same situation as previous entry], lot #61 to PATTERSON for $251; his seal; WIT: Isaac VORE, Sterling JOHNSTON; ack. Sterling JOHNSTON, J.P.; entered 22 Apr 1807, recorded 5 May 1807.

p. 110 - Indenture, 3 Jan 1807, Nicholas BOWERS, St. Clairsville, BCO; John DENT, BCO. $800, NW 1/4 of S 28 T 7 R 4, 160 acres, void if BOWERS pays DENT $800 on or before 1810; both seal; WIT: Saml. SULLIVAN, John THOMPSON; ack. Saml. SULLIVAN, J.P.; 12 Jul 1810 John DENT produced three notes that he had given to BOWERS dated 3 Jan 1807, calling in all for $800, supposed to be a full satisfaction for the above $800 mentioned in the above mortgage, WIT: Isaa [Isaac] VORE, Samuel SHARP, executors for Nick[l]. BOWERS.

p. 112 - Indenture, 27 Apr 1807, William GIBSON (wife Nancy), BCO; legal heirs of John FAIRHURST (late of BCO). Whereas FAIRHURST, deceased, did on 19 Apr 1806 purchase from GIBSON lots #151 and #152 in St. Clairsville for $380 and GIBSONs now convey; both seal; WIT: Sterling JOHNSTON, Josiah DILLON; ack. Sterling JOHNSTON, J.P.

p. 113 - Indenture, 6 Dec 1806, Andrew MARSHALL (wife Margaret), St. Clairsville, BCO; John EATON, Washington County, Pennsylvania. $500, lot #65 in St. Clairsville, 1/4 acre, conveyed to MARSHALL by David and Sally NEWELL and Benjamine and Jane NEWELL on 17 Apr 1801 in fee simple, recorded Book A, p. 35 (p. 32 of new book [p. 5 of abstracts]), fee simple; his seal, her mark; WIT: Saml. SULLIVAN, Jacob NAGLE; ack. Saml. SULLIVAN, J.P.; entered 30 Apr 1807, recorded 7 May 1807.

p. 114 - Indenture, 20 Apr 1807, Joseph SHARP (wife Nancy), BCO; John CAMPBELL, BCO. $160, part SE 1/4 of S 32 T 8 R 4, 40 acres, granted to SHARP by patent dated 18 Feb 1806; his seal, her mark; WIT: Moses MERRIT, Marget SHARP [her mark]; ack. Moses MERRIT, J.P.; entered 6 May 1807, recorded 19 May 1807.

p. 115 - Indenture, 7 Oct 1806, Daniel McELHERON (wife Amelia), Newark, New Jersey; Christian [HARR], Steubenville, Ohio. $288, land on McMahan's Creek, part S 36 T 2 R 2, Steubenville district, 32 acres 38 perches; both seal; WIT: Obadiah JENNINGS, Maria M. BROOKS; ack. New Jersey, William S. PENNINGTON, Justice of Supreme Court of Judicature.

p. 116 - Indenture, 31 Dec 1806, Borden STANTON (wife Charlotte), BCO; Horton HOWARD, BCO. $1,400, part of S 7 T 7 R 3, granted to STANTON as an assignee of HOWARD by patent dated 27 Aug 1805, 170 acres; both seal; WIT: James RILEY, Enoch STANTON; ack. 31 Dec 1806, Thos. MITCHELL [no position given]; entered and recorded 19 May 1807.

p. 118 - Indenture, 12 Feb 1807, Horton HOWARD (wife Hannah), BCO; Borden STANTON, BCO. $640, E 1/2 of S 8 T 7 R 3, granted by patent dated

10 Sep 1806; both seal; WIT: Isaac BOWMAN, John PIGGOTT, Levinah HALL; ack. Thos. MITCHELL [no position given]; entered 19 May 1807, recorded 21 May 1807.

p. 119 - Indenture, 29 Apr 1807, Borden STANTON (wife Charlotte), BCO; Moses PIGGOTT, BCO. $250, part of S 8 T 7 R 3, granted to Horton HOWARD by patent dated 10 Sep 1807, 50 acres, granted by HOWARD to STANTON by deed dated 12 Feb 1806; both seal; WIT: Job RIDGWAY, John BARNES; ack. Thos. MITCHELL [no position given]; entered 19 May 1807, recorded 21 May 1807.

p. 120 - Indenture, 13 Feb 1807, Horton HOWARD (wife Hannah), BCO; Borden STANTON, BCO. $320, NW 1/4 of S 7 T 9 R 7, Steubenville district, granted to HOWARD by patent dated 16 Dec 1806; both seal; [no witnesses given]; ack. Thos. MITCHELL [no position given]; entered 19 May 1807, recorded 21 May 1807.

p. 120 - Indenture, 19 May 1807, John LONG (wife Caly), BCO; James CALDWELL, BCO. $325, lot adjoining St. Clairsville, NBR: David NISWANGER (formerly Allen STEWART), 15 acres, fee simple; his seal, her mark; WIT: Sterling JOHNSTON, George PAULL; ack. Sterling JOHNSTON, J.P.; entered 19 May 1807, recorded 22 May 1807.

p. 122 - Indenture, 20 May 1807, Josiah HEDGES (wife Rebecca), BCO; Robert H. JOHNSTON, BCO. $700, lot #45 in St. Clairsville plus a right of way plus half of lot #46; both seal [her name Rebeckah]; WIT: John PATTERSON, Peter YARNALL; ack. John PATTERSON, J.P.; entered 20 May 1807, recorded 22 May 1807.

p. 123 - Indenture, 1 Sep 1806, Obadiah JENNINGS, JCO; Robert H. JOHNSTON, BCO. $50, lots #17, #18, #19, #20 in addition to St. Clairsville as laid out by William MATHERS; his seal; WIT: William CONGLETON, James JOHNSTON; ack. 1 Sep 1806, John PATTERSON, J.P.; entered 20 May 1807, recorded 22 May 1807.

p. 124 - Indenture, 19 Feb 1807, Joseph MERRIT (wife Mary), BCO; Alexander YOUNG, BCO. $100, lot #116 in St. Clairsville, 1/4 acre, conveyed from George and Mary MYERS to MERRIT on 1 Jan 1807, fee simple; both seal; WIT: Sterling JOHNSTON, Josiah DILLON; ack. Sterling JOHNSTON, J.P.; entered 25 May 1807, recorded 1 Jun 1807.

p. 125 - Indenture, 28 May 1807, Samuel HAWKINS, BCO; Jacob GRUBB, BCO. $105, lot #23 in addition to St. Clairsville as laid out by William

MATHERS, conveyed from William CONGLETON to HAWKINS on 4 Sep 1806, recorded in Book B, p. 61 [p. 92 of abstracts]; his mark; WIT: Sterling JOHNSTON, George PAULL; ack. Sterling JOHNSTON, J.P.; entered 28 May 1807, recorded 1 Jun 1807.

p. 126 - Indenture, 21 May 1807, Israel FRENCH, Junr., Frederick County, Maryland; Israel FRENCH, BCO. $320, SW 1/4 of S 17 T 8 R 6, 160 acres; his seal; WIT: Henry McELFRESH, Jesse WRIGHT; ack. Frederick County, Maryland, Henry McELFRESH, Jesse WRIGHT, J.P.'s, certified by Wm. RITCHIE, Clerk; entered 1 Jun 1807, recorded 2 Jun 1807.

p. 127 - Indenture, 18 Apr 1807, Samuel PAULTY [POULTNEY], Frederick County, Maryland; William WOOD, same. $100, lot #3 in addition to St. Clairsville as laid out by James BARNES, Notley HAYS, and William BROWN, 1/2 acre, fee simple; his seal; WIT: Silas BAILEY [BAILY], Jesse WRIGHT; ack. Frederick County, Maryland, Silas BAILEY, Jesse WRIGHT, J.P.'s, certified by Wm. RICHIE, Clerk; entered 1 Jun 1807, recorded 2 Jun 1807.

p. 128 - Indenture, 28 May 1807, James CALDWELL (wife Anne), BCO; Josiah DILLON, BCO. $200, lot #52 in St. Clairsville, 1/4 acre, fee simple; both seal; WIT: William MILLER, Sterling JOHNSTON; ack. Sterling JOHNSTON, J.P.; entered 2 Jun 1807, recorded 5 Jun 1807.

p. 129 - Indenture, 27 Jan 1807, Samuel GREGG (wife Anne), BCO; Joseph VANLAW, BCO. As S 33 T 7 R 4 was patented to GREGG (then of Ross County, Ohio) on 1 Oct 1806, GREGG now conveys to Joseph VANLAW for $480, 160 acres beginning at NW corner of S; both seal; WIT: James SINCLAIR, Samuel GREGG, Junr.; ack. 25 Apr 1807, Arthur IRWIN, J.P.; entered 4 Jun 1807, recorded 5 Jun 1807.

p. 130 - Indenture, 14 Apr 1807, David NEWELL (wife Sally), Richland twp., BCO; Robert GRIFFITH, same. $20, lot [number blank] in St. Clairsville, fee simple; his seal only; WIT: Sterling JOHNSTON, Michael McCLUNEY, Esqr.; ack. Sterling JOHNSTON, J.P.

p. 131 - Indenture, 28 May 1807, Richard SATERTHWAIT (bricklayer), BCO; John PICKERING (yeoman), BCO. $120, beginning SE corner of S 13 T 7 R 3, S granted to William SATERTHWAIT [SATTERTHWAIT] by patent dated 9 Mar 1803, conveyed to son Richard SATERTHWAIT by lw&t dated 29 Jul 1804, 10 acres, now conveyed to John PICKERING; his seal; WIT: Joseph GIBBONS, William GIBBONS; ack. Thos. THOMPSON, J.P.; entered 13 Jun 1807, recorded 23 Jun 1807.

p. 132 - Indenture, 26 Sep 1806, James BARNES (wife Nancy), St. Clairsville, BCO; William FARQUAHER [FAUQUIER], Wheeling, Ohio County, Virginia. $2,000, lots #71 and #72 in St. Clairsville, each 1/4 acre, both conveyed from David and Elizabeth KIRKPATRICK to BARNES by deed dated 9 Feb 1804, lots #1, #2, #5, #6 of town laid out by James BARNES, William BROWN, and Notley HAYS near the E end of town as recorded in Book A, pp. 504 and 505 (pp. 225 and 226 of new book [p. 36 of abstracts]), one other lot containing 3 acres conveyed by deed dated 13 Apr 1805 from Josiah HEDGES to BARNES and Moses MOREHEAD, MOREHEAD and his wife conveyed their moiety to BARNES on 25th day of this inst., NBR: (last lot) John LONG (his out lot); his seal, her mark; WIT: Saml. SPRIGG, John PATTERSON; ack. 10 Jun 1807, John PATTERSON, J.P.; entered 13 Jun 1807, recorded 23 Jun 1807.

p. 134 - Indenture, 11 Dec 1806, Merchant DEFORD, BCO; Noah LINSLEY [LINSLY], Ohio County, Virginia. To secure a debt of $248.92 due to Joseph HUSTON and for $1, part of S 34 T 6 R 3, 100 acres, tract where DEFORD now lives, land to LINSLEY but void if DEFORD pays HUSTON in installments ending second Tuesday of Dec 1809 with interest; DEFORD and LINSLEY both seal; WIT: Geo. PAULL, E. WOODS; ack. Sterling JOHNSTON, J.P.; entered 23 Jul [probably Jun] 1807, recorded 8 Jul 1807.

p. 135 - "Know all men," David HOWELL, BCO, in consideration of love and affection for son John HOWELL, BCO, conveys goods and chattles with one mare delivered at time of signing, 27 Jun 1807; his seal; WIT: Sterling JOHNSTON, James CLOYD; ack. James CLOYD, J.P. for Richland twp.; entered 27 Jun 1807, recorded 8 Jul 1807.

p. 136 - Indenture, 4 Jul 1807, William SMITH (wife Nancy), Richland twp., BCO; Moses MOREHEAD, BCO. $200, lot #120 in St. Clairsville (midtown), originally conveyed to SMITH by David and Sally NEWELL and Benjamine and Jane NEWELL on 13 Jan 1801, recorded in JCO Lib. A, p. 233, fee simple; his seal, her mark; WIT: Sterling JOHNSTON, Wm. BRYAN; ack. Sterling JOHNSTON, J.P.; entered 4 Jul 1807, recorded 8 Jul 1807.

p. 137 - Indenture, 5 Sep 1806, Richard ALLENDER, Washington County, Maryland, and John ALLENDER, Franklin County, Pennsylvania; William ALLENDER, Franklin County, Pennsylvania, and Nicholas ALLENDER, Cinton [probably Clinton] County, Pennsylvania. Whereas Daniel McELHERON by deed dated 10 Jun 1803 sold to Richard and John a tract of land in BCO containing 245 acres in S 30 T 2 R 2, now for $100 paid by Nicholas and William conveyed 122 1/2 acres, to be held as tenants in common (not joint); seals of Richard and John; WIT: Jno. BUCHANON; ack. Washington County, Maryland,

5 Sep 1806, Jno. BUCHANON, Chief Judge of Fifth Judicial District, certified by A. WILLIAMS, Clerk of County Court.

p. 139 - Indenture, 11 Jul 1807, George SNIDER [SNYDER] (wife Barbara), BCO; Nathan SPENCER, BCO. Whereas SNIDER was granted land by patent for S 31 T 7 R 4, Steubenville district, dated 1 Oct 1806, now for $320 paid by SPENCER conveying 160 acres of S 31 T 7 R 4; his seal, her mark; WIT: Sterling JOHNSTON, Robt. GRIFFITH; ack. Sterling JOHNSTON, J.P.; entered 11 Jul 1807, recorded 20 Jul 1807.

p. 140 - Indenture, 11 Jul 1807, George SNIDER [SNYDER] (wife Barbara), BCO; James CALDWELL, BCO. $1,000, part of S 31 T 7 R 4, granted to SNIDER by patent dated 1 Oct 1806, NBR: John WILKINS, Nathan SPENCER, 227 acres, 2 rods, 33 perches, fee simple; his seal, her mark; WIT: Sterling JOHNSTON, Robt. GRIFFITH; ack. Sterling JOHNSTON, J.P.; entered 11 Jul 1807, recorded 20 Jul 1807.

p. 141 - Indenture, 29 May 1807, Josiah DILLON, BCO, David MURPLE [MERPLE, MIRPLE], Muskingum County, Ohio. DILLON is indebted to MURPLE for $1,200, debt secured by conveyance of lot #52 in St. Clairsville, 1/4 acre, conveyed from James and Jane WOODS to James CALDWELL on 27 Aug 1805, from CALDWELL to DILLON, void if debt paid on or before 1 Oct 1808; his seal; WIT: George REYNOLDS, William WHITE; ack. 14 Jul 1807, Sterling JOHNSTON, J.P.; entered 21 Jul 1807, recorded 24 Jul 1807.

p. 143 - Indenture, 18 Jun 1807, David I. MARPLE, Zanesville, Ohio; James TAYLOR, Muskingum County, Ohio. $1,200, sells deed dated 9 May 1807 [though it is 29 in that entry] where Josiah DILLON sells lot [see previous entry for history] in St. Clairsville; his seal; WIT: Danl. CONVORSE, Charles WILLIAMS; ack. Muskingum County, Christian SPANGLER, J.P.

p. 143 - Indenture, 23 Jun 1807, Nathaniel UPDEGRAFF (wife Ann), Mountpleasant twp., JCO; James BAILEY [RAILEY], BCO. $500, SW 1/4 of S 2 T 7 R 3, 160 acres; both seal; WIT: Thomas MITCHELL, James GORDON; ack. Thos. MITCHELL, J.P.; entered 21 Jul 1807, recorded 24 Jul 1807.

p. 144 - Indenture, 26 Dec 1806, John BLY, Fairfield County, Ohio; John PATTERSON and McCALL, BCO. $70, lot #24 in St. Clairsville; his seal; WIT: Saml. SPRIGG, Noah ZANE; ack. Lancaster, Fairfield County, Ohio, 26 Dec 1806, Hugh BOYLE, J.P., certified 28 Jan 1807 by Hugh BOYLE, Clerk, Fairfield County, Ohio.

p. 146 - Indenture, 23 Jul 1807, William MOSELEY (wife Elizabeth), BCO; Samuel SULLIVAN, BCO. $150, out lot #6, 4 acres 3 rods 37 perches in plan laid out by Bazaleel WELLS adjoining the addition to St. Clairsville, originally conveyed from Obadiah JENNINGS to MOSELEY, as recorded in Book B, p. 25 (p. 86 of abstracts); both seal; WIT: James KNIGHT, Sterling JOHNSTON; ack. Sterling JOHNSTON, J.P.; entered 23 Jul 1807, recorded 27 Jul 1807.

p. 147 - Indenture, 23 Jul 1807, William MOSELEY (wife Elizabeth), BCO; James KNIGHT, BCO. $200, out lots #1 (2 acres 1 rod 1 perch) and #2 (2 acres 6 perches) adjoining addition to St. Clairsville as laid out by Bazaleel WELLS, originally conveyed from Obadiah JENNINGS to MOSELEY on 3 Sep 1806; both seal; WIT: Saml. SULLIVAN, Sterling JOHNSTON; ack. Sterling JOHNSTON, J.P.; entered 23 Jul 1807, recorded 28 Jul 1807.

p. 148 - Indenture, 23 Jul 1807, William MOSELEY (wife Elizabeth), BCO; James KNIGHT [WRIGHT], BCO. $250, lots #19 and #20 in addition to St. Clairsville as laid out by William MATHERS, conveyed from Obadiah JENNINGS to Robert H. JOHNSTON on 1 Sep 1806, from JOHNSTON to MOSELEY on 3 Nov 1806, fee simple; both seal; [no witnesses given]; ack. Sterling JOHNSTON, J.P.; entered 23 Jul 1807, recorded 28 Jul 1807.

p. 149 - Indenture, James KNIGHT, BCO; William MOSELEY, BCO. KNIGHT indebted to MOSELEY for $250, secures debt by conveying lots #19 and #20 in addition to St. Clairsville, fee simple, void if full amount paid by 23 Jul 1811; his seal; WIT: Saml. SULLIVAN, Sterling JOHNSTON; ack. Sterling JOHNSTON, J.P.; entered 23 Jul 1807, recorded 30 Jul 1807.

p. 150 - Indenture, 26 May 1807, Bazaleel WELLS (wife Sally), JCO; Francis COOPER, BCO. $506.25, part S 20 T 4 R 2, NBR: Andrew McMAHAN, 81 3/4 acres; both seal; WIT: Thomas ELLIOT, [Mergt. MUSHALL (Margt. MARSHALL?)]; ack. JCO, Thos. ELLIOT, J.P., certified by Jno. WARD, JCO; entered 25 Jul 1807, recorded 31 Jul 1807.

p. 151 - Indenture, 5 Mar 1807, William MOSELEY (wife Elizabeth), St. Clairsville, BCO; William ASKEW, same. $75, lots #17 and #18 in addition to St. Clairsville as laid out by William MATHERS, conveyed from Obadiah JENNINGS to Robert H. JOHNSTON on 1 Sep 1806, from JOHNSTON (wife Rosannah) to MOSELEY on 3 Nov 1806, fee simple; both seal; WIT: John PATTERSON, Josiah HEDGES; ack. John PATTERSON, J.P.; entered 27 Jul 1807, recorded 3 Aug 1807.

p. 152 - Indenture, 29 Apr 1807, Borden STANTON (wife Charlotte), BCO; John PIGGOTT, BCO. $260, part S 8 T 7 R 3, granted to Horton HOWARD by patent dated 10 Sep 1806, NBR: George WATKINS, 40 acres 69 perches, conveyed by HOWARD to STANTON on 12 Feb 1807; both seal; WIT: Job RIDGWAY, David BERRY; ack. Thos. MITCHELL, J.P.; entered 28 Jul 1807, recorded 3 Aug 1807.

p. 154 - Indenture, 20 Jun 1807, John PIGGOTT, BCO; Nathan PIGGOTT, BCO. $363 "and one third," part S 8 T 7 R 3, NBR: George WATKINS, 40 acres 69 perches (see previous entry for history); his seal; WIT: Joseph GIBBONS, Sarah GIBBONS; ack. Thos. MITCHELL, J.P.; entered 28 Jul 1807, recorded 3 Aug 1807.

p. 155 - Indenture, 7 Apr 1807, Dennis COSSAT [COSSOT, COSSET] (wife Lydia), Wheeling, Virginia; Anne MIFFLIN, Philadelphia, Pennsylvania. $30, lots #25 and #26 in Frankford in Muskingum County, Ohio; both seal; WIT: Joseph KERR, Saml. DAVIS, John DULLY; ack. Thos. THOMPSON, J.P.

p. 156 - Indenture, 18 Jun 1807, Barnet GROVES (wife Hannah), BCO; William GROVES, BCO. $426.67, 1/3 part of S 3 T 9 R 6; both seal; WIT: John WILSON, J. ISRAEL, ack. J. ISRAEL, J.P.; entered 12 Aug 1807, recorded 16 Aug 1807.

p. 157 - Indenture, 22 Jun 1807, Barnet GROVES (wife Hannah), BCO; Joseph GROVES, BCO. $328.--, part S 3 T 9 R 6, NBR: (stones marked I. G.), 164 acres; both seal; WIT: Nich. GASSAWAY, Jno. J. ISRAEL; ack. Jno. ISRAEL, J.P.; entered 12 Aug 1807, recorded 16 Aug 1807.

p. 158 - Indenture, 12 Aug 1807, Henry HUFFMAN, BCO; Leven OKEY, BCO. HUFFMAN indebted to OKEY for $100, to be paid before 1 Jan 1808, for securing of debt conveys 100 acres in NW corner of S 27 T 4 R 3 (all of 1/4 section except 60 acres claimed by William BROWN), fee simple, void if debt paid; his seal; WIT: Sterling JOHNSTON, Robt. GRIFFITH; ack. Sterling JOHNSTON, J.P.; entered 12 Aug 1807, recorded 15 Aug 1807.

p. 159 - Indenture, 9 Jul 1807, John WILFORD (wife Catharine), BCO; Abraham AMARINE, BCO. $50, part of S 28 T 6 R 3, 8 acres 1 rod 20 perches; his seal, her mark; WIT: E. WOODS, Ezred WILLIAMS; ack. Thos. THOMPSON, J.P.; entered 12 Aug 1807, recorded 18 Aug 1807.

p. 160 - Indenture, 9 Jul 1807, John WILFORD [WOLFORD] (wife Catharine), BCO; Nicholas LUNSFORD, Ohio County, Virginia. $178.50, part of S 28 T 6 R 3, NBR: Jacob [ENDLY], 59 1/2 acres 16 poles; his seal, her mark; WIT: E. WOODS, Thos. THOMPSON; ack. Thos THOMPSON, J.P.; entered 12 Aug 1807, recorded 18 Aug 1807.

p. 161 - Indenture, 27 Jul 1807, John WILFORD [WOLFORD] (wife Catharine), BCO; Jacob ENDLY [LINDLY], Fayette County, Pennsylvania. $1,175, part of S 28 T 6 R 3, NBR: Frederick AMRIN, 156 acres 1 rod 17 perches; both seal [?–this is puzzling as she had marked before]; WIT: William ECKELS, Thos. THOMPSON; ack. Thos. THOMPSON, J.P.; entered 12 Aug 1807, recorded 18 Aug 1807.

p. 162 - Indenture, 13 Jun 1807, Ebenezer ZANE (wife Elizabeth), Ohio County, Virginia; Ezra WILLIAMS, BCO. $50, land where WILLIAMS now lives, NBR: CARTER, FREEMAN; both seal; WIT: James CLOYD, E. WOODS; ack. James CLOYD, J.P.; entered 12 Aug 1807, recorded 18 Aug 1807.

p. 163 - Indenture, 14 Jun 1807, Ebenezer ZANE (wife Elizabeth), Ohio County, Virginia; Thomas THOMPSON, BCO. $58, land where Thomas now resides, NBR: CARTER, FREEMAN; both seal; WIT: James CLOYD, E. WOODS; ack. James CLOYD, J.P.; entered 12 Aug 1807, recorded 18 Aug 1807.

p. 164 - Indenture, 13 Jul 1807, Joseph PUMPHREY [PUMPHEY] (wife Sarah), JCO; William McFARLAND, BCO. $1,000, part of S 33 T 6 R 3, 164 acres 3 rods 26 perches, PUMPHREYs seized of estate of inheritance in fee simple; both seal; WIT: Jesse MARTIN, Abraham LEMASTERS; ack. JCO, Jesse MARTIN, J.P., certified by Jno. WARD, Clerk, JCO; entered 17 Aug 1807, recorded 19 Aug 1807.

p. 166 - Indenture, 14 May 1807, Borden STANTON (wife Charlotte), BCO; James RALEY, BCO. $80, part of S 8 T 7 R 3, granted to Horton HOWARD by patent dated 10 Sep 1806, 20 acres conveyed by HOWARD to STANTON on 12 Feb 1807; both seal; WIT: David BERRY, Borden STANTON, Junr.; ack. T. MITCHELL, J.P. for Peas twp.; entered 17 Aug 1807, recorded 19 Aug 1807.

p. 167 - Indenture, 14 Aug 1807, James KNIGHT (wife Mary), BCO; William ASKEW, BCO. $250, lots #19 and #20 in addition to addition to St. Clairsville as laid out by MATHERS, conveyed from Obadiah JENNINGS to Robert H. JOHNSTON on 1 Sep 1806, from JOHNSTON to William MOSELEY on 3 Nov 1806, from MOSELEY to KNIGHT on 23 Jul 1807, fee simple; both seal; WIT: Sterling JOHNSTON, William MOSELEY; ack. Sterling JOHNSTON, J.P.; entered 17 Aug 1807, recorded 19 Aug 1807.

p. 168 - Indenture, 18 Aug 1807, William ASKEW, St. Clairsville, BCO; James KNIGHT, same. KNIGHT indebted to ASKEW for $150, to secure debt conveys lots #19 and #20 in addition to St. Clairsville, void if debt paid by 23 Jul 1810;

his seal; James CLOYD, Michael GROVES; ack. James CLOYD, J.P.; entered 18 Aug 1807, recorded 20 Aug 1807.

p. 171 - Indenture, 14 Aug 1807, William FARQUHAR, Wheeling, Ohio County, Virginia; Thomas L. JUDGE, same. $100, lot #6 in St. Clairsville as laid out by James BARNES, William BROWN, and Notley HAYS, originally conveyed from James and Nancy BARNES to FARQUHAR by deed dated 26 Sep 1806; his seal [Wm.]; WIT: Israel UPDEGRAFF, Thos. CONARD; ack. Sterling JOHNSTON, J.P.; entered 19 Aug 1807, recorded 9 Sep 1807.

p. 172 - Indenture, 3 Jun 1807, Basil ISRAEL (wife Elenor), Richland twp., BCO; William BROWN, same. $160, part of out lot granted to ISRAEL by David NEWELL on 28 Sep 1803 of St. Clairsville, 3 acres, fee simple; his seal, her mark; WIT: Sterling JOHNSTON, Robert ISRAEL; ack. Sterling JOHNSTON, J.P.; entered 20 Aug 1807, recorded 9 Sep 1807.

p. 173 - "Know all men," James CALDWELL of St. Clairsville, in consideration of $.50 paid by Casper SEEVERS, same, conveys lots #83 and #75 in St. Clairsville, the two lots which SEEVERS by mortgage dated 30 Sep 1806 secured to Phillip WINDLE, who on 9 Jun 1807 secured to James CALDWELL, signed 24 Aug 1807; his seal; WIT: Sterling JOHNSTON; ack. ("on same day of the within release of mortgage") Sterling JOHNSTON, J.P.; entered 24 Aug 1807, recorded 9 Sep 1807.

p. 174 - Indenture, 22 Aug 1807, Casper SEEVERS (wife Ann), St. Clairsville, BCO; Isaac VORE, same. $54, lots #83 and #75 in St. Clairsville; his seal, her mark; Sterling JOHNSTON, William ROBERTSON; ack. Sterling JOHNSTON, J.P.; entered 21 Aug 1807, recorded 9 Sep 1807.

p. 175 - Indenture, 13 Aug 1807, Bazaleel WELLS (wife Sally), JCO; Charles McMANAS, BCO. $350.--, part of S 14 T 7 R 3, NBR: Robert McBRATNEY, Francis COOPER; both seal; WIT: Benj. HOUGH, Saml. SALMAN; ack. JCO, Benj. HOUGH, J.P., certified by Jno. WARD, Clerk, JCO; entered 25 Aug 1807, recorded 9 Sep 1807.

p. 176 - Indenture, 16 Apr 1807, Josiah HEDGES, Sheriff BCO; Charles HAMMON, Esqr. By virtue of writ of execution from Court of Common Pleas in chancery, 11 Mar 1807, John MICKLE at August term 1805 recovered a judgment against William MATHERS for $1,221.39 and $9.31 costs, at December term complained that William MATHERS had transferred lots #61, #67, and #68 in St. Clairsville to Daniel MATHERS, lots to be seized, sold, and costs of $25.26 added to amount to be recovered, now sells lot #67 to Charles

HAMMON, Esqr., for $25; his seal; WIT: John PATTERSON; ack. 31 Aug 1807, John PATTERSON, J.P.

p. 177 - Indenture, 23 Jun 1807, Nathan UPDEGRAFF (wife Ann), Mountpleasant twp., JCO; James GORDON, BCO. $960, SE 1/4 of S 2 T 7 R 3, 160 acres; both seal; WIT: Thos. MITCHELL, James RALEY; ack. Thos. MITCHELL, J.P.; entered 7 Sep 1807, recorded 19 Sep 1807.

p. 178 - Indenture, 16 Jan 1807, Andrew MOORE (wife Elizabeth), BCO; William ROBISON, BCO. $120.--, out lot #13 of 15 laid out by Bazaleel WELLS adjoining addition to St. Clairsville, 5 acres 3 rods 30 perches, conveyed by Obadiah JENNINGS to MOORE on 1 Sep 1806; both seal; WIT: Sam SPRIGG, Saml. SULLIVAN; ack. Saml. SULLIVAN, J.P.; entered 7 Sep 1807, recorded 22 Sep 1807.

p. 179 - Indenture, 12 Sep 1807, John PICKERING (wife Mary), BCO; Richard SATTERTHWAITE, BCO. $120, beginning SE corner S 13 T 7 R 3, 10 acres, same land which SATTERTHWAITE conveyed to PICKERING by indenture dated 28 May 1807, recorded in Book B, page 131 (p. 102 of abstracts); both seal; WIT: James CLOYD, Adam JOHNSTON; ack. James CLOYD, J.P.

p. 181 - Indenture, 14 Mar 1807, Obadiah JENNINGS (wife Ann), Steubenville, JCO; Thomas IRELAND, St. Clairsville. $50, lots #21 and #22 in the addition to St. Clairsville as laid out by William MATHERS; both seal; WIT: Jonathan JENNINGS, John McELROY; ack. 14 Mar 1807, JCO, Alexr. SNODGRASS, J.P.; entered 12 Sep 1807, recorded 24 Sep 1807.

p. 181 - Indenture, 14 Sep 1807, Abraham ENGE [ENGLE] (wife Patience) farmer, Richland twp., BCO; Job ENGLE, same. $530, land in Richland twp., beginning at SE corner of SW 1/4 of S 21 T 7 R 4, NBR: Abraham ENGLE, John HANES, 100 acres, part of tract conveyed to Abraham by Obadiah HARDESTY (wife Mary) of Richland twp. by indenture dated 27 Aug 1804, recorded Book A, p. 346 (p. 285 of new book [p. 46 of abstracts]); his seal, her mark; WIT: James CLOYD, Mahlon SMITH; ack. James CLOYD, J.P.

p. 183 - Indenture, 14 Sep 1807, Abraham ENGLE (wife Patience) farmer, Richland twp., BCO; John HAINES, same. $50, beginning NW corner of SW 1/4 of S 21 [T 7] R 4, NBR: Job ENGLE, Abraham ENGLE, 70 acres, part of land conveyed by Obadiah and Mary HARDESTY by indenture dated 27 Aug 1804 (see previous entry); his seal, her mark; WIT: James CLOYD, Mahlon SMITH; ack. James CLOYD, J.P.; entered 14 Sep 1807, recorded 30 Sep 1807.

p. 184 - Indenture, 16 Sep 1807, John CARNEY, BCO; William McCONALD, BCO. McCONALD bound as CARNEY's security on Sterling JOHNSTON's docket for a sum of about $24 or $25 in a suit with CARNEY as defendant and John EWING as plaintiff, and in order to secure McCONALD from any risk, conveys two horses (one black and the other bay) and 50 bushes of Indian corn, void if judgment discharged within six months from above date; his seal; WIT: Sterling JOHNSTON, Abraham LASH; ack. Sterling JOHNSTON, J.P.; entered 16 Sep 1807, recorded 30 Sep 1807.

p. 185 - Indenture, 3 Sep 1807, Notley HAY [HAYS] (wife Sally), Richland twp., BCO; William HULSE, same. $729, part of S 34 and 28, 364 acres 3 rods 2 perches, portion in S 34 granted to HAYS by patent dated 18 Feb 1806, portion in S 28 granted to Mordicai YARNELL by patent [no date], conveyed by YARNELL to HAYS on 6 Oct 1806, fee simple; his seal, her mark; WIT: Sterling JOHNSTON, William PHILPOT; ack. Sterling JOHNSTON, J.P.; entered 22 Sep 1807, recorded 30 Sep 1807.

p. 186 - Indenture, 11 Sep 1807, James BARNES (wife Nancy), BCO; Robert H. JOHNSTON, BCO. $1,000, 2 lots of land N of St. Clairsville, total of 16 acres 2 rods 10 perches, conveyed to BARNES by John and Sally THOMPSON by deeds dated 7 May 1804, school house located here); his seal, her mark; WIT: Saml. SPRIGG, Sterling JOHNSTON; ack. Sterling JOHNSTON, J.P.; entered 22 Sep 1807, recorded 30 Sep 1807.

p. 188 - Indenture, 11 Sep 1807, Robert H. JOHNSTON, St. Clairsville, BCO; Samuel SPRIGG, same. In order to secure debts of $58.69 to Josiah HEDGES (payable on 7 Apr 1808) and of $275.44 due to James CALDWELL (payable on 7 Apr 1808) and for $1, conveys to SPRIGG tract of land N of St. Clairsville containing 10 acres and tract containing 6 acres 2 rods and 13 perches, same conveyed to JOHNSTON by James and Nancy BARNES same date, void if debts paid before date of sale of land; both JOHNSTON and SPRIGG seal; WIT: Sterling JOHNSTON, James BARNES; ack. Sterling JOHNSTON, J.P.; entered 22 Sep 1807, recorded 1 Oct 1807; released 2 Nov 1807 as witnessed by Josiah HEDGES.

p. 189 - Indenture, 11 Sep 1807, Robert H. JOHNSTON, St. Clairsville, BCO; James BARNES, same. $1,000, lot #45 in St. Clairsville, also E 1/2 of lot #46; his seal; WIT: Saml. SPRIGG, Sterling JOHNSTON; ack. Sterling JOHNSTON, J.P.; entered 22 Sep 1807, recorded 1 Oct 1807.

p. 190 - Indenture, 29 Apr 1807, Borden STANTON, (wife Charlotte), BCO; George WALKER, BCO. $160, part of S 8 T 7 R 3, 39 acres 109 perches, NBR: James RALEY, Moses PIGGOT, section granted to Horton HOWARD by patent dated 10 Sep 1806, conveyed by HOWARD to STANTON Feb 1807; both seal; WIT: John BARNES, John PIGGOTT; ack. Thos. MITCHELL, [no office given]; entered 22 Sep 1807, recorded 2 Oct 1807.

p. 191 - Indenture, 28 Sep 1806, Moses MOREHEAD (wife Ann), BCO; James BARNES, St. Clairsville, BCO. $100, undivided moiety of land near St. Clairsville, due them by conveyance from Josiah HEDGES while Sheriff to both MOREHEAD and BARNES, NBR: John LONG; both seal; WIT: Saml. SPRIGG, John PATTERSON; ack. 1 Mar 1807, John PATTERSON, J.P.; entered 28 Sep 1807, recorded 3 Oct 1807.

p. 193 - Indenture, 14 Sep 1807, Richard SATTERTHWAITE, bricklayer, BCO; Samuel POTTS, yeoman, BCO. Whereas S 13 T 7 R 3 granted to William SATTERTHWAITE by patent dated 9 Mar 1803, and by his lw&t dated 29 Jul 1804 conveyed SW 1/4 of S 13 to his son Richard SATTERTHWAITE, and Richard conveyed 10 acres in SW portion of S 13 to John PICKERING by deed dated 28 May 1807, John and Mary PICKERING reconveyed to Richard by deed dated 12 Sep 1807, land resurveyed and error found, and now Richard conveys to Samuel POTTS for $1,219 "and one quarter" the SE 1/4 of S 13 T 7 R 3, NBR: Richard and Joseph and William SATTERTHWAITE, 121 acres 3 rods 28 perches; his seal; WIT: Joseph GIBBONS, Sarah GIBBONS; ack. Sterling JOHNSTON, J.P.

p. 195 - Indenture, 13 Jun 1807, Ebenezer ZANE (wife Elizabeth), Ohio County, Virginia; Elijah WOODS, BCO. $500, 80 acres, fee simple; both seal; WIT: James CLOYD, Thos. THOMPSON; ack. James CLOYD, J.P.; entered 6 Oct 1807, recorded 22 Oct 1807.

p. 196 - Indenture, 13 Jun 1807, Ebenezer ZANE (wife Elizabeth), Ohio County, Virginia; Richard CARTER and Richard FREEMAN, same. $37.50, NBR: Thomas THOMPSON, Ezra WILLIAMS; both seal; WIT: James CLOYD, Thos. THOMPSON; ack. James CLOYD, J.P.; entered 6 Oct 1807, recorded 22 Oct 1807.

p. 196 - Indenture, 21 Oct 1807, John EDWARDS, Senr., BCO; Thomas WILSON [WILLSON] BCO. $1,000, part of S 36 T 7 R 4, NBR: Thomas EDWARDS, Widow NORRISS, 174 acres, fee simple; his seal; WIT: Eleanor ISRAEL, Jno. ISRAEL; ack. Jno. ISRAEL, J.P.; entered 23 Oct 1807, recorded 4 Nov 1807.

p. 197 - Indenture, 17 Jun 1807, David TRINDLE, saddler, Hopewell twp., Cumberland County, Pennsylvania; Samuel SHANNON, Waun twp., JCO. $54, lot #117 in St. Clairsville, 1/4 acre, fee simple; his seal; WIT: James HOLMES,

John DOWNING; ack. Cumberland County, John CREIGH, Assoc. Judge, certified by Willm. LYON, Prothy; entered 26 Oct 1807, recorded 4 Nov 1807.

p. 198 - Indenture, 25 Apr 1807, Samuel GREGG (wife Ann), BCO; Joseph NICHOLSON, BCO. $180, part of S 33 T 7 R 4, granted to GREGG (then of Ross County, Ohio) by patent dated 1 Oct 1806, NBR: Joseph VANLAW, 60 acres; both seal; WIT: Joseph VANLAW, James SINCLAIR, Mary GREGG; ack. Arthur IRWIN, J.P.; entered 28 Oct 1807, recorded 5 Nov 1807.

p. 200 - Indenture, 28 Oct 1807, Thomas WILLSON (wife Nancy), BCO; Mary NORRIS, widow and executrix of William NORRIS, dec'd, BCO. $1,218, part of S 36 T 7 R 4, NBR: Thomas EDWARDS, 174 acres; his seal, her mark; WIT: Sterling JOHNSTON, Adam JOHNSTON; ack. Sterling JOHNSTON, J.P.; entered 28 Oct 1807, recorded 5 Nov 1807.

p. 201 - Indenture, 31 Oct 1807, John PATTERSON (wife Grezey [Gressey]), St. Clairsville, BCO; Ralph HEATH, BCO. $330, lot #61 in St. Clairsville; both seal; WIT: Wm. VANCE, George PAULL; ack. James CLOYD, J.P.; entered 31 Oct 1807, recorded 5 Nov 1807.

p. 202 - Indenture, 2 Nov 1807, Robert H. JOHNSTON, BCO; Josiah HEDGES, BCO. $800, two lots N of St. Clairsville, same conveyed by John and Sally THOMPSON to James BARNES by two deeds dated 7 May 1804, BARNES conveyed to JOHNSTON on 11 Sep 1807 (school house lot); his seal; WIT: James CLOYD, Sterling JOHNSTON; ack. Sterling JOHNSTON, J.P.; entered 2 Nov 1807, recorded 5 Nov 1807.

p. 203 - Indenture, 3 Nov 1807, Bazel ISRAEL (wife Elenor), BCO; Josiah DILLON, BCO. $1,000, lot N of St. Clairsville, NBR: William BROWN, John BROWN, 7 acres, same conveyed by David and Sally NEWELL to ISRAEL on 9 Nov 1803 as recorded in Book A, p. 266 (p. 208 in new book [p. 34 of abstracts]); his seal, her mark; WIT: Sterling JOHNSTON, George PAULL; ack. Sterling JOHNSTON, J.P.; entered 3 Nov 1807, recorded 6 Nov 1807.

p. 204 - Indenture, 3 Nov 1807, Bazel ISRAEL (wife Elenor), BCO; Josiah DILLON, BCO. $1,000, lots #59 and #60 in St. Clairsville, originally conveyed by David and Sally NEWELL on 9 Nov 1803, fee simple; his seal, her mark; WIT: Sterling JOHNSTON, George PAULL; ack. Sterling JOHNSTON, J.P.; entered 3 Nov 1807, recorded 6 Nov 1807.

p. 206 - "To all people," whereas Dunning McNAIR sued out of CCP against Isaac THOMPSON in a plea of debt returnable to August Term 1803 and obtained a judgment against THOMPSON at April Term following for $114.89

damages with $9.87 costs of suit, a writ of Fiere-Facias directed to Jacob COLEMAN, High Sheriff, BCO; levied against lot #6 in square #19 and lot #6 in square #3 in Pultney but went unsold due to lack of bidders, a writ of Vendition Exponas to Josiah HEDGES on 9 Jan 1805; sale on 30 Mar 1805 where lots purchased by William BROWN of St. Clairsville, carpenter, for $6, signed 1 Apr 1805; his seal; WIT: Moses MOREHEAD, James CLOYD; ack. 1 Apr 1805, Sterling JOHNSTON, J.P.; entered 13 Nov 1807, recorded 20 Nov 1807.

p. 207 - Indenture, 30 Nov 1807, Samuel SULLIVAN (wife Mary), St. Clairsville, BCO; John PATTERSON and Thomas McCALL, same. $460, part of lot #21 in St. Clairsville, NBR: John PATTERSON, Samuel SULLIVAN, 2,154 square feet; both seal; WIT: James CLOYD, Benjm. PEARSON; ack. James CLOYD, J.P.; entered 13 Nov 1807, recorded 20 Nov 1807.

p. 209 - Indenture, 14 Oct 1807, Abraham VAIL (wife Margaret), Fayette County, Pennsylvania; Stephen [Steven] VAIL, BCO. $90, part of S 2 T 8 R 5, Steubenville district, granted to Abraham by patent dated 6 Mar 1806, 218 acres 3 rods 27 poles; his seal only; WIT: Arthur IRWIN, Ann IRWIN; ack. BCO, Arthur IRWIN, J.P.; entered 13 Nov 1807, recorded 22 Nov 1807.

p. 210 - Indenture, 14 Oct 1807, Abraham VAIL (wife Margaret), Fayette County, Pennsylvania; Benjamine VAIL, BCO. $400, part of S 2 T 8 R 5, Steubenville district, granted to Abraham by patent dated 6 Mar 1806, 218 acres 3 rods and 27 poles; his seal only; WIT: Arthur IRWIN, Ann IRWIN; ack. BCO, Arthur IRWIN, J.P.; entered 13 Nov 1807, recorded 22 Nov 1807.

p. 211 - Indenture, 14 Oct 1807, Abraham VAIL (wife Margaret), Fayette County, Pennsylvania; Robert VAIL, BCO. $110, part of S 2 T 8 R 5, Steubenville district, granted to Abraham by patent dated 6 Mar 1806, 218 acres 3 rods and 27 poles; his seal only; WIT: Arthur IRWIN, Ann IRWIN; ack. BCO, Arthur IRWIN, J.P.; entered 13 Nov 1807, recorded 22 Nov 1807.

p. 212 - Indenture, 26 Nov 1807, Joseph SHARP (wife Nancy), BCO; Robert MILLER, Fayette County, Pennsylvania. $700, part of SW 1/4 of S 32 T 8 R 4, granted to SHARP by patent dated 18 Feb 1806, 94 acres; his seal, her mark; WIT: John STEWART, Moses MERRIT; ack. Moses MERRIT, J.P.; entered 27 Nov 1807, recorded 4 Jan 1808.

p. 213 - Indenture, 27 Nov 1807, William SMITH (wife Nancy), St. Clairsville, BCO; Samuel SHARP, same. $4,000, lots #129 and #130 in St. Clairsville, both 1/4 acre, both conveyed from John MARTIN (wife Elizabeth) to John THOMPSON on 10 Jan 1807, by THOMPSON (wife Sally) to SMITH on 11

Mar 1807 [recorded p. 74-75, p. 94 of abstracts], fee simple; his seal, her mark; WIT: James CLOYD, Josiah HEDGES; ack. James CLOYD, J.P.

p. 215 - Indenture, 29 Aug 1807, Borden [Bordon] STANTON (wife Charlotte), BCO; Joseph GAMBLE, BCO. S 8 T 7 R 3, granted to Horton HOWARD by patent dated 10 Sep 1806, Steubenville district, for $290 conveying 90 acres of E 1/2 of S conveyed by HOWARD to STANTON on 12 Feb 1807, NBR: Owen DEWEIS, John PIGGOTT, WALKER [George], RALEY [James]; both seal; WIT: David BERRY, Owen DEWEIS; ack. Thos. MITCHELL, J.P.; entered 28 Nov 1807, recorded 5 Jan 1808.

p. 217 - Indenture, 28 Nov 1807, Josiah DILLON (wife Dorothy), BCO; Hugh LYONS, BCO. $200, begin NW corner of S 35 T 6 R 3, Steubenville district, granted to DILLON by patent dated 14 Jul 1806, fee simple; both seal; WIT: James CLOYD, Robrt. THOMPSON; ack. James CLOYD, J.P.; entered 28 Nov 1807, recorded 6 Jan 1808.

p. 218 - Indenture, 30 Nov 1807, David NEISWANGER (wife Mary), BCO; John COPELAND, BCO. $400, lot #14 in St. Clairsville, conveyed from Josiah HEDGES, Esqr., High Sheriff, to Andrew MOORE, from MOORE (wife unnamed) to NEISWANGER, also lot #6 in St. Clairsville; his seal, her mark; WIT: James CLOYD, George PAULL; ack. James CLOYD, J.P.; entered 1 Dec 1807, recorded 7 Jan 1808.

p. 220 - Indenture, 29 Oct 1807, William COOK, Washington, Washington County, Pennsylvania; Vachel [Veichel] HALL, adjoining St. Clairsville, BCO. $35, lot adjoining St. Clairsville, NBR: "the land whereon said HALL lives formerly called Halam's purchase, 1 1/2 acres 39 perches, fee simple; his seal; WIT: James CUMMINS, H. WILSON; ack. Washington County, James ROBERTS, President of the Fifth Circuit; entered 3 Dec 1807, recorded 7 Jan 1808.

p. 221 - Indenture, 22 Jun 1807, Barnet GROVE (wife Hannah), BCO; Moses MILLIGAN, BCO. $150, part of S 3 T 9 R 6, 50 acres; both seal; WIT: Nich. GASSAWAY, Jno. ISRAEL; ack. 22 Jun 1807, Jno. ISRAEL, J.P.; entered 3 Dec 1807, recorded 7 Jan 1808.

p. 222 - Indenture, 34 Jan 1807, James BARNES (wife Nancy), St. Clairsville, BCO; Notley HAYS, Robt. DENT, John PATTERSON, Saml. SULLIVAN, Joseph MERRITT, William BROWN, David NIESWANGER [NESWANGER], Josiah DILLON, William MOSELEY, Saml. STEPHENSON, Mahlon [Malon] SMITH, Abraham LASH, Robert THOMPSON, Michael GROVE, Henry STONER, Sterling JOHNSTON, Phillip WINDLE, Joseph MARSHALL, Jacob

HALLS, William CONGLETON, Robert JOHNSTON, John THOMPSON, Moses MOREHEAD, and Saml. SPRIGG, BCO. $1, to all grantees "in the same ratio that they each have subscribed in the original article entered into between the subscribers and Notley HAYS and James BARNES for building the school house, $6 being considered one share, lot in corner of James's meadow on which the brick school house aforesaid now stands"; his seal, her mark; WIT: Benjn. PEARSON, Vachel HALL; ack. 5 Feb 1807, Saml. SULLIVAN, J.P.; entered 8 Dec 1807, recorded 7 Jan 1807.

p. 223 - Indenture, 28 May 1807, Jacob GRUBB, BCO; Samuel HAWKINS, BCO. $49, lot #23 in addition to St. Clairsville as laid out by William MATHERS, conveyed from William CONGLETON to HAWKINS on 4 Sep 1806, from HAWKINS to GRUBB on this date, void if GRUBB pays HAWKINS $49 by 1 Oct first ensuing in cabinet furniture; his seal; WIT: Sterling JOHNSTON; ack. Sterling JOHNSTON, J.P.; mortgage assigned by HAWKINS to William CONGLETON on 10 Dec 1807, released for full satisfaction in cabinet and carpenter work by Wm. CONGLETON.

p. 224 - Indenture, 9 Oct 1807, Josiah HEDGES, High Sheriff, BCO; James McELHENY, Pultney, BCO. Whereas Charles HAMMOND, assignee of Jacob Justice & Co., in CCP April Court 1806 obtained a judgment against George HEAP, BCO, for $123.44 damages costs, writ of Fiere Facias issued dated 23 Oct 1806 to seize HEAP's property and submit proceeds to December term, on second Tuesday of Nov 1806 levied upon lot #19 in square 3, T 2 R 2, and upon lot #10 in square 3, on 12 Dec 1806 sold two lots to James McELHENEY for $10; his seal; WIT: Sterling JOHNSTON,; ack. Sterling JOHNSTON, J.P.; entered 18 Dec 1807, recorded 8 Jan 1808.

p. 226 - Indenture, 15 Sep 1807, Samuel SHANNON, JCO; William KINDALL [KINDELL], Washington County, Pennsylvania. $100, lot #117 in St. Clairsville, 1/4 acre; his seal; WIT: Jesse MARTIN, Jenas KIMBERLY; ack. Jesse MARTIN, J.P.; entered 19 Dec 1807, recorded 9 Jan 1808.

p. 226 - Indenture, 26 Dec 1807, Sterling JOHNSTON, BCO; Samuel STOVER, Muskingum County, Ohio. $60, lots #15 and #16 in addition to St. Clairsville as laid out by William MATHERS, conveyed to JOHNSTON by Obadiah JENNINGS [JENNING] of JCO on 3 Sep 1806 as recorded in Book A, p. 694 (p. 513 in new book, [p. 80 of abstracts]), fee simple; his seal; WIT: David VANCE, Robert THOMPSON; ack. David VANCE, Assoc. Judge, CCP; entered 26 Dec 1807, recorded 9 Jan 1808.

p. 227 - Indenture, 23 Jul 1807, Bazaleel [Bezaleel] WELLS (wife Sally), JCO; Robert McBRATNEY, BCO. $770, part of S 14 T 7 R 3, 220 acres; both seal;

ack. Zachs. [BEGGS], J. JENKINSON; ack. JCO, 23 Jul 1807, J. JENKINSON, J.P., certified by Jno. WARD, Clerk, JCO; entered 26 Dec 1807, recorded 10 Jan 1808.

p. 229 - Indenture, 28 Dec 1807, David VANCE (wife Margaret), BCO; John BERRY, BCO. $70, part of S 36 T 6 R 3, 61 acres, 1 rod, 27 perches, granted to VANCE by patent dated 25 Sep 1807; his seal, her mark; WIT: Sterling JOHNSTON, James HANNAH; ack. Sterling JOHNSTON, J.P.; entered 29 Dec 1807, recorded 14 Jan 1808.

p. 230 - Indenture, 28 Dec 1807, David VANCE (wife Margaret), BCO; William DENHAM, BCO. $360, part of S 36 T 6 R 3, 111 acres 3 rods, part of land originally granted to VANCE by patent dated 25 Sep 1807, fee simple; his seal, her mark; WIT: Sterling JOHNSTON, James HANNAH; ack. Sterling JOHNSTON, J.P.; entered 29 Dec 1807, recorded 14 Jan 1808.

p. 231 - Indenture, 28 Dec 1807, David VANCE, Esqr. (wife Margaret), BCO; Hugh LYONS, BCO. $180, part of S 36 T 6 R 3, 60 acres, originally granted to VANCE by patent dated 25 Sep 1807, fee simple; his seal, her mark; WIT: Sterling JOHNSTON, James HANNAH; ack. Sterling JOHNSTON, J.P.; entered 29 Dec 1807, recorded 14 Jan 1808.

p. 232 - Indenture, 28 Dec 1807, David VANCE (wife Margaret),BCO; James HANNAH, BCO. $1,400, 161 acres, part of land granted to VANCE by patent dated 25 Sep 1807, NBR: Hugh LYONS, fee simple; his seal, her mark; WIT: Sterling JOHNSTON, William DENHAM; ack. Sterling JOHNSTON, J.P.; entered 29 Dec 1807, recorded 14 Jan 1808.

p. 234 - Indenture, 8 Sep 1807, William MOSELEY, BCO; Sterling JOHNSTON, BCO. MOSELEY indebted to JOHNSTON for $387.60, secures debt by conveying lots #1 and #2 in addition to St. Clairsville as laid out by Bazaleel WELLS, another lot [unnumbered] in addition to St. Clairsville and one sorrel horse, void if 77,520 brick delivered from his brickyard on premises of David NIESWANGER on 10th day of this Instant; his seal; WIT: Robt. THOMPSON, Amos BRYAN; ack. 10 Dec 1807, James CLOYD, J.P.; entered 29 Dec 1807, recorded 20 Jan 1808.

p. 235 - Indenture, 21 Dec 1807, William SMITH (wife Margaret), BCO; John MOORE, BCO. $640, 1/2 N part of S 13 T 10 R 6, 320 acres, part of S granted to SMITH by patent dated 22 Sep 1807, fee simple; his seal, her mark; WIT: Levi LAW, Wm. WEBSTER; ack. D. MORRISON, J.P.; entered 29 Dec 1807, recorded 20 Jan 1808.

p. 235 - Indenture, 29 Sep 1807, Richard McKIBBENS (wife Sarah), Pease twp., BCO; Mary McKIBBENS, BCO. $276.37, part of S 27 T 4 (fractional) R 2, 50 acres 1 rod 6 perches, NBR: Joseph MOORE, John McCLURE, Richard McKIBBENS, (by survey 40 acres 1 rod 6 perches); both seal; WIT: Thos. MITCHELL, James MITCHELL; ack. 3 Dec 1807, Thos. MITCHELL, J.P.; entered 2 Jan 1808, recorded 21 Jan 1808.

p. 237 - Indenture, 2 Jan 1808, John PICKERING (wife Mary), yeoman, BCO; James BARNES, same. $267, W part of NW 1/4 of S 10 T 6 R 3 (formerly in JCO), 53 acres 1 rod 28 perches, granted to Horton HOWARD by patent 22 Jan 1806, HOWARD to PICKERING NW 1/4 of S on 8 Jul 1806; his seal, her mark; WIT: Sterling JOHNSTON, Wm. CONGLETON; ack. Sterling JOHNSTON, J.P.; entered 2 Jan 1808, recorded 21 Jan 1808.

p. 238 - Indenture, 18 Jan 1808, Michael CARROL (wife Sally), BCO; Samuel BROWN, BCO. $320, NW 1/4 of S 12 T 7 R 4, 173 acres 3 rods 31 perches, granted to CARROL by patent dated 8 May 1806, fee simple; both seal; WIT: Sterling JOHNSTON, Robt. H. JOHNSTON; ack. Sterling JOHNSTON, J.P.; entered 19 Jan 1808, recorded 23 Jan 1808.

p. 239 - Indenture, 18 Jun 1807, William GROVES (wife Rebecah), BCO; John WILLSON, Junr., BCO. $280, part of S 3 T 9 R 6, NBR: stones marked I.W., 73 acres; his seal, her mark; WIT: N. GASSAWAY, Jno. ISRAEL; ack. 19 Jun 1807, Jno. ISRAEL, J.P.; entered 19 Jan 1808, recorded 25 Jan 1808.

p. 240 - "Whereas," John BROWN, William ROBINSON [ROBISON], and Daniel McCURDY entered into a partnership trading as joint traders under name of Brown Robinson and McCurdy, now ROBINSON and McCURDY "being desirous by the consent of the said John BROWN to alien and ___ in said partnership as well as real as personal to Conrod Kotts ROBINSON" now of New Jersey but soon to relocate to St. Clairsville, Ohio; now William ROBINSON (wife Sarah) and Daniel McCURDY (wife Priscilla) in consideration that Conrod Kotts ROBINSON [ROBERTSON] undertakes all debts or incumbrances [sic] against them and for $2 convey their interest in all of business including lots #28, #27, #19 [NBR: Jacob HOLTZ] in St. Clairsville plus lot of 4 1/4 acres 9 poles N of St. Clairsville, conveyed by deed dated 9 [6] Nov 1806 from John THOMPSON (wife Sally) to partners as recorded in Book A [actually Book B], p. 22 and 23 [p. 86 of abstracts], signed 12 May 1807; all seal; WIT: George MAXWELL, Paul I. [ZUHL?]; ack. 12 May 1807, New Jersey, George MAXWELL, "one of the masters of the High Court of Chancery of the State of New Jersey," certified by James LINN, Clerk in Chancery and Secretary of State; entered 19 Jan 1808, recorded 26 Jan 1808.

p. 242 - Indenture, 18 Jan 1808, James MACKEY (wife Jenny [Jenney]), BCO; William MISKIMMONS [MISKIMMINS], Muskingum County, Ohio. $120, 2 lots at west end of St. Clairsville, 1/2 and 1/4 acre, conveyed from Henry STONER (wife Elizabeth) on 24 Dec 1807; his seal, her mark; WIT: Sterling JOHNSTON, Ezar DILLON; ack. Sterling JOHNSTON, J.P.; entered 19 Jan 1808, recorded 27 Jan 1808.

p. 244 - Indenture, 25 Jan 1808, Robert T. FINNEY (wife Peggy), BCO; Robert FINNEY (wife Phebe), BCO. $850, part of Ss 20 and 26 T 4 R 2, NBR: John HANNAH (sold by Bazaleel WELLS), 67 acres, for their natural lives; his seal, her mark; WIT: Thos. MITCHELL, Hariet MITCHELL; ack. Thos. MITCHELL, J.P.; entered 27 Jan 1808, recorded 27 Jan 1808.

p. 245 - Indenture, 10 Jan 1808, John THOMPSON (wife Sally), St. Clairsville, BCO; Notley HAYS, BCO. [Money amount not given], 60 acres, same conveyed by James BARNES (wife Nancy) to THOMPSON on 7 May 1804, part of S 4 T 7 R 4, fee simple; his seal, her mark; WIT: Sterling JOHNSTON, John COPELAND; ack. Sterling JOHNSTON, J.P.; entered 27 Jan 1808, recorded 2 Feb 1808.

p. 246 - Indenture, 21 Oct 1807, Robert H. JOHNSTON, St. Clairsville, BCO; Thomas LOVE, same. $500, fee simple, lot #33 in St. Clairsville, to be void if JOHNSTON delivers at Sharpless Mill in BCO on Indian Wheeling Creek $200 worth of "merchanable" [merchantable?] wheat flour on 1 Mar 1808 (plus freighting, storage and delivery to Charlestown, Brook County, Virginia, price at the ware house at Thomas THOMPSONs on the Ohio River) for use of LOVE, also pay $300 over next three years (ending Mar 1811), further stipulation that the wheat is to be barrelled, 2/3 superfine, 1/3 fine; his seal; WIT: James CLOYD, Jacob NAGLE; ack. James CLOYD, J.P.; entered 29 Jan 1808, recorded 2 Feb 1808; released 23 Jul 1808 by Thomas LOVE.

p. 247 - Indenture, 8 Jan 1808, James WILKINS (wife Lydia), BCO; John HINDS [HINES], BCO. $200, part of S 34 T 6 R 3, NBR: William HOULTZ, 10 acres, granted to Notley HAYS by patent dated 18 Feb 1806, from HAYS to WILKINS on 7 Aug 1806, fee simple; both seal; WIT: Sterling JOHNSTON; ack. Sterling JOHNSTON, J.P.; entered 2 Feb 1808, recorded 4 Feb 1808.

p. 248 - Indenture, 24 Dec 1807, Henry STONER (wife Elizabeth), BCO; James MACKEY, BCO. $100, lot at W end of St. Clairsville containing 1/2 acre conveyed by John DUGAN (wife Hannah) to STONER on 19 Apr 1805, another lot beginning at (NBR:) George MYERS out lot, 1/4 acre, which was conveyed from Robert JOHNSTON to STONER on 21 Apr 1806; his seal, her mark; WIT: Sterling JOHNSTON, David NEISWANGER; ack. 4 Dec 1807 [probably a clerical error], Henry only, Sterling JOHNSTON, J.P., 29 Feb 1808 for Elizabeth; entered 4 Feb 1808, recorded 4 Feb 1808.

p. 249 - Indenture, 3 Jan 1807 [?], James WRIGHT (wife Mary), BCO; George McWILLIAMS, BCO. $200, part of S 19 T 8 R 4, Steubenville district, part of S granted to John WINTER by patent dated 11 Feb 1806, conveyed by WINTER to WRIGHT; both mark; WIT: James CLOYD, Sterling JOHNSTON; ack. 18 Feb 1808, Sterling JOHNSTON, J.P.; entered 18 Feb 1808, recorded 18 Feb 1808.

p. 250 - Indenture, 11 Feb 1808, Jacob HOULTZ (wife Peggy), BCO; James WILKINS, BCO. $170, lots #37 and #38 in St. Clairsville, each lot 1/4 acre, fee simple; both mark; WIT: Sterling JOHNSTON, Robt. GRIFFITH; ack. Sterling JOHNSTON, J.P.; entered 18 Feb 1808, recorded 19 Feb 1808.

p. 252 - Indenture, 10 Feb 1808, Jacob KUHN (wife Barbara), BCO; Peter WIRICH, Senr., BCO. $320, E 1/2 of S 14 T 8 R 4 excepting 60 [50?] acres conveyed by KUHN to John RYANS on 9 Feb 1808, entire S granted to KUHN by patent dated 27 Aug 1805; his seal, her mark; WIT: Sterling JOHNSTON, John STEWART; ack. Sterling JOHNSTON, J.P.; entered 18 Feb 1808, recorded 22 Feb 1808.

p. 253 - Indenture, 9 Feb 1808, Jacob KUHN (wife Barbara), BCO; John RYANS, Senr., BCO. $250, part of S 14 T 8 R 4, granted to KUHN by patent dated 22 Aug 1805, 50 acres, in NE corner, fee simple; his seal, her mark; WIT: Sterling JOHNSTON, John STEWART; ack. Sterling JOHNSTON, J.P.; entered 18 Feb 1808, recorded 22 Feb 1808.

p. 254 - Indenture, 20 Aug 1807, Borden STANTON (wife Charlotte), BCO; Owen DEWEES, BCO. $240, part of S 8 T 7 R 3, 80 acres, granted to Horton HOWARD by patent dated 10 Sep 1806, E 1/2 conveyed from HOWARD (wife Hannah) to STANTON on 12 Feb 1807; both seal; WIT: David BERRY, Horton HOWARD; ack. 20 Aug 1807, Thos. MITCHELL, J.P.; entered 19 Feb 1808, recorded 23 Feb 1808.

p. 256 - Indenture, 2 Feb 1808, Joseph GAMBLE (wife Elizabeth), BCO; John FARIS, BCO. S 8 T 7 R 3, Steubenville district, granted to Horton HOWARD on 10 Sep 1806, conveyed E 1/2 to Borden STANTON on 12 Feb 1807, STANTON conveyed 90 acres to GAMBLE on 12 Feb 1807, now GAMBLE (wife Elizabeth) for $180 convey tract to FARIS, beginning at (NBR:) Owen DEWEES, 30 acres; his seal, her mark; WIT: Sarah SUPLER, Joseph GIBBONS; ack. 3 Jan 1808, Thos. MITCHELL, J.P.

p. 257 - Indenture, 18 Feb 1808, Isaac HILL, BCO; George SHARPLESS, BCO. $1,020, part of S 17 T 6 R 3, NBR: Francis TOWNSEND, John BELL, 164 acres, tract conveyed from Francis TOWNSEND to HILL on 2 Feb 1806 with TOWNSEND reserving a stream in case he wants to build a mill; his seal; WIT: James CLOYD, Robt. GRIFFITH; ack. James CLOYD, J.P.; entered 20 Feb 1808, recorded 23 Feb 1808.

p. 258 - Indenture, 2 Jan 1808, John STEWART (wife Mary), BCO; John LISK, Ohio County, Virginia. $300, tract in Ohio County, Virginia, NBR: John MILLIGAN, John STEWART, Senr., heirs of Robt. STEWART, Stephen BURKHAM; both seal; WIT: Arthur IRWIN, Ann IRWIN; ack. BCO, Arthur IRWIN, J.P.; entered 20 Feb 1808, recorded 24 Feb 1808.

p. 259 - Indenture, 25 Feb 1808, William PHILPOT (wife Ruth), BCO; Joseph WRIGHT, BCO. $416, W side of S 12 T 7 R 5, Steubenville district, granted to PHILPOT by patent dated 15 Nov 1807, surveyed by John ISRAEL, 211 acres, NBR: Wm. PHILPOT, Joseph DONNY, and others, fee simple; both seal; WIT: James CLOYD, Samuel SHARP; ack. James CLOYD, J.P.; entered 25 Feb 1808, recorded 25 Feb 1808.

p. 260 - "Whereas" William PHILPOT was granted S 12 T 7 R 5 by patent dated 15 Nov 1807, for $388.50 paid by Ralph HEATH, St. Clairsville, now convey E end of S 12 T 7 R 5, bounded by line run by John ISRAEL in 1803 and blazed by William PHILPOT and Ralph HEATH on 24 Feb 1808, 222 acres, fee simple, signed 25 Feb 1808; both seal; WIT: James CLOYD, Saml. SHARP; ack. James CLOYD, J.P.; entered 20 Feb 1808, recorded 26 Feb 1808.

p. 262 - Indenture, 24 Feb 1808, Notley HAYS (wife Sally), BCO; Robert DENT, BCO. $50, lot #10 with additional being annexed to E end of St. Clairsville, 22 1/2 perches, fee simple; his seal, her mark; WIT: Sterling JOHNSTON, Mary NORRIS; ack. Sterling JOHNSTON, J.P.; entered 25 Feb 1808, recorded 26 Feb 1808.

p. 263 - Indenture, 27 Feb 1808, Hugh PARKS (wife Mary), BCO; David BALEY, BCO. $42, part of NW 1/4 of S 10 T 6 R 3, 107 1/2 acres 12 perches, granted to Horton HOWARD by patent dated 22 Jan 1806, NW 1/4 of S 10 conveyed by HOWARD to John PICKERING on 8 Jul 1806, by PICKERING to PARKS on 13 Feb 1807; both seal; WIT: Sterling JOHNSTON, Robert THOMPSON; ack. Sterling JOHNSTON, J.P.; entered 27 Feb 1808, recorded 1 Mar 1808.

p. 264 - Indenture, 16 Oct 1807, Samuel GREGG, Senr. (wife Ann), BCO; Samuel GREGG, Junr., BCO. Whereas patent granted to Samuel, Senr., then of

Ross County, Ohio, for S 33 T 7 R 4, Steubenville district, dated 1 Oct 1806, now for $150 paid by Samuel GREGG, Junr., conveys 58 acres 3 rods 1 perch; both seal; WIT: David BERRY; ack. Arthur IRWIN, J.P.; entered 29 Feb 1808, recorded 1 Mar 1808.

p. 266 - Indenture, 12 Feb 1808, David VANCE (wife Margaret), BCO; Phillip McGRAW, BCO. $686, W 1/2 of S 6 T 7 R 4, 320 acres, granted to VANCE by patent dated 12 Feb 1798, fee simple; his seal, her mark; WIT: Sterling JOHNSTON, James JOHNSON; ack. Sterling JOHNSTON, J.P.; entered 2 Mar 1808, recorded 11 Mar 1808.

p. 267 - Indenture, 3 Mar 1808, Robert H. JOHNSTON (wife Polly), BCO; James CORROTHERS, Washington County, Pennsylvania. $500, lot #33 in St. Clairsville, 1/4 acre, fee simple; his seal, her mark; WIT: James CLOYD, William B. JOHNSTON; ack. James CLOYD, J.P.; entered 4 Mar 1808, recorded 11 Mar 1808.

p. 268 - Indenture, 4 Mar 1808, Benjamine NEWELL, Champaign County, Ohio; Robert JOHNSTON and William CONGLETON, BCO. $25, lot #113 in St. Clairsville, to both as tenants in common and not as joint tenants; his seal; WIT: George PAULL, Sterling JOHNSTON; ack. Sterling JOHNSTON, J.P.; entered 4 Mar 1808, recorded 11 Mar 1808.

p. 269 - Indenture, 4 Mar 1808, Ralph HEATH (wife Elizabeth), St. Clairsville, BCO; Samuel SHARP, same. Whereas William PHILPOT (wife Ruth) by deed dated 25 Feb 1808 sold to HEATH E end of S 12 T 7 R 5, Steubenville district, line run by John ISRAEL in 1803, for 222 acres, recorded Book B, p. 243 (seems to be on p. 260 [p. 120 of abstracts]), fee simple; both seal; WIT: William SMITH, James CLOYD; ack. James CLOYD, J.P.; entered 5 Mar 1808, recorded 11 Mar 1808.

p. 270 - Indenture, 16 Jan 1808, James ALEXANDER, Junr. (wife Isabel), farmer, BCO, and James CLARK, BCO; James STRAIN, weaver, BCO. $120, part of S 32 T 4 R 2, 30 acres; all seal; WIT: Thos. MITCHELL, Margaret ALEXANDER [her mark]; ack. Thos. MITCHELL, J.P.; entered 5 Mar 1808, recorded 14 Mar 1808.

p. 271 - Indenture, 31 Mar 1807, Joseph SCOTT (wife Elizabeth), BCO; Richard McKIBBEN, BCO. $200, part of S "numbered in the general draught" 27 T 4 (fractional) R 2, granted on 15 Nov 1797, this conveyance for 52 1/2 acres, NBR: MOORE, [LIN?], Richard McKIBBEN, Andrew EAGLESON; his seal, her mark; WIT: Andrew GILLESON, Thos. MITCHELL; ack. Thos. MITCHELL, J.P.; entered 7 Mar 1808, recorded 15 Mar 1808.

p. 272 - Indenture, 9 Mar 1808, Samuel BROWN (wife Mary), BCO; Archibald CRAWFORD, Brook County, Virginia. $175, part of S 12 T 7 R 4, 50 acres, part of 1/4 S conveyed to BROWN by Michael CARROL [CARLL] on __ Feb 1808 [18 Jan 1808], fee simple; his seal, her mark; WIT: Sterling JOHNSTON, Robt. GRIFFITH; ack. Sterling JOHNSTON, J.P.; entered 10 Mar 1808, recorded 15 Mar 1808.

p. 273 - Indenture, 10 Mar 1808, Archibald CRAWFORD, Brook County, Virginia; William WOODS, BCO. $82.50, part of S 12 T 7 R 4, conveyed from Samuel BROWN to CRAWFORD on 9 Mar 1808, fee simple, void if CRAWFORD pays $82.50 to WOODS by 10 Mar 1810, possession by CRAWFORD until he defaults; his seal; WIT: Sterling JOHNSTON, Henry HUFFMAN; ack. Sterling JOHNSTON, J.P.; entered 10 Mar 1808, recorded 15 Mar 1808.

p. 275 - Indenture, 10 Mar 1808, Andrew MARSHALL (wife Margaret), St. Clairsville, BCO; Robert H. JOHNSTON, same. $500, lot #85 in St. Clairsville, 1/4 acre, conveyed by David NEWELL (wife Sally) and Benjamine NEWELL (wife Jane) by deed dated 7 Apr 1801 in fee simple, recorded in Book A, p. 35 (p. 32 in new book [p. 5 of abstracts]), fee simple; his seal, her mark; WIT: Sterling JOHNSTON, Archibald CRAWFORD; ack. Sterling JOHNSTON, J.P.; entered 10 Mar 1808, recorded 16 Mar 1808.

p. 276 - Indenture, 9 Mar 1808, Reverend Joseph ANDERSON (wife Betsey), BCO; Robert H. JOHNSTON, BCO. $150, land in Richland twp., adjoining St. Clairsville, NBR: William CONGLETON, John THOMPSON, 3 acres, fee simple; both seal; WIT: Sterling JOHNSTON, Robt. LAUGHLIN; ack. Sterling JOHNSTON, J.P.; entered 10 Mar 1808, recorded 16 Mar 1808.

p. 277 - Indenture, 10 Mar 1808, Robert H. JOHNSTON, BCO; Andrew MARSHALL, BCO. $700, lot #65 in St. Clairsville plus another lot in Richland twp., BCO, 3 acres, NBR: William CONGLETON, John THOMPSON, fee simple, void if JOHNSTON pays full $700 in payments ending 1 Apr 1811; his seal; WIT: Sterling JOHNSTON, Archibald CRAWFORD; ack. Sterling JOHNSTON, J.P.; entered 10 Mar 1808, recorded 17 Mar 1808; released 12 Aug 1808 signed by A. MARSHALL.

p. 278 - Indenture, 7 Oct 1807, Fielding PHILLIPS, BCO; John SCATTERDAY, BCO. Whereas James MARTIN and John SCATTERDAY bound in a note or obligation given to Samuel CONALD and Hance WILEY, executors to Easter HOULTS, dec'd, bearing date 6 Oct 1807 for $66 payable in 12 months, secured by transfer to MARTIN and SCATTERDAY of a black mare bought at the "Vandeu" [vendue] of HOULTS, void if PHILLIPS pays $66 to

CONALD and WILEY without putting MARTIN and SCATTERDAY to any damage; his mark; WIT: Sterling JOHNSTON, Thos. WILLSON; ack. 7 Oct 1807, Sterling JOHNSTON, J.P.; entered 13 Mar 1808, recorded 17 Mar 1808.

p. 279 - Indenture, 13 May 1807, Charles ECKELS (wife Mary), BCO; James ROBERTSON [ROBINSON], BCO. $1.50 per acre, part of S 13 T 6 R 3, 15 acres 3 rods 22 perches; both seal; WIT: Jacob DAVIS, Calep TILTON; ack. 30 May 1807, Jacob DAVIS; entered 14 Mar 1808, recorded 18 Mar 1808.

p. 280 - Indenture, 5 Mar 1808, Josiah HEDGES, Sheriff of BCO; Thomas BARR, BCO. Whereas Caleb RUSSEL, in Supreme Court of BCO at September term 1805 obtained judgment against David BARR, BCO, for $120 costs, an allias writ of fiere facias issued dated 19 Nov 1807 commanding HEDGES to seize enough of BARR's property to cover judgment, seized 100 acres in S 31 T 7 R 3, same purchased by BARR from David VANCE, put on sale 4 Mar 1808 and sold to Thomas BARR for $161; his seal; WIT: James CLOYD, John BROWN, Junr.; ack. James CLOYD, J.P.; entered 14 Mar 1808, recorded 18 Mar 1808.

p. 281 - Indenture, 14 Mar 1808, Thomas IRELAND (wife Sarah), St. Clairsville, BCO; Samuel SULLIVAN, BCO. $300, lots #21 and #22 in addition to St. Clairsville as laid out by William MATHERS, conveyed by Obadiah JENNINGS (wife Ann) to IRELAND on 14 Mar 1807; his seal, her mark; WIT: John PATTERSON, James BARNES; ack. John PATTERSON, J.P.; entered 15 Mar 1808, recorded 21 Mar 1808.

p. 282 - Indenture, 14 Mar 1808, James ROBERTSON (wife Elizabeth), BCO; Samuel CLARK, BCO. $960, two lots, part of S 13 T 6 R 3, first 107 or 108 acres which was granted to Robert JOHNSTON by patent dated 17 Apr 1788, from JOHNSTON to Absalom MARTIN on 24 May 1799, from MARTIN to ROBERTSON on 16 Aug 1800, second containing 15 acres 3 rods and 22 perches, part of above section conveyed to ROBERTSON by Charles ECKLES on 13 May 1807, fee simple; his seal, her mark; WIT: Sterling JOHNSTON, William GIFFEN; ack. Sterling JOHNSTON, J.P.

p. 284 - Indenture, 11 Jun 1807, Horton HOWARD (wife Hannah), BCO; John LLOYD, Callawissa, Northumberland County, Pennsylvania. $2,000, begin NW corner S 9 T 7 R 3, 320 acres, S 9 granted to Horton HOWARD in fee by patent dated 22 Jan 1806; both seal; WIT: John MITCHELL, John STEWART; ack. 11 Jun 1807, Thos. MITCHELL, J.P.; entered 14 Mar 1808, recorded 24 Mar 1808.

p. 286 - Indenture, 12 Jan 1808, John DEVERS, BCO; John VANPELT, BCO. $240, 133 acres in S 13 T 9 R 5, beginning at NW corner of NW 1/4, fee simple;

his mark; WIT: John REAGH, Isaac BRANSON; ack. Union twp., BCO, John WILEY, acting J.P.; entered 17 Mar 1808, recorded 25 Mar 1808.

p. 286 - Indenture, 11 Dec 1807, Charles HAMMOND; David NIESWANGER, [no locations given]. $50, lot #67 in St. Clairsville; his seal; WIT: Jacob NAGLE, James CLOYD; ack. James CLOYD, J.P.; entered 19 Mar 1808, recorded 25 Mar 1808.

p. 287 - Indenture, 19 Mar 1808, Phillip McGRAW (wife Margaret), BCO; David HUTCHISON, BCO. $600, part of S 6 T 7 R 4, beginning NW corner, 101 acres 3 rods 20 perches, S granted to David VANCE by patent dated 12 Feb 1798, conveyed by VANCE (wife Margaret) to McGRAW on 12 Feb 1808 as recorded in Book B, p. 247 (p. 266 in this book [p. 121 of abstracts]); his seal, her mark; WIT: Sterling JOHNSTON, George PAULL; ack. Sterling JOHNSTON, J.P.

p. 288 - Indenture, 1 Oct 1807, Daniel MERRIT (wife Nancy), Richland twp., BCO; Moses MERRIT, same. $45, part of NE 1/4 of S 31 T 8 R 4, 15 acres 9 perches, granted to Daniel by patent dated 27 Aug 1805; both seal; WIT: John WILEY, William COEN; ack. 1 Oct 1807, John WILEY, J.P.; entered 18 Mar 1808; recorded 28 Mar 1808.

p. 289 - Indenture, 1 Oct 1807, Daniel MERRIT (wife Nancy), Richland twp., BCO; Moses MERRIT, same. $340, NW 1/4 of S 31 T 8 R 4, granted to Daniel by patent dated 27 Aug 1805; both seal; WIT: John WILEY, William COEN; ack. 1 Oct 1807, John WILEY, J.P.; entered 19 Mar 1808, recorded 28 Mar 1808.

p. 290 - Indenture, 8 Dec 1807, Merchant DEFORD, BCO; James CALDWELL, St. Clairsville, BCO. $176.61, tract of land on which DEFORD now lives, part of Ss 34, 35, 28 T 6 R 3, beginning at NE corner S 28, 100 acres 2 rods 20 perches, conveyed to DEFORD by Notley HAYS by deed dated 18 Apr 1807, avoid if DEFORD pays $176.61 plus interest by 1 Apr "next ensuing"; both seal; WIT: Hugh McCOY, Adam JOHNSTON, Junr.; ack. Sterling JOHNSTON, J.P.; entered 26 Mar 1808, recorded 30 Mar 1808; released 24 May 1808 by James CALDWELL.

p. 292 - Indenture, 19 Feb 1808, David HUTCHISON, BCO; Josiah DILLON and Sterling JOHNSTON, BCO. To secure $341.10 due to Jacob LOWRY of Fayette County, Pennsylvania, by HUTCHISON for which DILLON and JOHNSTON stand bound as security and for $1 HUTCHISON conveys land on which he now lives which was conveyed to him on present date, part of S 6 T 7 R 4, 101 acres 3 rods 20 perches, void if payments completed by 19 Mar 1813;

all seal; WIT: Geo. PAULL, James CLOYD; ack. James CLOYD; entered 26 Mar 1808, recorded 12 Apr 1808; released 28 Feb 1833 by Sterling JOHNSTON and Josiah DILLON, Wm. FARIS a wit. to S. JOHNSTON.

p. 294 - Indenture, 19 Mar 1808, Phillip McGRAW, BCO; Josiah DILLON and Sterling JOHNSTON, BCO. To secure a debt of $411.25 due to Jacob LOWRY of Fayette County, Pennsylvania, by Phillip McGRAW, for which DILLON and JOHNSTON stand bound as security and for $1 McGRAW conveys land on which he now lives, part of S 6 T 7 R 4, about 220 acres, part of land conveyed to McGRAW by David VANCE (wife Margaret) on 12 Jan 1808, void if payments completed by 19 Mar 1813; all seal; WIT: George PAULL, Merchant DEFORD; ack. James CLOYD, J.P.; entered 26 Mar 1808, recorded 12 Apr 1808; released 3 Jul 1810 by DILLON and JOHNSTON, by George PAULL, Esqr, attorney for Jacob LOWRY.

p. 296 - "Know all men," Robert TROUP, Judge of U.S. in New York, for $13 paid by Jacob LEWIS, Pennsylvania, lot #4 in square #33 in Pultney in T 2 R 2 on map made by LEWIS and deposited in the secretary's office of the State of New York, signed 16 Jun 1707 [probably 1797]; his seal; WIT: Robt. MURRY, A. WAUGH; ack. 22 Jun 1797, New York, Jno. [Slon] HOBART [HOBARTS], Justice of Supreme Court of Judicature of New York; entered 28 Mar 1808, recorded 12 Apr 1808.

p. 296 - Indenture, 13 Mar 1807, Elijah WOODS (wife Hettey), BCO; James McELHENEY, BCO. $100, donation lot #10 in square #3 in Pultney; both seal; WIT: Tho. THOMPSON, Joel ZANE; ack. 13 Mar 1807, Tho. THOMPSON, J.P.; entered 28 Mar 1808, recorded 13 Apr 1808.

p. 297 - Indenture, 11 Sep 1802, Samuel DANNELL [DANNEL], JCT, James McELHENEY, [no location given]. $40, lot #4, square #33, BCT, granted to DANNEL by instrument dated 27 Apr 1801 from Jacob LEWIS of Ohio County, Virginia; his seal; WIT: Thos. RICHARD, Wm. B. KING; ack. 11 Sep 1802, Jacob REPSHER, J.P.; entered 28 Mar 1808, recorded 13 Apr 1808.

p. 298 - "Know all men," George HEAP, Wells twp., Muskingum County, Ohio, for $7.50 paid by James McELHENEY, Pultney twp., BCT, lot #19, square #3 in Pultney, in the Wegee Bottom in T 2 R 2, signed 17 Mar 1807; his seal; WIT: Richd. McELHENEY, Mathew McELHENEY, Junr.; ack. 7 Mar 1807, Michael McCLUNEY, Esqr., J.P. for Pultney twp.; entered 28 Mar 1808, recorded 13 Apr 1808.

p. 299 - Indenture, 27 Apr 1801, Jacob LEWIS, Ohio County, Virginia; Samuel DANNELL [DANNEL], [no location given]. $20, lot #4, square #33 in JCT, land granted to LEWIS by instrument of writing from Robert TROUP, Esqr., State of New York, dated 16 Jun 1796; his seal; WIT: James EVANS, D. McELHERON; ack. BCO, 1 Feb 1802, Jacob REPSHER, J.P.

p. 299 - "Know all men," Daniel McELHERON, town of Pultney, BCO, for $50 paid by George HEAP, Esqr., of same, lot #19, square #3 in Pultney, in Wegee Bottom, T 2 R 2, signed 19 Jul 1805; his seal; WIT: John WEST; ack. Pultney twp., BCO, 12 Aug 1805, Jacob [DAVISS], Esqr., J.P. for Pultney twp. [but no seal]; entered 28 Mar 1808, recorded 13 Apr 1808.

p. 300 - Indenture, 13 Mar 1808, David NEWELL (wife Sally), Richland twp., BCO; Sterling JOHNSTON, same. $40, lots #105 and #106 in St. Clairsville, fee simple; both seal; WIT: George PAULL, James CLOYD; ack. James CLOYD, J.P.; entered 28 Mar 1808, recorded 13 Apr 1808.

p. 301 - "Know all men," John TIMBERLAKE, Campbell County, Virginia, gives Charles PIDGEON, BCO, power of attorney to sell SE 1/4 of S 24 T 7 R 5, signed 6 Feb 1808; his seal; WIT: M. LAMBETH, Rodk. [Roderick?] TALEAFERE; Terence COONEY; ack. Campbell County, Corporation of Lynchburg, John SCHOOLFIELD, James STEWART, and in Virginia, certified by Thomas W. COOKE, Notary Public, "recorded in A, p. 482."

p. 302 - Indenture, 14 Jan 1808, John DIVERS, BCO; Abraham DIVERS, BCO. $164, 110 acres 3 rods 13 poles in S 13 T 9 R 5, fee simple; his mark; WIT: John VANPELT, John REAGH; ack. 12 Jan 1808, John WILEY, acting J.P.; entered 13 Apr 1808, recorded 29 Apr 1808.

p. 303 - Indenture, 7 Mar 1808, Bazaleel WELLS (wife Sally), JCO; John PICKERING, BCO. $127, part of S 18 T 6 R 3, 36 1/4 acres; both seal; WIT: Jonathan TAYLOR, Butler WELLS [WILES]; ack. JCO, J. JENKINSON, J.P., certified by Jno. WARD, Clerk, JCO; entered 13 Apr 1808, recorded 29 Apr 1808.

p. 304 - Indenture, 7 Mar 1808, Bazaleel WELLS, JCO; Hugh PARKS, BCO. $380, part of S 18 T 6 R 3, 80 acres; both seal; WIT: Jonathan TAYLOR, Butler WELLS; ack. JCO, J. JENKINSON, J.P., certified by Jno. WARD, Clerk, JCO.

p. 305 - Indenture, 16 Feb 1808, John McCLURE (wife Mary), BCO; Joseph MOORE, BCO. $505.75, part of tract purchased jointly by MOORE and McCLURE from Archibald WOODS, Ohio County, Virginia, by deed dated 21 Jun 1804, as recorded in Book A, p. 337 (p. 278 in new book [p. 44 of abstracts], [additional note that document recorded in p. 337 had been done in error]) dated 21 Jun 1804, part of S 27 T 4 (fractional) R 2, grant issued 15 Nov

1797, NBR: Francis HARDESTY, Mr. HARVY, John McCLURE, Mr. [Joseph] SCOTT, 102 acres 36 perches; his seal, her mark; WIT: Thos. MITCHELL, Charles McMANAS; ack. Thos. MITCHELL, J.P.; entered 13 Apr 1808, recorded 30 Apr 1808.

p. 307 - Plat of Belmont, by Joseph WRIGHT of BCO, signed 8 Apr 1808; ack. Sterling JOHNSTON, J.P. (See Appendix.)

p. 308 - Indenture, 12 Apr 1808, Charles PIDGEON [PEDGION], BCO, attorney for John TIMBERLAKE, Campbell County, Virginia; Caleb GREGG, BCO. $800, 160 acres, square piece in SE corner of S 24 T 7 R 5, S granted to James RATKINS by patent, conveyed by RATKINS to TIMBERLAKE on 13 Oct 1806 as recorded in Book B, p. 10 [p. 84 of abstracts]; PIDGEON's seal for TIMBERLAKE; WIT: Brice RICKEY, Sterling JOHNSTON; ack. Sterling JOHNSTON, J.P.; entered 13 Apr 1808, recorded 3 May 1808.

p. 309 - Indenture, 11 Mar 1808, Joseph WRIGHT, BCO; John ROBERTS and James ROBERTS, merchants, of Baltimore. Joseph bound to John and James in penal sum of $1,160 conditioned for the payment of $580 with interest, to secure debt and for $1 conveying W side of S 12 T 7 R 5, Steubenville district, patented on 15 Nov 1807, NBR: John ISRAEL, William PHILPOT, Joseph DONNER, and others, 211 acres, void if $580 paid by 11 Mar 1809; his seal [Josh. WRIGH]; WIT: Joseph H. [M.] NICHOLSON; ack. Maryland, Joseph H. NICHOLSON, Chief Judge of 6th Judicial District, certified by Wm. GIBSON, Clk., Baltimore County; entered 14 Apr 1808, recorded 3 May 1808.

p. 311 - Indenture, 7 Apr 1808, Henry HUFMAN (wife Mary), BCO; Jacob BREWER, BCO. $200, part of E 1/2 of S 27 T 4 R 3, Marietta district, NBR: Able BROWN, 100 acres; his seal, her mark; WIT: Levin OKEY, Easter OKEY [her mark]; ack. Levin OKEY, J.P.

p. 312 - Indenture, 7 Apr 1808, Henry HUFMAN (wife Mary), BCO; Able BROWN, BCO. $500, part of E 1/2 of S 27 T 4 R 3, Marietta district, 192 acres; his seal, her mark; WIT: Levin OKEY, Easter OKEY [her mark]; ack. Levin OKEY, J.P.; entered 14 Apr 1808, recorded 4 May 1808.

p. 313 - Indenture, 22 Feb 1808, Ebenezer ZANE (wife Elizabeth), gentleman, Wheeling; Jacob BURKETT (wife Mary Ann) [no location given]. For natural affection and other good causes, S 28 (fractional) T 3 R 2, 150 acres, for providing a ferry; both seal; WIT: Noah ZANE, Thos. THOMPSON; ack. Thos. THOMPSON, J.P.; entered 14 Apr 1808, recorded 4 May 1808.

p. 315 - Indenture, 4 May 1804, Ebenezer ZANE, Ohio County, Virginia; Samuel ZANE, his son [no location given]. For love and natural affection, Ss 18 (fractional) and 24 T 3 R 2, S 18 equals 86 1/2 acres, S 24 a full section adjoining S 18 on W and should contain 340 acres; NBR: heirs of Absalom MARTIN, now dec'd; both seal; WIT: Noah ZANE, Thos. THOMPSON; ack. BCO, [no date given], Thos. THOMPSON, J.P.; entered 14 Apr 1808, recorded 4 May 1808.

p. 316 - Indenture, 22 Apr 1808, James NEWELL, BCO; John LONG, BCO. $22, lots #94, #102, #110 in St. Clairsville, fee simple; his seal [J. E. NEWELL]; WIT: Sterling JOHNSTON, James JOHNSON; ack. Sterling JOHNSTON, J.P.; entered 22 Apr 1808, recorded 4 May 1808.

p. 317 - Indenture, 18 May 1807, Christopher CLOUSE (wife Catharine), Pennsylvania; Nicholas BOWERS, BCO. $120, lots #135 and #136 in St. Clairsville, each 1/4 acre, fee simple; both seal; WIT: Sterling JOHNSTON, Leonard I. DEVEN [his mark]; ack. Washington County, 18 May 1807, Isaac LEONARD, J.P., certified 17 Jun 1807 by W. McKENNON, Prothonotary of CCP; entered 22 Apr 1808, recorded 5 May 1808.

p. 318 - Indenture, 16 Apr 1808, Josiah HEDGES, Sheriff of BCO; John WINTERS, BCO. By virtue of a writ serie facias from Calvin PEASE, Esqr., president of court, dated 24 Dec 1807 where Sterling JOHNSTON had recovered a judgment at December term 1807 against William MOSELEY for $229.85 and $10.15 for costs, HEDGES levies two lots (#1 and #2) adjoining addition to St. Clairsville as laid out by Bazaleel WELLS, and lot #__ in addition to St. Clairsville, conveys lots #1 and #2 to John WINTERS for $101, estimated at 4 to 5 acres; his seal; WIT: S. SPRIGGS, John PATTERSON, James HUGHES; ack. John PATTERSON, J.P.; entered 22 Apr 1808, recorded 5 May 1808.

p. 319 - Indenture, 27 Oct 1807, Daniel MERRIT (wife Nancy), Richland twp., BCO; William McWILLIAMS, same. $340, SW 1/4 of S 31 T 8 R 4, granted to MERRIT by patent dated 27 Aug 1805; both seal; WIT: Moses MERRIT, Ann BELL; ack. Moses MERRIT, J.P.; entered 27 Apr 1808, recorded 9 May 1808.

p. 320 - Indenture, 22 Apr 1808, Joseph POSEY (wife Susanna), BCO; Isiah ALLON, BCO. $603, part of S 20 T 7 R 4, 100 acres 2 rods 20 perches, conveyed to Joseph POSEY by John MARTIN on 8 Dec 1806 as recorded in Book B, p. 44 [p. 83 of abstracts], fee simple; both seal; WIT: Sterling JOHNSTON, James JOHNSON; ack. Sterling JOHNSTON, J.P.; entered 22 Apr 1808, recorded 9 May 1808.

p. 321 - Indenture, 26 Apr 1808, James MARTIN (wife Agness), BCO; John LONG, BCO. $300, parts of lots #160 and #159 in St. Clairsville, NE corner of

#160, on this date conveyed from William WOODS, Joseph MARSHALL and Jeremiah FAIRHURST, executors of John FAIRHURST, dec'd, to James MARTIN, fee simple; both seal; WIT: Sterling JOHNSTON, Wm. CONGLETON; ack. Sterling JOHNSTON, J.P.

p. 322 - Indenture, 25 Apr 1808, John LONG (wife Catharine), BCO; James MARTIN, BCO. $610, lots #94, #110, and #102 in St. Clairsville according to plat laid out by David NEWELL, fee simple; his seal, her mark; WIT: Sterling JOHNSTON, Wm. CONGLETON; ack. Sterling JOHNSTON, J.P.; entered 27 Apr 1808, recorded 10 May 1808.

p. 323 - Indenture, Indenture, 26 Apr 1808, John LONG (wife Catharine), BCO; John BROWN, Junr., BCO. $300, part of lots #160 and #159 in St. Clairsville, fee simple; his seal, her mark; WIT: Sterling JOHNSTON, Wm. CONGLETON; ack. Sterling JOHNSTON, J.P.; entered 27 Apr 1808, recorded 10 May 1808.

p. 325 - Indenture, 27 Apr 1808, James MARTIN, BCO; John LONG, BCO. MARTIN is indebted to LONG for $230, secured by conveying lots #94, #102, and #110 in St. Clairsville, void if payments made by 1 Dec 1811; his seal; WIT: Robt. GRIFFITH, Sterling JOHNSTON; ack. Sterling JOHNSTON, J.P.; entered 27 Apr 1808, recorded 10 May 1808; released 13 Jun 1812 by John LONG.

p. 326 - Indenture, 26 Apr 1808, John BROWN, Junr., BCO; John LONG, BCO. BROWN bound to LONG in sum of $250, secured by conveying part of lots #160 and <u>#59</u> in St. Clairsville, void if payments made by 27 Apr 1802 [1812]; his seal; WIT: Sterling JOHNSTON, Wm. CONGLETON; ack. Sterling JOHNSTON, J.P.; entered 27 Apr 1808, recorded 11 May 1808.

p. 327 - Indenture, 26 Apr 1808, William WOODS, Joseph MARSHALL, and Jeremiah FAIRHURST, BCO (executors of lw&t of John FAIRHURST, dec'd); James MARTIN, BCO. $168, part of lot #160 and #159 in St. Clairsville, conveyed from William GIBSON (wife Nancy) to heirs of John FAIRHURST, dec'd on 27 Apr 1807, as recorded in Book B, p. 109 (p. 112 of new book [p. 99 of abstracts]), fee simple; WOODS mark, MARSHALL and FAIRHURST seal; WIT: Sterling JOHNSTON, John BROWN; ack. Sterling JOHNSTON, J.P.; entered 27 Apr 1808, recorded 11 May 1808.

p. 328 - Indenture, 11 Apr 1808, Sterling JOHNSTON (wife Mary) and James CLOYD, BCO; Thomas L. JUDGE, Ohio County, Virginia. $100, E 1/2 of lot #16 in St. Clairsville, 1/8 acre; all seal; WIT: John PATTERSON, Robert JOHNSTON; ack. John PATTERSON, J.P.; entered 2 May 1808, recorded 11 May 1808.

p. 329 - Indenture, 30 Apr 1808, Sterling JOHNSTON (wife Mary), BCO; James CLOYD [CLAUD], BCO. $1 and for other considerations, W 1/2 of lot #16 in St. Clairsville, conveyed to CLOYD and Robert JOHNSTON by William CONGLETON of Virginia on 26 Mar 1806, Robert JOHNSTON's part conveyed to Sterling JOHNSTON on 23 Feb 1807; both seal; WIT: John PATTERSON, Robert JOHNSTON; ack. John PATTERSON, J.P.; entered 2 May 1808, recorded 12 May 1808.

p. 330 - Indenture, 4 May 1808, Robert H. JOHNSTON (wife Mary), BCO; James CORRATHERS [CARROTHERS?], BCO. $100, lot adjoining the public commons of St. Clairsville, NBR: Vitchel HALL, William CONGLETON, 1 acre, conveyed by Reverend Joseph ANDERSON (wife Betsey) to JOHNSTON on 9 Mar 1808 as recorded in Book B, p. 256 (p. 276 in new book [p. 123 of abstracts]), fee simple; his seal, her mark; WIT: Sterling JOHNSTON, Wm. CONGLETON; ack. Sterling JOHNSTON, J.P.; entered 4 May 1808, recorded 13 May 1808.

p. 331 - Indenture, 7 Mar 1808, Bazaleel WELLS (wife Sally), JCO; Sampson ROBISON [ROBSON], BCO. $196, part of S 18 T 6 R 3, NBR: Hugh PARKS, 56 acres; both seal; WIT: Jonathan TAYLOR, Butler WELLS; ack. JCO, J. JENKINSON, J.P., certified by Jno. WARD, Clk., JCO; entered 5 May 1808, recorded 14 May 1808.

p. 332 - Indenture, 7 May 1808, Robert JOHNSTON, BCO; Robert H. JOHNSTON, BCO. $40, lot #114 in St. Clairsville, fee simple; his seal; WIT: James [Jamars] CLOYD, George PAULL; ack. James CLOYD, J.P.; entered 7 May 1808, recorded 14 May 1808.

p. 333 - Indenture, 26 Nov 1807, Samuel PATTON (wife Jane), BCO; Benjamine MERIDITH [MERRIDITH], BCO. $60, land in S 19 T 8 R 4, Steubenville district, NBR: George McWILLIAMS, Samuel PATTON, Benjamine MERIDITH, part of S granted to John WINTER by patent dated 11 Jan 1806, fee simple; both seal; WIT: Moses MERRIT, William McWILLIAMS; ack. 26 Nov 1807, Moses MERRIT, J.P.; entered 14 May 1808, recorded 17 May 1808.

p. 334 - Indenture, 24 Dec 1807, John YOUNG (wife Elisabeth), Washington County, Pennsylvania; James McMILLEN, Peas twp., BCO. $1,000, N part of S 36 T 8 R 6, NBR: John THOMPSON and others, 224 acres; his seal, her mark; WIT: Thomas MITCHELL, George MITCHELL; ack. 24 Dec 1807, BCO, Thos. MITCHELL, J.P.; entered 21 May 1808, recorded 24 May 1808.

p. 335 - Indenture, 18 Oct 1802, Bazaleel [Bezaleel, Bezoleel] WELLS (wife Sally, Sall), JCT; Henry HANNAH, BCT. $484, part of Ss 20 and 26 T 4 R 2,

NBR: Andrew McMAHAN, Francis HARDISTY; both seal; WIT: Archibald COLE, Ph. CABLE; ack. JCT, 18 Oct 1802, Phillip CABLE, J.P.; entered 21 May 1808, recorded 24 May 1808.

p. 336 - Indenture, 30 Apr 1808, William BROWN (wife Sally), BCO; John HINDS, BCO. $153.75, NBR: William BROWN, Notley HAYS, 2 acres 2 rods 10 perches at $60 per acre, fee simple, BROWN promises to leave a piece of ground leading from the above mentioned and sold lot to intersect with the S commons of St. Clairsville as a public road; both seal; WIT: Sterling JOHNSTON, David NEISWANGER; ack. Sterling JOHNSTON, J.P.

p. 337 - Indenture, 30 Apr 1808, Moses MOREHEAD (wife Ann), BCO; William BROWN, BCO. $16, NBR: David RUSSLE, William BROWN, fee

simple; both seal; WIT: James McCONNEL, Sterling JOHNSTON; ack. Sterling JOHNSTON, J.P.; entered 25 May 1808, recorded 25 May 1808.

p. 338 - Indenture, 24 May 1808, Frederick AULTFATHER, Summerset County, Pennsylvania; Samuel STONEBREAKER, BCO. $600, part of S 19 T 7 R 4, Steubenville district, 206 acres; his seal; WIT: Robert JOHNSTON, James CLOYD; ack. James CLOYD, J.P.; entered 25 May 1808, recorded 25 May 1808.

p. 339 - Indenture, 24 May 1808, Frederick AULTFATHER, Summerset County, Pennsylvania; Adam AULTFATHER, same. $600, part of S 19 T 7 R 4, 206 acres; his seal; WIT: Robert JOHNSTON, James CLOYD; ack. James CLOYD, J.P.; entered 25 May 1808, recorded 25 May 1808.

p. 340 - Indenture, 24 May 1808, Frederick AULTFATHER, Summerset County, Pennsylvania; Jacob AULTFATHER, same. $120, part of S 19 T 7 R 4, Steubenville district, NBR: Samuel STONEBREAKER, Adam AULTFATHER, 40 acres 3 rods 25 perches; his seal; WIT: Robert JOHNSTON, James CLOYD; ack. James CLOYD, J.P.

p. 341 - Indenture, 24 May 1808, Frederick AULTFATHER, Summerset County, Pennsylvania; Casper KEIFFER, same. $600, part of S 19 T 7 R 4, Steubenville district, NBR: Samuel STONEBREAKER, 206 acres; his seal; WIT: Robert JOHNSTON, James CLOYD; ack. James CLOYD, J.P.

p. 342 - Indenture, 26 Apr 1808, Bezeleel WELLS, Steubenville, JCO, and Elias VAN ARSDALE, Newark, Essex County, New Jersey, executors of lw&t of Daniel McELHERAN, dec'd; James GREENLEE, JCO. McELHERAN's lw&t dated 25 May 1807, other executor was William HILL of New York City, merchant. $1, part of S 1 T 6 R 3, 160 acres; both seal; WIT: (VAN ARSDALE) Thomas WARD, Joseph HORNBLOWER, WIT: (Bazaleel WELLS), Zachs. BEGGS, Obadiah JENNINGS; ack. (VAN ARSDALE) Essex County, New Jersey, 26 Apr 1808, Thomas WARD, Judge of Inferior CCP, ack. (WELLS) JCO, 20 May 1808, J. JENKINSON, J.P., certified by Geo. LUCKEY for John WARD [WORK], Clerk, JCO; entered 26 May 1808, recorded 30 May 1808.

p. 344 - Indenture, 25 May 1808, James GREENLEE, JCO; Abraham WORKMAN, BCO. $150, E part of SW 1/4 of S 1 T 6 R 3, conveyed to GREENLEE on 26 Apr 1808 [see preceding entry for history], 66 1/2 acres, fee simple; his seal; WIT: Sterling JOHNSTON, James CALDWELL; ack. Sterling JOHNSTON, J.P.; entered 26 May 1808, recorded 30 May 1808.

p. 345 - Indenture, 23 Mar [probably May] 1808, Merchant DEFORD (wife Elizabeth), BCO; Robert GREENLEE, BCO. $1,000, part of Ss 34, 35, 28 T 6 R 3, Steubenville district, 100 acres 2 rods 20 perches, land granted to Notley HAYS by patent, Josiah DILLON (wife Dorothy) and Mordicai YARNELL [YARNEL] (wife Phebe), from HAYS (wife Sally) to DEFORD on 18 Apr 1807, as recorded in Book B, p. 104 (p. 106 in new book [p. 98 of abstracts]), fee simple; both seal; WIT: Sterling JOHNSTON, James CALDWELL; ack. Sterling JOHNSTON, J.P.

p. 346 - 23 May 1808, James GREENLEE, JCO; Merchant DEFORD, BCO. $499, part of S 1 T 6 R 3, part of land conveyed go GREENLEE by executors of lw&t of Daniel McELHERAN, dec'd [see transaction on beginning on p. 342 of book, preceding page of abstracts], 93 1/2 acres, fee simple; his seal; WIT: Sterling JOHNSTON, James CALDWELL; ack. Sterling JOHNSTON, J.P.; entered 26 May 1808, recorded 30 May 1808.

p. 347 - 23 May 1808, Merchant DEFORD, BCO; James CALDWELL, BCO. $262.49, part of S 1 T 6 R 3, 93 1/2 acres, conveyed to DEFORD by James GREENLEE on 23 May 1808, void if DEFORD pays CALDWELL $272.49 by 24 Nov 1808; both seal; WIT: Sterling JOHNSTON, Robert GREENLEE; ack. Sterling JOHNSTON, J.P. [additional note regarding conditions of default]; entered 26 May 1808, recorded 31 May 1808.

p. 349 - "Whereas" Register of Land Office on 17 Sep 1804 granted a certificate to Horton HOWARD, BCO, where HOWARD was entitled to a patent for SE 1/4 of S 29 T 7 R 5, Steubenville district, for $240 paid by John PIGGOTT, BCO, conveys rights of this patent, signed 6 Jun 1808; his seal; WIT: Levinah HALL, Henry HOWARD; ack. Sterling JOHNSTON, J.P.; entered 6 Jun 1808, recorded 7 Jun 1808.

p. 350 - Indenture, 31 May 1808, Robert H. JOHNSTON (wife Mary); BCO; William GREENLEE, BCO. $40, lot #114 in St. Clairsville, conveyed to Robert H. JOHNSTON from Robert JOHNSTON on 7 May 1808; his seal, her mark; WIT: Sterling JOHNSTON, William B. JOHNSTON; ack. Sterling JOHNSTON, J.P.

p. 351 - Indenture, 2 Jun 1808, Robert T. FINNEY (wife Peggy), BCO; William STRINGER, Junr., BCO. $500, part of Ss 20 and 26 T 4 R 2, NBR: Henry HANNAH (land sold by Bazaleel WELLS), 67 acres; both seal; WIT: Malcom STRINGER, Thos. THOMPSON; ack. Thos. THOMPSON, J.P.; entered 7 Jun 1808, recorded 20 Jun 1808.

p. 352 - Indenture, 16 Jan 1807, William HODGEN (wife Agness), Kirkwood twp., BCO; Rebeckah TODD and Robert TODD [no relationship given], BCO. $267.60, SE corner of S 8 T 8 R 6, 106 acres 1 rod, fee simple; his seal, her mark; WIT: Nathan SIDWELL, John GREER; ack. John GREER, J.P.; entered 7 Jun 1808, recorded 20 Jun 1808.

p. 353 - [different handwriting] ack. by William CHAPLIN of plat of Morristown, 22 Jun 1808, Sterling JOHNSTON, J.P.; entered 21 Jun 1808, recorded 21 Jun 1808 [previous plat on p. 51 of Book A (p. 8 of abstracts)].

p. 354 to 355 - Plat of Morristown, as laid out by William CHAPLIN. (See Appendix.)

p. 356 - Indenture, 12 Jun 1808, William GREENLEE, BCO; Soloman WADDLE, BCO. $42, lot #114 in St. Clairsville, conveyed to GREENLEE by Robert H. JOHNSTON (wife Mary) on 31 May 1808; his seal; WIT: John PATTERSON, Sterling JOHNSTON; ack. Sterling JOHNSTON, J.P.; entered 12 Jun 1808, recorded 22 Jun 1808.

p. 357 - Indenture, 11 Jun 1808, John McCLAIN (wife Martha), Ohio County, Virginia; William PORTER, same. $100, land on E end of St. Clairsville, 1/4 acre, fee simple; both mark; WIT: Sterling JOHNSTON, John NICHOL; ack. BCO, Sterling JOHNSTON, J.P.; entered 13 Jun 1808, recorded 22 Jun 1808.

p. 358 - Indenture, 11 Jun 1808, John McCLAIN (wife Martha), Ohio County, Virginia; James ROSE [ROSS], Fayette County, Pennsylvania. $100, paid by George BRADSHAW, two lots at E end of St. Clairsville, each 1/4 acre, fee simple; both mark; WIT: Sterling JOHNSTON, John NICHOL; ack. Sterling JOHNSTON, J.P.; entered 13 Jun 1808, recorded 22 Jun 1808.

p. 359 - Indenture, 16 Feb 1808, Joseph MOORE (wife Jane), BCO; John McCLURE, BCO. $214.99, part of tract purchased jointly by MOORE and McCLURE from Archibald WOODS, Ohio County, Virginia, on 21 Jun 1804, as recorded in Book A, p. 337 (p. 278 in new book [p. 44 of abstracts], part of S 27 T (fractional) 4 R 2, patent issued 15 Nov 1797, NBR: Mr. HARVEY, Richard McKIBBENS, Joseph MOORE, 47 acres 3 rods 4 perches; his seal, her mark; WIT: Thos. MITCHELL, Charles McMANAS; ack. 18 Feb 180_, Thos. MITCHELL, J.P.; entered 15 Jun 1808, recorded 23 Jun 1808.

p. 360 - Indenture, 30 Mar 1808, William ROBINSON, St. Clairsville, BCO; Thomas ROBINSON, BCO. $160, out lot #13 of 5 acres 3 rods 30 perches as laid out by Bazaleel WELLS adjoining addition to St. Clairsville as laid out by William MATHERS, sold to Andrew MOORE by Obadiah JENNINGS by deed dated 1 Sep 1806, conveyed by MOORE to William ROBINSON on 16 Jan 1807, void if William pays Thomas $160 by 30 Mar 1809; William's seal; WIT: John PATTERSON, John HAZLETT; ack. John PATTERSON, J.P., entered 22 Jun 1808, recorded 23 Jun 1808.

p. 361 - Indenture, 1 Sep 1806, Obadiah JENNINGS, JCO; Andrew MOORE, BCO. $200.--, out lot #8 (6 acres 11 perches) and #13 (5 acres 3 rods 30 perches) in plan laid out by Bazaleel WELLS adjoining addition to St. Clairsville; his seal; WIT: Geo. PAULL, Saml. SPRIGG; ack. 1 Sep 1806, John PATTERSON, J.P.; entered 28 Jun 1808, recorded 29 Jun 1808.

p. 362 - Indenture, 20 Dec 1807, Andrew MOORE (wife Elizabeth), Muskingum County, Ohio; Samuel SULLIVAN, St. Clairsville, BCO. $150, out lot #8 in tract adjoining addition to St. Clairsville, 6 acres 11 perches, conveyed from Obadiah JENNINGS to MOORE on 1 Sep 1806 [see previous entry]; both seal; [no witnesses given]; ack. Muskingum County, 15 Jan 1808, Hans MORRISON, J.P.; entered 28 Jun 1808, recorded 29 Jun 1808.

p. 363 - Indenture, 29 Jun 1808, John COPELAND (wife Caroline), St. Clairsville, BCO; James POLLOCK, Mount Pleasant twp., JCO. For stud horse valued at $380, part of S 25 T 8 R 4, Steubenville district, NBR: [Bolton, Jackson & Co.], 60 acres; his seal, her mark; WIT: Sterling JOHNSTON, Kotts ROBINSON; ack. BCO, Sterling JOHNSTON, J.P.; entered 30 Jun 1808, recorded 11 Jul 1808.

p. 364 - Indenture, 12 Jan 1808, John DEVERS [DEVENS], BCO; Isaac BRANSON, BCO. $780, 138 acres in S 13 T 9 R 5, fee simple; his mark; [no witnesses given]; ack. John WILEY, J.P.; entered 1 Jul 1808, recorded 12 Jul 1808.

p. 365 - Indenture, 26 Dec 1808 [probably 1807], Nicholas GASSAWAY (wife Amelia), BCO; James SINCLAIR, BCO. Whereas S 2 T 9 R 6, Steubenville district, was granted to GASSAWAY by patent dated 5 Apr 1806, now GASSAWAY conveys 320 acres for $800 paid by SINCLAIR; both seal; WIT: Samuel GREGG, James SINCLAIR, Junr.; ack. 26 Dec 1807, Arthur IRWIN, J.P.; entered 6 Jul 1808, recorded 12 Jul 1808.

p. 366 - Indenture, 12 Mar 1808, Robert McBRATNEY (wife Jane), BCO; John McFADDEN, BCO. $335.40, part of S 14 T 7 R 3, NBR: Charles McMANUS, Robert McBRATNEY, 69 acres 3 rods 13 perches; his seal, her mark [name Jean]; [no witnesses given]; ack. 12 Mar 1808, Thos. MITCHELL, J.P.; entered 5 Jul 1808, recorded 12 Jul 1808.

p. 367 - "Know all men," Josiah DILLON (wife Dorothy) conveyed on 6 Oct 1806 to Alexander BOGGS, George IRELAND, Alexander GASTON, and David RUSK [RUSKE], trustees of Reverend Joseph ANDERSON's congregation, an out lot for building a house of public worship (part of lot sold to DILLON by Robert JOHNSTON) as recorded in Book B, p. 8 [p. 84 of abstracts], but the house won't be built so land is transferred back to DILLON for $.25; all seal; WIT: Sterling JOHNSTON, William BROWN; ack. Sterling JOHNSTON, J.P.; entered 5 Jul 1808, recorded 12 Jul 1808.

p. 368 - Indenture, 24 Jun 1808, George SNIDER (wife Barbara), BCO; John WILKINSON, BCO. Whereas SNIDER was granted a patent dated 1 Oct 1806 for S 31 T 7 R 4, now conveying 100 acres 2 rods 20 perches of that S for $200; his seal, her mark; WIT: James CLOYD, Batteal HARRISON; ack. James CLOYD, J.P.; entered 12 Jul 1808, recorded 13 Jul 1808.

p. 369 - Indenture, 19 Nov 1807, Conrod Kotts ROBINSON and John BROWN (wife Phebe), St. Clairsville, BCO; Lucius Horatio STOCKDON, Trenton, Huntington County, New Jersey. $2,2__.00, lots #28, #27, and #19 (NBR: Jacob HOLTZ) in St. Clairsville, each 1/4 acre, plus a tract N of the town containing 4 1/4 acres 9 poles, all conveyed to John BROWN, William ROBINSON, and Daniel McCURDY by John THOMPSON (wife Sally) by deed dated 6 Nov 1806 and recorded Book A, pp. 22-23 [this is probably Book B, p. 89 of abstracts], some already conveyed to Conrod Kotts ROBINSON by William ROBINSON (wife Sarah) and Daniel McCURDY (wife Prescilla) by deed dated 12 May 1807 (p. 240 [p. 117 of abstracts]); Conrod Kotts ROBINSON and John BROWN seal, Phebe mark; WIT: Saml. SPRIGGS, Ralph PHILLIPS; ack. John PATTERSON, J.P.; entered 12 Jul 1808, recorded 14 Jul 1808.

p. 371 - Indenture, 23 Jul 1808, James CORRATHERS, BCO; Thomas LOVE, BCO. $500, lot #33 in St. Clairsville, void if CORRATHERS pays LOVE $500 by 1 Mar 1811; his seal; WIT: George PAULL, James CLOYD; ack. James CLOYD, J.P.; entered 23 Jul 1808, recorded 29 Jul 1808; $129 paid at signing, $316.37 paid on 1 Mar 1810, release signed by Thos. LOVE [no date].

p. 372 - Indenture, 23 Jul 1808, William CONGLETON (wife Nancy), BCO; Alexander GASTON and Robert THOMPSON, BCO. $140, lots #33 and #34 in addition to St. Clairsville as laid off by William MATHERS, sold by Josiah HEDGES to CONGLETON on 5 May 1806 as recorded in Book B, p. 659 (I think this is Book A, p. 484 of the new book [p. 76 of abstracts]), fee simple; both seal; WIT: Notley HAYS, Sterling JOHNSTON; ack. Sterling JOHNSTON, J.P.; entered 24 Jul 1808, recorded 29 Jul 1808.

p. 373 - Indenture, 25 Jul 1808, William FARQUHAR, Wheeling, Ohio County, Virginia; John THOMPSON, St. Clairsville, BCO. $250, lot adjoining St. Clairsville, NBR: John LONG, 3 acres, conveyed to FARQUHAR by James BARNES (wife Nancy) by deed dated 26 Sep 1806; his seal; WIT: Sterling JOHNSTON, George PAULL; ack. Sterling JOHNSTON, J.P.; entered 25 Jul 1808, recorded 29 Jul 1808.

p. 374 - "Whereas" Register of the land office at Steubenville on 20 Jul 1804 granted a certificate to John CLARK of BCO that on conditions he is entitled to a patent for the NW 1/4 S 29 T 5 R 3, 160 acres, now conveys rights of certificate for $430 paid by John KING, BCO, signed 10 Aug 1807; his seal; WIT: Thomas BROWN, Thos. THOMPSON; ack. 10 Aug 1808 [suspect this date is incorrect as document was recorded in Jul 1808], Thos. THOMPSON, J.P., certified by Elijah WOODS [WOOD], Clerk, CCP, 27 Jul 1808.

p. 375 - Indenture, 27 Jun 1808, William CHAPLIN (wife Mary), Ohio County, Virginia; Duncan MORRISON, BCO. $415, part of S 20 T 8 R 5, 17 acres 1 rod 26 perches, land granted to CHAPLIN by patent dated 7 Jan 1808, fee simple; both seal; WIT: Sterling JOHNSTON; ack. Sterling JOHNSTON, J.P.; entered 28 Jul 1808, recorded 30 Jul 1808.

p. 376 - Indenture, 23 Jun 1808, William CHAPLIN (wife Mary), Ohio County, Virginia; John SCOTT, same. $400, part of S 20 T 8 R 5, 200 acres, land granted to CHAPLIN by patent dated 7 Jan 1808, fee simple; both seal; WIT: Robert MORRISON, Sterling JOHNSTON; ack. BCO, Sterling JOHNSTON, J.P.; entered 28 Jul 1808, recorded 30 Jul 1808.

p. 377 - 25 Jun 1808, Wm. CHAPLIN (wife Mary), Ohio County, Virginia; Leonard HEART, BCO. $771, part of S 20 T 8 R 5, 257 acres, land granted to CHAPLIN by patent dated 7 Jan 1808; both seal; WIT: Sterling JOHNSTON; ack. Sterling JOHNSTON, J.P.; entered 28 Jul 1808, recorded 30 Jul 1808.

p. 378 - Indenture, 25 Jun 1808, William CHAPLIN, Ohio County, Virginia; Leonard HEART, BCO. $87, part of S 20 T 8 R 5, NBR: Duncan MORRISON, 29 acres, land granted to CHAPLIN by patent dated 7 Jan 1808, fee simple; he and wife Mary seal [though she is not mentioned at the first of document]; WIT: Sterling JOHNSTON; ack. Sterling JOHNSTON, J.P.; entered 28 Jul 1808, recorded 30 Jul 1808.

p. 379 - Indenture, 27 Jun 1808, William CHAPLIN (wife Mary), Ohio County, Virginia; Caleb ENGLE, BCO. $1,376, all of S 36 T 6 R 4, granted to CHAPLIN by patent dated 8 Sep 1807, fee simple; both seal; WIT: Sterling JOHNSTON; ack. Sterling JOHNSTON, J.P.; entered 28 Jul 1808, recorded 1 Aug 1808.

p. 380 - Indenture, 24 Jun 1808, William CHAPLIN (wife Mary), Ohio County, Virginia; Leonard HEART [HART], BCO. $10, lot #90 in Morristown as laid off by CHAPLIN; both seal; WIT: Robert JOHNSTON; ack. Sterling JOHNSTON, J.P.

p. 381 - Indenture, 25 Jun 1808, William CHAPLIN (wife Mary), Ohio County, Virginia; Lenard HART [HEART], Senr., BCO. $21, lot #1 in Morristown; WIT: Duncan MORRISON, Jacob DOVANBARGOR; ack. Sterling JOHNSTON, J.P.; entered 28 Jul 1808, recorded 1 Aug 1808.

p. 382 - Indenture, 25 Jun 1808, William CHAPLIN (wife Mary), Ohio County, Virginia; Lenard HART, Senr., BCO. $21, lot #2 in Morristown; both seal; WIT: Duncan MORRISON, Jacob DOVENBARGAR; ack. Sterling JOHNSTON, J.P.; entered 28 Jul 1808, recorded 2 Aug 1808.

p. 383 - Indenture, 22 Jun 1808, William CHAPLIN (wife Mary), Ohio County, Virginia; Lenard HART, Senr., BCO. $10, lot #15 in Morristown; both seal; WIT: Duncan MORRISON, Jacob DOVENBARGAR; ack. Sterling JOHNSTON, J.P.; entered 28 Jul 1808, recorded 2 Aug 1808.

p. 384 - Indenture, 25 Jun 18008, William CHAPLIN (wife Mary), Ohio County, Virginia; George HART, BCO. $20, lot #48 in Morristown; both seal; WIT: Duncan MORRISON, Levi LAE--- [possibly LAW?]; ack. Sterling JOHNSTON, J.P.; entered 28 Jul 1808, recorded 2 Aug 1808.

p. 385 - Indenture, 24 Jun 1808, William CHAPLIN (wife Mary), Ohio County, Virginia; Lenard HART, BCO. $20, lot #46 in Morristown; both seal; WIT: Robert JOHNSTON; ack. Sterling JOHNSTON, J.P.; entered 28 Jul 1808, recorded 2 Aug 1808.

p. 385 - Indenture, 22 Jun 1808, William CHAPLIN (wife Mary), Ohio County, Virginia; Margaret HAZLETT, BCO. $110, lot #10 in Morristown; both seal; WIT: Samuell SPRIGG, Josiah HEDGES; ack. Sterling JOHNSTON, J.P.; entered 28 Jul 1808, recorded 2 Aug 1808.

p. 386 - Indenture, 24 Jun 1808, William CHAPLIN (wife Mary), Ohio County, Virginia; Margaret HASLET [HAZLETT], BCO. $20, lot #11 in Morristown; both seal; WIT: Dunan [Duncan] MORRISON; ack. Sterling JOHNSTON, J.P.; entered 28 Jul 1808, recorded 2 Aug 1808.

p. 387 - Indenture, 24 Jun 1808, William CHAPLIN (wife Mary), Ohio County, Virginia; Dunkin [Duncan] MORRISON, BCO. $10, lot #22 in Morristown; both seal; WIT: Wm. RIDDELE, Jacob DOVENBARGAR; ack. Sterling JOHNSTON, J.P.; entered 28 Jul 1808, recorded 3 Aug 1808.

p. 388 - Indenture, 24 Jun 1808, William CHAPLIN (wife Mary), Ohio County, Virginia; Dunkin MORRISON, BCO. $10, lots #17 and #18 in Morristown; both seal; WIT: Moses MILLIGAN; ack. Sterling JOHNSTON, J.P.; entered 28 Jul 1808, recorded 3 Aug 1808.

p. 389 - Indenture, 27 Jun 1808, William CHAPLIN (wife Mary), Ohio County, Virginia; John MORRISON, BCO. $10, lot #55 in Morristown; both seal; WIT: Samuel HOLLOWAY, Jacob DOVENBARGAR; ack. Sterling JOHNSTON, J.P.; entered 28 Jul 1808, recorded 3 Aug 1808.

p. 390 - Indenture, 24 Jun 1808, William CHAPLIN (wife Mary), Ohio County, Virginia; Elizabeth MORRISON, BCO. $10, lot #16 in Morristown; both seal; WIT: James HAZLETT; ack. Sterling JOHNSTON, J.P.; entered 28 Jul 1808, recorded 3 Aug 1808.

p. 391 - Indenture, 24 Jun 1808, William CHAPLIN (wife Mary), Ohio County, Virginia; Mary MORRISON, BCO. $10, lot #60 in Morristown; both seal; WIT: James HAZETT [HAZLETT]; ack. Sterling JOHNSTON, J.P.; entered 28 Jul 1808, recorded 4 Aug 1808.

p. 392 - Indenture, 23 Jun 1808, William CHAPLIN (wife Mary), Ohio County, Virginia; William GROVE, BCO. $10, lot #34 in Morristown; both seal; WIT: Dunan [Duncan] MORRISON; ack. Sterling JOHNSTON, J.P.; entered 28 Jul 1808, recorded 8 Aug 1808.

p. 393 - Indenture, 24 Jun 1808, William CHAPLIN (wife Mary), Ohio County, Virginia; Moses MILLIGAN, BCO. $10, lot #94 in Morristown; both seal;

WIT: Robert JOHNSTON; ack. Sterling JOHNSTON, J.P.; 28 Jul 1808, recorded 4 Aug 1808.

p. 393 - Indenture, 22 Jul Jun 1808, William CHAPLIN (wife Mary), Ohio County, Virginia; John MELLOR, BCO. $25, lot #29 in Morristown; both seal; WIT: Dunan MORRISON, Samuel HALLAWAY; ack. Sterling JOHNSTON, J.P.; entered 28 Jul 1808, recorded 4 Aug 1808.

p. 394 - Indenture, 22 Jun 1808, William CHAPLIN (wife Mary), Ohio County, Virginia; John MELLOR, BCO. $10, lot #14 in Morristown; both seal; WIT: Dunan MORRISON, Sammuel HOLLOWAY; ack. Sterling JOHNSTON, J.P.; entered 28 Jul 1808, recorded 4 Aug 1808.

p. 395 - Indenture, 23 Jun 1808, William CHAPLIN (wife Mary), Ohio County, Virginia; David CHAMBERS, BCO. $10, lot #47 in Morristown; both seal; WIT: Dunan MORRISON; ack. Sterling JOHNSTON, J.P.; entered 28 Jul 1808, recorded 4 Aug 1808.

p. 396 - Indenture, 25 Jun 1808, William CHAPLIN (wife Mary), Ohio County, Virginia; David CHAMBERS, BCO. $37.50, lot #31 in Morristown; both seal; WIT: Dunan MORRISON, James PARK; ack. Sterling JOHNSTON, J.P.; entered 28 Jul 1808, recorded 5 Aug 1808.

p. 397 - Indenture, 22 Jun 1808, William CHAPLIN (wife Mary), Ohio County, Virginia; Jacob DOVENBARGER, BCO. $10, lot #51 in Morristown; both seal; WIT: Dunan MORASON, Samuel HALLOWAY; ack. Sterling JOHNSTON, J.P.; entered 28 Jul 1808, recorded 5 Aug 1808.

p. 398 - Indenture, 22 Jun 1808, William CHAPLIN (wife Mary), Ohio County, Virginia; Jacob DAVENBARIGER, BCO. $10, lot #13 in Morristown; both seal; WIT: Dunan MORRISON, Samuel HALLAWAY; ack. Sterling JOHNSTON, J.P.; entered 8 Aug 1808, recorded 8 Aug 1808.

p. 399 - Indenture, 27 Jun 1808, William CHAPLIN (wife Mary), Ohio County, Virginia; Nicholas [Nicobos] LUNSFORD, same. $10, lot #57 in Morristown; both seal; WIT: Samuel HALLAWAY, Jacob DOVENBARGER; ack. Sterling JOHNSTON, J.P.; entered 28 Jul 1808, recorded 8 Aug 1808.

p. 400 - Indenture, 27 Jun 1808, William CHAPLIN (wife Mary), Ohio County, Virginia; Nicholas LUNSFORD, same. $10, lot #79 in Morristown; both seal; WIT: Samuel HALLAWAY, Jacob DOVENBARGAR; ack. Sterling JOHNSTON, J.P.; entered 28 Jul 1808, recorded 8 Aug 1808.

p. 401 - Indenture, 27 Jun 1808, William CHAPLIN (wife Mary), Ohio County, Virginia; William GAULT, BCO. $10, lot #19 in Morristown; both seal; WIT: Samuel HALLAWAY, Jacob DOVENBARGAR; ack. Sterling JOHNSTON, J.P.; entered 28 Jul 1808, recorded 8 Aug 1808.

p. 402 - Indenture, 27 Jun 1808, William CHAPLIN (wife Mary), Ohio County, Virginia; William GAULT, BCO. $10, lot #20 in Morristown; both seal; WIT: Samauel HALLAWAY, Jacob DOVENBARGAR; ack. Sterling JOHNSTON, J.P.; entered 28 Jul 1808, recorded 8 Aug 1808.

p. 402 - Indenture, 27 Jun 1808, William CHAPLIN (wife Mary), Ohio County, Virginia; Joseph SMITH, Muskingum County, Ohio. $10, lot #3 in Morristown; both seal; WIT: Samuel HALLAWAY, Jacob DOVENBARGAR; ack. Sterling JOHNSTON, J.P.; entered 28 Jul 1808, recorded 9 Aug 1808.

p. 403 - Indenture, 22 Jun 1808, William CHAPLIN (wife Mary), Ohio County, Virginia; Thomas THOMPSON, BCO. $10, lot #7 in Morristown; both seal; WIT: Jacob DOVENBARGAR, Samuel HALLAWAY; ack. Sterling JOHNSTON, J.P.; entered 28 Jul 1808, recorded 9 Aug 1808.

p. 404 - Indenture, 24 Jun 1808, William CHAPLIN (wife Mary), Ohio County, Virginia; David WHERRY, BCO. $10, lot #59 in Morristown; both seal; WIT: Dunan MORRISON; ack. Sterling JOHNSTON, J.P.; entered 28 Jul 1808, recorded 17 Aug 1808.

p. 405 - Indenture, 24 Jun 1808, William CHAPLIN (wife Mary), Ohio County, Virginia; Peter WELLER [WELLON/WILLON], BCO. $10, lot #24 in Morristown; both seal; WIT: Dunan MORRISON, Jacob DOVENBARGAR; ack. Sterling JOHNSTON, J.P.; entered 28 Jul 1808, recorded 17 Aug 1808.

p. 406 - Indenture, 24 Jun 1808, William CHAPLIN (wife Mary), Ohio County, Virginia; Thomas McCRANY, BCO. $10, lot #96 in Morristown; both seal; WIT: Dunan MORRISON; ack. Sterling JOHNSTON, J.P.; entered 28 Jul 1808, recorded 17 Aug 1808.

p. 407 - Indenture, 22 Jun 1808, William CHAPLIN (wife Mary), Ohio County, Virginia; Samuel GRIMES, JCO. $30, lots #37, #42, and #5 in Morristown; both seal; WIT: Dunan MORRISON, Caleb ENGLE; ack. Sterling JOHNSTON, J.P.; entered 28 Jul 1808, recorded 17 Aug 1808.

p. 408 - Indenture, 25 Jun 1808, William CHAPLIN (wife Mary), Ohio County, Virginia; Samuel PILLERS [PILLORS], BCO. $30, lot #35 in Morristown; both seal; WIT: Dunan MORRISON, David CHAMBERS; ack. Sterling JOHNSTON, J.P.; entered 28 Jul 1808, recorded 23 Aug 1808.

p. 409 - Indenture, 23 Jun 1808, William CHAPLIN (wife Mary), Ohio County, Virginia; John SHAY, BCO. $10, lot #77 in Morristown; both seal; WIT: Dunan MORRISON; ack. Sterling JOHNSTON, J.P.; entered 28 Jul 1808, recorded 23 Aug 1808.

p. 410 - Indenture, 22 Jun 1808, William CHAPLIN (wife Mary), Ohio County, Virginia; Samuel HOLLAWAY, BCO. $10, lot #21 in Morristown; both seal; WIT: Dunan MORRISON, John MILLER; ack. Sterling JOHNSTON, J.P.; entered 28 Jul 1808, recorded 23 Aug 1808.

p. 411 - Indenture, 13 Feb 1808, Alexander GRAY (wife Jane), Richland twp., BCO; Richard TRAVIS, same. $190, part of S 32 T 7 R 3, granted to GRAY by patent dated 27 Aug 1807, 58 acres 1 rod 20 perches, fee simple; both mark; WIT: James CLOYD, Jacob NAGLE; ack. James CLOYD, J.P.; entered 9 Aug 1808, recorded 23 Aug 1808.

p. 412 - Indenture, 15 Jun 1808, Christopher WINTER (wife Catherine), Washington County, Pennsylvania; Hugh GILLELAND, BCO. $1,280, S 25 T 9 R 6, 640 acres, fee simple; his seal [WINR?], her mark; [no witnesses given]; ack. Washington County, Jacob LEFFLER, J.P.

p. 413 - Indenture, 24 Dec 1807, Obadiah JENNINGS (wife Ann), JCO; Jacob HOULTZ, BCO. $250.--, out lots #11 (5 acres 20 perches) and #12 (6 3/4 acres) in land adjoining addition (laid out by William MATHERS) to St. Clairsville as laid out by Bazaleel WELLS, conveyed by WELLS (wife Sally) [to JENNINGS]; both seal; WIT: James JOHNSTON, John M. DOWELL, Junr.; ack. Sampn. [Sampson?] V. KING, J.P.; entered 10 Aug 1808, recorded 24 Aug 1808.

p. 414 - Indenture, 5 Apr 1808, Casper SEVERS (wife Anne), St. Clairsville, BCO; James CALDWELL, same. $350, lots #92 and #91 in St. Clairsville, 1/4 acre each, fee simple; his seal, her mark; WIT: Isaac VORE, Jas. CLOYD; ack. Jas. CLOYD, J.P.; entered 16 Aug 1808, recorded 24 Aug 1808.

p. 415 - Indenture, 27 May 1808, Samuel GREGG (wife Ann), BCO; Joseph GRIFFITH, BCO. Whereas S 33 T 7 R 4, Steubenville district, was granted to GREGG (then of Ross County, Ohio) by patent dated 1 Oct 1806, now conveys part of S 33, 100 acres, for $1,175, NBR: Joseph NICHOLSON; both seal; WIT: Thomas NICHOLS, Thos. [CROM], Abraham [CROEN]; ack. 18 Aug 1808, Arthur IRWIN, J.P.; entered 19 Aug 1808, recorded 24 Aug 1808.

p. 417 - Indenture, 23 Aug 1808, Leonard HEART (wife Jemima), BCO; William GAULT, BCO. $126, part of S 20 T 8 R 5, NBR: Duncan MORRISON, granted to HEART by William CHAPLIN on 25 Jun 1808, fee simple; both mark [HART]; WIT: Sterling JOHNSTON, David VANCE; ack. Sterling JOHNSTON, J.P.; 23 Aug 1808, recorded 25 Aug 1808.

p. 418 - Indenture, 23 Jun 1808, William CHAPLIN (wife Mary), Ohio County, Virginia; Isaac BRODERICK, BCO. $200, part of S 20 T 8 R 5, 60 acres, fee simple; both seal; WIT: Robert JOHNSTON; ack. Sterling JOHNSTON, J.P.; entered 19 Aug 1808, recorded 29 Aug 1808.

p. 419 - Indenture, 12 Apr 1808, John McCOLLOCK (wife Mary), Ohio County, Virginia; Robert WADDLE, BCO. $320, part of S 9 T 9 R 6, granted to McCOLLOCK by patent dated 6 Mar 1806; both seal; [no witnesses given]; ack. David LOCKWOOD, Assoc. Judge, BCO.

p. 420 - Indenture, 12Aug 1808, Robert H. JOHNSTON (wife Mary), BCO; James and Samuel CORRATHERS, BCO. $200, 2 acres of land adjoining commons of St. Clairsville, tenants in common and not joint tenants, NBR: John THOMPSON, balance of lot conveyed from JOHNSTON and wife to James CORRATHERS on 4 May 1808, fee simple; his seal, her mark; WIT: Sterling JOHNSTON, George PAULL; ack. Sterling JOHNSTON, J.P.; entered 19 Aug 1808, recorded 29 Aug 1808.

p. 421 - Indenture, 20 Aug 1808, Alexander YOUNG (wife Jenny), BCO; Samuel MUCHMORE, BCO. $508, part of S 18 T 7 R 4, 101 acres 2 rods 12 perches, S granted to YOUNG by patent dated 10 Nov 1807, fee simple; both seal; WIT: Sterling JOHNSTON, Jacob NAGLE; ack. Sterling JOHNSTON, J.P.; entered 21 Aug 1808, recorded 10 Sep 1808.

p. 422 - Indenture, 20 Aug 1808, Alexander YOUNG (wife Jenny), BCO; Abraham GARIDY, BCO. $403, part of S 18 T 7 R 4, NBR: MUTCHMORE [MUCHMORE], granted to YOUNG by patent dated 10 Nov 1807, fee simple; both seal [her name Jean]; WIT: Sterling JOHNSTON, Jacob NAGLE; ack. Sterling JOHNSTON, J.P.; entered 21 Aug 1808, recorded 10 Sep 1808.

p. 423 - Indenture, 20 Aug 1808, Alexander YOUNG (wife Jenny), BCO; Martha JOHNSTON, BCO. $30, part of S 18 T 7 R 4, granted to YOUNG by patent dated 10 Nov 1807, NBR: Adam JOHNSTON, Alexander YOUNG, fee simple; both seal [her name Jean]; WIT: Sterling JOHNSTON, Jacob NAGLE; ack. Sterling JOHNSTON, J.P.; entered 21 Aug 1808, recorded 10 Sep 1808.

p. 425 - Indenture, 20 Aug 1808, Alexander YOUNG (wife Jenny), BCO; Adam JOHNSTON, BCO. $920, W 1/2 of S 18 T 7 R 4, Steubenville district, granted to YOUNG by patent dated 10 Nov 1807; both seal; WIT: Sterling JOHNSTON, Jacob NAGLE; ack. Sterling JOHNSTON, J.P.; entered 21 Aug 1808, recorded 12 Sep 1808.

p. 426 - Indenture, 29 Mar 1808, Robert GIFFEN (wife Hetty), Muskingum County, Ohio; George GIFFEN, BCO. $482, 192 1/2 acres, beginning at SE corner of S 9 T 6 R 3, granted to Robert GIFFEN by patent dated 1806; both seal; WIT: Sterling JOHNSTON, William SHARPLESS; ack. Sterling JOHNSTON, J.P.; entered 27 Aug 1808, recorded 12 Sep 1808.

p. 427 - Indenture, 13 May 1807, Rebeckah TODD and Robert TODD (wife Sarah), Kirkwood twp., BCO; Thomas HUNNICUT [HUNNICUTT] and Micajah BAILEY, BCO. $424, SE corner of S 8 T 8 R 6, 160 acres, fee simple; all seal; WIT: Sibbilla TODD, Rody GRIER [her mark]; ack. John GRIER, J.P.; entered 10 Sep 1808, recorded 13 Sep 1808.

p. 428 - Indenture, 12 Sep 1808, Job ENGLE (wife Sarah), Richland twp., BCO; Isaac BRODERICK, same. $900, beginning at SE corner of S 21 T 7 R 4, NBR: Abraham ENGLE, John HANES, 100 acres, part of land in Richland twp. conveyed by Obadiah HARDESTY to Abraham ENGLE on 27 Aug 1804, as recorded in Book A, p. 346 (p. 285 of new book [p. 46 of abstracts]); both seal; WIT: Sterling JOHNSTON, Adam JOHNSTON; ack. Sterling JOHNSTON, J.P.; entered 12 <u>Aug</u> [Sep written in above] 1808, recorded 15 <u>Aug</u> 1808.

p. 430 - Indenture, 18 "first month (called April)" [suspect should have been "fourth month"] 1808, Horton HOWARD (wife Hannah), BCO; John NICHOLS, BCO. $1,120, S 1/2 of S 10 T 6 R 3, tract purchased at land office in Steubenville and granted to HOWARD by patent dated 22 Jan 1806, 320 acres, subject to taxes; both seal; WIT: Levinah HALL, Aquila M. BOTTON; ack. James ALEXANDER, Judge; entered 21 Sep 1808, recorded 24 Sep 1808.

p. 431 - Indenture, 20 Aug 1808, Borden STANTON (wife Charlotte), BCO; Thomas CAMPBELL, BCO. $500, 145 acres, NE 1/4 of S 11 T 6 R 3, except 15 acres sold to Thomas THOMPSON on S side of 1/4, NBR: Thomas CAMPBELL, S granted to STANTON by patent dated 18 Feb 1806; both seal; WIT: Thos. MITCHELL, Enoch STANTON; ack. Thos. MITCHELL, J.P.; entered 22 Sep 1808, recorded 24 Sep 1808.

p. 432 - Indenture, 26 Sep 1808, Abraham LASH (wife Mary), BCO; Moses MOREHEAD, BCO. $640, part of S 4 T 7 R 4, 60 acres, NBR: Volentine [Valentine] AULT, conveyed from Bazaleel WELLS (wife Sally) to LASH on 18

Dec 1798, fee simple; his seal, her mark; WIT: Sterling JOHNSTON, John THOMPSON; ack. Sterling JOHNSTON, J.P.; entered 26 Sep 1808, recorded 27 Sep 1808.

p. 434 - Indenture, 28 Sep 1808, Caleb ENGLE (wife Mary), BCO; William WILLSON, BCO. $460, part of S 36 T 6 R 4, 166 acres, granted to William CHAPLIN by patent dated 8 Sep 1807, conveyed by CHAPLIN (wife Mary) to ENGLE on 27 Jun 1808, fee simple; both seal; WIT: Isaac MERRIT, Sterling JOHNSTON; ack. Sterling JOHNSTON, J.P.; entered 28 Sep 1808, recorded 1 Oct 1808.

p. 435 - Indenture, 11 Dec 1807, Borden STAUNTON [STANTON] (wife Charlotte), BCO; Thomas THOMPSON, BCO. $500, SE 1/4 of S 11 T 6 R 3, Steubenville district, 160 acres; both seal; WIT: Thos. MITCHEEL [MITCHELL], Enock STANTON; ack. 11 Dec 1807, Thos. MITCHELL, J.P.; entered 5 Oct 1808, recorded 1 Nov 1808.

p. 436 - Indenture, 20 Aug 1808, Borden STANTON (wife Charlotte), BCO; Thomas THOMSON [THOMPSON], BCO. $1__.00, land in SW side of NE 1/4 of S 11 T 6 R 3, 15 acres, granted to STANTON by patent dated 18 Feb 1806; both seal; WIT: Thos. MITCHELL, Enock STANTON; ack. Thos. MITCHELL, J.P.; entered 6 Oct 1808, recorded 2 Nov 1808.

p. 437 - Indenture, 6 Aug 1808, Jonathan TAYLOR (wife Ann), Mount Pleasant twp., JCO; William PARKS, BCO. $500, land beginning in center of S 12 T 6 R 3, 85 3/4 acres, granted to TAYLOR by patent dated 10 Aug 1807; both seal; WIT: George KINSAY, John BARNS; ack. James ALEXANDER, Assoc. Judge; entered 8 Oct 1808, recorded 2 Nov 1808.

p. 438 - Indenture, 10 Oct 1808, Peter WIRICH (wife Catharine), BCO; Robert COUGHRON, BCO. $225, part of S 14 T 8 R 4, NBR: John RYAN, 50 acres, part of a piece conveyed to WIRICH by Jacob COON [KUHN] (wife Barbara) on 10 Feb 1808 as recorded in Book B, p. 236 (p. 252 of new book [p. 119 of abstracts]), fee simple; both mark; WIT: Sterling JOHNSTON, Jacob FRANCIS [his mark]; ack. Sterling JOHNSTON, J.P.; entered 10 Oct 1808, recorded 4 Nov 1808.

p. 440 - "Know all men," Matilda WAY of Sadsberry twp., Lancaster County, Pennsylvania, appoint Thomas VICKERS of East Calm twp., Chester County, Pennsylvania, as attorney to deal with land in BCO, 3 Sep 1808; his seal; WIT: Robert MILLER, Warwick MILLER; ack. Chester County, Pennsylvania, 3 Sep 1808, Robert MILLER, J.P., certified by P. HIESTER; entered 24 Oct 1808, recorded 8 Nov 1808.

p. 441 - Indenture, 23 Sep 1808, Alexander BOGGS (wife Hannah), BCO; John WITCHELL, Wheeling, Virginia. $1,008, part of S 10 T 7 R 4, NBR: William BOGGS, David McWILLIAMS, 166 acres 2 rods, same land conveyed by Ezekiel BOGGS by indenture dated 11 Jun 1805, recorded in Book A, p. 444 (p. 375 of new book [p. 60 in abstracts]) granted to Alexander BOGGS; his seal, her mark; WIT: Joseph GIBBONS, Mahlon SMITH; ack. John PATTERSON, J.P.

p. 442 - Indenture, 23 Sep 1808, Charles McMANAS [McMANUS], BCO; John WITCHELL, Wheeling, Virginia. $900, part of S 14 T 7 R 3, NBR: Robert McBRATNY, Francis COOPER, 160 acres, conveyed to McMANUS by Bazaleel WELLS (wife Sally) on 13 Aug 1807 as recorded in Book B, p. 170 (p. 175 in new book [p. 108 of abstracts]); his seal; WIT: Mahlon SMITH, Joseph GIBBONS; ack. John PATTERSON, J.P.; entered 25 Oct 1808, recorded 11 Nov 1808.

p. 444 - Indenture, 25 Oct 1808, Michael GROVES (wife Elizabeth), BCO; Henry Hawkens Haislep EVANS, BCO. $180, lot #77 in St. Clairsville; his seal, her mark; WIT: Sterling JOHNSTON, W. BOOKER; ack. Sterling JOHNSTON, J.P.; entered 25 Oct 1808, recorded 14 Nov 1808.

p. 445 - Indenture, 30 Aug 1808, Robert GILKISON [ATKISON] (wife Mary), BCO; Josiah DILLON, BCO. $300, part of S 4 T 5 R 4, 60 acres 33 perches; his seal, her mark; WIT: Levin OKEY, James ____; ack. Levin OKEY; 25 Oct 1808, recorded 15 Nov 1808.

p. 446 - Indenture, [28 Oct 1808], Jacob WINLIN (wife Margaret), BCO; Richard POWEL, BCO. $200, 30 acres 16 1/2 perches, part of survey of 100 acres to WINLIN by James EDGINGTON out of S 4 T 4 R 4, both mark; WIT: Levin OKEY, Edw. BRYSON; ack. Levin OKEY, J.P.

p. 447 - Indenture, 26 Oct 1808, William BROWN (wife Sally), BCO; Michael GROVES, BCO. $180, lot #14 in land adjoining addition to St. Clairsville as laid out by Bazaleel WELLS, 5 acres 3 rods 30 perches, conveyed to BROWN by Obadiah JENNINGS on 2 Sep 1806 as recorded in Book B, p. 1 [p. 83 of abstracts], fee simple; both seal; WIT: Sterling JOHNSTON, Mary JOHNSTON; ack. Sterling JOHNSTON, J.P.; entered 31 Oct 1808, recorded 15 Nov 1808.

p. 448 - "Whereas" register of lands in Steubenville on 20 Feb 1806 granted a certificate to Matilda WAY of Sadsbury twp. in Lancaster County, Pennsylvania to patent NE 1/4 S 23 T 8 R 6, 160 acres, by Thomas VICKELS of East Caln twp., Chester County, Pennsylvania, for $320 paid by Samuel SULLIVAN, St. Clairsville, BCO, conveys certificate and rights, signed 24 Oct 1808; his seal;

WIT: Sterling JOHNSTON, Enos PICKERING; ack. Sterling JOHNSTON, J.P.; entered 5 Nov 1808, recorded 16 Nov 1808.

p. 449 - Indenture, 12 Aug 1808, James EDGERTON (wife Sarah) and George STARBUCK (wife Elizabeth), BCO; Jacob WINDLAND, BCO. $200, part of S 4 T 5 R 4, Marietta district, 100 acres; all seal; WIT: Isaac MOORE, Joseph COX; ack. Isaac MOORE; entered 6 Nov 1808, recorded 16 Nov 1808.

p. 450 - Indenture, 12 Nov 1808, John VANY [VANVEY, VANWAY], BCO; Daniel McPEEK, BCO. VANY owes McPEEK $35.21, secures by conveying personal property (cow and heifer, set of carpenter tools, wind mill, some flax, bed and bedding, 2,000 feet of boards, grind stone, 2 hogs, peach trees, spinning wheel, 2 chairs, 2 chests, looking glass, pot and skillet, wash tub, churn, bucket), transaction void if $23.33 paid with interest by 1 Jun 1809, plus $11.66 before 1 Jun 1810; [VANVEY's] seal, McPEEK's mark; WIT: Sterling JOHNSTON, Robt. GRIFFITH; ack. Sterling JOHNSTON, J.P.; entered 12 Nov 1808, recorded 16 Nov 1808.

p. 451 - Indenture, 14 Nov 1808, James CALDWELL (wife Nancy), St. Clairsville, BCO; John HINDS [HINES, HANES], BCO. $300, lot #96 in St. Clairsville, conveyed to CALDWELL by David NEWELL on 28 Sep 1803, fee simple; both seal; WIT: Am. JOHNSTON, Junr., Sterling JOHNSTON; ack. Sterling JOHNSTON, J.P.; entered 14 Nov 1808, recorded 17 Nov 1808.

p. 452 - Indenture, 16 Nov 1808, Mahlon SMITH and Isaac VORE, BCO; James MOORE, Loudon County, Virginia. $260, 1/2 of lot #68 in St. Clairsville, 1/8 acre; both seal; WIT: Sterling JOHNSTON, Jos. JOHNSTON; ack. Sterling JOHNSTON, J.P.; entered 15 Nov 1808, recorded 17 Nov 1808.

p. 454-455 - Plat of Barnesville. (See Appendix.)

p. 456 - ack. of plat by James BARNES, Ss 15 and 21 T 8 R 6, dated 9 Nov 1808; his seal; certified by Sterling JOHNSTON, J.P.; entered 9 Nov 1808, recorded 23 Nov 1808.

p. 457 - Indenture, 7 Sep 1808, Barnet GROVES (wife Hannah), BCO; Henry WOLGAMOAT, BCO. $112.50, part of S 3 T 9 R 6, Steubenville district, [references a patent but no details as to date or recording], NBR: William GROVES, Moses MILLIGAN, Robt. MORRIS and others, 50 acres; both seal; WIT: John ISRAEL, Alexander DALLAS, Junr.; ack. Duncan MORRISON, J.P.

p. 458 - "Know all men," Thomas HOWELL, BCO, for natural love and affection for his six children--sons John HOWELL and Aaron HOWELL, daughters Hannah CAIN, Ruth HOWELL, Rhode HOWELL, and Emma HOWELL--Thomas moving, signed 24 Nov 1808; his seal; WIT: Alexander NOBLE, Reuben PREBBLE; ack. David RUBLE, Justice of BCO and York twp.

p. 459 - Indenture, 9 Oct 1805, John CLARK, BCO; Phillip DODDRIDGE [no location given]. $1,000, E 1/2 of S 4 T 6 R 3, 320 acres except for 40 acres in NE corner sold to John PURDY, void if CLARK pays debt with interest from 17 Aug 1802 by 1 Jul 1807; both seal; WIT: Zee SPRIGG, John GOODEN, G. MILLER; ack. Thos. THOMPSON, J.P.; entered 16 Nov 1808, recorded 24 Nov 1808.

p. 460 - Indenture, 2 Jul 1808, Thomas WILSON, BCO; John EDWARDS, BCO. $630, part of NW 1/4 of S 13 T 10 R 6; his seal; WIT: John MOORE, Robert McBRIDE; ack. 2 Jul 1808, BCO, Barnet GROVES, J.P.; entered 8 Dec 1808, recorded 26 Dec 1808.

p. 461 - Indenture, 1 Jul 1808, John MOORE (wife Hannah), BCO; Thomas WILSON, BCO. $450, NW 1/4 of S 13 T 10 R 6, fee simple; his seal, her mark; WIT: Robert McBRIDE, Barnet GROVES; ack. 1 Jul 1808, Barnet GROVES, J.P.; entered 8 Dec 1808, recorded 27 Dec 1808.

p. 462 - Indenture, 27 Aug 1808, Jacob ENDLY (wife Mary), Fayette County, Pennsylvania; David MOORE, Fayette County, Pennsylvania. $1,106, part of S 28 T 6 R 3, NBR: Frederick AMRINE, 158 acres 1 rod 17 perches; both seal; WIT: Isaac ROGERS, Jno. M. C. HEZLIP; ack. Fayette County, Nathaniel BREADING, 1st Assoc. Judge, CCP; entered 10 Dec 1808, recorded 22 Dec 1808.

p. 463 - Indenture, 22 Oct 1808, Henry WILLIAMS (wife Zelpha), Warren twp., BCO; George STARBUCK, BCO. $300, NW 1/4 of S 1 T 8 R 6, 160 acres; his seal, her mark; WIT: John GRIER, Robert GRIER; ack. John GRIER, J.P.; entered 12 Dec 1808, recorded 28 Dec 1808.

p. 464 - Indenture, 28 Nov 1808, Hugh BRYSON (wife Sarah [Saras]), BCO; Edward BRYSON, BCO. $500, beginning at NW corner of S 33 T 4 R 3, 100 acres; his mark, her seal; WIT: Dannel THOMAS, John BRYSON; ack. David RUBLE, J.P.; entered 13 Dec 1808, recorded 29 Dec 1808.

p. 465 - Indenture, 1 Oct 1808, Robert COUGHRON (wife Rebecah), BCO; Mathew PATTON, BCO. $216, part of S 20 T 4 R 2, NBR: Mathew PATTON, 87 acres 16 perches; both mark; [no witnesses given]; ack. Thos THOMPSON, J.P.; entered 14 Dec 1808, recorded 29 Dec 1808.

p. 466 - Indenture, 12 Aug 1808, James EDGERTON (wife Sarah) and George STARBUCK (wife Elizabeth), BCO; John BROWN, BCO. $100, part of S 4 T 5 R 4, Marietta district, 50 acres; all seal; WIT: Isaac MOORE, Joseph COX; ack. Isaac MOORE, J.P.; entered 14 Dec 1808, recorded 31 Jan 1808 [suspect Dec].

p. 467 - Indenture, Indenture, 15 Dec 1808, Archibald KERR, BCO; Samuel CLARK, BCO. KERR owes CLARK $300, to secure debt conveys personal property (brown horse, red cow, black steer, . . . note of $25, void if conveyance of property made to John WORKMAN for land KERR sold to WORKMAN; his seal; WIT: William BELL, Campbell LEFEVER; ack. Sterling JOHNSTON, J.P.; entered 15 Dec 1808, recorded 6 Feb 1809.

p. 468 - Indenture, 5 Nov 1808, Henry JOHNSTON (wife Martha), BCO; Jacob RILEY, JCO. $200, lots #1 and #2 in addition to St. Clairsville as laid out by William MATHERS, conveyed to JOHNSTON by MATHERS on 25 Mar 180_ [5, recorded on p. 380 of book (p. 61 of abstracts)]; his seal, her mark; [no witnesses given]; ack. Sterling JOHNSTON, J.P.; entered 21 Dec 1808, recorded 5 Feb 1809.

p. 469 - "Know all men," Jacob RIELY, JCO, for $1 paid by Zenas KIMBERLY, JCO, lots #1 and #2 in [addition to?] St. Clairsville, void if obligation dated 2 Jun 1806 for payment of $100 to KIMBERLY is made within 1 year of this date ($36.36 paid on 29 Oct 1808), signed 12 Nov 1808; his seal; WIT: Benedict WELLS; released 30 Mar 1812, WIT: John FERGUSON, Junr.; release entered 8 Apr 1812, recorded 8 Apr 1812.

p. 470 - Indenture, 23 Nov 1808, Jonathan TAYLOR (wife Ann), Mountpleasant twp., JCO; John PICKERING, BCO. $600, NW 1/4 of S 12 T 6 R 3, granted to TAYLOR by patent dated 10 Aug 1807; both seal; WIT: Nathan UPDEGRAFF, Thos. MITCHELL; ack. Thos. MITCHELL, J.P.; entered 21 Dec 1808, recorded 7 Feb 1809.

p. 471 - Indenture, 23 Nov 1808, Jonathan TAYLOR (wife Ann), Mountpleasant twp., JCO; Abner LAMBERT, BCO. $200, beginning at NE corner of S 12 T 6 R 3, NBR: Wm. PARKS, 85 3/4 acres, granted to TAYLOR by patent dated 10 Aug 1807; both seal; WIT: Nathan UPDEGRAFF, Ann UPDEGRAFF; ack. Thos. MITCHELL, J.P.; entered 21 Dec 1808, recorded 8 Feb 1809.

p. 472 - Indenture, 29 Dec 1806, James SINCLAIR (wife Mary), BCO; Ignetious BYRNES, Loudoun County, Virginia. Whereas SINCLAIR received patent for S 17 T 7 R 5, Steubenville district, dated 6 Jun 1806, for $440, SW 1/4 of S 17 T 7 R 5; both seal; WIT: Samuel GREGG, David NICHOLS, James HOGE,

Asahel TOMKINS, James SINCLAIR, Junr.; ack. 25 Apr 1807, BCO, Arthur IRWIN, J.P.; entered 26 Dec 1808, recorded 8 Feb 1809.

p. 473 - Indenture, 12 Aug 1808, Garret SNEDEKER (wife Elizabeth), Brook County, Virginia; Rudolph WILLMAN, BCO. $400, 104 acres, part of NW 1/4 of S 1 T 9 R 5, granted to SNEDEKER by patent dated 10 Sep 1806, fee simple; both seal; WIT: Moses MERRIT, William V. MARQUIS; ack. 12 Aug 1808, Moses MERRIT, J.P.; entered 10 Jan 1809, recorded 9 Feb 1809.

p. 474 - Indenture, 20 Aug 1808, Adam JOHNSTON (wife Peggy), BCO; Richard TRUAX, BCO. $707, beginning at NE corner of S 18 T 7 R 4, 107 acres 3 rods 38 perches, granted to Alexander YOUNG by patent dated 10 Nov 1807, YOUNG conveyed to JOHNSTON on this date; both seal [her name Marget]; WIT: Robert JOHNSTON, Sterling JOHNSTON; ack. 6 Jan 1809, Sterling JOHNSTON, J.P.; entered 6 Jan 1809, recorded 11 Feb 1809.

p. 475 - Indenture, 13 Aug 1808, John EDWARDS (wife Margret), Richland twp., BCO; John BELL, same. $400, 65 acres 80 perches on waters of Wheeling Creek, part of S 36 T 7 R 4, granted to John EDWARDS, Senr., by patent dated 7 Apr 1806, conveyed by John Senr., to John EDWARDS, Junr., by deed dated 28 May 1806; John's mark; WIT: Moses MERRIT, Polly MERRIT; ack. 13 Aug 1808, Moses MERRIT, J.P.; entered 16 Jan 1809, recorded 14 Feb 1809.

p. 477 - Indenture, 15 Dec 1808, Thomas SHARP (wife Jenny), Washington County, Pennsylvania; John McFADDEN, JCO. $600, 300 acres, W 1/2 of S 9 T 8 R 5, S granted to SHARP by patent dated 8 May 1806; both seal; WIT: Emos PICKERING, David BALDWIN, Josiah RODGERS; ack. Emos PICKERING, J.P. for Union twp., BCO; entered 20 Jan 1809, recorded 14 Feb 1809.

p. 478 - Indenture, 15 Dec 1808, Thomas SHARP (wife Jenny), Washington County, Pennsylvania; Elizabeth TAYLOR, BCO. $100, part of SE 1/4 of S 9 T 8 R 5, 50 acres, S granted to SHARP by patent dated 8 May 1806; both seal; WIT: Emos PICKERING, David BALDWIN, Josiah RODGERS; ack. Emos PICKERING, J.P.; entered 20 Jan 1809, recorded 15 Feb 1809.

p. 479 - Certification over signature of Thomas Jefferson, President, that Thomas SHARP of Washington County, Pennsylvania, having deposited a certificate at Steubenville that he has made full payment for S 9 T 8 R 5, grant is thereby made over seal of U.S. in Washington on 8 May 1806, by Tho. Jefferson, James MADISON, Secretary of the State.

p. 480 - "Know all men," Chalkley RAKESTRAW, BCO, for $60 paid by Jas. KIRKWOOD, BCO, convey personal property (wagon, horse, 3 cows, etc.) on property now occupied by RAKESTRAW, signed 21 Nov 1808; his seal; WIT: Andrew MITCHELL; entered 23 Jan 1809, recorded 15 Feb 1809.

p. 480 - Indenture, 12 Aug 1808, Garret SNEDEKER (wife Elizabeth), Brook County, Virginia; John SNEDEKER, BCO. $640, 221 acres, part of W 1/2 of S 1 T 9 R 5, granted to Garret by patent dated 10 Sep 1806; his seal, her mark; WIT: Moses MERRIT; William V. MARQUIS; ack. 12 Aug 1808, Moses MERRIT, J.P.; entered 2 Feb 1809, recorded 16 Feb 1809.

p. 482 - Certification of J. M. BECKETT, Recorder of BCO, certifies copy of Book B, made by order of the County Commissioners at their Spring Session 1889, signed 1 Apr 1890.

[end of Vol. B]

Deed Abstracts, Belmont County, Ohio

Volume C (Feb 1809 - Feb 1811)

p. 1 - Thos. COHOON allows his patented invention of "a new and useful improvement in flax and hemp machine" to be made, used, and vended within the state of Ohio by Oliver PERSON of Nelson twp., Madison County, New York, for fourteen years, sgn: 24 Nov 1808; WIT: [none given]; PERSON then assigns rights to Horton HOWARD, BCO, for areas of Jefferson, Belmont, or Columbiana Counties, Ohio; sgn: 8 Feb 1809; WIT: Martin PIERSON, Henry HOWARD; ack. 8 Feb 1809, [Oliver PIERSON], Sterling JOHNSTON, J.P.; ent. 8 Feb 1809, rec. 16 Feb 1809.

p. 2 - Indenture, 2 Feb 1809, William FROST (wife Nancy), Richland twp., BCO; William PORTER, Finley twp., Washington County, Pennsylvania. $500, lot #157 in St. Clairsville, 1/4 acre, plat recorded in Book A, p. 31; also two back Lots #150 and #108, fee simple; both seal; WIT: John PATTERSON, James HEDGES; ack. 13 Feb 1809, John PATTERSON, J.P.; ent. 14 Feb 1809, rec. [16] Feb 1809.

p. 3 - Indenture, 14 Feb 1809, Samuel ROSE [however, second part of deed refers to <u>James</u> ROSE], Feyatte County, Pennsylvania; Obadia STILLWELL, Ohio County, Virginia. $100, two lots in or near St. Clairsville, 1/4 acre each, fee simple; WIT: Robt. GRIFFITH, Sterling JOHNSTON; ack. Sterling JOHNSTON, J.P., ent. 14 Feb 1809, rec. 16 Feb 1809.

p. 4 - Indenture, 2 Dec 1808, David RUBLE (wife Susanna), BCO; George KITTZS, BCO. $300, lot on Capteen Creek, part S 20 T 4 R 3, deed by U.S. to RUBLE, 200 acres; both seal [her name Susany]; WIT: Liven OKEY, [Aethen] OKEY; ack. 2 Dec 1808, Liven OKEY, justice, [her name Susannah], ent. 21 Feb 1809, rec. <u>17</u> Feb 1809.

p. 6 - Indenture, 22 Feb 1809, George MIRES, <u>Licken</u> County, Ohio; William CRAIG; BCO. $35, NBR: John DUGAN, 1.5 acre, 22 rods, conveyed from David NEWALL (wife Sally) on 18 Oct 1803, near west end of St. Clairsville, fee simple; his seal; WIT: Sterling JOHNSTON, Mary JOHNSTON; ack. Sterling JOHNSTON, J.P., ent. 22 Feb 1809, rec. 27 Feb 1809.

p. 7 - Indenture, 23 Feb 1809, Alexander McWILLIAMS, Junr. (wife Peggy), farmer, BCO; John McWILLIAMS, farmer, BCO. $300, S 25 T 4 R 2, NBR: Peter ALEXANDER, 140 acres, 1 rod, 25 perches, and dwelling house; his seal, her mark; WIT: William BARNES, John ALEXANDER; ack. James ALEXANDER, Assoc. Judge, ent. 4 Mar 1809, rec. 9 Mar 1809.

p. 8 - Indenture, 23 Feb 1809, Alexander WILLIAMSON [but later McWILLIAMS], Junr., (wife Peggy), farmer; John McWILLIAMS, farmer, BCO. $70, NE corner S 25 T 4 R 2, 50 acres 35 perches; his seal, her mark; WIT: William BARNES, John ALEXANDER; ack. James ALEXANDER, Assoc. Judge, ent. 4 Mar 1809, rec. 9 Mar 1809.

p. 9 - Indenture, 4 Feb 1809, James POLLOCK [POLLICK] (wife Mary), Jefferson County, Ohio; John COPELAND [COPLAND], BCO. $400, 60 acres, part of S 25 T 8 R 4, conveyed from COPLAND to POLLICK on 29 Jun 1808; his seal, her mark; WIT: Sterling JOHNSTON, Jacob NAGLE,; ack. 1 Mar 1809, Sterling JOHNSTON, J.P.

p. 11 - Indenture, 13 Feb 1809, Thomas IRELAND (wife Sally), BCO; George PAULL, BCO. $200, lots #33 and #34 in addition on south side of St. Clairsville; his seal, her mark; WIT: James CLOYD, Robert GRIFFITH; ack. James CLOYD, J.P., ent. 5 Mar 1809, rec. 15 Mar 1809.

p. 12 - Indenture, 17 Jan 1809, Philip McGRAW (wife Margaret), BCO; James PAULL, Junr., Feyatte [sic] County, Pennsylvania. $930, part of S 6 T 7 R 4, NBR: David HUTCHINSON, 232 acres 1 rod 39 perches, plus buildings; his seal, her mark; WIT: James CLOYD, John PATTERSON; ack. James CLOYD, ent. 5 Mar 1800, rec. 16 Mar same.

p. 13 - Indenture, 24 Mar 1809, Jacob HOLTZ (wife Peggy), BCO; William GOUGH, BCO. $285, out lot #11, 5 acres 20 perches, out lot #12, 6 3/4 acres, in addition to St. Clairsville laid out by Bazaleel WELLS adjoining addition laid out by William MATHERS, conveyed to HOLTZ by Obediah JENNINGS (wife Ann) on 24 Dec 1807, in Book B, p. 497, fee simple; both mark; WIT: Joseph HAINS, Robert H. JOHNSTON; ack. Sterling JOHNSTON, J.P., ent. 6 Mar 1809, rec. 16 same.

p. 14 - Indenture, 25 Feb 1809, Allen BOND (wife Sarah), BCO; heirs and assigns of Enos BROOMHALL deceased, "agreeable to a contract between them bearing date March the eleventh one thousand eight hundred and five," BCO. $800, NE side of S 13 T 8 R 5, Steubenville district, patented [to BOND] on 21 Mar 1808, 320 acres, NBR: Allen BOND, Wm. EWERS, and others, fee simple; both seal; WIT: Samuel HOLLAWAY, Thomas DUNN; ack. Duncan MORRISON, J.P., ent. 7 Mar 1809, rec. 18 same.

p. 16 - Indenture, 18 Oct 1808, Richard TRAVASS, BCO; Mathew [Mathias] CRAY, Senr., BCO. For personal estate, to be void if $40 plus interest paid by 18 Oct 1809; both parties seal; WIT: Samuel ISRIAL, Sterling JOHNSTON; ack. 27 Feb 1809, Sterling JOHNSTON, J.P., ent. 27 Mar 1809, rec. 28 same.

p. 17 - Indenture, 27 Mar 1809, Ami MUSSARD, Green County, Pennsyslvania; James SMITH, BCO. For delivery by MUSSARD of 2,400 gallons of whiskey due on 15 Mar 1812 at landing place on property, secured by tract of land deeded on that date to MUSSARD by SMITH, void if whiskey delivered; WIT: Briggs STEWART, Cornelius BELVEAL; ack. 28 Mar 1809 [to be her act], David LOCKWOOD, Assoc. Judge, ent. 28 Mar 1809, rec. 10 Apr 1809; release 9 May 1812 by James SMITH, WIT: Sampson COLE.

p. 18 - Indenture, 18 Mar 1809, Henry SMITH (wife Mary), Ohio County, Virginia; James SMITH, Washington County, NWT. For "one-third part of tract of land in Ohio County, Virginia in the great bend of Wheeling Creek, formerly property of our father James SMITH, Senr., deceased, who willed the same to Henry Thomas & James SMITH at his decease and on a devetion taken place by mutual consent of us three brothers" the portion with father's residence goes to James, total of land is 400 acres, patent of which in hands of Henry SMITH, now for James's one-third Henry transfers 160 acres, part of lot [S?] 35 T 1 R 2, NWT, Washington County, 160 acres out of total of 200, remaining 40 acres previously sold by Henry to Martin SHEENY, originally granted to Henry by Absolem MARTIN of same territory by deed dated 13 May 1795; WIT: Cornelius STEENROD, Valentine SAUERHEBER, John EVANS [his mark]; ack. 20 Mar 1809 by SAUERHEBER and EVANS as witnesses to signing of deed, David LOCKWOOD, Assoc. Judge, ent. 28 Mar 1809, rec. 10 Apr same.

p. 20 - Indenture, 20 Mar 1809, Morten [Martin] and Catrine SHUE, BCO; James SMITH, BCO. $400, 40 acres in lot [S?] 35 T 1 R 2, NBR: Benjamin LOCKWOOD, part of 200 acres that Henry SMITH bought of Absalom MORTEN, conveyed by Henry to James; both mark; WIT: Valentine SAUERHEBER, Peter FARRIL; ack. [giving relationship of Catharine as wife of Martin] David LOCKWOOD, Assoc. Judge, ent. 28 Mar 1809, rec. 11 Apr same.

p. 21 - Indenture, 27 Mar 1809, James SMITH (wife Mary), BCO; Ami MUSSARD, Green County, Pennsylvania. $2,200, 200 acres, part of lot [S?] 35 T 1 R 2, originally granted by U.S. of Jno. HOPKINS, conveyed by HOPKINS to William DUER, by DUER to Laben BRONSON, by BRONSON to Absalom MARTIN, by MARTIN to Henry SMITH, by Henry 40 acres to Martin SHUE which has now been conveyed to James SMITH, 160 acres to James SMITH, total now conveyed by James SMITH (wife Mary) to Ami MUSSARD, patent registered in Book A in treasury office of the U.S., deeds recorded in recorder's office at Marietta and St. Clairsville, [MUSSARD referred to as male]; WIT: Cornelius BELVOAL, Briggs STEWART, Miles HART; ack. David LOCKWOOD, Assoc. Judge, ent. 28 Mar 1809, rec. 11 Apr same.

p. 22 - Indenture, 29 Mar 1809, Robert CARNES [CAINES], BCO; Robert HOPPER, BCO. HOPPER bound in a joint bond or obligation with BARNES to Joseph GILL, Washington County, Ohio, for $100 to be paid by 29 Sep 1811, securing debt by conveying lot #39 in St. Clairesville, conveyed to CARNES by Sterling JOHNSTON on 15 Oct 1805, void if debt paid; WIT: Sterling JOHNSTON; ack. Sterling JOHNSTON, J.P., ent. 29 Mar 1809, rec. 12 Apr same.

p. 23 - Indenture, 28 Dec 1808, James SMITH, BCO; Sterling JOHNSTON, BCO. $20, lot in St. Clairsville, NBR: Robert LAUGHLIN; his mark; WIT: James CLOYD, Robert JOHNSTON; ack. 28 Dec 1808, James CLOYD, J.P., ent. 4 Apr 1809, rec. 14 same.

p. 24 - Indenture, 20 Mar 1809, David VANCE, Esqr., BCO; Sterling JOHNSTON, BCO. $10, land lying between Henry CLOSE, James WILKINS, and Sterling JOHNSTON; WIT: James CLOYD; ack. James CLOYD, J.P.

p. 24 - Indenture, 20 Mar 1809, James JOHNSTON, BCO; Sterling JOHNSTON, BCO. $15, tract of land at SE corner of land where James now lives to land belonging to Sterling, ; WIT: James CLOYD; ack. 20 Mar 1809, James CLOYD, J.P., ent. 10 Apr 1809, rec. 14 same.

p. 25 - Indenture, 21 Mar 1809, Sterling JOHNSTON (wife Mary), BCO; Zacheus [Zachariah] HAYS and John NORRIS, BCO. $1,000, NBR: William WOODS, 99 acres 2 rods 26 perches, fee simple; WIT: Notley HAYS, Joseph HARRIS; ack. 25 Mar 1809, James CLOYD, J.P.

p. 26 - Indenture, 13 Oct 1808, John EDWARDS, Senr. (wife Eleanor), BCO; James EDWARDS, BCO. $160, part of NW 1/4 S 13 T 10 R 6, 80 acres, conveyed by John MOORE to Thomas WILLSON by deed dated 1 Jul 1808, conveyed by WILLSON to John EDWARDS, Senr., by deed dated 2 Jul 1808; WIT: Thos. WILSON, Dorsay WILSON; ack. 13 Oct 1808, Thos. WILSON, J.P., ent. 10 Apr 1809, rec. 15 same.

p. 28 - Know all men, 2 day of ____ 1802, Jacob REPSHER [RAPSHEAR] (wife Elizabeth) of town of Pulling, BCT, for $90 paid by Aaron DILLE, BCT, out lot D near Pultney, 7 acres, conveyed to REPSHER by instrument dated 3 Oct 1800 from Daniel McELHERON to REPSHER; WIT: Phillip DOVER, Samuel DILLE, D. McELHERON; act. BCT, 19 Jan 1802, Daniel McELHERON, J.P., ent. 10 Apr 1809, rec. 17 same.

p. 28 - Indenture, 23 Feb 1809, Alexander McWILLIAMS, Junr., (wife Peggy), BCO; John ALEXANDER, wheelright, BCO. $60.50, land previously sold to

MITCHELL and MONTGOMERY in SW corner S 25 T 4 R 2, 22 acres 1 rod 29 perches; his seal, her mark; WIT: John McWILLIAMS, William BARNES; ack. James ALEXANDER, Assoc. Judge, ent. 13 Apr 1809, rec. 17 same.

p. 30 - Indenture, 15 Apr 1809, David VANCE, BCO; William McFARLAND, James DUFF, Robert HOPPER, and David WALLACE, BCO. $10, "in trust for lower [branch] of the Wheeling congregation under the pastoral care of the Reverand Alexander CALDERHEAD, member of the Monongehala Presbetry," part of NE 1/4 S 6 T 7 R 4, near spring called meeting house spring, 2 acres; WIT: [John] WARDELL, Sterling JOHNSTON; ack. Sterling JOHNSTON, J.P., ent. 15 Apr 1809, rec. 25 same.

p. 31 - Indenture, 13 Apr 1809, David VANCE (wife Margaret), BCO; James WILKINS, BCO. $400, part of S 36 T 6 R 3, granted to VANCE by patent dated 25 Sep 1807, NBR: William GIFFEN, 65 acres 2 rods 12 perches; his seal, her mark; WIT: Sterling JOHNSTON, Mary JOHNSTON; ack. 17 Apr 1809, Sterling JOHNSTON, J.P., ent. 17 Apr, rec. 26 same.

p. 32 - Indenture, [1 or 4] Mar 1809, John COPELAND (wife Caroline), St. Clairsville, BCO; John BELL, BCO. $400, part of S 25 T 8 R 4, Steubenville dist., NBR: Robert JACKSON and Co., 60 ares, fee simple; his seal, her mark; WIT: James CLOYD, Jacob NAGLE; ack. James CLOYD, J.P.

p. 33 - Know all men, whereas land office at Steubenville on 20 Feb 1806 granted to Matilda WAY [MAY] of "Salls berry township" in Lancaster County, Pennsylvania, NE 1/4 S 23 T 8 R 6, 160 acres, whereas Samuel SULLIVAN on 24 Oct 1808 got a conveyance or certificate from Thomas TUCKER, attorney for MAY, for $480 paid by John PERRY [PENY?], BCO, transfer of certificate, 24 Apr 1809; WIT: Saml. SHARPLESS, Sterling JOHNSTON; ack. Sterling JOHNSTON, J.P., ent. 25 Apr 1809, rec. 1 May 1809.

p. 34 - Indenture, 26 Apr 1809, Caleb DILLE (wife Rebeckah), BCO; Obediah HARDESTY, BCO. $800, land surveyed by Robert JOHNSTON, within S 35 T 5 R 3, granted to DILLE by patent dated 29 Dec 1808; his seal, her mark; WIT: George PAULL, Sterling JOHNSTON; ["and from thence to the place of beginning were interlined by consent of parties, 27 Feb 1813]; ack. 26 Apr 1809, Sterling JOHNSTON, J.P., ent. 26 Apr 1809, rec. 2 May same.

p. 35 - Indenture, 26 Apr 1809, Caleb DILLE (wife Rebeckah), BCO; Josiah JOHNSTON, BCO. $268, part of S 35 T 5 R 3, granted to DILLE by patent dated 29 Dec 1808, 67 3/4 acres, fee simple; his seal, her mark; WIT: George PAULL, Sterling JOHNSTON; ack. Sterling JOHNSTON, J.P., ent. 26 Apr 1809, rec. 2 May 1809.

p. 37 - Indenture, 26 Apr 1809, Caleb DILLE (wife Rebeckah), BCO; John MELOT, BCO. $160, NBR: Obediah HARDESTY, 64 acres, part of S 35 T 5 R 3, Steubenville dist., granted to DILLE by patent dated 29 Dec 1808; his seal, her mark; WIT: George PAULL, Sterling JOHNSTON; ack. Sterling JOHNSTON, J.P., ent. 26 Apr 1809, rec. 10 May.

p. 38 - Indenture, 22 Apr 1809, Samuel SULLIVAN (wife Mary), St. Clairsville, BCO; Joseph GILL, now of Mount Pleasant, JCO. Whereas James BARNES (wife Nancy) by deed dated 3 Oct 1804 granted to SULLIVAN lot #21 in St. Clairsville, SULLIVAN by deed dated 13 Nov 1807 sold to John PATTERSON lot containing 2,154 square feet, now SULLIVAN (wife Mary) for $2,200 sell entire lot except portion conveyed to PATTERSON; she signs Polly; WIT: John PATTERSON, Saml. SHARPLESS; ack. John PATTERSON, J.P.

p. 40 - Indenture, 22 Apr 1809, Samuel SULLIVAN (wife Mary), of St. Clairsville, BCO; Joseph GILL, Mount Pleasant, JCO. $300, lot #6 of 15 out lots to St. Clairsville, 4 acres 3 rods 37 perches, as recorded in Book A, p. 429, conveyed by Obadiah JENNINGS on 3 Sep 1806 to William MOSLEY, MOSLEY (wife Elizabeth) conveyed to Samuel SULLIVAN on 23 Jul 1807; sgn: Saml. and Polly; WIT: John PATTERSON, Samuel SHARPLESS, ack. John PATTERSON, J.P., ent. 26 Apr 1809, rec. 12 May same.

p. 41 - Indenture, 22 Apr 1809, Samuel SULLIVAN (wife Mary), of St. Clairsville, BCO; Joseph GILL, Mount Pleasant, JCO. Josiah HEDGES, Sheriff, by Indenture dated 19 Apr 1805 sold to SULLIVAN lot #22 in St. Clairsville seized as property of William MOSELEY upon a judgment in the court of common pleas and supream [sic] court, plaintiffs James ROSS and James BOND (trading as Ross and Bond) for the use of Thomas FOULKE, William MATHERS, Joseph [SHUD] and Andrew MARSHALL defendants, now for $200 paid by GILL; he signs Saml., she signs Polly; WIT: John PATTERSON, Saml. SHARPLESS, ack. John PATTERSON, J.P., ent. 26 Apr 1809, rec. 12 May same.

p. 42 - Indenture, 30 Apr 1809, Jacob DOVENBARGER; Simon MONTAGUE. For debt and $.50, lots #51, #44, #45, and schoolhouse lot in Morristown, void if $50 debt repaid within one year as contained in condition of note dated 22 Oct 1807, penal sum of $50; WIT: Samuel HOLLOWAY, Levi LAC, ack. Duncan MORRISON, J.P., ent. 1 May 1809, rec. 12 same.

p. 43 - Indenture, 2 May 1809, Isaac BRODERICK (wife Beauleh [Beaulah]), BCO; Samuel WILSON, Pennsylvania. $420, part of S 20 T 8 R 5, 60 acres, fee simple; WIT: Wm. W. GAULT, Jacob DOVENBARGER, ack. Duncan MORRISON, J.P.

p. 44 - Indenture, 5 May 1809, John YOUNG (wife Polly), BCO; John FRITCH, BCO. $90, lot near west end of St. Clairsville, NBR: Samuel CRAWFORD, conveyed from John DUGAN (wife Hannah) to Henry STONER on 19 Apr 1805, from STONER (wife Elizabeth) to YOUNG on 6 Jan 1806, as recorded in Book A, pp. 491 and 492, fee simple; his seal, her mark; WIT: John PATTERSON, James HUGHES, ack. John PATTERSON, J.P.

p. 45 - Indenture, 6 May 1809, Jacob DOVENBARGER; Moses CAMPBELL [CAMPBLE]. To secure debt and $.25 paid by CAMPBELL, house on lot #13 in Morristown, void if $40 paid in one year; WIT: Samuel HOLLIWAY, Levi LAC, ack. Duncan MORRISON, J.P., ent. 8 May 1809, recorded 8 same; Moses CAMPBELL [his mark] acknowledges satisfaction of debt on 30 May 1818; WIT: Wm. FARIS, Junr., Recorder.

p. 46 - Indenture, 4 Apr 1809, James CALDWELL (wife Nancy), BCO; John INSKEEP, BCO. $46, lot #96 in St. Clairsville, conveyed to CALDWELL by David NEWALL on 28 Sep 1803, fee simple; WIT: John PATTERSON, James SIMPSON, ack. John PATTERSON, J.P.

p. 47 - Indenture, 29 Apr 1809, John BELL (wife Elizabeth), BCO; Joseph SMITH, BCO. $270, part S 25 T 8 R 4, Steubenville dist., NBR: Robert JACKSON & Co., 60 acres, conveyed from John COPELAND (wife Caroline) to BELL on 4 Mar 1809, fee simple; his seal, her mark; WIT: Solomon WADELL, Sterling JOHNSTON; ack. 8 May 1809, Sterling JOHNSTON, J.P., ent. 8 May 1809, rec. 13 same.

p. 48 - Indenture, 8 Mar 1809, Mordecai YARNELL (wife Phebe), Virginia; Abraham AMRINE, Ohio. For 1/4 S 27 T 6 R 3, 160 acres, $4 per acre; he signs Mo.; WIT: Henry SMITH, Thos. SHARPLESS, ack. 8 Mar 1809, Thos. THOMPSON, J.P., ent. 8 May 1809, rec. 22 same.

p. 49 - Indenture, 21 May 1809, Joshua HUTCHER [HATCHER] (wife Jane), BCO; Christley WINE, BCO. $153, NE 1/4 S 18 T 9 R 7, 151 acres 1 rod 15 perches, fee simple; his seal, her mark; WIT: Sarah HATCHER, Sterling JOHNSTON, ack. 20 May 1809, Sterling JOHNSTON, J.P., ent. 22 May 1809, rec. 23 same.

p. 50 - Indenture, 28 Dec 1808, David NEWALL (wife Sally), BCO; Sterling JOHNSTON, BCO. $25, lot #98 in St. Clairsville, fee simple, [her seal "Saley"], WIT: James CLOYD, Geo. PAULL, ack. James CLOYD, J.P.

p. 51 - Indenture, 17 Mar 1809, James CALDWELL (wife Nancy), BCO; John SPENCER, Loudon County, Virginia. $1,200, part SE corner S 31 T 7 R 4, granted to George SNYDER by patent dated 1 Oct 1806, SNYDER to CALDWELL by deed dated 11 Jul 1807, NBR: John WILKINSON and Nathan SPENCER, fee simple; WIT: John PATTERSON, William BROWN, Senr., ack. 11 Apr 1809, John PATTERSON, J.P. Richland twp.

p. 52 - Indenture, 8 Mar 1809, Mordecai YARNELL (wife Phebe), Virginia; Matthias CRAY, Ohio. Part of E 1/4 S 29 T 6 R 3, $3.00 per acre [but no acreage given]; WIT: Henry SMITH, Thos. THOMPSON, ack. Thomas THOMPSON, J.P., ent. 29 May 1809, rec. 29 same.

p. 53 - Indenture, 2 Jun 1809, Philip ROSEMAN (wife Mary), Oxford twp., BCO; John WICHELL [MITCHELL, WITCHELL], Wheeling, Virginia. $350, NW corner of S 1/2 S 24 T 7 R 4, NBR: Wm. McWILLIAMS, conveyed by Archibald McELROY (wife Sally) by indenture dated 22 Jan 1805, recorded Book A, p. 389, granted to ROSEMAN in fee; WIT: Peter YARNELL, Podrick McGLAUGHLIN [his mark], WIT of consideration money Absalom BRODERICK [his mark], ack. John PATTERSON, J.P.

p. 54 - Know all men, Joseph TANNEY, Loudon County, Virginia, son Enos TANNEY appointed attorney to dispose of land in S 2 T 9 R 5, sgn: 13 Feb 1808, WIT: Daniel D---, Thomas WILKINSON, Joshua OSBORN, ack. 14 Mar 1808, Stacy TAYLOR, [Motley, Notley] C. WILLIAMS, ack. Loudon County, Virginia, Charles BINNS, Clerk, BINNS certified by Francis PEYTON.

p. 55 - Indenture, 1 d 4 m 1809, Jonathan TAYLOR (wife Ann), JCO; John GREER [GRIER], BCO. $480, part of NW 1/4 S 9 T 8 R 6, granted to Jonathan by patent dated 18 d 3 m 1805, 160 acres; WIT: Thos. MITCHELL, John MITCHELL, ack. Thos. MITCHELL, J.P.

p. 57 - Indenture, 22 Apr 1809, James McMILLION [McMILLON] (wife Jane), BCO; Abraham DAVIS, same. $1,400, parts of two fractional S 15 and 24 T 4 R 2, 100 acres, granted to Archibald WOODS by patent of Philadelphia dated 15 Nov 1797, WOODS conveyed half to Absolem MARTIN, parts conveyed by MARTIN to John CONNELL by deed; WIT: Malcolm STRINGER, Andrew McMILLEN, ack. Thos. MITCHELL, J.P.

p. 58 - Indenture, 8 Mar 1809, Mordecai YARNELL (wife Phebe), Virginia; Valentine HORN, Ohio. 1/2 of 1/4 S 29 T 6 R 3, $3.00 per acre; WIT: Henry SMITH, Thos. THOMPSON, ack. Thos. THOMPSON, J.P.

p. 58 - Know all men, William CONGLETON (wife Nancy), of St. Clairsville, BCO, for $200 convey to Mary Ann KINNARD, dau of John KENNARD, Chester County, Pennsylvania, 1/2 of lot #73 in St. Clairsville, 1/8 acre, conveyed by David NEWALL (wife Sally) to CONGLETON by deed dated 28 Dec 1802, fee simple, except free possession and occupation of Sarah BOYD (now known as Sarah ROBINSON) guaranteed during her natural life; WIT: John PATTERSON, Jacob NAGLE, ack. John PATTERSON, J.P., ent. 9 Jun 1809, rec. 26 same.

p. 60 - Indenture, 18 Mar 1809, Henry HUFFMAN (wife Mary), BCO; David RUBLE, Edward BRYSON, and Susannah DAVIS, admrs. of John DAVIS. $300, land on Capteen Creek, part of S 27 T 4 R 3, NBR: Henry HOOVER, William BROWN, 103 acres; his seal, her mark], WIT: Leven OKEY, Samuel FORDICE, ack. Leven OKEY, J.P., ent. 12 Jun 1809, rec. 26 same.

p. 61 - Indenture, 8 May 1809, Marshall JENKINS (wife Sarah), BCO; Samuel LEWES, BCO. $600, SW 1/4 S 20 [original transcriber had written seventy, someone had corrected it to 20 in superscript] T 8 R 4, granted to JENKINS by patent dated 10 Oct 1806, fee simple; WIT: Moses MERRITT, Polly MERRITT, ack. Moses MERRITT, J.P., ent. 17 Jun 1809, rec. 27 same.

p. 62 - Indenture, 23 d 11 m 1808, Borden STANTON (wife Charlotte), BCO; Jonathan TAYLOR, JCO. $600, NW 1/4 S 11 T 6 r 3, granted to STANTON by patent dated 18 d 2 m 1806, 160 acres; WIT: Nathan UPDEGRAFF, Thos. MITCHELL, ack. 23 d 11 m 1808, Thos. MITCHELL, ent. 17 Jun 1809, rec. 27 same.

p. 63 - Indenture, 23 d 11 m 1808, Nathan UPDEGRAFF (wife Ann), Mount Pleasant twp., JCO; Jonathan TAYLOR, same twp. and county. $600, NW 1/4 S 2T 7 R 3, granted to UPDEGRAFF by patent dated 8 d 10 m 1805, 160 acres; WIT: Thos. MITCHELL, Nancy MITCHELL, ack. 23 d 11 [not specified as month] 1808, Thos. MITCHELL, J.P., ent. 17 Jun 1809, rec. 27 same.

p. 64 - Indenture, 9 May 1809, Amos JENNEY, Columbiana County, Ohio, atty. for Joseph JENNEY; Garrett [Garret] SNEDEKER, Brook County, Virginia. $330, part S 2 T 9 R 2, 80 acres, fee simple; WIT: Moses MERRITT, Peter SNEDEKER, ack. Moses MERRITT, J.P., ent. 22 Jun 1809, rec. 27 same.

p. 65 - Indenture, 21 Jun 1809, Jeremiah FAIRHURST (wife Nancy), BCO; Robert THOMPSON, BCO. $110, 7 acres 3 rods and 38 perches, NBR: William WOODS, HAYS, NORRIS, part of land conveyed from David VANCE (wife Margaret) to Sterling JOHNSTON, from JOHNSTON (wife Mary) to Magdalene PIPER, from PIPER to FAIRHURST, fee simple; his seal, her mark, WIT: Sterling JOHNSTON, ack. Sterling JOHNSTON, J.P.

p. 66 - Indenture, 3 Apr 1809, James McMILLAN (wife Jane), BCO; Isaac VAN METRE [VANMETRE], BCO. $900, NBR: John THOMPSON on south "and others," part S 36 T 8 R 6, 224 acres, north part of S; his seal, her mark, WIT: Malcolm STRINGER, Andrew McMILLEN, ack. 3 Apr 1809, Thomas MITCHELL, Esq., ent. 26 Jun 1809, rec. 28 same.

p. 67 - City of New Orleans, Territory of Orleans, Know all men, Robert McCOMB, of St. Clairsville, BCO, appoint Samuel SPRIGG, Esq., BCO, to be his attorney to convey lot in St. Clairsville which he bought of James BARNES to Thomas IRELAND, 25 Jun 1808, WIT: John MARIS, ack. [Robert McCOMBS], Eliphalet FITCH, Notary Public, ent. 24 Jun 1809, rec. 28 same.

p. 68 - Indenture, 13 Mar 1809, Robert McCOMB, St. Clairsville, BCO, by Samuel SPRIGG, his atty; Thomas IRELAND, same town, county, state. [No dollars given here], lot in west end of St. Clairsville, conveyed to McCOMB by James BARNES (wife Nancy) by deed dated 13 May 1804; WIT: James CLOYD, Josiah HEDGES, ack. 14 Mar 1809, James CLOYD, J.P., ent. 24 Jun 1809, rec. 28 same.

p. 69 - Indenture, 24 Jun 1809, Archd. WOODS (wife Ann), Ohio County, Virginia; John STRINGER, BCO. $1,500, to STRINGER ("who purchased of Nehemiah CRAVENS), 300 acres, part of S's 21 and 27 T 4 R 2, patent dated [13] Nov 1797 granted to Archd. WOODS, [assigne] of Absalom MARTIN, NBR: Joseph MOORE, John McCLURE, "land sold to Joseph SCOTT," WOODS's own land; WIT: Thos. THOMPSON, Bayle IRWIN, ack. Thos THOMPSON, J.P., ent. 28 Jun 1809, rec. 29 same.

p. 70 - Indenture, 8 Mar 1808, Mordecai YARNELL (wife Pheby), Virginia; Elizabeth BEAM [no location given]. 1/4 S 29 T 6 R 3, $3.00 per acre; WIT: Henry SMITH, Thos. THOMPSON, ack. Thos. THOMPSON, J.P., ent. 28 Jun 1809, rec. 29 same.

p. 71 - Indenture, 14 Apr 1809, Evan JENKINS (wife Elizabeth), BCO; Stephen BROCK, BCO. $308, 77 acres 2 rods 38 perches, part NW 1/4 S 24 T 8 R 5, granted to JENKINS by patent dated 7 Jan 1808; his seal [Evin], her mark, WIT: Peter TALLMAN, John WILEY, ack. Union twp., 14 Aapr 1809, John WILEY, J.P., ent. 30 Jun 1809, rec. same.

p. 72 - Indenture, 14 Apr 1809, Evans JENKINS (wife Elizabeth), BCO; David PARKINS, BCO. $300, part of SW 1/4 S "20 four" T 8 R 3, granted to JENKINS by patent dated 7 Jan 1808; his seal [Even], her mark; WIT: Peter TALLMAN, John WILEY, ack. 14 Apr 1809, John WILEY, J.P., ent. 30 Jun 1809, rec. same.

p. 73 - Indenture, 17 Jun 1809, John ALEXANDER, BCO; Charles COLLENS [COLLINS], St. Clairsville, BCO. $50, SE corner of lot #13 on south side of St. Clairsville, fee simple; WIT: James CLOYD, George BOYD, John HARRIS, ack, James CLOYD, J.P., ent. 30 Jun 1809, rec. 5 Jul same.

p. 74 - Indenture, 4 Feb 1809, John EDWARDS, Senr., (wife Elenor), BCO; Mary LAPPEN, BCO. $10, 61 acres 3 rods 20 perches, part of S 36 T 7 R 4, granted to EDWARDS by patent dated 7 Apr 1806; only John seals, WIT: Thomas [LAWSON, LARSON], Moses MERRITT, ack. 4 Feb 1809 [John only], Moses MERRITT, ent. 1 Jul 1809, rec. 6 same.

p. 75 - Indenture, 14 Apr 1809, Mordecai YARNELL (wife Phebe), Virginia; William FARQUHAR, same state. Middle 1/2 of S 27 T 6 R 3, 820 acres, also a tract in S 28 T 6 R 3 adjoining the other, NBR: Joseph FLORY, John MAXWELL, Valentine SHEARUS, 100 acres 101 perches, $5 per acre paid by Joseph UPDEGRAFF for the said William FARQUHAR; WIT: Thomas THOMPSON, ack. 4 Apr 1809, Thos. THOMPSON, J.P., ent. 3 Jul 1809, rec. 6 same.

p. 76 - Indenture, 4 Jul 1809, David NEISWANGER (wife Mary), BCO; John BROWN, Junr., BCO. $71, part of lot #67, NBR: William PERRINE, in a town but only streets mentioned; his seal, her mark; WIT: Sterling JOHNSTON, Elisha BROWN, ack. 13 Jul 1809, Sterling JOHNSTON, J.P., ent. 4 Jul 1809, rec. 13 same.

p. 78 - Indenture, 10 Jul 1809, James GORDON, Senr., (wife Jenet), BCO; James GORDEN, Junr., his son, BCO. $480, part S 2 T 7 R 3, 80 acres 32 perches; his seal, her mark; WIT: Thomas MITCHELL, Harriet MITCHELL, ack. Thos. MITCHELL, ent. 10 Jul 1809, rec. 19 same.

p. 79 - Indenture, 1 d 6 m 1809, Jonathan TAYLOR (wife Ann), JCO; James BAYLES [BOYLES], BCO. $60, part of SE 1/4 S 12 T 6 R 3, granted to TAYLOR by patent dated 10 d 8 m 1807; WIT: Thos. MITCHELL, Nancy MITCHELL, ack. date of instrument, Thos. MITCHELL, ent. 15 Jul 1809, rec. 19 same.

p. 80 - Indenture, 18 Jul 1809, William CONGLETON (wife Nancy), St. Clairsville, BCO; Charles FRYMAN, same place. $25, lot #28 in addition to St. Clairsville, Conveyed to CONGLETON by Obediah JENNINGS dated 1 Sep 1806; WIT: Sterling JOHNSTON, Geo. PAULL, ack. Sterling JOHNSTON, J.P., ent. 18 Jul 1809, rec. 20 same.

p. 81 - Indenture, 21 Jul 1809, Samuel HOLLOWAY, BCO; Nicholas GASSOWAY, BCO. $75, lot #21 in Morristown laid of by William CHAPLINE of Ohio County, Virginia, sold by CHAPLINE (wife Mary) to HOLLOWAY by deed dated 22 Jun 1808; WIT: William W. GARRETT, Benjamin [HARONS], ack. Duncan MORRISON, J.P., ent.. 22 Jul 1809, rec. 3 Aug same.

p. 82 - Indenture, 27 Oct 1808, David RUSSELL (wife Hannah), Frederick County, Virginia; Mahlon SMITH, St. Clairsville, BCO. $216.66, lot #97 in St. Clairsville, conveyed to RUSSELL by David NEWALL (wife Sally) on 21 Jan 1801 as recorded in Book A, p. 6, plus a second lot adjacent, NBR: Notley HAYS, William BROWN, and others, sold to RUSSELL by the NEWALLS on 3 Dec 1801, recorded in Book A, p. 23; his seal, her mark, WIT: Leml. BENT, Jos. H. LINGAN, Jesse D. RUSSELL, RUSSELL received payment in Winchester 28 Oct 1808, WIT: Leml. BENT, ack. in court in Frederick County on 5 Dec 1808, ack. 15 Jul 1809, Jas. KEITH, ent. 24 Jul 1809, rec. 3 Aug same.

p. 83 - Indenture, 19 Jul 1809, Josiah HEDGES (wife Rebecca), St. Clairsville, BCO; Vachal HALL, Henry HOSIER, Henry JOHNSTON, Robert DENT, Joseph HARRIS (trustees for the Methodist Episcopal Church). $70, 1 acre in SE corner of meadow north of commons of St. Clairsville for church with exception of land for school conveyed by James BARNES (wife Nancy), reserved in sale to Robert H. JOHNSTON, by JOHNSTON to HEDGES; WIT: John PATTERSON, Samuel BARNES, ack. John PATTERSON, J.P., ent. 27 Jul [1809], rec. 3 Aug same.

p. 85 - Indenture, 1 Aug 1809, David BARTON (wife Nancy), BCO; James PATTON, Wheeling, Ohio County, Virginia. $400, 160 acres, SE 1/4 S 13 T 8 R 4; WIT: Sterling JOHNSTON, Archibald McELROY, ack. Sterling JOHNSTON, J.P., ent 2 Aug 1809, rec. 4 same.

p. 86 - 2 Aug 1809, David BARTON (wife Nancy), BCO; Archibald McELROY, BCO. $200, NW corner S 13 T 8 R 4, 100 acres, adjoining land where Archibald now lives, fee simple; WIT: Sterling JOHNSTON, William HOLMES, ack. Sterling JOHNSTON, J.P., ent. 2 Aug 1809, rec. 7 Aug.

p. 87 - Indenture, 2 Aug 1809, David BARTON (wife Nancy), BCO; William HOLMES, BCO. $200, NBR: Archibald McELROY, 60 acres, part of S 13 T 8 R 4, granted to BARTON by patent dated 20 Dec 1808, fee simple; WIT: Sterling JOHNSTON, Archibald McELROY, ack. Sterling JOHNSTON, J.P., ent. 2 Aug 1809, rec. 7 Aug same.

p. 88 - Indenture, 1 Aug 18809, Moses MOREHEAD, BCO; Mahlon SMITH, BCO. $8, NBR: Moses MOREHEAD, Mahlon SMITH, [no S T R given]; WIT: Sterling JOHNSTON, Jos. JOHNSTON, ack. Sterling JOHNSTON, J.P., ent. 4 Aug 1809, rec. 7 Aug same.

p. 89 - Indenture, 25 d 5 m 1809, Nathan UPDEGRAFF (wife Ann), Mount Pleasant twp., JCO; Isaac PERKINS, Frederick County, Virginia. $800, S 36 T 9 R 7, Steubenville district, granted to UPDEGRAFF; WIT: Thomas MITCHELL, Nancy MITCHELL, ack. 25 May 1809, Thomas MITCHELL, J.P., ent. 7 Aug 1809, rec. same.

p. 90 - Indenture, "twentieth seventh day" May 1809, Alexander GRAY (wife Jane), BCO; John GRAY. $1, S 32 T 7 R 3, Steubenville district, patented to Alexander GRAY, 106 acres 1 rod 5 perches, fee simple; his seal, her mark [name Jean here], WIT: David MARSHALL, Esq., John NIBLOCK, Ann MARSHALL, ack. 27 May 1809, David MARSHALL, Esq., J.P., ent. 9 Aug 1809, rec. 15 same.

p. 91 - Testimony by Allan BOND and William EWERS [written as in first part of record MORS] relative to a contract entered into between Enos BROOMHALL, deceased, and Daniel McFUSON, Phebi BROOMHALL, admx., and Joseph WRIGHT, admr., present at examination. BOND affirms that BROOMHALL told him at his house that he had sold to Daniel McPHERSON 50 acres in the NE corner of S 13 T 8 R 5, bounded by McMahon's Creek, sold at $4 per acre, conversation took place Aug or Sep 1806, sgn: 8 Aug 1809, WIT: David VANCE, James ALEXANDER. EWERS confirmed BOND's story, sgn: St. Clairsville, Richland twp., BCO, 8 Aug 1809; WIT: David VANCE, James ALEXANDER, Assoc. Judges, ent. 11 Aug 1809, rec. 15 same.

p. 92 - Indenture, 25 Jul 1809, Josiah DILLON, BCO; George PAULL, BCO. For trust and confidence and $5, lots #59 and #60 in St. Clairsville, conveyed by David NEWALL (wife Sally) to Bazil ISREAL [sic] (wife Eleanor), ISRAEL and wife to DILLON, lots now in possession of Mr. Zebulon WARNER, Inkeeper [sic], also a lot north of commons, NBR: William BROWN, John BROWN, 7 acres, same conveyed by NEWALL and wife to ISREAL and wife, and from ISREAL to DILLON, also another lot north of commons, NBR: Jacob HOUTZ, 7 acres, also a lot which is part of land where Robert THOMPSON now lives, 3 acres 18 perches, land held in trust, whereas DILLON is indebted to the bank of Marietta for $2,500, and Samuel SHARP, William SMITH, and Ezar DILLON are liable to same bank and Josiah DILLON endorsed, and Josiah DILLON indemnifies Danniel SHORT [sic!], William SMITH, and Ezar DILLON, sgn: Josiah DILLON and George PAULL, WIT: Zebulon WARNER, David HOGE, ack. 25 Jul 1809, John PATTERSON, J.P., ent. 11 Aug 1809, rec. 15 same.

p. 94 - Indenture, 3 Jul 1807, Anthony KENNEDY and Benjamin C. CALHOUN, Baltimore, Maryland, merchants; John CARTER, Josiah UPDEGRAFF, and William FARQUHAR, St. Cclairsville, Ohio. $625, lots #8 and #7 in St. Clairsville, each 1/4 acre, sold to KENNEDY and CALHOUN by John THOMPSON (wife Sally) by deed dated 23 Jan 1806, recorded in Book A, p. 498; WIT: (KENNEDY's signature) N. DAVIDSON, Coleman SELLEN, WIT: (CALHOUN's signature) E. J. COALS, Jno. PROUD, ack. (WHARTON) 7 Jul 1807, Philadelphia, Robert WHARTON, Mayor, ack. (CALHOUN) 10 Jul 1807, Baltimore, Maryland, [Thorangood] SMITH, Mayor, ent. 14 Aug 1809, rec. 16 same.

p. 96 - Indenture, 3 Apr 1809, John EATON (wife Catharine), Washington County, Pennsylvania; John PATTERSON, BCO. $350, lot #65 in St. Clairsville, 1/4 acre, sold by David NEWALL (wife Sally) and Benjamin NEWALL (wife Jane) to Andrew MARSHALL on 17 Apr 1801, recorded Book A, p. 35, and by MARSHALL (wife Margret) to EATON on 6 Dec 1806; WIT: A. MARSHALL, John BUCHANAN, ack. 3 Apr 1809, Washington County, Pennsylvania, John BUCHANAN, J.P., certified 18 May 1809 by Alexr. MURDOCK, Prothonotary of court of Common Pleas.

p. 98 - Indenture, 4 Apr 1809, Robert H. JOHNSTON (wife Mary), BCO; John PATTERSON, BCO. $300, lot #65 in St. Clairsville, 1/4 acre, conveyed by David NEWALL (wife Sally) and Benjamin NEWALL (wife Jane) to Andrew MARSHALL on 17 Apr 1801, recorded Book A, p. 35, by MARSHALL and wife JOHNSTON; his seal, her mark; WIT: A. MARSHALL, Sterling JOHNSTON, ack. Sterling JOHNSTON, J.P.

p. 99 - Indenture, 23 Nov 1808, Obediah JENNINGS (wife Ann), of Steubenville, [JCO]; William WOODBURN [no location]. $30, lot #31 in addition to St. Clairsville; WIT: James JOHNSTON, Zach. BIGGS, ack. 25 Nov 1808, Jefferson County, Ohio, [Samp.] J. KING, J.P., ent. 22 Aug 1809, rec. same.

p. 101 - Indenture, 5 Sep 1809, Ezar DILLON (wife Elizabeth), BCO; Solomon BENTLEY and Samuel GILL, BCO. $700, lot #85 in St. Clairsville, 1/4 acre, conveyed by James KNOX to William CONGLETON on 16 Jun 1804, by CONGLETON to DILLON on 1 Apr 1806, fee simple; his seal, her mark, WIT: Zebulon WARNER, George THOMPSON, ack. Zebulon WARNER, J.P.

P. 102 - Indenture, 29 Jun 1809, James WILKINS (wife Lydia), BCO; James BARNES, BCO. $125, part of lot #37 in St. Clairsville, NBR: John WINTER, and part of #38, conveyed to WILKINS by Jacob HOLTZ (wife [Beggy]) on 11

Feb 1808, fee simple; WIT: Sterling JOHNSTON, ack. 7 Sep 1809, Sterling JOHNSTON, J.P., ent. 7 Sep 1809, rec. 9 same.

p. 103 - Indenture, 5 Sep 1809, BENTLY and GILL, St. Clairsville, BCO; Ezar DILLON, BCO. BENTLY and GILL bound in five written obligations of $80 each, secure to DILLON by conveying lot #85 in St. Clairsville, void if payments [but in the $1,000s] finished by 1 Jul 1814; sgn: Solomon BENTLEY, Samuel GILL, WIT: Sterling JOHNSTON, Wm. BROWN, ack. Sterling JOHNSTON, J.P., ent. 5 Sep 1809, rec. 25 same.

p. 104 - Indenture, 11 Sep 1809, John EDWARDS, BCO; John PRICE, BCO. $240, NW 1/4 S 13 T 10 R 6, except 80 acres previously conveyed by John EDWARDS to James EDWARDS on 13 Oct 1808, this piece also 80 acres, fee simple; WIT: Sterling JOHNSTON, Jos. JOHNSTON, ack. Sterling JOHNSTON, J.P., ent. 11 Sep 1809, rec. 26 same.

p. 106 - Indenture, 11 Sep 1809, John PRICE, BCO; John EDWARDS, BCO. PRICE bound to EDWARDS to allow him to live in cabin and provide materials for him, PRICE conveying 80 acres in S 18 T 10 R 6, except portion previously conveyed to James EDWARDS, property to revert to PRICE if conditions met; PRICE's mark; WIT: Sterling JOHNSTON, Joseph JOHNSTON, ack. Sterling JOHNSTON, J.P., ent. 11 Sep 1809, rec. 28 same.

p. 107 - Indenture, 23 Sep 1809, William CONGLETON (wife Nancy), BCO; Thomas ROBERTSON, BCO. $250, NBR: Nicholas STONER, Jacob AULT, 50, part S 2 T 7 R 4, fee simple; WIT: Sterling JOHNSTON, Jacob MEYERS, ack. Sterling JOHNSTON, J.P., ent. 23 Sep 1809, rec. 28 same.

p. 108 - Indenture, 13 Jun 1808, James WILKINS (wife Lydia), BCO; John WINTER, BCO. $125, part of lot #17 in St. Clairsville; WIT: James CLOYD, Benj. PEARSON, ack. 14 Jun 1808, James CLOYD, J.P., ent. 25 Sep 1809, rec. 14 Oct same.

p. 109 - Indenture, 23 Aug 1809, John McENTIRE (wife Sarah), Muskingham County, Ohio; Archibald WOODS, Ohio County, Virginia. McENTIRE purchased fractional S 1 and 7 T 4 R 3, by patent, sections never divided and Archibald "sill" [sic, probably "still"] holds an undivided equitable estate in fee in a certain proportion of part of S's, $1,060 paid by WOODS, McENTIRE releases his rights; WIT: Saml. THOMPSON, Samuel KIRKLAND, ack. 23 Aug 1809, Muskingum County, Ohio, Samuel THOMPSON, J.P., ent. 28 Sep 1809, rec. 16 Oct same.

p. 111 - Indenture, 26 d 7 m 1809, Joseph NICHOLSON, BCO; Joseph VANLAW, BCO. $620, 60 acres, beginning at corner in S 33 T 7 R 4, NBR: Joseph VANLAW, same that Samuel GREGG (and wife) conveyed on 25 Apr 1807 to VANLAW, recorded in Book B, p. 191; sgn: Joseph J. NICHOLSON, WIT: Arthur IRWIN, Ann IRWIN, ack. 26 Jul 1809, Arthur IRWIN, J.P.

p. 112 - Indenture, 2 f 9 m 1809, William MILHOUSE (wife Hannah), BCO; Horton HOWARD, BCO. $2,500, 240 acres, conveyed by HOWARD and wife to MILHOUSE on 11 d 6 m 1807 in fee, first beginning NE corner S 9 T 7 R 3, second part of S 3 T 7 R 3, 25 acres, conveyed by Thomas MITCHELL (wife Agnes) by Indenture dated 11 Jun 1807 to MILHOUSE in fee; WIT: Thos. MITCHELL, Joseph GIBBONS, ack. 12 Sep 1809, Thos. MITCHELL, J.P., receipt of payment ack. by MILHOUSE, ent. 3 Oct 1809, rec. 23 same.

p. 115 - Indenture, 11 d 6 m 1807, Horton HOWARD (wife Hannah), BCO; William MILHOUSE, BCO. $2,400, 240 acres beginning at NE corner S 9 T 7 R 3, same granted to HOWARD by patent dated 22 Jan 1806; WIT: John MITCHELL, John STEWART, ack. 11 Jun 1807, Thomas MITCHELL, J.P., receipt of money ack. and WIT: by John MITCHELL, John STEWART, ent. 3 Oct 1809, rec. 24 same.

p. 117 - Indenture, 11 Jun 1807, Thomas MITCHELL (wife Agnes), BCO; William MILHOUS, BCO. $112.50, part S 3 T 7 R 3, 25 acres, granted to MITCHELL by patent dated 18 Jan 1806; WIT: John MITCHELL, John STEWART, ack. 11 Jun 1807, James ALEXANDER, receipt of money ack. and WIT: John MITCHELL, John STEWART, ent. 3 Oct 1809, rec. 25 same.

p. 118 - Indenture, 23 Sep 1809, Jacob MYERS (wife Elizabeth), BCO; Peter AULT, BCO. $600, NBR: Leonard DIVAN, Philip AULT, 110 acres, part S 2 T 7 R 4, fee simple; his seal, her mark, ack. John GRIER, J.P., ent. 10 Oct 1809, rec. 27 same.

p. 119 - Indenture, 13 Jul 1809, Sterling JOHNSTON (wife Mary), BCO; John DUGAN, BCO. $35, lot on north side of main street of St. Clairsville, NBR: Robert LAUGHLIN; WIT: James CLOYD, William JOHNSTON, ack. 14 Jul 1809, James CLOYD, J.P., ent. 14 Oct 1809, rec. 3 Nov same.

p. 120 - Indenture, 17 Aug 1809, Sterling JOHNSTON (wife Mary), St. Clairsville, BCO; William WOODS, BCO. $37, part S 5 T 7 R 4, 3 acres 2 rods 38 perches, conveyed from David VANCE, Esqr. (wife Margaret) to Sterling JOHNSTON; WIT: James CLOYD, William JOHNSTON, ack. 7 Oct 1809, James CLOYD, J.P., ent. 14 Oct 1809, rec. 3 Nov same.

p. 122 - Indenture, 9 Aug 1809, Abraham PLUMMER, Warren twp., BCO; John SIMPSON, BCO. For "sarvises" received by SIMPSON [?], 100 acres beginning at SE corner S 6 T 8 R 6; WIT: John PLUMMER, Robert PLUMMER, ack. 9 Aug 1809, John GREIR, Esqr., ent. 22 Oct 1809, rec. 3 Nov same.

p. 123 - Indenture, 20 Oct 1809, David RUBLE (wife Susannah), BCO; William BONER, BCO. $200, part S 20 T 4 R 3, Marietta district, NBR: George [RILLS] and James McENTIRE, 100 acres; his seal, her mark, WIT: Edw. BRYSON, George [GET], ack. 20 Oct 1809, Edward BRYSON, J.P., ent. 14 Nov 1809, rec. same.

p. 124 - Indenture, 22 Dec 1808, Hugh McCAY (wife Martha), BCO; James McCAY, BCO. $80, SW corner of S 1/4 of S 24 T 7 R 4; WIT: Sterling JOHNSTON, Jos. JOHNSTON, ack. 14 Nov 1809, Sterling JOHNSTON, J.P., ent. 14 Nov 1809, rec. 22 same.

p. 125 - Indenture, 2 Nov 1809, Bazalel [Bazaleel] WELLS (wife Sally), JCO; Mordecai BALDERSTON, same. $325, part of S 20 T 7 R 3, part of S sold to Jane VANWAY, 93 acres; WIT: Samp.. J. KING, Aaron THOMPSON, ack. JCO, 2 Nov 1809, Samp. J. KING, J. P., KING certified by Jno. WARD, Clk., ent. 16 Nov 1809, rec. 17 same.

p. 126 - Whereas register of land office at Steubenville did on 2 Jan 1805 grant a certificate to William WEBB of Wheeling, Ohio County, Virginia, WEBB entitled to patent for SE 1/4 S 26 T 3 R 2; WEBB transfers patent to Matthew SCOTT of Wheeling, Ohio County, Virginia, for $380, sgn: 20 Jul 1809; WIT: John [Jen] WRIGHT, Edward WEBSTER, John [McLUERR], ack. Ohio County, produced at August term, sgn: 15 Aug 1809, Moses CHAPLIN, C.O.C.

p. 127 - Indenture, 10 Jul 1809, Jacob GREGG (wife Mary), BCO; John LARUE, BCO. GREGG of Loudon County, Virginia, received patent for S 7 T 8 R 5, Steubenville district, dated 19 Oct 1808, for $1,080 transfer to LARUE 60 acres in that S, NBR: Jacob GREGG; WIT: William EWEN, Absalom HOGE, Mary GREGG, Senr., ack. 10 Jul 1809, Duncan [Dunken] MORRISON, J.P., rec. 15 Nov 1809.

p. 128 - Indenture, 11 Nov 1809, Abraham LASH (wife Mary), BCO; Samuel HATCHER, Virginia. $12, lot #153 in St. Clairsville, 1/4 acre, conveyed from David NEWALL (wife Sally) on 8 Jan 1802; his seal, her mark, WIT: Sterling JOHNSTON, Eleanor KINNEY, ack. Sterling JOHNSTON, J.P., ent. 16 Nov 1809, rec. 20 same.

p. 129 - Whereas register of land office in Steubenville on 19 Jun 1807 granted certificate to Cyrus BOYD, BCO, to patent SW 1/4 S 19 T 7 R 5, Steubenville district, 161 acres 22/100, for $161 paid by Matthew WOOD, BOYD conveys benefit of certificate, sgn: 25 Nov 1809; WIT: Sterling JOHNSTON, Nathan UPDEGRAFF, ack. Sterling JOHNSTON, ent. 25 Nov 1809, rec. same.

p. 130 - Indenture, 23 Sep 1809, Leonard HART (wife Mary), BCO; William WAGGONER, BCO. $40, lot #90 in Morristown as laid out by William CHAPLINE; both mark; WIT: Robert MORRISON, William DUNN, ack. 27 Sep 1809, Duncan MORRISON, J.P., ent. 26 Nov 1809, rec. 30 same.

p. 131 - Indenture, 1 d 9 m 1809, Horton HOWARD, BCO; William MILHOUSE, BCO. HOWARD bound to MILHOUSE for $4,900, payment of $2,450 secured by five shillings and transfer of land part of S 7 T 7 R 3 containing 170 acres, same conveyed by Borden STANTON (wife Charlotte) by indenture dated 31 d 12 m 1806, recorded Book B, p. 118, granted to HOWARD in fee, other tract in S 13 T 7 R 3 containing 30 acres, same which Joseph W. SATTERTHWAITE conveyed by indenture dated 22 d 12 m 1806 to HOWARD in fee, recorded Book B, pp. 83-84, void if debt paid; WIT: Thomas MITCHELL, Joseph GIBBONS, ack. 12 Sep 1809, Thos. MITCHELL, J.P., ent. 1 Dec 1809, rec. 16 same; mortgage satisfied, no date.

p. 134 - Indenture, 24 d 6 m1809, William SATTERTHWAITE, BCO; Samuel POTTS, BCO. $818.44, begin in S 13 T 7 R 3, NBR: Samuel POTTS, Joseph H. SATTERTHWAIT, Thomas SATTERTHWAIT, 96 acres 1 rod 6 perches, part of large tract divided to William SATTERTHWAIT by his father William SATTERTHWAITE, deceased; sgn: Wm. W. SATTERTHWAITE, WIT: William GIBBONS, Joseph GIBBONS, receipt of money ack., WIT: Joseph GIBBONS, Wm. GIBBONS, ack. 1 Dec 1809, Sterling JOHNSTON, J.P.

p. 135 - Indenture, 31 Oct 1809, Mordecai YARNELL (wife Phebe), Virginia; Jacob PICKERING, Ohio. S 14 T 9 R 5 for $10 per acre; WIT: [John] KING, Thomas THOMPSON, ack. 31 Oct 1809, Thos. THOMPSON, J.P., ent. 1 Dec 1809, rec. 20 same.

p. 136 - Indenture, 10 Jul 1809, Jacob GREGG (wife Mary), BCO; William EWERS, BCO. Patent granted to GREGG of Loudon County, Virginia, for S 7 T 8 R 5, Steubenville district, dated 19 Oct 1808, for $647.50 paid by EWERS, GREGGs convey 202 acres 72 poles, NBR: John [LAWES*], Samuel GREGG; WIT: John LARUE*, Absalom HOGE, Rebecca GREGG, ack. Duncan MORRISON, J.P., 10 Jul 1809, ent. 10 Dec 1809, rec. 20 same.

p. 137 - Indenture, 6 Aug 1809, David VANCE (wife Margaret), BCO; John PATTERSON, BCO. $[none mentioned], part S 5 T 7 R 4, 15 acres 1 rod 30 perches; his seal, her mark; WIT: Robert VANCE, Robert JOHNSTON, ack. 10 Dec 1809, Sterling JOHNSTON, J.P., ent. 10 Dec 1809, rec. 20 same.

p. 138 - Indenture, 14 Aug 1809, Noah LINSLEY, Ohio County, Virginia; Archibald WOODS [WOOD], same. $480, SE 1/4 S 26 T 8 R 5, Steubenville district, granted to LINSLY by patent dated 9 Nov 1808, also NW 1/4 S 1 T 10 R 7, patented 15 Jun 1808, fee simple; WIT: J. McGEE, Sterling JOHNSTON, ack. 13 Dec 18809, Sterling JOHNSTON, J.P.

p. 139 - Indenture, 27 Nov 1809, Absalom GRAHAMS (wife Eleanor), JCO; "Rowlin Craig & Co.," same. $30, lots #37, #42, #5 in Morristown as laid off by William CHAPLINE; both mark, WIT: James CROW, James IRWIN, ack. BCO, 28 Nov 1809, Jacob MARTIN, Judge of CCP, ent. 14 Dec 1809, rec. 20 same.

p. 140 - Whereas register of land in Steubenville on 18 Jan 1806 granted John LEWES, JCO, a certificate to patent NW 1/4 S 20 T 7 R 5, for $400 paid by Cyrus BOYD, LEWES conveys rights; sgn: 15 Dec 1809, WIT: Joseph POSEY, Sterling JOHNSTON, ack. Sterling JOHNSTON, J.P.

p. 141 - Indenture, 29 Jun 1809, Jacob GREGG (wife Mary), BCO; Samuel GREGG, BCO. Jacob GREGG, Loudon County, Virginia, patented S 7 T 8 R 5, Steubenville district, on 19 Oct 1808, for $275 paid by Samuel GREGG, convey 72 1/4 acres 29 perches in that S; WIT: Stephen SHARP, George SHARP, ack. 10 Jul 1809, Duncan MORRISON, J.P.

p. 142 - Indenture, 24 Dec 1807, Obediah JENNINGS (wife Ann), JCO; Edward WILLSON, St. Clairsville, [BCO]. $36, lots #11 and #12 in addition to St. Clairsville as laid out by William MATHERS, late proprietor, conveyed by Bazaeel [sic] WELLS (wife Sally) to JENNINGS; WIT: James JOHNSTON, John McDOWELL, Junr., ack. BCO [?], 24 Dec 1807, Samp. J. KING, J.P., ent. 18 Dec 1809, rec. 22 same.

p. 143 - Indenture, 25 Oct 1809, Amos JENNEY, BCO, attorney for Joseph JENNEY [JENNEN first written, but JENNEY at signing] of Loudon County, Virginia; Robert LEE, Washington County, Pennsylvania. $682.50, 136 acres in S 2 T 9 R 5; Amos JENNEY, attorney for Joseph JENNEY, WIT: William WILEY, John ELLIOT, John PATTERSON, ack. 25 Oct 1809, Enos PICKERING, J.P. for Union twp, ent. 19 Dec 1809, rec. 22 same.

p. 144 - Indenture, 11 Sep 1809, James EDWARDS (wife Margaret), BCO; John PRICE, BCO. $220, part of NW 1/4 Ss 13 T 10 R 6, granted to John EDWARDS by Thomas WILLSON on 2 Jul 1808, from John EDWARDS to James EDWARDS on 13 Oct 1808, 80 acres; his seal, her mark, WIT: Sterling JOHNSTON, Joseph JOHNSTON, ack. 12 Dec 1809, Thos. WILSON, J.P., ent. 19 Dec 1809, rec. 22 same.

p. 146 - Indenture, 29 Nov 1809, Alexander GRAY (wife Jane), BCO; Robert GRAY, BCO. $300, 107 acres 3 rods 24 perches on Barr's Run, part of S 32 T 7 R 3, Steubenville district, fee simple; both mark, WIT: James GRAY, John GRAY, ack. 29 Nov 1809, David MARSHALL, J.P.

p. 147 - Indenture, 26 Dec 1809, John FRITCH, BCO; John FOREST [FORREST], BCO. $100, NBR: Samuel CRAWFORD, near St. Clairsville, 1/8 acre, E 1/2 of lot conveyed to FRITCH by John YOUNG (wife Polly) on 5 May 1809; his mark, WIT: Sterling JOHNSTON, Henry MITCHELL, ack. Sterling JOHNSTON, J.P., ent. 26 Dec 1809, rec. 30 same.

p. 148 - Indenture, 26 Dec 1809, John FRITCH, BCO; Henry MITCHELL, BCO. $75, near St. Clairsville, NBR: Samuel CRAWFORD, 1/8 acre, W 1/2 of lot conveyed by John YOUNG (wife Polly) to FRITCH; his mark, WIT: Sterling JOHNSTON, Robert JOHNSTON, ack. Sterling JOHNSTON, J.P., ent. 26 Dec 1809, rec. 30 same.

p. 149 - Indenture, 7 May 1808, Henry W. LIVINGSTONE (wife Mary), Columbiana County, New York; William Nicholson JEFFERS, lawyer, of New York, New York County, New York. $5,000, fractional T 1 R 3 on Ohio River made by Thomas HUTCHINS Geographer of U.S.; sgn: H. W. LIVINGSTON, WIT: Geo. JEFFERS, Junr., J. SEVAN, ack. Albany County, 8 May 1808, Jno. N. QUACKENBUSH, Master in Chancery.

p. 151 - To all persons, William Nicholson JEFFERS, City of New York, for $5,000 paid by James JOHNSTON and East SPROAT, both of Ohio, convey fractional T 1 R 3 on Ohio River, about 5,500 acres, surveyed in 1788, granted to Henry W. LIVINSTON, being in the Counties of Washington and Belmont, Ohio, sgn: 28 Oct 1809, WIT: Wood CRAIGE, Joseph WOOD, ack. BCO [?], 28 Oct 1809, Jeremiah DARE, J.P., ent. 27 Dec 1809, rec. 28 same.

p. 152 - Indenture, 4 Dec 1809, Samuel LEWES, BCO; Titus SHOTWELL, BCO. LEWES owes SHOTWELL $600, securing payment by conveying pesonal property, void if LEWES executes a deed for a piece of land conveyed to SHOTWELL by writing on 2 Dec 1809 on or before 2 Dec 1810; both seal, WIT:

Sterling JOHNSTON, ack. Sterling JOHNSTON, J.P., ent. 28 Dec 1809, rec. 10 Jan 1819 [sic--1810?] mortgage satisfied 2 Jun 1810.

p. 154 - Indenture, 6 Dec 1809, David BARTON (wife Nancy), BCO; Thomas WHITACKER, BCO. $600, NE 1/4 S 13 T 8 R 4,160 acres, granted to BARTON by patent dated13 Dec 1808, fee simple; WIT: Sterling JOHNSTON, William HOLMES, ack. Sterling JOHNSTON, J.P., ent. 28 Dec 1809, rec. 10 Jan 1810.

p. 155 - Indenture, 6 Jan 1810, Notley HAYS (wife Sally), BCO; John ELLIOT, BCO. $20, lot #11 in town laid out by HAYS, James BARNES, and William BROWN containing 1 rod 20 perches; his seal, her mark, WIT: Sterling JOHNSTON, ack. Sterling JOHNSTON, ent. 12 Jan 1810, rec. same.

p. 156 - Indenture, 18 Aug 1809, Jacob HOULTZ (wife Margaret), BCO; George PAULL and John THOMPSON, BCO. $120, out lot #9 laid out by Bazaleel WELLS adjoining addition to St. Clairsville laid out by William MATHERS, 6 acres 9 perches, conveyed by Robert JOHNSTON to HOULTZ; both mark, WIT: James CLOYD, Adam JOHNSTON, ack. James CLOYD, 18 Aug 1809.

p. 157 - Indenture, 28 Oct 1809, William ROBERTSON, BCO; Abner BURRIS, BCO. $250, out lot #13 in plan laid out by Bazaleel WELLS on south side of St. Clairsville, 5 acres 3 rods 30 perches, conveyed from Obediah JENNINGS, JCO, to Andrew MOORE, from MOORE (wife Elizabeth) to ROBERTSON on 17 Jan 1807, fee simple; WIT: Sterling JOHNSTON, ack. 28 Oct 1809, Sterling JOHNSTON, J.P., ent. 13 Jan 1810, rec. 16 same.

p. 158 - Indenture, 6 Aug 1809, Ebenezer ZANE (wife Elizabeth), Ohio County, Virginia; Sarah PALMER (daughter of Jo. PALMER of town of Wheeling), Virginia. $100, lot in town of Canton laid out by ZANE in fractional s 28 T 3 R 2, part of square 8, fee simple; WIT. Thos. THOMPSON, E. WOODS, ack. 6 Aug 1809, Thos. THOMPSON, J.P., ent. 13 Jan 1810, rec. 16 same.

p. 159 - Indenture, 11 Jan 1810, Sterling JOHNSTON (wife Mary), BCO; William CONGLETON, BCO. $120, lots #105 and #106 in St. Clairsville, conveyed to JOHNSTON by David NEWALL (wife Sally) on 13 Mar 1808, recorded Book B, p. 282, fee simple; WIT: Nathaniel WHITE, James CLOYD, ack. James CLOYD, J.P., ent. 14 Jan 1810, rec. 17 same.

p. 160 - Indenture, 11 d 1 m 1810, John BROWN [PICKERING?] (wife Mary), BCO; Levi HOLLINGSWORTH, BCO. $640, SW 1/4 S 26 T 9 R 5, granted to "said John PICKERING" [?] by patent dated 3 d 12 m 1808, 160 acres; WIT:

Thos. THOMPSON, William BARNES, ack. Thos. THOMPSON, ent. 23 Jan 1810, rec. 27 same.

p. 161 - Indenture, 26 Jan 1810, Henry MITCHELL, BCO; Jeremiah BURRIS, BCO. $55, lot near W end of St. Clairsville, 1/8 acre, W 1/2 of lot conveyed from John YOUNG (wife Polly) to John FRITCH, from FRITCH to MITCHELL on 26 Dec 1809, fee simple; WIT: Sterling JOHNSTON, Wm. CONGLETON, ack. Sterling JOHNSTON, J.P., ent. 26 Jan 1810, rec. 27 same.

p. 162 - Indenture, 20 Jan 1810, Philip DOODRIDGE, Brook County [Virginia]; Noah ZANE, Wheeling [Virginia]. Whereas John CLARK by deed of 9 Oct 1805 conveyed to Philip in fee simple 320 acres in BCO, E 1/2 S 4 T 6 R 3 except 40 acres to secure debt of $513, deed proved before Thomas THOMPSON, J.P., on 12 Nov 1808, payment still in arrears, $1,020.07 is the best price Philip can obtain in ready cash, land conveyed to ZANE with assent of CLARK; WIT: C. HAMMOND, S. SPRIGG, CLARK's assent dated 20 Mar 1810, WIT: S. SPRIGG, C. HAMMOND, receipt of money ack. 20 Jan 1810, WIT: C. HAMMOND, ack. 29 Jan 1810, of Charles HAMMOND and Samuel SPRIGG, Esqr., verifying their having witnessed the above document, Zebulon WARNER, J.P.

p. 164 - Articles of Agreement, 20 Mar 1810, between John CLARK and Noah ZANE, Noah has paid to Mecker & Canman $2,100 "discharging a judgement recovered in Belmont against the said John for which the said John had engaged to give a mortgage on the premises to the said Noah," Noah now to hold property as mortgage; both seal, WIT: C. HAMMOND, Saml. SPRIGG, ack. 29 Jan 1810, Zebulon WARNER, J.P., ent. 29 Jan 1810, rec. 31 same.

p. 165 - Indenture, 20 Jan 1810, Noah ZANE, Wheeling, Ohio County, Virginia; Ebenezer ZANE, same. $1,020.07 and agreement by Ebenezer to enter agreement in his will to make good the debt on John CLARK paid for by Noah to Mecker and Denman, E 1/2 S 4 T 6 R 3 except 40 acres, subject to CLARK's redeeming it; WIT: C. HAMMOND, Saml. SPRIGG, ack. 29 Jan 1810, Zebulon WARNER, ent. 7 Jan 1810, rec. 31 same.

p. 166 - Know all men, Jacob DILLON, BCO, for $2,200 paid by Samuel SPRIGG, BCO, sold 7 acres on which there is a [home] mill and distillery and situate adjoining the commons of St. Clairsville in S 4 T 7 R 4, conveyed to DILLON by Thomas VANSWEARINGIN by mortgage deed dated 13 Apr 1802, also lot #52 in St. Clairsville, 1/4 acre, "that I conveyed by morgage deed dated the ninth day of May 1809, to David MARPOLE of the county of Muskindum [sic]"; sgn: 26 Nov 1809, WIT: Zebulon WARNER, Wynkoop WARNER, ack. 26 Nov 1809, Zebulon WARNER, J.P., ent. 29 Jan 1810, rec. 31 same.

p. 167 - Indenture, 11 d 1 m 1810, John PICKERING (wife Mary), BCO; Levi HOLLINGSWORTH, BCO. $640, recorded on p. 139. [NOTE: I'm not sure what this means as there is no reference to this transaction on p. 139 of this book. However, there is one that matches these details on p. 160. Perhaps a change in pagination due to recopying book?]

p. 167 - Indenture, 13 Jan 1810, William GOUGH, BCO; William HATFIELD, JCO. $300 to be paid in installments, HATFIELD gives bonds to GOUGH with William CRAIG of BCO security for said payments, lots #91 and #92 in St. Clairsville, same bought by GOUGH of James CALDWELL, to secure title GOUGH conveys to HATFIELD lots #12 and #12 whereon GOUGH now lives, this to be void if GOUGH makes deed; GOUGH's mark, HATFIELD's seal, WIT: Joseph FLORA, Sterling JOHNSTON, ack. 30 Jan 1810 receipt of $10 on agreement, GOUGH's mark, WIT: Sterling JOHNSTON, ack. 30 Jan 1810, Sterling JOHNSTON, J.P., ent. 30 Jan 1810, rec. 5 Feb same.

p. 168 - Indenture, 2 Dec 1809, James NEWALL (wife Elizabeth), BCO; William FROST, BCO. $10, lots #149, #150, #158, #157, one acre, fee simple; WIT: Robert GRIFFITH, Robert ELWOOD, ack. 5 Dec 1809, Robert GRIFFITH, J.P., ent. 10 Feb 1810, rec. 23 same.

p. 170 - Know all men, Joseph POSEY sold to Sterling JOHNSTON and Ch. HAMMOND for $500, 120 acres, W end of S 1/2 S 20 T 7 R 4, where POSEY now lives, POSEY to indemnify JOHNSTON and HAMMOND from all risk which may happen in consequence of endorsing the said Joseph note for $500 offered for discount and discounted at the bank of Washington, then this is void, other wise in effect; POSEY sgn: 18 Jan 1810, WIT: George PAULL, James CLOYD, ack. 18 Jan 1810, James CLOYD, J.P., ent. 19 Feb 1810, rec. 23 same.

p. 170 - Indenture, 19 Feb 1810, Robert BELL (wife Sarah), BCO; William WOODS, BCO. $100, part of NW 1/4 S 21 T 8 R 5, patented to BELL, NBR: James CALDWELL, Archibald WOODS, 40 acres 3 rods 25 perches; both mark [her name Sally here], WIT: James HAZLETT, John McWILLIAMS, ack. Duncan MORRISON, J.P., ent. 20 Feb 1810, rec. 23 same.

p. 172 - Indenture, 21 Feb 1810, John THOMPSON (wife Sally) and George PAULL, all BCO; Robert THOMPSON, BCO. $200, out lot #9 in plan laid off by Bazaleel WELLS adjoining the addition to St. Clairsville, 6 acres 9 perches, same conveyed from Jacob HOLTZ (wife Margaret) to THOMPSON and PAULL on 18 Aug 1809, recorded in Book C, p. 135, fee simple; all seal, her name given as Sarah, WIT: Sterling JOHNSTON, James HUGHS, ack. Sterling JOHNSTON, J.P., ent. 221 Feb 1810, rec. 24 same.

p. 173 - Indenture, 19 d 7 m 1809, James EGERTON (wife Sarah) and George STARBUCK (wife Elizabeth), BCO; John BROWN, executors of the ["Henry Frane Titus Denast"], BCO. $100, sell Caty, Susannah, George, and Jacob TEELER, heirs of Francis TEELER deceased, part S 4 T 5 R 4, Marietta district, 50 acres; all seal, WIT: Jordon NEWSOM, Robert GREER, ack. 19 Jul 1809, John GRIER, J.P., ent. 21 Feb 1810, rec. 26 same.

p. 174 - Indenture, 26 d 8 m 1809, Horton HOWARD (wife Hannah), BCO; John GARRETSON, BCO. $340, part NW 1/4 S 8 T 7 R 3, granted to HOWARD by patent dated 10 d 9 m 1806, NBR: Owen DEWEES, Josiah BUNDAY, William MILHOUSE, GAMBLLE, FERRIS, 77 acres; WIT: Thos. MITCHELL, William BARNES, ack. [not dated] Thos. MITCHELL, J.P., ent. 21 Feb 1810, rec. 27 same.

p. 176 - Indenture, 26 d 8 m 1809, Horton HOWARD, (wife Hannah), BCO; Josiah BUNDAY, BCO. $240, part of NW 1/4 S 8 T 7 R 3, granted to HOWARD by patent dated 10 d 9 m 1806, NBR: GARRETSON, William MILHOUSE, 83 acres; WIT: Thos. MITCHELL, William BARNES, ack. Thos. MITCHELL, additional ack. 16 Feb 1810, by Phebe BROWN, wife of John BROWN, "who acknowledged that she signed sealed and delivered the above deed of conveyance Lewus Horatio STOCKDON for the purpose therein mentioned" on 19 Nov 1807, Zebulon WARNER, J.P., ent. 21 Feb, rec. 28 same.

p. 178 - Indenture, 14 Dec 1809, James MACKEY (wife Jane), Ohio County, Virginia; Archibald HAMILTON, Wheeling, Ohio County, Virginia. $150, lots in St. Clairsville, alias Newelston, BCO, lot numbers omitted, conveyed to MACKEY by Henry STONER, and by John DUGAN and Robert JOHNSTON to STONER; his seal, her mark; WIT: James DAVIES, John DAVIES, ack. Ohio County, 14 Dec 1809, receipt of $150, ack. BCO, 20 Jan 1810, Jacob DAVIS, J.P., ent. 22 Feb 18180, rec. 28 same.

p. 179 - Indenture, 22 Feb 1810, James BARNES (wife Nancy), St. Clairsville, BCO; Notley HAYS, BCO. $520, part of NE 1/4 S 4 T 7 R 4, 26 acres, NBR: Notley HAYS, William GIBSON, conveyed to BARNES by Francis SUNDERLAND (wife Ann) on 4 May 1804, fee simple; his seal, her mark; WIT: Sterling JOHNSTON, John H. BARNES, ack. Sterling JOHNSTON, J.P., ent. 22 Feb 1810, rec. 28 same.

p. 180 - Indenture, 29 Jan 1810, John DUGAN, BCO; Robert LAUGHLIN, David NEISWANGER, and Samuel CRAWFORD, BCO. $17, land at W end of St. Clairsville, to be a public street or highway; WIT: Robert DENT, Sterling

JOHNSTON, ack. 29 Jan 1810, Sterling JOHNSTON, J.P., ent. 23 Feb 1810, rec. 1 Mar same.

p. 181 - Know all men, Andrew BLAIR, BCO, for $100 paid by Thomas BARR [later BLAIR], household goods, sgn: 10 Feb 1810, WIT: Robert JOHNSTON, John RYANS, Sterling JOHNSTON, ack. Sterling JOHNSTON, J.P., ent. 24 Feb 1810, rec. 2 Mar same.

p. 182 - To all people, John FARGUSON [FERGUSON], Richland twp., BCO, for $60 payable to William FARGUSON [FERGUSON], BCO, and obligations and rents which John paid to Joseph GILL, William to get goods and chattles, sgn: 4 Dec 1809, WIT: John C. GILKISON, Edward WILLSON, ack. 4 Dec 1809, Zebulon WARNER, J.P., delivery of goods certified 4 Dec 1809, WIT: William DUKEY, Margaret DEHAVEN [her mark], ent. 27 Feb 1810, rec. 2 Mar same.

p. 183 - Indenture, 19 Feb 1810, Mordecai YARNELL (wife Phebe), of Wheeling, Virginia; Job. DILLON, Ohio [BC not specified]. $350, part of S 29 T 6 R 3, 100 acres, fee simple; WIT: Thos. THOMPSON, Asa DILLON, ack. BCO, Thos. MITCHELL, J.P., ent. 28 Feb 1810, rec. 8 Mar same.

p. 184 - Indenture, 25 d 12 m 1809, Borden STANTON and Nathan UPDEGREFF, extrs. of Benjamin STANTON dec'd, JCO and BCO; John FORREST, BCO. $75, in the NE 1/4 S 36 T 5 R 3, 30 acres; WIT: David BERRY, Thos. MITCHELL; ack. JCO, 4 Jan 1810, Thos. MITCHELL, J.P., ent. 1 Mar 1810, rec. 12 same.

p. 185 Indenture, 23 Aug 1809, John WORKMAN (wife Eleanor), BCO; Thomas THOMPSON, BCO. $107.60, land in SE 1/4 S 2 T 6 R 3, 26 9/10 acres, part of tract deeded by Daniel McELHERON (wife Emelia) to John WORKMAN [no date given]; both mark, WIT: Amos WORKMAN, Isaac McALLISTER, ack. [Emos first], 23 Aug 1809, Amos WORKMAN, J.P. of Pultney twp., ent. 8 Mar 1810, rec. 15 same.

p. 186 - Indenture, 22 Feb 1810, Thomas IRELAND (wife Sally), BCO; Charles ACKLER [ACKLES], BCO. $110, lot near W end of St. Clairsville, conveyed to Robert McCOMBS by James BARNES (wife Nancy) by deed dated 13 May 1804, by McCOMBS (by atty. Samuel SPRIGG) on 13 Mar 1809, fee simple; his seal, her mark; WIT: Sterling JOHNSTON, Henry H. EVANS, ack. Sterling JOHNSTON, J.P., ent. 9 Mar 1810, rec. 16 same.

p. 187 - Indenture, 10 Mar 1810, Robert THOMPSON, BCO; William WOODS, BCO. $90, 7 acres 3 rods 38 perches, near (NBR) William WOODS property, conveyed from Jeremiah FAIRHURST to THOMPSON on 21 Jun 1809, fee simple; WIT: Sterling JOHNSTON, Alexander GASTON, ack. Sterling JOHNSTON, J.P., ent. 10 Mar 1810, rec. 18 same.

p. 188 - Indenture, 10 Mar 1810, William WOODS, BCO; Robert THOMPSON, BCO. $90, 3 acres 37 perches, near (NBR) Josiah DILLON, William BOGGS, same conveyed from David NEWALL to Daniel CHURCH, from CHURCH to WOODS on 19 Jun 1804, fee simple; "William WOODS by Sterling JOHNSTON" [?], WIT: Alexander GASTON, Marmaduke DAVIS, ack. Sterling JOHNSTON, J.P., ent. 10 Mar 1810, rec. 13 same.

p. 189 - Indenture, 23 Jan 1808, Joseph PUMPHREY (wife Sarah), JCO; Nicholas PUMPHREY, Brooke County, Virginia. $766, land beginning on range line near (NBR) Widow McCONALL's spring, William HULSE, William BELL, MEEKS, WELCH, McFARLAND, 383 1/4 acres 8 perches, part of S 33 T 6 R 3, granted to Joseph PUMPHREY by patent dated 3 Oct 1805; WIT: Jesse MARTIN, John FLOWERS, ack. JCO, 7 Mar 1809, Jesse MARTIN, J.P., MARTIN certified by Jno. WARD, Clk., ent. 12 Mar 1810, rec. 20 same.

p. 192 - Indenture, 15 Mar 1810, William BOGGS (wife Elizabeth), BCO; John CARTER and Josiah UPDEGRAFF, BCO. $140, part of NE 1/4 of S 10 T 7 R 4, transferred to BOGGS by Bazaleel WELLS by deed dated 13 Jun 1800, 1/2 acre on north side of Wheeling road; [she signs Elisebeth], WIT: Sterling JOHNSTON, Thomas CONNELLY, ack. Sterling JOHNSTON, J.P., ent. 13 Mar 1810, rec. 26 same.

p. 193 - Indenture, [3] Feb 1810, Ebenezer ZANE (wife Elizabeth), Ohio County, Virginia; Andrew SCOTT, BCO. $500, SW 1/4 S 4 T 6 R 3, however, subsequently refers to "this half section of land"; WIT: Archb. WOODS, Thos. THOMPSON, ack. 27 Feb 1810, Thos. THOMPSON, J.P., ent. 24 Mar 1810, rec. 30 same.

p. 194 - Indenture, 22 Mar 1810, Josiah DILLON (wife Dority), BCO; James IRELAND, George IRELAND, and Thomas IRELAND, BCO. $486.31, SE 1/4 S 35 T 6 R 3, NBR: Joseph GILL, Josiah DILLON, Notley HAYS, 103 acres 20 perches; sgn: "Dorthy" DILLON, WIT: John [SHOPHER], John REID [his mark], ack. Robert GRIFFITH, J.P.

p. 195 - Indenture, 19 Mar 1810, William CHAPLINE (wife Mary), Ohio County, Virginia; Abner MURPHEY [MURPHY], BCO. $30, lot #62 in Morristown as laid off by CHAPLINE; WIT: Duncan MORRISON, ack. Sterling JOHNSTON, J.P., ent. 27 Mar 1810, rec. 5 Apr same.

p. 196 - Indenture, Josiah DILLON (wife Dorotha/Dorothea/Dorothy), BCO; Micheal [sic] GROVES, BCO. $205, out lot #15 in Bazaleel WELLS' plat adjoining addition of St. Clairsville; sgn: 13 Nov 1809 [she signs Dorithy], WIT: Zebulon WARNER, Edward WILLSON, ack. Zebulon WARNER, J.P., ent. 29 Mar 1810, rec. 5 Apr same. [Written in margin: "See old record "C" page 169."]

p. 197 - Indenture, 31 Mar 1800 [although the ack. is dated 1810], Obediah STILLWELL, Ohio County, Virginia; John TURNER, same. $150, two lots at east end of St. Clairsville, each 1/4 acre, conveyed from James ROSE to STILLWELL on 14 Feb 1809, as recorded in Book C, p. 3; WIT: Sterling JOHNSTON, John WINTER, ack. Sterling JOHNSTON, J.P., ent. 31 Mar 1810, rec. 6 Apr 1810.

p. 198 - Indenture, 2 Apr 1810, William BOGGS (wife Elizabeth), BCO; Samuel C. CLARK, BCO. $50, land near west end of St. Clairsville, 1 rod 30 perches, fee simple; WIT: Wm. VANCE, Sterling JOHNSTON, ack. Sterling JOHNSTON, J.P., ent. 2 Apr 1810, rec. 6 same.

p. 199 - Indenture, 2 Apr 1810, William BOGGS (wife Elizabeth), BCO; Samuel C. CLARK, BCO. $150, land near west end of St. Clairsville, NBR: John CARTER [whose land was also sold to him by BOGGS], 1/4 acre, fee simple; WIT: Wm. VANCE, Sterling JOHNSTON, ack. Sterling JOHNSTON, J.P., ent. 2 Apr 1810, rec. 7 same.

p. 200 - Indenture, 24 Mar 1810, Andrew CAMPBELL (wife Mary), BCO; Isaac MOORE, BCO. $202, part of NE 1/4 S 12 T 8 R 6, 50 1/2 acres 20 perches, fee simple; his seal, her mark, WIT: Thomas MOORE, John DOUGHERTY, ack. John GRIER, J.P., ent. 10 Apr 1810, rec. 20 same.

p. 201 - Indenture, 24 Mar 1810, William CAMPBLE [CAMPBELL] (wife Margaret), BCO; Isaac MOORE, BCO. $44, part of SW 1/4 S 1 T 9 R 6, 20 1/4 acres 7 perches, fee simple; WIT: Thomas MOORE, William McCORMACK, ack. John GRIER, J.P., ent. 11 Apr 1810, rec. 20 same.

p. 202 - Indenture, 20 Dec 1809, Joseph HODGIN (wife Elizabeth), Warren twp., BCO; Stephen TODD, same. $280, beginning S of NE corner S 11 T 8 R 6, 140 acres, fee simple; WIT: John GRIER, Amos DAVIS, ack. 20 Dec 1809, John GRIER, J.P., ent. 11 Apr 1810, rec. 20 same.

p. 204 - Know all men, Philip DOVER, of Pultney, BCO; James FARIS, same. $50, lot #13 in Square No. 32 in Pultney in the Wegee Bottom T 2 R 2; sgn: 29 Jan 1810, WIT: Jacob DAVIS, Patrick McELHONEY, ack. Jacob DAVIS, J.P., ent. 11 Apr 1810, rec. 21 same.

p. 204 - Indenture, 2 Apr 1810, Amos [Emos] JENNEY, attorney for Joseph JENNEY of Loudon County, Virginia; William EWERS, BCO. $300, part of S 2 T 9 R 5, 175 acres, fee simple; WIT: Jacob GREGG, Rebecca GREGG, Sarah SHARP, ack. William SINCLAIR, J.P., ent. 11 Apr 1810, rec. 21 same.

p. 206 - Indenture, 19 d 1 m 1810, Joseph COX (wife Elizabeth), BCO; James EDGERTON, BCO. $20, NW corner of NW 1/4 S 29 T 3 R 5, near Captina Creek, 5 acres; WIT: Isaac HALL, Thomas GRIER, ack. 27 Mar 1810, John GRIER, J.P., ent. 12 Apr 1810, rec. 21 same.

p. 207 - Indenture, 11 Apr 1810, William CHAPLINE, Brook County, Virginia; Obediah JENNINGS, Steubenville. $107, lots #109, #110, and #111 in Morristown, as well as land adjoining town in S 20 T 8 R 5, Steubenville district, near a horse mill, 19 1/2 acres 20 perches, ; WIT: James CARRATHERS, James McELHERAN, ack. Sterling JOHNSTON, J.P.

p. 208 - Indenture, 27 d 3 m 18810, Isaac HALL (wife Dinah), BCO; Joseph COX, BCO. $550, E 1/2 S 33 T 6 R 5, Marietta district; WIT: James EDGERTON, John GRIER, Senr., ack. 27 Mar 1810, John GRIER, J.P., ent. 18 Apr 1810, rec. 23 same.

p. 209 - Indenture, 19 Mar 1810, William CHAPLIN (wife Mary), Ohio County, Virginia; Nicholas RODGERS, BCO. $30, lots #49 and #30 in Morristown as laid off by CHAPLIN; WIT: Duncan MORRISON, ack. 13 Apr 1810, Sterling JOHNSTON, J.P., ent. 13 Apr 1810, rec. 23 same.

p. 210 - Indenture, 16 Apr 1810, John RYANS (wife Elizabeth), BCO; George ARMSTRONG, late of same. $245, part of NE corner S 14 T 8 R 4, 50 acres, conveyed to RYANS by Jacob KUHN (wife Barbara) on 9 Feb 1808, recorded in Book B, p. 237, fee simple; his mark, her seal, WIT: John COTTLE, Sterling JOHNSTON, ack. Sterling JOHNSTON, J.P., ent. 16 Apr 1810, rec. 23 same.

p. 211 - Indenture, 17 Apr 1810, William GIBSON, Guernsey County, Ohio; Notley HAYS, BCO. $60, part of S 4 T 7 R 4, 2 acres, conveyed to William GIBSON by William GIBSON (senior his father) on 9 Jun 1806, recorded in Book A, p. 666; WIT: Adam JOHNSTON, Sterling JOHNSTON, ack. Sterling JOHNSTON, J.P., ent. 17 Apr 1810, rec. 24 same.

p. 212 - Indenture, 11 Apr 1810, Joshua HATCHER (wife Jane), BCO; James DILLON, BCO. $320, part S 18 T 9 R 7, NBR: David WHERRY, 160 acres, fee simple; WIT: David VANCE, Sterling JOHNSTON, ack. Sterling JOHNSTON, J.P., ent. 17 Apr 1810, rec. 24 same.

p. 213 - Indenture, 1 Nov 1809, Mary CAMPBELL, widow, William CAMPBELL (wife Eleanor), James CAMPBELL (wife Margaret), David CAMPBELL (wife Ann), Benjamin BAY (wife Grasy), William FALLON (wife Polly), Charles CAMPBELL, Junr., George CAMPBELL, Elizabeth CAMPBELL, legal heirs and representatives of John CAMPBELL, late of Cross Creek twp., Washington County, Pennsylvania, deceased; John CAMPBELL, BCO. John died intestate leaving relict Mary CAMPBELL and legal issue six sons and three daughters, viz. John, William, James, David, Charles, George, and Grasy, Polly, and Elizabeth, and previous to decease expressed intention of dividing a section of land between his four oldest sons--John, William, James, and David, and land in Cross Creek twp., Washington County, Pennsylvania be divided between two younger sons Charles and George, land in Ohio valued at $3 per acre, and in Pennsylvania at $5 per acre, John now receives title to part of S 26 T 8 R 4, 131 acres, sgn: Mary, Wm., Nelly, James, Peggy, David, Ann CAMPBELL, Benjamin and Grasie BAY, William and Mary FULTON, Charles, George, and Betsy CAMPBELL, WIT: William KERR, James CAMPBELL, Joseph CAMPBELL, ack. 1 Nov 1809, Washington County, Samuel MILLER, J.P., ent. 20 Apr 1810, rec. 25 same.

p. 215 - Indenture, 1 Nov 1809, [same individuals as above except John (wife Polly) included and David excluded from first party list)]; David CAMPBELL, BCO. David receives part of S 26 T 8 R 4, 171 acres, sgn: same list except includes John and Mary CAMPBELL, and there are small "x's" after Mary CAMPBELL and Nelly CAMPBELL's first names, WIT: William KERR, James CAMPBELL, Jesse CAMPBELL, ack. 1 Nov 1809, Washington County, Pennsylvania, Samuel MILLER, J.P., ent. 20 Apr 1810, rec. 25 same.

p. 217 - Indenture, 1 Nov 1809, [same individuals minus William]; William CAMPBELL, BCO. 171 acres in S 26 T 8 R 4; WIT: William KERR, James CAMPBELL, Jesse CAMPBELL, ack. BCO, 1 Nov 1809, Samuel MILLER, J.P., ent. 20 Apr 1810, rec. 25 same.

p. 219 - Indenture, 31 Mar 1810, Moses MERRIT (wife Polly), Wheeling twp., BCO; William DIXON, Fayette County, Pennsylvania. $757, NW 1/4 S 31 T 8 R 4, granted to Moses MERRIT by patent dated 1 Oct 1807, also 15 acres; WIT: John CAMPBELL, Caleb JEFFEIRS [sic], ack. 31 Mar 1810, John CAMPBELL, J.P., ent. 21 apr 1810, rec. 26 same.

p. 220 - Indenture, 21 Aug 1808, [Knonis/Knowis] DOUDNA (wife Hannah), BCO; John COLYAR, BCO. $400, NE 1/4 S 7 T 8 R 6, patented to DOUDNA on 9 Mar 1807; WIT: John GREIR [sic], Senr., Henry DOUDNA, ack. 22 Aug 1808, John GRIER, J.P.

p. 221 - Indenture, 22 Jan 1810, Samuel SULLIVAN (wife Mary), Zanesville, Muskingum County, Ohio; William ASKEW, St. Clairsville, BCO. $250, out lot #8 adjoining addition to St. Clairsville as laid out by William MATHERS, conveyed by Obediah JENNINGS to Andrew MOORE by deed dated 1 Sep 1806, conveyed by MOORE (wife Elizabeth) to SULLIVAN by deed dated 20 Dec 1807; WIT: Ruban REIVES, Saml. THOMPSON, ack. 7 Mar 1810, Saml. THOMPSON, J.P., ent. 27 Apr 1810, rec. 28 same.

p. 222 - Whereas patent dated 3 Oct 1805 granted to Francis TOWNSEND, assignee of Joseph TOWNSEND for S 17 T 6 R 3. Now for bond Benjamin BAILEY has granted Joseph TOWNSEND, Francis TOWNSEND (wife Marrah), of JCO, delivered by George SHARPLESS, BCO, SHARPLESS receives part of S 17 T 6 R 3, NBR: Aaron NEWPORT (near Yost run), George SHARPLESS, Jacob LASH, 30 acres; sgn: 26 Mar 1810, she signs [Mart], WIT: John MORTON, Preston SHARPLESS, ack. JCO, John MORTON, J.P.

p. 224 - Indenture, 1 Nov 1809, [same CAMPBELL list as on pp. 213-217, less James]; James CAMPBELL, BCO. James receives his 171 acres in S 26 T 8 R 4; WIT: William KERR, James CAMPBELL, Jesse CAMPBELL, ack. 1 Nov 1809, Washington County, Pennsylvania, Saml. MILLER, J.P., ent. 28 Apr 1810, rec. 30 same.

p. 226 - Indenture, 12 Apr 1810, Abraham DAVIES [DAVIS], BCO, James McMILLION [McMILLAN], Lickin County, Ohio. DAVIS indebted to McMILLION for $700, conveys to McMILLION part of S 15 and S 21 in T 4 R 2, originally conveyed to Archibald WOODS, from WOODS to Absalom MARTIN, from MARTIN to John CONNELL, etc., and conveyed from McMILLAN to DAVIS on 22 Apr 1809, fee simple, void if debt paid by 1 Apr 1814; sgn: Abraham DAVIS and Abigail DAVIS, WIT: Thos. MITCHELL, Hariat MITCHELL, ack. Thos. MITCHELL, J.P., ent. 16 Apr 1810, rec. 7 May same.

p. 227 - Indenture, 2 May 1810, John FORREST (wife Rachel), BCO; Henry ARFORD, BCO. $90, part of NE 1/4 S 36 T 5 R 3, 30 acres, conveyed to FORREST by Nathan UPDEGRAFF and Borden STANTON, extrs. of Benjamin STANTON, dec'd, on 25 d 12 m 1809, recorded Book C, p. 158, fee simple; his seal, her mark, WIT: Isaac COOK, Wm. VANE, ack. Sterling JOHNSTON, J.P., ent. 2 May 1810, rec. 8 same.

p. 228 - Indenture, 1 May 1810, Neal MAHAN (wife Mary), and William DEVLIN (wife Jane), BCO; Issacher FOULKE [no location specified]. $740, part of S 23 T 7 R 4, 80 acres, NBR: Evan PHILIPS, William DEVLIN, conveyed to John HOPKINS by Samuel OSGOOD and Walter LIVINGSTON on

3 Mar 1789; MAHANs' marks, DEVLINs' seals, WIT: John WILCHILL, Susanna [BURCDAY, BINCDAY], ack. Sterling JOHNSTON, J.P., ent. 4 May 1810, rec. 8 same.

p. 230 - Indenture, 6 Nov 1809, Bazaleel WELLS (wife Sally), JCO; Jesse FINCH, BCO. $620, part of S 18 T 6 R 3, 172 acres; WIT: Margt. MARSHALL, J. JINKENSON, ack. JCO, 6 Nov 1809, J. JENKINSON, J.P., JENKINSON certified by Jno. WARD at Steubenville, 6 Nov 1809, ent. 5 May 1810, rec. 8 same.

p. 231 - Indenture, 1 May 1810, Neal MAHAN (wife Mary), BCO; William DEVLIN, BCO. ". . . in consideration of certain particular reasons by them agreed to," part of S 23 T 7 R 4, NBR: Issachar FOULKE, Evan PHILIPS, Isaac HOGE, George KELLAR, 80 acres, conveyed to John HOPKINS by Samuel OSGOOD and Walter LIVINGSTON dated 3 Mar 1789; [seals here--?], WIT: Sterling JOHNSTON, Henry HARDY, ack. Sterling JOHNSTON, J.P., ent. 6 May 1810, rec. 8 same.

p. 232 - Indenture, 11 d 6 m 1807, Horton HOWARD (wife Hannah), BCO; William MILHOUSE, BCO. $1,280, SW 1/4 S 8 T 7 R 3, granted to HOWARD in fee by patent dated 10 Sep 1806; WIT: John MITCHELL, John STEWART, ack. of payment WIT: John MITCHELL, John STEWARD, ack. 11 d 6 m 1807, Thomas MITCHELL, J.P., ent. 8 May 1810, rec. 10 same.

p. 234 - Indenture, 1 d 1 m 1810, Borden STANTON (wife Charlotte), BCO; Joseph GIBBONS, BCO. $1,280, SW 1/4 S 7 T 7 R 3, 160 acres, granted to STANTON by fee patent dated 27 Aug 1805; WIT: Horton HOWARD, Joseph BISHOP [his mark], ack. 4 Jan 1810, Thos. MITCHELL, J.P., payment WIT: same.

p. 235 - Indenture, 4 Apr 1810, Thomas WILSON, Kirkwood twp., BCO; James CALDWELL, St. Clairsville, BCO. $200, SE 1/4 S 18 T 9 R 6, Steubenville district, 169 acres, granted to John HART, BCO, which HART assigned to WILSON, payment due by 1812; [sgn: listed as Thos. MITCHELL's seal--?], WIT: Sterling JOHNSTON, Jacob NAGLE, ack. Sterling JOHNSTON, J.P., CALDWELL signs that he received "the interest on the within two hundred dollars say twenty two dollars in having paid himself two dollars in the bank 7 Apr 1810," ent. 10 May 1810, rec. 12 same.

p. 236 - Indenture, 26 Feb 1810, James STANTON [subsequently MARTIN] (wife Agnes), BCO; Charles PIGION and William GREGG, BCO. $550, purchasers to be tenants in common, lots #94, #110, and #102 in St. Clairsville, conveyed from John LONG (wife Catharine) to said James MARTIN on 25 Apr

1808, recorded Book B, p. 303; WIT: Sterling JOHNSTON, Jonah GORE, ack. 26 Feb 1810, Sterling JOHNSTON, J.P., ent. 16 May 1810, rec. 22 same.

p. 237 - Indenture, 25 Nov 1809, John SIMINSON [SIMONSON], Washington, Pennsylvania; Bazaleel WELLS and Obediah JENNINGS of Steubenville. $1,000, lot #125 in St. Clairsville, conveyed to SIMONSON by John ISRAEL (wife Rachel) by deed dated 11 Aug 1806; WIT: J. JENKINSON, Mary WILLSON, ack. 25 Nov 1809, J. JENKINSON, J.P., ent. 16 May 1810, rec. 22 same.

p. 238 - Indenture, 10 Apr 1810, James [rest of document refers to Jonas] PICKERING (wife Ruth), BCO; Thomas BUFKIN, Union twp., BCO. $255, land in Union twp., part of the N 1/2 S 20 T 9 R 5, Steubenville district, 81 acres, patented to Jonas PICKERING on 17 Jul 1808; WIT: John PICKERING, Isaac WILSON, ack. 10 Apr 1810, Zebulon WARNER, J.P., ent. 18 May 1810, rec. 23 same.

p. 240 - Indenture, 23 d 4 m 1810, John STANLEY (wife Elizabeth); Aaron WOOD [no locations given]. $100, part of SW 1/4 S 10 T 6 R 5, Marietta district, 51 3/4 acres 37 poles; WIT: Isaac MOORE, George HALL, ack. Isaac MOORE, J.P., ent. 22 may 1810, rec. 23 same.

p. 241 - Indenture, 15 Aug 1809, David CHAMBERS (wife Prudence), Muskingum County, Ohio; Samuel WILSON, BCO. $55, lot #31 in Morristown; his seal, her mark, WIT: Wm. W. GANT, Levi WHIPPLE, ack. Muskingum County, 13 Feb 1810, Levi WHIPPLE, J.P., ent. 25 May 1810, rec. 27 same.

p. 242 - Indenture, 24 Mar 1810, Samuel WILSON (wife Ann), Washington County, Pennsylvania; Joseph HANDERSON, same. $120, lot #31 in Morristown; WIT: John BUCHANNON, Walter CRAIG, ack. Washington County, 24 ____ 1810, ent. 25 May 1810, rec. 29 same.

p. 243 - Indenture, 8 Dec 1809, Bazaleel WELLS (wife Sally), JCO; Daniel McPECK [probably McPEEK], BCO. $612, part S 18 T 6 R 3, NBR: John FINCH; WIT: Alex. HOLMES, Buttler[?] WELLS, ack. JCO, 8 Dec 1809, J. JENKINSON, J.P., JENKINSON certified by Jno. WARD, Clk., ent. 29 May 1810, rec. 30 same.

p. 244 - Indenture, 29 Mar 1810, James CALDWELL (wife Nancy), BCO; John HINES, BCO. $40, lot #25 in St. Clairsville, fee simple; WIT: Samuel A. BOOKER, Sterling JOHNSTON, ack. 29 Mar 1810, Sterling JOHNSTON, J.P., ent. 30 May 1810, rec. 1 Jun same.

p. 245 - Indenture, 30 May 1810, Edward WILSON (wife Amy), Richland twp., BCO; Samuel WILSON, BCO. $25, N 1/2 of lots #11 and #12 in addition to St. Clairsville, as laid out by William MATHERS, conveyed by Hadiah [Obediah?] JENNINGS (wife Ann) to WILSON; WIT: Zebulon WARNER, Isaac WILSON, ack. 13 May 1810, Zebulon WARNER, J.P., ent. 31 May 1810, rec. 1 Jun same.

p. 246 - Indenture, 10 Apr 1810, Jonas [later referred to erroneously as Joseph] PICKERING (wife Ruth), BCO; Joseph FAUCET, Union twp., BCO. $243.50, 121 3/4 acres, part of S 20 T 9 R 5, Steubenville district, in Union twp., patented to PICKERING on 20 Jul 1808; WIT: John PICKERING, Isaac WILSON, ack. 10 Apr 1810, Zebulon WARNER, J.P.

p. 247 - Indenture, 10 Apr 1810, Jonas PICKERING (wife Ruth), Kirkwood twp., BCO; Mary FAUCET, Union twp., BCO. $296.68, land in Union twp. [Flushing is written in above Union], 74 17/100 acres, part of NW 1/4 S 20 T 9 R 5, Steubenville district, patented to PICKERING on 20 Jul 1808; WIT: John PICKERING, Isaac WILSON, ack. 10 Apr 1810, Zebulon WARNER, J.P., ent. 1 Jun 1810, rec. 4 same.

p. 249 - Indenture, 4 Jun 1810, David WALLACE, BCO; Alexander McCONNELL, BCO. $146, 73 acres 2 rods 28 perches, part of SW 1/4 S 8 T 8 R 4, patented to WALLACE on 30 Dec 1807; WIT: Sterling JOHNSTON, David MARSHALL, ack. 4 Jun 1810, Sterling JOHNSTON, J.P., ent. 4 Jun 1810, rec. 5 same.

p. 250 - Indenture, 29 d 5 m 1810, Borden STANTON (wife Charlotte), BCO; David BERRY, BCO. $560, part of S 1 T 7 R 3, patented to Borden on 20 d 12 m 1810, bordered by N side of Glen's run, NBR: FRAZIER, WILLIAMS, [SLEEL--possibly STEEL?], 270 acres; WIT: Borden STANTON, Junr., Stafford MILTON, ack. 29 May 1810, Thos. MITCHELL, Justice.

p. 251 - Whereas William CHAPLINE, Ohio County, Virginia, on 14 Jun 1804 purchased SW 1/4 S 34 T 8 R 5, Steubenville district, certificate dated 23 Jul 1804, for $100 paid by Moses CAMBELL [CAMPBELL], BCO, and it looks like CAMPBELL takes over future payments on land; sgn: 3 Nov 1805, [no WIT given], ack. 3 Nov 1805, J. ISRAEL and Duncan MORRISON, J.P.'s, ent. 5 Jun 1810, rec. same.

p. 252 - Indenture, 10 Apr 1810, Jonas PICKERING (wife Ruth), BCO; George SMITH, Union twp., BCO. $600, land in Union twp., 104 1/4 acres, part of S 20 T 9 R 5, Steubenville district, patented to PICKERING on 20 Jul 1808; WIT: John PICKERING, Isaac WILSON, ack. 10 Apr 1810, Zebulon WARNER, J.P., ent. 6 Jun 1810, rec. 15 same.

p. 253 - Indenture, 6 d 6 m 1810, Jacob MOORE (wife Elizabeth), BCO; Joseph NICHOLSON, [no location given]. $320, E 1/2 of SW 1/4 S 17 T 6 R 5, Marietta district; both mark, WIT: Isaac MOORE, Hannah MOORE, ack. 6 d 6 m 1810, Isaac MOORE, ent. 8 Jun 1810, rec. 15 same.

p. 254 - Indenture, 23 d 4 m 1810, John STANLEY (wife Elizabeth); George HALL, [no locations given]. $109, 54 1/2 acres, part of SW 1/4 S 10 T 6 R 5, Marietta district; his seal, her mark, WIT: Isaac MOORE, Aaron WOOD, ack. 23 d 4 m 1810, Isaac MOORE, J.P., ent. 8 Jun 1810, rec. 15 same.

p. 255 - Indenture, 6 d 6 m 1810, Jacob MOORE (wife Elizabeth), BCO; Samuel EDGERTON, BCO. $320, W 1/2 of SW 1/4 S 17 T 6 R 5, Marietta district; both mark, WIT: Isaac MOORE, Hannah MOORE [her mark], ack. 6 d 6 m 1810, Isaac MOORE, J.P., ent. 8 Jun 1810, rec. 16 same.

p. 256 - Indenture, Herman DAVIS (wife Hannah), BCO; Moses DAVIS, BCO. $80, 40 acres, part of S 14 T 8 R 6; WIT: Dunsey BOSWELL, John [written "Jehn"] MIDDLETON, ack. 31 May 1810, John GRIER, J.P., ent. 8 Jun 1810, rec. 16 same.

p. 257 - Indenture, 12 Jun 1810, John PRICE (wife Elizabeth), BCO; John MITCHELL, BCO. $330, part of S 36 T 7 R 4, patented to John EDWARDS, Senr., on 7 Apr 1806, EDWARDS conveyed to PRICE on 28 May 1806, bordering Wheeling Creek, 61 acres 3 rods 20 perches, fee simple; both mark, WIT: Isaac VORE, Sterling JOHNSTON, ack. Sterling JOHNSTON, J.P., ent. 12 Jun 1810, rec. 16 same.

p. 259 - Indenture, 15 d 4 m 1810, Thomas SATTERTHWAITE, BCO; John WILSON, BCO. $140, part of S 13 T 7 R 3, 13 acres 2 rods 15 poles, NBR: Joseph W. SATTERTHWAIT, Saml. POTTS, part of tract given by lw&t of father William SATTERTHWAIT, dec'd, to Thomas SATTERTHWAIT, patented to William on 9 d 3 m 1803; WIT: Peter TALLMAN, John McWILLIAMS, ack. 13 Jun 1810, Sterling JOHNSTON, J.P., ent. 13 Jun 1810, rec. 18 same.

p. 260 - Indenture, 7 May 1810, Bazaleel WELLS (wife Sally), JCO; Thomas SATTHERTHWAITE, BCO. $200, part S 19 T 7 R 3, Steubenville district, NBR: land sold by WELLS to Samuel [T.] IDEN, 177 acres 144 perches; WIT: Jonathan TAYLOR, J. JENKINSON, ack. JCO, 7 May 1810, J. JENKINSON, J.P., [however, here the certification says JENKINSON's first name is Isaac!], Jno WARD, Clerk, ent. 18 Jun 1810, rec. 18 same.

p. 261 - Indenture, 7 May 1810, Bazaleel WELLS (wife Sally), JCO; Samuel T. IDEN, Burks County, Pennsylvania. $1,260, part S 19 T 7 R 3, NBR: Thomas BLACKLEDGE, Thomas SATTERTHWAITE, 307 acres; WIT: Jonathan TAYLOR, J. JENKINSON, ack. JCO, 7 May 1810, J. JENKINSON, J.P., [again Isaac in certification] certification of JENKINSON by Jno. WARD, Clk., ent. 13 Jun 1810, rec. 13 same.

p. 262 - Indenture, 14 Jun 1810, Jacob RIPPLEAGLE, Montgomery County, Ohio; James McCOY [McCAY], BCO. $100, part of SW 1/4 S 30 T 7 R 4, 20 acres; WIT: Sterling JOHNSTON, John McWILLIAMS, ack. BCO 14 Jun 1810, Sterling JOHNSTON, J.P., ent. 14 Jun 1810, rec. 18 same.

p. 264 - Indenture, 2 Jun 1810, Isaac VORE and Samuel SHARP, BCO, admrs. Nicholas BOWERS, dec'd; Richard TRUAX, BCO. $94.30, lots #135 and #136 in St. Clairsville, conveyed from David NEWELL (wife Sally) to Christopher CLOUSE (Senr.) on 1 May 1802, from CLOSE (wife Catharine) to BOWERS; WIT: Sterling JOHNSTON, Joseph JOHNSTON, ack. Sterling JOHNSTON, J.P., ent. 14 Jun 1810, rec. 22 same.

p. 265 - Indenture, 7 Jun 1810, Richard TRUAX (wife Mary), BCO; David BARTON, BCO. $200, lots #135 and #136 in St. Clairsville, [history as in previous indenture]; his seal, her mark, WIT: Sterling JOHNSTON, William MOSELY, ack. Sterling JOHNSTON, J.P., ent. 14 Jun 1810, rec. 23 same.

p. 266 - Indenture, 26 Mar 1810, Richard TRUAX (wife Mary), BCO: David BARTON, BCO. $1,400, 106 acres 6 perches, part of S 18 T 7 R 4, patented to Alexander YOUNG on 10 Nov 1807; his seal, her mark, WIT: Sterling JOHNSTON, William MOSELY, ack. 7 Jun 1810, Sterling JOHNSTON, J.P., ent. 14 Jun 1810, rec. 22 same.

p. 267 - Indenture, 26 May 1810, David BARTON (wife Nancy), BCO; Richard TRUAX, BCO. $1,800, NBR: Richard TRUAX, Joshua CLARK, 99 acres 2 rods 32 perches, part of S 13 T 8 R 4, patented to BARTON on 20 Dec 1808; WIT: Wm. MOSELY, Sterling JOHNSTON, ack. 7 Jun 1810, Sterling JOHNSTON, J.P., ent. 14 Jun 1810, rec. 23 same.

p. 269 - Indenture, 26 May 1810, David BARTON (wife Nancy), BCO; Joshua CLARK, BCO. $362, bordered by N side of Wheeling Creek, NBR: Holmes WHITACRE, PATTON, Richard TRUAX, Joshua CLARK, 60 acres 1 rod 11 perches, part of S 13 T 8 R 4, patented to BARTON on 20 Dec 1808; WIT: Wm. MOSELY, Sterling JOHNSTON, ack. 7 Jun 1810, Sterling JOHNSTON, J.P., ent. 14 Jun 1810, rec. 23 same.

p. 271 - Indenture, 16 Jun 1808, David NEISWANGER (wife Mary), Richland twp., BCO; William PERRINE, St. Clairsville, BCO. Josiah HEDGES, Esqr., high sheriff of BCO granted to Charles HAMMOND, Esqr., lot #67 in St. Clairsville, HAMMOND sold to NISWONGER on 11 Dec 1807, 1/4 acre, for $25 now sold to PERRINE; his seal, her mark, WIT: Robert GRIFFITH, Sterling JOHNSTON, ack. 16 Jun 1808, Sterling JOHNSTON, J.P., ent. 17 Jun 1810, rec. 23 same.

p. 272 - Indenture, 16 Jun 1810, Samuel GREGG, BCO, atty. for Jonah HOUGH and Pleasant HOUGH (wife) of Loudon County, Virginia; Joseph PANCOAST [originally written PANCOATS], BCO. $364.50, NW 1/4 S 1 t 8 R 5, patented to HOUGH on 15 Aug 1808, fee simple; WIT: Wm. CONGLETON, Sterling JOHNSTON, ack. 17 Jun 1810, Sterling JOHNSTON, J.P., ent. 17 Jun 1810, rec. 25 same.

p. 273 - Know all men, Jonah HOUGH (wife Pleasant), Loudon County, Virginia, power of atty. to Samuel GREGG, BCO, to convey to Charles PIDGION, Charles GREGG, Abner GREGG, and Joseph PANCOST, S 1 T 8 R 5, sgn: 19 Jul 1806; WIT: Samuel HOUGH, Samuel [MUNY--probably MURRY], Obediah CLIFFORD, ack. Loudon County, 19 Jun 1806, Samuel MURRY, Obediah CLIFFORD, MURRY and CLIFFORD certified by C. BINNS, Clk, BINNS certified by Francis PEYTON, first J.P., 21 Jul 1806, ent. 17 Jun 1810, rec. 25 same.

p. 274 - Indenture, 18 Jun 1810, Neal MAHON (wife Mary), BCO; William DEVLIN [DEVLON] [no location given]. Whereas MAHON and DEVLIN purchased a lot on 4 Sep 1800 as joint tenants from Stephen MILLER of New York by his atty. George MILLER, 220 acres, part of S 23 and 24 T 7 R 4, recorded in Jefferson County, Lib. A, p. 128, whereas MAHON on 1 May past sold to John MITCHELL 80 acres to which DEVLON has relinquished all right, for which MITCHELL paid $740, the total of which went to MAHON, MAHONs are now quit claiming to DEVLON 80 acres in that section, NBR: Issacher FOULKS, Evan PHILIPPS, Isaac HOGE, George KELLER; both mark, WIT: James CLOYD, Sterling JOHNSTON, ack. Sterling JOHNSTON, J.P., ent. 18 Jun 1810, rec. 25 same.

p. 275 - Indenture, 31 d 5 m 1810, Harmon [Herman] DAVIS (wife Hannah), Warren twp., BCO; Joseph MIDDLETON, same. $112, beginning in NE corner S 14 T 8 R 6, 56 acres, fee simple; his seal, her mark, WIT: William BOSWELL, Thomas BOUDY, ack. 31 May 1810, John GRIER, J.P., ent. 23 Jun 1810, rec. 25 same.

p. 276 - Indenture, 27 Apr 1810, Joseph SHARP (wife Nancy), BCO; Jacob RIPPLEAGLE, Montgomery County, Ohio. $555, SE 1/4 S 30 T 7 R 4, patented to SHARP on 20 Jun 1809, Steubenville district; only Joseph signs, WIT: John CAMPBELL, Mary CAMPBELL, ack. 27 Apr 1810, John CAMPBELL, J.P., ent. 23 Jun 1810, rec. 25 same.

p. 277 - Indenture, 23 Jun 1810, Jacob HOULTS (wife Peggy), BCO; Jacob MYERS, BCO. $540, part S 2 T 7 R 4, 120 acres, fee simple; both mark, WIT: Sterling JOHNSTON, Wm. CONGLELTON, ack. Sterling JOHNSTON, J.P., ent. 23 Jun 1810, rec. 26 same.

p. 278 - Indenture, 10 Apr 1810, Jonas PICKERING (wife Ruth), BCO; Samuel FAUCET, Union twp., BCO. $205, 46 acres, part of NE 1/4 S 20 T 9 R 5, Steubenville district, patented to PICKERING on 20 Jul 180_; WIT: John PICKERING, Isaac WILSON, ack. 10 Apr 1810, Zebulon WARNER, J.P., ent. 25 Jun 1810, rec. 26 same.

p. 279 - Indenture, 10 Apr 1810, Jonas PICKERING (wife Ruth), BCO; Samuel FAUCET, Union twp., BCO. $100, 50 acres, part of SW 1/4 S 20 T 9 R 5, Steubenville district, patented to PICKERING on 20 Jun 1810; WIT: John PICKERING, Isaac WILSON, ack. 10 Apr 1810, Zebulon WARNER, J.P., ent. 25 Jun 1810, rec. 27 same.

p. 280 - Indenture, 23 Jun 1810, James CALDWELL (wife Nancy), St. Clairsville, BCO; William CONGLETON, same. $200, 219 acres 53 perches 8 links, part of S 2 T 7 R 4, part of land patented to CALDWELL on 24 Aug 1807; WIT: Sterling JOHNSTON, James HEDGES, ack. Sterling JOHNSTON, J.P., ent. 28 Jun 1810, rec. same.

p. 281 - Indenture, 23 Jun 1810, James CALDWELL (wife Nancy), BCO; Jacob HOULTS [HOLTS], BCO. $313, 219 acres 5 perches 8 links, part of S 2 T 7 R 4, patented to CALDWELL on 24 Aug 1807; WIT: Sterling JOHNSTON, Wm. CONGLETON, ack. Sterling JOHNSTON, J.P., ent. 28 Jun 1810, rec. same.

p. 282 - Indenture, 23 Jun 1810, Mahlon SMITH (wife Mary), BCO; George HARTSHORN, Senr., JCO. $40, part of lot #97 of St. Clairsville, conveyed to David RUSSEL by David NEWALL (wife Sally) and Benjamin NEWALL (wife Jane) on 21 Jan 1801 as recorded in Book A, p. 6, from RUSSELL (wife Hannah) to SMITH on 27 Oct 1808, recorded in Book C, p. 71, fee simple; WIT: John DUGAN, Sterling JOHNSTON, ack. Sterling JOHNSTON, J.P., ent. [no data].

p. 283 - Indenture, 29 Jun 1810, John CARLOW, BCO; William BROWN, BCO. BROWN bound to CARLOW in judgment obtained before Sterling

JOHNSTON on 21 May 1810 foro $64.37 1/2 in favor of Jacob HOULTS, BCO, for better securing of bail and $1 CARLOW sells to BROWN his half interest in printing press now in possession of John C. GILKISON, void if debt paid by 29 Dec; WIT: Sterling JOHNSTON, Joseph JOHNSTON, ack. Sterling JOHNSTON, J.P., ent. 29 Jun 1810, rec. same.

p. 284 - Indenture, 29 Jun 1810, John HARDESTY (wife Elizabeth), Muskingum County, Ohio; William McMILLON [McMILLAN], BCO. $900, land bordering on Wheeling Creek, 100 acres, patented to Robert JOHNSTON on 17 Apr 1788, conveyed by JOHNSTON to HARDESTY on 31 Jan 1794, part of S 23 and 24 T 6 R 3, fee simple; his mark, WIT: Sterling JOHNSTON, Jos. JOHNSTON, ack. Sterling JOHNSTON, J.P.

p. 285 - Indenture, 7 Mar 1810, Joseph GILL (wife Ann), Mount Pleasant, JCO; John TAGERT, JCO. $3,000, part of S 35 T 6 R 3, Steubenville district, NBR: Notley HAYS, George IRELAND, John BERRY, Hugh LYON, 403 acres, patented to Josiah DILLON on 14 Jul 1806, fee simple; WIT: John GILL, John WATSON, ack. 17 Mar 1810, John WATSON, J.P., ent. 21 Jul 1810, rec. same.

p. 286 - Indenture, 5 May 1810, Garret SNEDEKER (wife Elizabeth), Brook County, Virginia; James FLAHARTY, BCO. $40, 9 3/4 acres, part of SE 1/4 S 1 T 9 R 5, patented to SNEDEKER on 10 Sep 1806; Elizabeth doesn't sgn, WIT: John CAMPBELL, Joseph RANKIN, ack. 5 May 1810, Garrett only, "his wife being unable to attend," John CAMPBELL, J.P., ent. 21 Jul 1810, rec. same.

p. 287 - Indenture, 18 Jun 1810, Jacob RIPLOGAIL (wife Elizabeth), Montgomery County, Ohio; John MITCHELL, BCO. $40, 10 acres, part of SE 1/4 S 30 T 7 R 4, patented to Joseph SHARP on 20 Jun 1809, SHARP to RIPLOGAL by deed dated 27 Apr 1810, NBR: James McCOY, John MITCHELL; his seal, her mark; WIT: Wm. JOHNSTON, Junr., Sterling JOHNSTON, ack. BCO, 18 Jun 1810, Sterling JOHNSTON, J.P., ack. Montgomery County, John FOLKERTH, J.P., FOLKERTH certified by Benjamin VAN CLEVE, Clerk, FOLKERTH a J.P. for Dayton twp., sgn: 5 Jul 1810, ent. 24 Jul [1810], rec. same.

p. 290 - Know all, Jeremiah BURRIS, BCO, to secure Josiah HEDGES and Samuel SPRIGG who have endorsed note for $600 to be discounted at the Bank of Steubenville, sells to Charles HAMMOND 160 acres in S 6 T 3, purchased by BURRIS from Enoch RUSH, Peter BLASER now living there, and 50 acres adjoining the tract of 160 acres purchased from Samuel MEEKS, purchased by MEEKS from Joseph PUMPHREY, where Wm. FROST now lives, void if BURRIS pays debt, sgn: ___ Feb 1810; his mark, WIT: Zebulon WARNER,

James HEDGES, ack. 21 Feb 1810, Zebulon WARNER, J.P., ent. 1 Aut 1810, rec. same.

p. 291 - Indenture, 26 Jun 1810, Robert VERNON, BCO; Otho FRENCH, BCO. $165, part of NW 1/4 S 26 T 7 R 5, 60 acres; WIT: Henry GIER[?], Thomas SHANNON, ack. 26 Jun 1810, John GRIER, J.P., ent. 4 Aug 1810, rec. 6 same.

p. 291 - Indenture, 2 Aug 1810, William HOLMES (wife Mary), BCO; James MOORE, JCO. $300, part S 13 T 8 R 4, NBR: Archibald McELROY, 60 acres, patented to David BARTON on 20 Dec 1808; his seal, her mark, WIT: Wm. BARTON, John CAMPBELL, ack. John CAMPBELL, J.P., ent. 6 Aug 1810, rec. 7 same.

p. 292 - Indenture, 29 d 5 m 1810, Borden STANTON (wife Charlotte), BCO; Anna WILLIAMS, BCO. $110, part of S 1 T 7 R 3, patented to STANTON on 20 d 12 m 1808, 50 acres, NBR: David BERRY, Bennajah [STEEL or STEET]; WIT: David BERRY, Borden STANTON, Junr., ack. 29 May 1810, Thos. MITCHELL, J.P., ent. 13 Aug 1810, rec. same.

p. 294 - To all people, Israel FRENCH, BCO, for love and good will and affection to two daus, Ann GIVEN, wife to Moses GIVEN, and Emma FRENCH, BCO, W 1/2 of S 17 T 8 R 6, NW 1/4 S to GIVEN, SW 1/4 S to Emma, sgn: 14 Aug 1810; WIT: Robert JOHNSTON, Sterling JOHNSTON, ack. Sterling JOHNSTON, J.P., ent. 14 Aug 1810, rec. same.

p. 294 - Thomas JEFFERSON, President, Samuel STEWART, BCO, certificate for NE 1/4 S 35 T 8 R 6, Steubenville district; sgn: 18 Feb 1806, ent. 14 Aug 1810, rec. same [James MADISON, Sec. of State].

p. 295 - Indenture, 31 Jul 1810, Joseph WRIGHT (wife Eleanor), BCO; William WARNER, printer, Baltimore, Maryland. $20, lot #13 in town of Belmont, 28 rods, plat recorded in Book B, p. 288; WIT: William SMITH, Allen BOND, ack. 12 Aug 1810, William SMITH, J.P., ent. 14 Aug 1810, rec. 16 same.

p. 296 - Indenture, 12 Aug 1810, Joseph WRIGHT (wife Eleanor), BCO; John HAYES, late a printer of Baltimore, Maryland. $30, lots #6 (39 rods 9 links) and #122 (28 rods) in Belmont; WIT: William SMITH, Allen BOND, ack. William SMITH, J.P., ent. 14 Aug 1810, rec. 16 same.

p. 297 - Indenture, 21 Jul 1810, Joseph WRIGHT (wife Eleanor), BCO; Andrew HANNA, printer of Baltimore, Maryland. $20, lot #9 in Belmont, 28 rods; WIT: William SMITH, Allen BOND, ack. 12 Aug 1810, William SMITH, J.P., ent. 14 Aug 1810, rec. 17 same.

p. 298 - Indenture, 12 Aug 1810, Joseph WRIGHT (wife Eleanor), BCO; John ROBERTS, merchant, of Baltimore, Maryland. $30, lot #28 in Belmont, 28 rods; WIT: William SMITH, Allen BOND, ack. William SMITH, J.P., ent. 14 Aug 1810, rec. 17 same.

p. 299 - Indenture, 12 Aug 1810, Joseph WRIGHT (wife Eleanor), BCO; Isak PROCTER, merchant, of Baltimore, Maryland. $27, lot #33 in Belmont, 28 rods; WIT: William SMITH, Allen BOND, ack. Wm. SMITH, J.P., ent. 14 Aug 1810, rec. 17 same.

p. 300 - Indenture, 12 Aug 1810, Joseph WRIGHT (wife Eleanor), BCO; Martin Fielding MAGHER, merchant, of Baltimore, Maryland. $70, lots #1, #3, #5, #7, and #8 in Belmont, total of 135 rods 38 links; WIT: William SMITH, Allen BOND, ack. William SMITH, J.P., ent. 14 Aug 1810, rec. 17 same.

p. 301 - Indenture, 31 Jul 1810, Joseph WRIGHT (wife Eleanor), BCO; Isaac ATCHINSON, merchant of Baltimore, Maryland. $20, lot #45 in Belmont, 28 rods; WIT: William SMITH, Allen BOND, ack. 12 Aug 1810, William SMITH, J.P., ent. 14 Aug 1810, rec. 17 same.

p. 302 - Indenture, 12 Aug 1810, Joseph WRIGHT (wife Eleanor), BCO; Thomas MEETIER, merchant, Baltimore, Maryland. $60, lots #24, #23, each 28 rods, and #37, 20 rods, in Belmont; WIT: William SMITH, Allen BOND, ack. William SMITH, J.P.

p. 303 - Indenture, 12 Aug 1810, Joseph WRIGHT (wife Eleanor), BCO; Abagail [Abigail] MEDCALF, of Baltimore, Maryland. $20, lot #37, 28 rods, in Belmont; WIT: William SMITH, Allen BOND, ack. William SMITH, J.P., ent. 14 Aug 1810, rec. 18 same.

p. 304 - Indenture, 31 Jul 1810, Joseph WRIGHT (wife Eleanor), BCO; Daniel Evans REESE, of Baltimore, Maryland. $40, lots #44 and #48, each 28 rods, in Belmont; WIT: William SMITH, Allen BOND, ack. William SMITH, J.P., ent. 14 Aug 1810, rec. 18 same.

p. 305 - Indenture, 12 Aug 1810, Joseph WRIGHT (wife Eleanor), BCO; Micijah [Micajah] ALLY and James SUMMERS, cordwainers, of Baltimore, Maryland. $70, lots #73 (35 rods), #74, #75, #76, #77, #78, and #79 (last each 28 rods); WIT: William SMITH, Allen BOND, ack. William SMITH, J.P., ent. 14 Aug 1810, rec. 18 same.

p. 306 - Indenture, 12 Aug 1810, Joseph WRIGHT (wife Eleanor), BCO; Cassandra Webster BREVITT, of Baltimore, Maryland. $24, lots #58 and #62, each 28 rods, in Belmont; WIT: William SMITH, Allen BOND, ack. William SMITH, J.P., ent. 14 Aug 1810, rec. 18 same.

p. 307 - Indenture, 12 Aug 1810, Joseph WRIGHT (wife Eleanor), BCO; James LYNES, coach-maker, of Baltimore, Maryland. $50, lots #29 and #40, each 28 rods, in Belmont; WIT: William SMITH, Allen BOND, ack. William SMITH, J.P., ent. 14 Aug 1810, rec. 18 same.

p. 308 - Indenture, 10 Apr 1810, Jonas PICKERING (wife Ruth), Richland twp., BCO; Samuel PICKERING, of Union twp., BCO. $500, 161 acres, SE 1/4 S 20 T 9 R 5, Steubenville district, patented to PICKERING on 20 Jul 1808; WIT: John PICKERING, Isaac WILSON, ack. Zebulon WARNER, J.P., ent. 15 Aug 1018, rec. 20 same.

p. 309 - Indenture, 10 Apr 1810, Jonas PICKERING (wife Ruth), Richland twp., BCO; Grace BEAR, Union twp., BCO. $60, 20 acres in NW 1/4 S 20 T 9 R 5, Steubenville district, patented to PICKERING on 20 Jul 1808; WIT; John PICKERING, Isaac WILSON, ack. Zebulon WARNER, J.P., ent. 15 Aug 1810, rec. 20 same.

p. 310 - Indenture, 10 Dec 18810, Jonas PICKERING (wife Ruth), Richland twp., BCO; Jonathan ELLIS and Jacob BRANSON of Union, in trust for use of Plainfield Monthly meeting. $20, 4 acres in S 20 T 9 R 5, Steubenville district, patented to PICKERING on 20 Jul 1808, WIT: John PICKERING, Isaac WILSON, ack. Zebulon WARNER, J.P., ent. 15 Aug 1810, rec. 20 same.

p. 312 - Indenture, 16 Jun 1810, James CALDWELL (wife Nancy), BCO; Lenard DIVER [DIVEN], BCO. $1,200, part of S 2 T 7 R 4, 219 acres 53 perches, fee simple; WIT: Zebulon WARNER, Isaac HOLMES, ack. Zebulon WARNER, J.P., ent. 16 Aug 1810, rec. 20 same.

p. 313 - Know all men, John PRIOR agrees with Samuel LUCAS to pay him for cleaning his part of improvement on S of NE 1/4 S 28 T 6 R 4, Steubenville district, which belongs to the adjoining quarter at rate of $4 per acre, plus use of sugar trees below PRIOR's meadow on 30 acres lying on W side of said 1/4 S, sgn: 9 Jul 1810 [John PRYOR], WIT: Obediah JENNINGS, ent. 15 Aug 1810, rec. 21 same.

p. 313 - Indenture, 14 Aug 1809, Alexander YOUNG, BCO; Cuff DAVIS ("Black Man"), BCO. DAVIS binds himself to YOUNG for 12 months, YOUNG will pay jail fees of $30; YOUNG's seal, DAVIS's mark; WIT: Joseph JOHNSTON, ack. of completion of indenture, 15 Aug 1810, Sterling JOHNSTON, J.P., ent. 16 Aug 1810, rec. 21 same.

p. 314 - Indenture, 24 Mar 1810, Alexander GRAY (wife Jane), Colerain twp., BCO; David MARSHALL, same. $243, part of S 32 T 7 R 3, Steubenville district, patented to GRAY on 27 Aug 1807, 124 acres 1 rod and 22 perches, fee simple; WIT: Agness WALLACE Mary WALLACE, ack. 24 Mar 1810, David WALLACE, J.P., ent. 17 Aug 1810, rec. 22 same.

p. 315 - Indenture, 7 Jul 1810, Thomas MITCHELL (wife Nancy), BCO; James ALEXANDER, Senr., BCO. $650, E 1/2 S 6 T 5 R 3, Pultney twp., 326 acres; WIT: James ALEXANDER, George COPE, ack. 7 Jul 1810, James ALEXANDER, Judge, CCP, ent. 17 Aug 1810, rec. 23 same.

p. 316 - Indenture, 18 Aug 1810, Samuel GREGG, BCO, atty for Josiah HOUGH (wife Plesant), of Loudon County, Virginia; Caleb GREGG, BCO. $405, [Caleb heir of the relict], NE 1/4 S 1 T 8 R 5, 162 acres, patented to HOUGH on 15 Aug 1808, fee simple; WIT: William SMITH, Isaac WHITE, ack. William SMITH, J.P., ent. 20 Aug 1810, rec. 25 same.

p. 317 - Indenture, 29 d 5 m 1810, Borden STANTON (wife Charlotte), BCO; Stafford MILTON [MELTON], same. $206, part of N 1/2 S 1 T 7 R 3, NBR: Benajah STEEL, FRAZIER, 103 acres, patented to STANTON on 20 Dec 1808; WIT: David BERRY, Borden STANTON, Junr., ack. Thos. MITCHELL, J.P., ent. 22 Aug 1810, rec. 23 same.

p. 318 - Indenture, 26 Apr 1810, Robert GRIFFITH (wife Sarah), BCO; John THOMPSON, BCO. $70, out lot #4 in 15 out lots laid out by Bazaleel WELLS adjoining addition to St. Clairsville; his seal, her mark, WIT: Sterling JOHNSTON, Henry MITCHELL, ack. Sterling JOHNSTON, J.P., ent. 22 Aug 1810, rec. 24 same.

p. 319 - Know all men, Nicholas GASSOWAY, BCO, sells to James CALDWELL, BCO, for $1,280 land on which he lived and on which Thomas and Wm. HINTON now live, SE 1/4 S 2 T 9 R 6, Steubenville district, 160 acres, in force if GASSOWAY fails to pay CALDWELL $640.86 with interest by 20 Jul 1811, void if paid, sgn: 1 Aug 1810, Nh. GASSAWAY, WIT: Wm. BROWN, Junr., Sterling JOHNSTON, ack. Sterling JOHNSTON, J.P. for Richland twp.

p. 320 - Indenture, 11 Apr 1810, William RIDDLE, BCO; Obediah JENNINGS, Steubenville [JCO]. $100, lots #32 and #63 in Morristown; WIT: David VANCE, C. HAMMOND, ack. Sterling JOHNSTON, ent. 28 Aug 1810, rec. same.

p. 321 - Indenture, James JOHNSTON, BCO; Bazaleel WELLS, Steubenville. $450, part of NE 1/4 S 5 T 7 R 4, Steubenville district, 100 acres, tract on which James now lives, to WELLS in trust for officers of bank of Steubenville, conditions: 6 Apr 1810 David VANCE had a note for $450 of that date, due within 60 days, void if either VANCE or JOHNSTON pays bank debt; sgn: 16 Aug 1810, WIT: William JOHNSTON, Sterling JOHNSTON, ack. Sterling JOHNSTON, J.P., ent. 28 Aug 1810, rec. same.

p. 322 - Indenture, 30 Jun 1810, Samuel GREGG (wife Ann), BCO; Jacob GREGG, BCO. Whereas Samuel GREGG, then of Ross County, Ohio, was patented S 33 T 7 R 4 on 1 Oct 1806, now Samuel and Ann sell to Jacob GREGG for $260 69 acres 9 poles, part of that section, NBR: Joseph VANLAW, Joseph GRIFFITH, Samuel GREGG, Junr.; WIT: Jacob DOVENBERGER, John MERCER, ack. 30 Jun 1810, Duncan MORRISON, J.P., ent. 31 Aug 1810, rec. same.

p. 323 - Indenture, 9 Apr 1810, Samuel HATCHER (wife Sarah), Loudon County, Virginia; Charles PIGEON and Jacob GREGG, trustees, on behalf of Plainfield meeting, BCO. $4.25, land in SE corner of S 3 T 8 R 5, for use of friends meeting house and grave yard, patented to HATCHER on 13 Jul 1803; WIT: John BEANS, John MEAD, Hamilton RODGERS, ack. Loudon County, 9 apr 1810, Stacy TAYLOR, Burr POWELL, J.P., latter certified by Charles BINNS, clerk, and preceding certificate verified by William ELLZEY, J.P., 10 Apr 1810, ent. 1 Sep 1810, rec. 3 same, {"received of Noah HATCHER $2.02 my fee and seal - C. BINNS, Clk.}

p. 324 - Indenture, 9 Apr 1810, Samuel HATCHER (wife Sarah), Loudon County, Virginia; Noah HATCHER, same. $300, 1/4 of S 3 T 8 R 5, 160 acres, patented to Samuel on 13 Jul 1803; WIT: Blackston JENNEY, Hamilton RODGERS, John BEANS, ack. Loudon County, 9 Apr 1810, Stacy TAYLOR, Burr POWELL, J.P., latter certified by Charles BINNS, Clerk, and him by William <u>ELLEZEY</u>, J.P., ent. 1 Sep 1810, rec. 3 same.

p. 326 - Indenture, 16 Aug 1810, Benjamin VAIL, BCO; Joshua HATCHER, Charles PIDGEON, and Jacob GREGG, trustees on behalf of Plainfield meeting, BCO. $20, part of S 2 T 8 R 5, 5 acres, patented to VAIL on 6 Mar 1806, for society of friends; WIT: Nathan SPENCER, William EWERS, Robert VAIL, ack. William SINCLAIR, J.P., ent. 1 Sep 1810, rec. 3 same.

p. 326 - Indenture, 31 d 5 m 1810, Harmon DAVIS (wife Hannah), BCO; James VERNON, BCO. $200, part of S 14 T 8 R 6, 100 acres; WIT: John MIDDLETON, Dernsey BOSWELL, ack. 31 May 1810, John GRIEF[?], J.P., ent. 7 Sep 1810, rec. same.

p. 328 - Indenture, 10 Jul 1810, William GIBSON (wife Evish), Virginia; Notley HAYS, BCO. $307, part of 1/4 S 4 T 7 R 4, part of land conveyed to GIBSON by Francis SUNDERLAND (wife Ann) on 19 May 1804, 11 acres 3 rods 10 perches; both mark, WIT: Robert JOHNSTON, Sterling JOHNSTON, ack. 10 Jul 1810, Sterling JOHNSTON, J.P., ent 10 Sep 1810, rec. 11 same.

p. 329 - Indenture, 19 Sep 1810, Jacob HOLTZ [HOLTS], Union twp., BCO; John THOMPSON, St. Clairsville, BCO. $35, for part of claim to a well of water in land on which John THOMPSON now lives, lot #4 in St. Clairsville, dug by HOLTZ and THOMPSON "in Co. Partnership, agreeable to articles bearing date the third day of December" 1803, recorded in Book A, p. 275, BCO; his mark, WIT: Wm. FARIS, Junr., Robert GRIFFITH, ack. Robert GRIFFITH, J.P., ent. 19 Sep 1810, rec. 20 same.

p. 330 - Indenture, 22 Sep 1810, Samuel FAWCETT (wife Rachel), BCO; Abel WALKER, Frederick County, Virginia. $230, land in Union twp., 46 acres, part of NE 14 S 20 T 9 R 5, Steubenville district, patented 20 Jul [no year]; WIT: Wm. W. GAULT, Thomas LENNEN[?], ack. William DUNN, J.P., ent. 22 Sep 1810, rec. same.

p. 331 - Indenture, 11 Apr 1810, Joseph SHARP (wife Nancy), BCO; Jacob GOSSER, BCO. $555, SW 1/4 S 30 T 7 R 4, patented to SHARP on 20 Jun 1809, fee simple; WIT: Robert GRIFFITH, Robert THOMPSON, ack. 12 Apr [no year], Zebulon WARNER, J.P., ent. 25 Sep 1810, rec. 27 same.

p. 332 - Know all men, David VANCE and Sterling JOHNSTON, BCO, to secure to the President directors and company of Bank of Marietta $402.97 in one year from that date and for $1, all of S 31 T 7 R 3 belonging to David VANCE and unnumbered lot in St. Clairsville on which the Brick Hotel is situated where Sterling now lives, Samuel SPRIGG [officcr of bank?] authorized in case of default to sell land, void if VANCE and JOHNSTON satisfy debt; sgn: 11 Apr 1810, WIT: John McWILLIAMS, David BERRY, ack. 22 Sep 1810, Robert GRIFFITH, J.P., ent. 26 Sep 1810, rec. 28 same.

p. 333 - Indenture, 10 Sep 1810, Alexander McCALL (wife Margaret), Washington County, Pennsylvania; Joseph SHARP, BCO. For half of the purchase money of whole section paid as partner in original purchase, S 1/2 S 33 T 8 R 4, Steubenville district, patented to McCALL on 26 Jan 1809; WIT: Joseph GRIMES, John CAMPBELL, ack. John CAMPBELL, J.P., ent. 27 Sep 1810, rec. 1 Oct same.

p. 334 - Indenture, 24 Feb 1810, Henry HUFFMAN (wife Mary), BCO; David GILASPEY [first spelling looked like GELALSPEY], BCO. $200, land on

Capteen Creek, Marietta district, in S 27 T 4 R 3 (near a grave yard), NBR: Abel BROWN, 78 acres, fee simple; his seal, her mark, WIT: Levin OKEY, Henry HOOVER, ack. 24 Feb 1810, Levin OKEY, J.P., ent. 29 Sep 1810, rec. 2 Oct same.

p. 335 - Indenture, 24 Feb 1810, Henry HUFFMAN (wife Mary), BCO; John STUKEY, BCO. $200, land on Capteen Creek in S 27 T 4 R 3 in SW 1/4, NBR: Abel BROWN, 78 acres, fee simple; his seal, her mark, WIT: Levin OKEY, Henry HOOVER, ack. 24 Feb 1810, Levin OKEY, J.P., ent. 29 Sep 1810, rec. 2 Oct same.

p. 336 - Indenture, 24 Feb 1810, Henry HUFMAN (wife Mary), BCO; Henry HOOVER, BCO. $100, land on main branchc of Capteen Creek, part of S 27 T 4 R 3, 22 acres 10 perches; his seal, her mark, WIT: Levin OKEY, David PILES, ack. 24 Feb 1810, Levin OKEY, J.P., ent. 29 Sep 1810, rec. 2 Oct same.

p. 336 - Indenture, 1 d 6 m 1810, Jonathan TAYLOR (wife Ann), JCO; Daniel McPEAK, BCO. $480, part of SE 1/4 S 12 T 6 R 3, patented to TAYLOR on 10 d 8 m 1807, NBR: James BOYLES, 151 acres 40 poles; WIT: Thos. MITCHELL, Nancy MITCHELL, ack. 1 d 6 m 1810, Thos. MITCHELL, J.P., ent. 2 Oct 1810, rec. same.

p. 337 - Indenture, 1 Nov 1809, Bezeliel WELLS and Elias VAN ARSDALE, two of extrs. of LW&T of Daniel McELHERAN; Benjamin SCRICHFIELD, BCO. LW&T dated 25 May 1807 authorized extrs. to sell in fee simple his real estate, appointed extrs. William HILL of New York City, New York, merchant, Bezeliel WELLS of Steubenville, JCO, and Elias VAN ARSDALE of Newark, Essex County, New Jersey, now for $280 paid by SCRICHFIELD convey part of S 2 T 6 R 3, 160 acres; WIT: Wm. WHITEHEAD, Phillip C. HAY, ack. 16 Jun 1810, Essex County, New Jersey, Thomas WARD, one of the judges of Inferior CCP, WARD certified 16 Jun 1810 by Silas CONDIT, clerk of Inferior CCP, ack. BCO, 14 Sep 1810, Jacob DAVIS, J.P., ent. 2 Oct 1810, rec. 3 same.

p. 339 - 18 Aug 1810, Samuel STOVER, Muskingum County, Ohio; Andrew FENEFROCK, BCO. $60, lots #15 and #16 in addition to St. Clairsville laid out by William MATHERS, conveyed to STOVER by Sterling JOHNSTON of BCO on 26 Dec 1807, as recorded in Book B, p. 214, fee simple; WIT: Robert GRIFFITH, Margaret GRIFFITH, ack. 18 Aug 1810, Robert GRIFFITH, J.P.

p. 340 - Indenture, 30 May 1810, John CADWALLADER, Junr., (wife Ruth), of Nottingham twp., Tuscarawas County, Ohio; William HOGG, Brownsville, Fayette County, Pennsylvania. $324.65, SW 1/4 S 9 T 7 R 5, Steubenville district, patented to CADWALLADER on 1 Dec 1809, 162.33 acres; WIT:

Samuel FAWCETT, Jonathan FAWCETT, ack. BCO, 30 May 1810, Enos PICKERING, J.P., ent. 11 Oct 1810, rec. 12 same.

p. 341 - Indenture, 30 May 1810, John CADWALLADER, Junr., (wife Ruth), of Nottingham twp., Tuscarawas County, Ohio; William HOGG, Brownsville, Fayette County, Pennsylvania. $324.36, SW 1/4 S 10 T 7 R 5, patented to CADWALLADER on 1 Dec 1809, 162.18 acres; WIT: Samuel FAWCETT, Jonathan FAWCETT, ack. 30 May 1810, Enos PICKERING, J.P., ent. 11 Oct 1810, rec. 12 same.

p. 342 - Indenture, 8 Sep 1810, Isaac PATTEN (wife Ellenor), BCO; Otho FRENCH, BCO. $80, part of NE 1/4 S 32 T 7 R 5, 40 acres; his seal, her mark [there is an X between her first and last name, but no "her mark" indicated], WIT: Thomas WILLIAMS, David SMITH, ack. 8 Sep 1810, John STRALL, J.P., ent. 12 Oct 1810, rec. 13 same.

p. 343 - Know all men, William WRIGHT, BCO, gave note to Michael ENLOW, now of BCO, to amount of $60, note dated 1 Apr 1808, now wants to lift note out of hands of ENLOW, receipt of which he now acknowledges. In consideration of note, WRIGHT sells to ENLOW livestock and personal property amounting to $60; sgn: 26 Sep 1810, WIT: Elaas E. ELLMAKER, Nathaniel BEAL, ent. 20 Oct 1810, rec. 22 same.

p. 343 - Indenture, 29 d 5 m 1810, Borden STANTON (wife Charlotte), BCO; Benajah STEEL, BCO. $300, part of NE 1/4 S 1 T 7 R 3, 150 acres, patented to STANTON in fee on 20 Dec 1808; WIT: David BERRY, Bordon STANTON, Junr., ack. 29 d 5 m 1810, Thos. MITCHELL, J.P., ent. 22 Oct 1810, rec. 23 same.

p. 345 - Indenture, 12 Jun 1810, Robert GIFFEN (wife Hetty), Muskingum County, Ohio; William SHARPLESS, BCO. $5,000, NW 1/4 S 9 T 6 R 3, 160 acres, patented to GIFFEN in 1806; WIT: Sterling JOHNSTON, Wm. CONGLETON, ack. 12 Jun 1810, Sterling JOHNSTON, J.P., ent. 24 Oct, rec. same.

p. 346 - Indenture, 27 Oct 1810, Benjamin SCRICHFIELD, BCO; Wallice McALLISTER, BCO. $130, two adjoining lots in BCO, part of SW 1/4 S 2 T 6 R 3, conveyed to SCRICHFIELD by Bazaleel WELLS and Elias VAN ARSDALE, extrs. of Daniel McELHERAN by LW&T dated 1 Nov 1809, NBR: KIZER, 33 acres 2 rods 3 poles, and second lot containing 28 acres 1 rod 26 poles, total 61 acres 3 rods 29 poles; WIT: Robert GRIFFITH, Wm. FARIS, Junr., ack. Robert GRIFFITH, J.P., ent. 27 Oct 1810, rec. 29 same.

p. 347 - Indenture, 29 d 5 m 1810, Borden STANTON (wife Charlotte), BCO; Daniel FRAZIER, BCO. $134, part of NW 1/4 S 1 T 7 R 3, NBR: BERRY, 67 acres, part of land patented to STANTON on 20 Dec 1808; WIT: David BERRY, Borden STANTON, Junr., ack. 29 d 5 m 1810, Thos. MITCHELL, J.P., ent. 27 Oct 1810, rec. 29 same.

p. 348 - Indenture, 27 Oct 1810, Benjamin SCRICHFIELD, BCO; Christopher HINKLE, BCO. $20, part of SW 1/4 S 2 T 6 R 3, 1/4 S conveyed to SCRICHFIELD by Bazaleel WELLS and Elias VAN ARSDALE, extrs. of Daniel McELHERAN on 1 Nov 1809, NBR: KEIZER, McALLISTER, R. KING, 14 acres 2 rods 32 poles; WIT: Robert GRIFFITH, Wm. FARIS, Junr., ack. Robert GRIFFITH, J.P., ent. 27 Oct 1811, rec. 29 same.

p. 349 - Indenture, 27 Oct 1810, Benjamin SCRICHFIELD, BCO; William GIFFEN, BCO. $42, part of SW 1/4 S 2 T 6 R 3, conveyed to SCRICHFIELD by Bazeliel WELLS and Elias VAN ARSDALE, extrs. of Daniel McELHERAN, dated 1 Nov 1809, NBR: John KING's spring, 21 acres 1 rod 23 poles; WIT: Robert GRIFFITH, Wm. FARIS, Junr., ack. Robert GRIFFITH, J.P., ent. 27 Oct 1810, rec. 29 same.

p. 351 - Indenture, 10 Sep 1810, Elias HUGHES, Loudon County, Virginia; John SPENCER, same. $406, NW 1/4 S 10 T 7 R 5, Steubenville district, patented to HUGHES on 23 Mar 1810; no WIT given, ack. Loudon County, Virginia, 10 Sep 1810, C. BINNS, Clk, BINNS certified by Francis PEYTON, J.P., ent. 27 Oct 1810, rec. 30 same.

p. 352 - Indenture, 29 Sep 1810, James LYNES (wife Eliza), City of Baltimore; Thomas KENNY, same. $50, lots #29 and #40 in town of Belmont, both 28 rods; his seal, her mark, WIT: Edwd. JOHNSON, John HARGROVE, ack. Baltimore County, Maryland, 29 Sep 1810, Edwd. JOHNSON, Mayor of Baltimore, ent. 27 Oct 1810, rec. 30 same.

p. 353 - Indenture, 28 Jul 1810, Thomas HUGHES, Loudon County, Virginia; Abijah SANDS, same. $400, NW 1/4 S 8 T 10 R 6, Steubenville district, patented to HUGHES on 21 Oct 1807; WIT: Benjamin WHITE, Isaael[?] JENNEY, Giles GRAVEN, ack. Loudon County, Virginia, 10 Sep 1810, C. BINNS, Clk., BINNS certified by Francis PEYTON, J.P., ent. 27 Oct [1810], rec. 30 same.

p. 354 - Indenture, 4 Jul 1810, William HODGIN (wife Agness), BCO; William CHILDRE, BCO. $215, begin SW corner of S 8 T 8 R 6, 100 acres; his seal, her mark, WIT: John GRIER, John HODGIN, ack. 4 Jul 1810, John GRIER, J.P., ent. 2 Nov 1810, rec. 5 same.

p. 355 - Indenture, 3 Nov 1810, Wallice McALLISTER (wife Elizabeth), BCO; Thomas THOMPSON, BCO. $10, part of Sw 1/4 S 2 T 6 R 3, conveyed to Benjamin SCRICHFIELD by Bazeliel WELLS and Elias VAN ARSDALE, extrs., of Daniel McELHERAN dated 1 Nov 1809, conveyed to McALLISTER by SCRICHFIELD on 27 Oct 1810, 9.4 acres; both mark, WIT: Wm. FARIS, Junr., Robert GRIFFITH, ack. Robert GRIFFITH, J.P., ent. 3 Nov 1810, rec. 6 same.

p. 356 - Know all men, Samuel PILLERS, Springfield, Muskingum County, Ohio, seized[?] in fee of a lot of ground in Morristown, appoints William W. GAULT lawful attorney (GAULT living in Morristown), to sell lot, sgn: 15 Aug 1809, WIT: William CRAIG, Michael HALM, ack. 15 Aug 1809, William NEWEL, Esqr., ent. 12 Nov 1810, rec. same.

p. 357 - Indenture, 12 Jul 1810, William CONGLETON (wife Nancy), BCO; Joseph MORRISON, BCO. $325, beginning at line of (NBR:) John TOMPSON, Thomas CONLEY, Thomas HELLOM, William COOK, to land formerly claimed by William VANCE, 10 acres 27 perches, conveyed to CONGLETON by David NEWALL (wife Sally) 28 Sep 1803, part of S that the town of St. Clairsville now stands on, fee simple; WIT: Sterling JOHNSTON, Nathaniel WHITE, ack. 12 Jul 1810, Sterling JOHNSTON, J.P., ent. 21 Nov 1810, rec. 23 same.

p. 358 - Indenture, 26 d 8 m 1809, Horton HOWARD (wife Hannah), BCO; Joseph STUBBS, BCO. $640, NW and SE 1/4 S 3 T 8 R6, each 160 acres; WIT: Thos. MITCHELL, William BARNES, ack. Thos. MITCHELL, one of the Justices, ent. 29 Nov 1810, rec. 1 Dec same.

p. 359 - Indenture, 1 Dec 1810, David WALLACE, BCO; James DUFF, BCO. $320, 160 1/2 acres, part of S 8 T 8 R 4, patented to WALLACE on 30 Dec 1807; WIT: William THAKER, Alexander SMILEY, ack. Zebulon WARNER, J.P., ent. 1 Dec 1810, rec. 3 same.

p. 360 - Indenture, 30 Nov 1810, David WALLACE, BCO; Samuel and William ROBINSON, BCO. $388, 131 acres 32 perches, part of S 8 T 8 R 4, patented to WALLACE on 30 Dec 1807, NBR: Alexander McCONNELL; WIT: Zebulon WARNER, John STEWART, ack. Zebulon WARNER, J.P., ent. 1 Dec 1810, rec. 3 same.

p. 360 - Indenture, 26 d 8 m 1809, Horton HOWARD (wife Hannah), BCO; Camm THOMAS, BCO. $320, NW 1/4 S 2 T 8 R 6, 640 acres; WIT: Thos. MITCHELL, William BARNES, ack. Thos. MITCHELL, J.P., ent. 6 Dec 1810, rec. 7 same.

p. 361 - Indenture, 9 Mar 1810, Charles CAMPBELL, surviving executor of LW&T of James CAMPBELL of Washington County, Pennsylvania; John WILEY, BCO. According to order in CCP of Belmont held on 11 Aug 1819, CAMPBELL empowered to make deed in fee simple to WILEY, for $900 paid to James CAMPBELL in his lifetime and balance to Charles CAMPBELL, W 1/2 S 6 T 8 R 5, 238 acres; WIT: John CAMPBELL, John LYLE, ack. BCO, 9 Mar 1810, John CAMPBELL, J.P., ent. 11 Dec 1810, rec. same.

p. 362 - Indenture, 9 Aug 1810, Robert PLUMMER (wife Rachel), Warren twp., BCO; John PLUMMER, same. For conveyance of the right of a parcel of land to Robert from John (wife Ann), Robert and Rachel convey their part of land in SE and NE 1/4s of S 6 T 8 R 6, fee simple; WIT: John GRIER, John SIMSON, ack. 9 Aug 1810, John GRIER, J.P., ent. 11 Dec 1810, rec. same.

p. 363 - Indenture, 9 Aug 1810, John PLUMMER (wife Ann), Warren twp., BCO; Robert PLUMMER, same. For conveyance of the right of a parcel of land from Robert (wife Rachel) to John, John and Ann convey their part of the land in SE 1/4 S 1 T 9 R 6, fee simple; WIT: John GRIER, John SIMSON, ack. 9 Aug 1810, John GRIER, J.P., ent. 11 Dec 1810, rec. 12 same.

p. 364 - Know all men, Samuel SPRIGG, BCO, for $1,750 sells to John WHITE of Wheeling, Ohio County, Virginia, lot #52 in St. Clairsville, 1/4 acre, where George Thompson & Co., and James MARTIN now lives, conveyed by Josiah DILLON to SPRIGG by deed dated 26 Nov 1809; sgn: 14 Aug 1810, WIT: Joseph CALDWELL, Peter YARNALL, ack. 14 Aug 1810, Zebulon WARNER, J.P., ent. 11 Dec 1810, rec. 12 same.

p. 365 - Indenture, 4 Dec 1810, Noah LINSLEY, Ohio County, Virginia; John WISE, BCO. $501, NW 1/4 S 32 T 3 R 2, patented to LINSLY on 15 Jun 1808; WIT: Georg WISE, ack. 11 Dec 1810, Zebulon WARNER, J.P., ent. 11 Dec 1810, rec. 13 same.

p. 365 - Indenture, 10 Nov 1810, James STRAIN (wife Elizabeth), BCO; James ALEXANDER, Junr., BCO. $160, part of S 32 T 4 R 2, Pease twp., 30 acres; WIT: Obed WHITAKER, John RUSH, ack. Thos. MITCHELL, J.P., ent. 12 Dec 1810, rec. 13 same.

p. 366 - Indenture, 12 Jan 18__, John DEVER, BCO; Joseph HOLLOWAY, BCO. $320, 60 acres, part of S 13 T 9 R 5, fee simple; his mark [two "o"s], WIT: John VANPELT, John REAGH, ack. 12 Jan 1808, John WILEY, J.P., ent. 12 Dec 1810, rec. 17 same.

p. 367 - Indenture, 21 Jun 1810, Joseph PUMPHREY (wife Sarah), JCO; Jeremiah BURROWS, BCO. $400, part of S 33 T 6 R 3, NBR: Nicholas PUMPHREY, McFARLAND, 87 acres 3 rods 34 perches; WIT: George HUMPHREY, David HUMPHREY, ack. 21 Jun 1810, JCO, George HUMPHREY, J.P., in Steubenville on 15 Dec 1810, HUMPHREY certified as J.P. in Warren twp. by Thomas PATTON, Clerk of CCP, ent. 18 Dec 1810, rec. same.

p. 368 - Indenture, 5 Dec 1810, Joseph SHARP (wife Nancy), BCO; Isaac FARMER, BCO. $320, 80 acres, NW corner S 30 T 7 R 4, patented to SHARP on 20 Jun 1809, fee simple; his seal, her mark, WIT: John HENDERSON, John CAMPBELL, ack. John CAMPBELL, J.P., ent. 19 Dec 1810, rec. same.

p. 369 - Indenture, 2 Aug 1810, Henry HUFMAN, BCO; James HUFMAN, BCO. $60, personal property, void if James pays $60 by 1 Mar 1811; WIT: Thos. THOMPSON, ack. Thos. THOMPSON, J.P., ent. 22 Dec 1810, rec. same.

p. 370 - Know all men, Alexander McCALL, Washington County, Pennsylvania, for $211.50 paid by Andrew WALKER, BCO, 50 acres, part of NW corner S 33 T 8 R 4; sgn: 10 Sep 1810 by Alexander and Marget McCALL, WIT: Joseph GRIMES, followed immediately by "We do assign our righ[t] and title forever to Zacheriah BARLOW, sgn: Andrew WALKER and Elizabeth WALKER, ack. 10 Sep 1810, by "Alexander McCall and Margret his wife," John CAMPBELL, J.P., ent. 22 Dec 1810, rec. same.

p. 371 - Know all men, Andrew WALKER, BCO, for $350 paid by Zachariah BARLOW, BCO, 50 acres in NW corner of NW 1/4 S 33 T 8 R 4, NBR: Joseph BARLOW; sgn: 22 Dec 1810 by his seal and mark of Elizabeth WALKER, WIT: John CAMPBELL, Robert MILLER, ack. by Alexander WALKER and Betsey his wife, John CAMPBELL, J.P., ent. 24 Dec 1810, rec. 25 same.

p. 371 - Know all men, Alexander McCALL, Washington County, Pennsylvania, for $217 convey to Joseph BARLOW, BCO, 50 acres in SW of NW 1/4 S 33 T 8 R 4; sgn: 10 Sep 1810, Alexander and Marget McCALL, WIT: John CAMPBELL, Joseph GRIMES, ack. 10 Sep 1810, by Alexander McCALL and Magret, John CAMPBELL, J.P., ent. 24 Dec 1810, rec. 25 same.

p. 372 - Indenture, 31 d 5 m 1810, Hermon DAVIS (wife Hannah), BCO; Thomas BUNDY, BCO. $92.50, 45 acres, part of S 14 T 8 R 6; WIT: Demsey BOSWELL, James VERNON, ack. 31 May 1810, by Harmon DAVIS, John GRIER, J.P., ent. 29 Dec 1810, rec. same.

p. 373 - Indenture, 31 d 5 m 1810, Hermon DAVIS (wife Hannah), BCO; William BOSWELL, BCO. $120, 60 acres, part of S 14 T 8 R 6; here it is Harmon DAVIS's seal and her mark, WIT: Thomas BUNDY, John MIDDLETON, ack. 31 May 1810, John GRIER, J.P., ent. 29 Dec 1810, rec. 31 same.

p. 375 - Indenture, 31 d 5 m 1810, Harmon DAVIS (wife Hannah), BCO; Demsey BOWELL [probably BOSWELL], BCO. $80, 40 acres, part of S 14 T 8 R 6; his seal, her mark, WIT: Thomas BUNDY, James VERNON, ack. 31 May 1810, John GRIER, J.P., ent. 29 Dec 1810, rec. 1 Jan 1811.

p. 376 - Indenture, 22 d 12 m 1810, Isaac COPPOCK (wife Mary), BCO; Demsey BOSWELL, BCO. $50, 21 1/4 acres, part of S 13 T 8 R 6; WIT: James PATTERSON, William BUNDY, ack. John GRIER, J.P., ent. 29 Dec 1810, rec. 1 Jan 1811.

p. 377 - Indenture, 29 Dec 1810, Adam SEEBERT, BCO; Christopher COROTHERS, BCO. $260, 50 acres, part of SW 1/4 S 9 T 8 R 4, patented to SEEBERT on 28 Dec 1807; his mark [name given as Adam SEBERT], WIT: David WALLICE, William ROBINSON, ack. Dd. WALLACE, J.P., ent. 31 Dec 1810, rec. 2 Jan 1811.

p. 378 - Indenture, 1 Nov 1810, Robert BELL (wife Sarah), BCO; Nathaniel BELL, BCO. $80, part of NW 1/4 S 26 T 8 R 5, patented to Robert BELL, but no date given, NBR: William WOODS, 40 acres 1 rod 30 perches; both mark, WIT: Lenart H. HEART, William + LAM [NOTE: It would appear that the middle letters of these names were marks, but there is no written indication to that effect], ack. [no date], Duncan MORRISON, J.P., ent. 31 Dec 1810, rec. 2 Jan 1811.

p. 379 - Indenture, 31 Dec 1810, Joseph GRIFFITH (wife Catharine), BCO; John SPENCER, BCO. Patent granted to Samuel GREGG then of Ross County, Ohio, for S 33 T 7 R 4, Steubenville district, dated 1 Oct 1806, since sold to GRIFFITH, now for $1,600, selling 100 acres of that section, NBR: Joseph NICKELSON; his seal, her mark, WIT: Nathan SPENCER, Henry ROBERTS, William SINCLAIR, ack. William SINCLAIR, J.P., ent. 1 Jan 1811, rec. 3 same.

p. 380 - Indenture, 24 Feb 1810, Henry HUGHMAN, BCO; William BROWN, BCO. $300, part of S 27 T 4 R 3, Marietta district, NBR: John DAVIS on land sold by HUGHMAN, John STOKEY (near Capteen Creek), 60 acres; his seal [HUFMAN], mark of Mary HUFMAN, WIT: Levin OKEY, Henry HOOVER, ack. 24 Feb 1810, Levin OKEY, ent. 8 Jan 1811, rec. 9 same.

p. 381 - Indenture, 22 Dec 1810, Daniel McPEAK (wife Elizabeth), BCO; James BOYLES, BCO. $150, part of SE 1/4 S 12 T 6 R 3, granted to McPEAK by Jonathan TAYLOR (wife Ann) by deed dated 1 d 6 m "year aforesaid", recorded in Book C, p. 297, NBR: Charles IRWIN, 15 acres; both mark, WIT: Sterling JOHNSTON, Henry STEWART, ack. 22 Dec 1810, Sterling JOHNSTON, J.P., ent. 8 Jan 1811, rec. 10 same.

p. 382 - Indenture, 31 Dec 1810, Saml. GREGG (wife Ann), BCO; John SPENCER, BCO. Patent granted to GREGG then of Ross County, Ohio, for S 33 T 7 R 4, Steubenville district, dated 1 Oct 1806, now for $663, 102 acres 2 rods 16 poles; WIT: Robert MORRISON, Enos WEST, ack. Duncan MORRISON, J.P., ent. 17 Jan 1811, rec. 18 same.

p. 383 - Indenture, 17 Aug 1810, Samuel STEWART, BCO; Thomas MITCHELL and William GIBSON, BCO. STEWART extr. of estate of William THOMPSON, to secure money in hands of STEWART for payment to heirs, of whom MITCHELL and GIBSON are guardians, NE 1/4 S 35 T 8 R 6, in trust for heirs and whoever should afterwards be their guardians of those orphans, to be void if patent obtained in name of heirs on or before 15 Aug 1814; sgn: by STEWART and GIBSON, but not MITCHELL, WIT: James CLOYD, Sterling JOHNSTON, ack. 17 Aug 1810, Sterling JOHNSTON, J.P., ent. 22 Jan 1811, rec. same.

p. 384 - Indenture, 12 Jan 1808, John DEVERS, BCO; Thomas REIGH, BCO. $200, 104 acres, in S 13 T 9 R 5, fee simple; his mark, no WIT given, ack. Union twp., 12 Jan 1808, John WILEY, J.P.

p. 384 - Know all men, Josiah DILLON, BCO, being indebted to John and George RINIKER (for $400) and Jonathan MANROE (for $992.91), Merchants, and George BAILEY (for $128.25), Druggist, of City of Baltimore. For purpose of securing debts conveying to Charles HAMMOND, BCO, livestock and personal property, to remain in DILLON's possession until 1 Jun 1811, void if debt paid with interest, sgn: 11 Jun 1810, WIT: Zebulon WARNER, ack. 11 Jun 1810, Zebulon WARNER.

p. 386 - Indenture, 11 Jan 1811, James CARLOW (wife Mary), St. Clairsville, BCO; Zebulon WARNER, same; Peter YARNALL, same. CARLOW is indebted to YARNALL for $60.25 rent money, CARLOW conveys a house and lot in St. Clairsville plus for other lots of 1/4 acre each known as the Spring lots, purchased by CARLOW from William CONGLETON (formerly of St. Clairsville, BCO), to remain in WARNER's possession as trust in case debt is not repaid within six months; sgn: James CARLOW, Polly CARLOW, Zebulon

WARNER, Peter YARNALL, ack. David MOORE, J.P., ent. 25 Jan 1811, rec. 28 same.

p. 387 - Indenture, 1 Aug 1810, Nicholas GASSAWAY (wife Amelia), BCO; John ISRAEL, BCO. $161, 160 acres, part of S 2 T 9 R 6, fee simple; only Nicholas signs, WIT: Sterling JOHNSTON, Henry HARDY, ack. 1 Aug 1810, [only Nicholas comes] Sterling JOHNSTON, J.P., ent. 28 Jan 1811, rec. 29 same.

p. 388 - Indenture, 18 Aug 1810, Caleb GREGG (wife Hannah), BCO; Mahlon SMITH, BCO. $400, 80 acres in N side of NE 1/4 S 1 T 8 R 5, which 1/4 conveyed to GREGG by Samuel GREGG attorney for Jonah HOUGH (wife Pleasant) dated 18 Aug 1810, patented to Jonah HOUGH on 15 Aug 1808, fee simple; his seal, her mark, WIT: William SMITH, Samuel GREGG, ack. 18 Aug 1810, William SMITH, J.P., ent. 30 Jan 1811, rec. same.

p. 389 - Indenture, 28 d 1 m 1811, Joseph W. SATTERTHWAITE (wife Ann), BCO; Francis COOPER, BCO. $96, 12 acres 2 rods __ perches on N side of S 13 T 7 R 3, NBR: Horton HOWARD, COOPER, part of land given to Joseph W. SATTERTHWAITE by William SATTERTHWAITE, deceased, by will; WIT: Joseph VANLAW, Thomas VANLAW, ack. 31 Jan 1811, William SINCLAIR, J.P., ent. 31 Jan 1811, rec. 1 Feb same.

p. 390 - Know all men, Joseph SHARP, BCO, for $480 paid by Robert MILLER, BCO, convey SW 1/4 S 33 T 8 R 4, 160 acres; sgn: 10 Sep 1810, seal of Joseph SHARP, mark of Nancy SHARP, WIT: John CAMPBELL, Joseph GRIMES, ack. 10 Sep 1810, John CAMPBELL, J.P., ent. 2 Feb 1811, rec. same.

p. 391 - Indenture, 20 Dec 1810, John WINTER, BCO; John SUTTON, BCO. $60, part of S 2 T 7 R 4, 10 acres, fee simple; WIT: Robert GRIFFITH, Samuel CONNELL, ack. 4 Feb 1811, Robert GRIFFITH, J.P., ent. 4 Feb 1811, rec. same.

p. 392 - Indenture, 17 Dec 1810, Daniel McPEAK (wife Elizabeth), BCO; Samuel FINNEY, BCO. $734, part of S 12 T 6 R 3, part of land conveyed to McPEAK on 1 d 6 m 1810 by Jonathan TAYLOR, 117 acres 2 rods 37 perches, begin at "post standing by the road that leads from Martins Ferry to the Town of St. Clairsville," NBR: Charles IRWIN, fee simple; both mark, WIT: Sterling JOHNSTON, Henry STEWART, ack. 22 Dec 1810, Sterling JOHNSTON, J.P., ent. 5 Feb 1811, rec. same.

p. 393 - Indenture, 12 Oct 1810, Garret SNEDAKER (wife Elizabeth), Brook County, Virginia; Nicholas SNEDAKER, BCO. $80, 145 1/4 acres, part of SE 1/4 S 1 T 9 R 5, fee simple; only Garret seals, WIT: David CAMPBELL, John LYLE, ack. 12 Oct 1810 (wife being unable to attend), John CAMPBELL, ent. 8 Feb 1811, rec. same.

p. 394 - Indenture, 12 Oct 1810, Garret SNEDAKER (wife Elizabeth), Brook County, Virginia; Peter SNEDAKER, BCO. $80, 160 ares, NE 1/4 S 1 T 9 R 5, fee simple; only Garret seals, WIT: David CAMPBELL, John LYLE, ack. 12 Oct 1810 (wife unable to attend), John CAMPBELL, ent. 8 Feb 1811, rec. 9 same.

p. 395 - Indenture, 18 Aug 1810, Caleb GREGG (wife Hannah), BCO; Isaac WHITE, BCO. $410, 82 acres, conveyed to Caleb GREGG by Samuel GREGG, attorney for Jonah HOUGH (wife Pleasant) dated 18 Aug 1810, granted to HOUGH by patent dated 15 Aug 1808, part of NE 1/4 S 1 T 8 R 5; his seal, her mark, WIT: Mahlon SMITH, Samuel GREGG, ack. 18 Aug 1810, William SMITH, J.P., ent. 15 Feb 1811, rec. same.

p. 396 - Indenture, 15 Sep 1810, John STRAHL (wife Ann), BCO; Isaac STRAHL, BCO. $163, W 1/2 of SW 1/4 S 34 T 7 R 5, 71.12 acres; WIT: John GRIER, Rhoda GRIER [her mark], ack. 15 Sep 1810, John GRIER, J.P., ent. 16 Feb 1811, rec. same.

p. 397 - Indenture, 25 Oct 1810, Ebenezer ZANE (wife Elizabeth), Ohio County, Virginia; Jacob CLARK, BCO. $225, part of N 1/2 of S 29 T 3 R 2, NBR: E. WOODS, 50 acres; WIT: E. WOODS, Thos. THOMPSON, ack. BCO, 25 Oct 1810, Thos. THOMPSON, J.P., ent. 25 Feb 1811, rec. same.

p. 398 - "The State of Ohio, Belmont Co. ss. I, J. M. BECKETT, Recorder of the County aforesaid Certify that the foregoing is a true and correct copy of Deed Book Vol. "C." Belmont County Record of Deeds. This copy was made by order of the County Commissioners at their Spring Session A.D. 1889. Witness my signature this April 1, 1890. J. M. BECKETT, Recorder.

[end of Vol. C]

APPENDIX

Township Map, Belmont County, Ohio

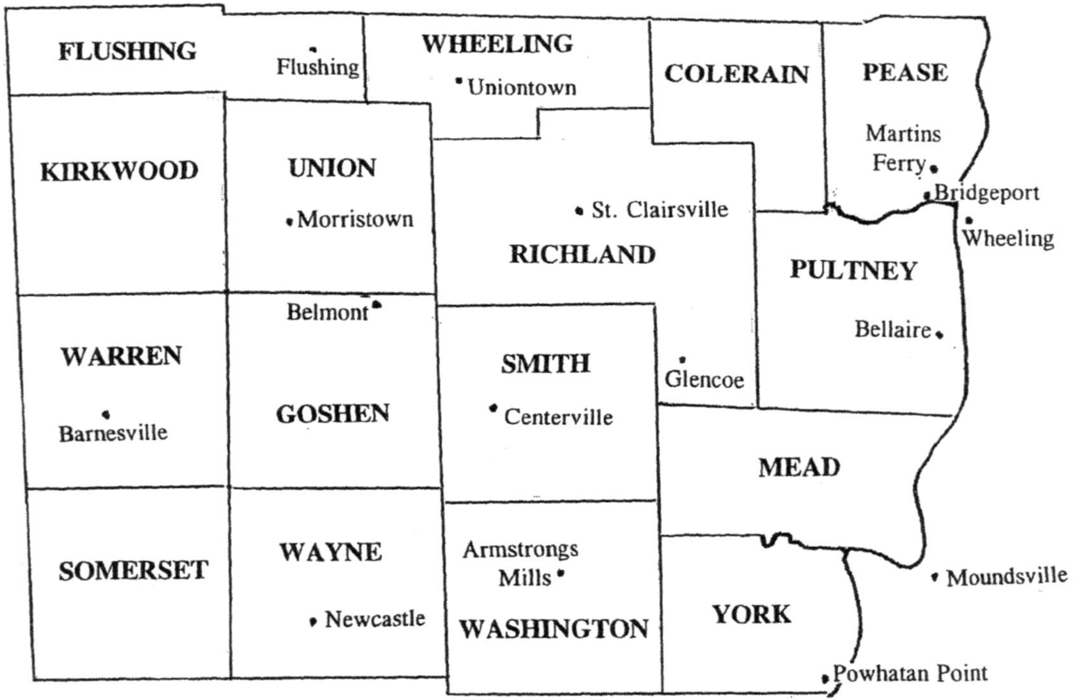

FLUSHING
Flushing
WHEELING
Uniontown
COLERAIN
PEASE
Martins Ferry
Bridgeport
Wheeling
KIRKWOOD
UNION
Morristown
St. Clairsville
RICHLAND
PULTNEY
Belmont
Bellaire
WARREN
Barnesville
GOSHEN
SMITH
Centerville
Glencoe
MEAD
SOMERSET
WAYNE
Newcastle
Armstrongs Mills
WASHINGTON
YORK
Moundsville
Powhatan Point

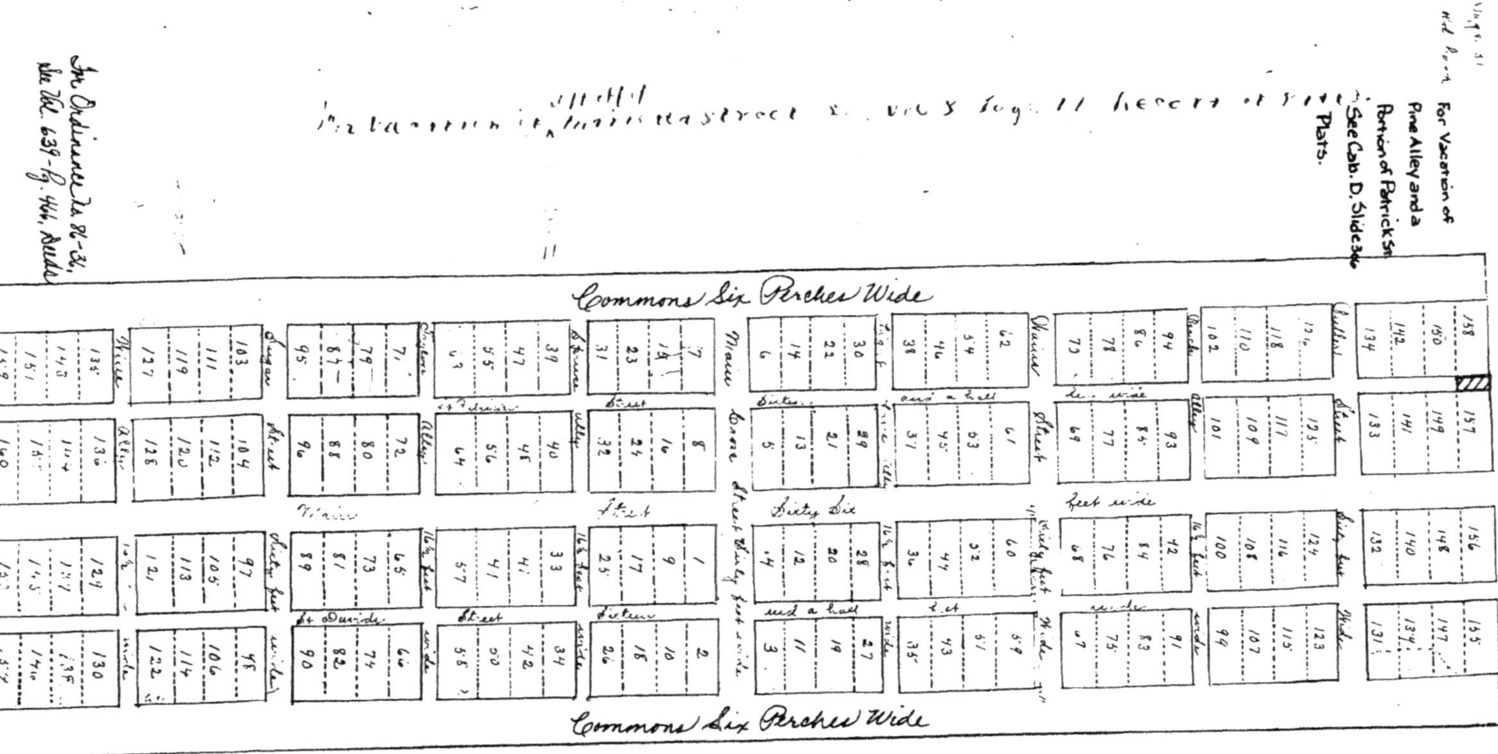

Plat of St. Clairsville, Ohio (Vol. A, p. 27 of new book, p. 31 of old book)

Plat of Pultney (south half) (Vol. A, part of p. 42)

[NOTE: According to the pattern evident in the other sections of this plat, the compiler assumes that the lots written in by hand between the two portions on this page may have disappeared in the gutter of the book when the copy was made.]

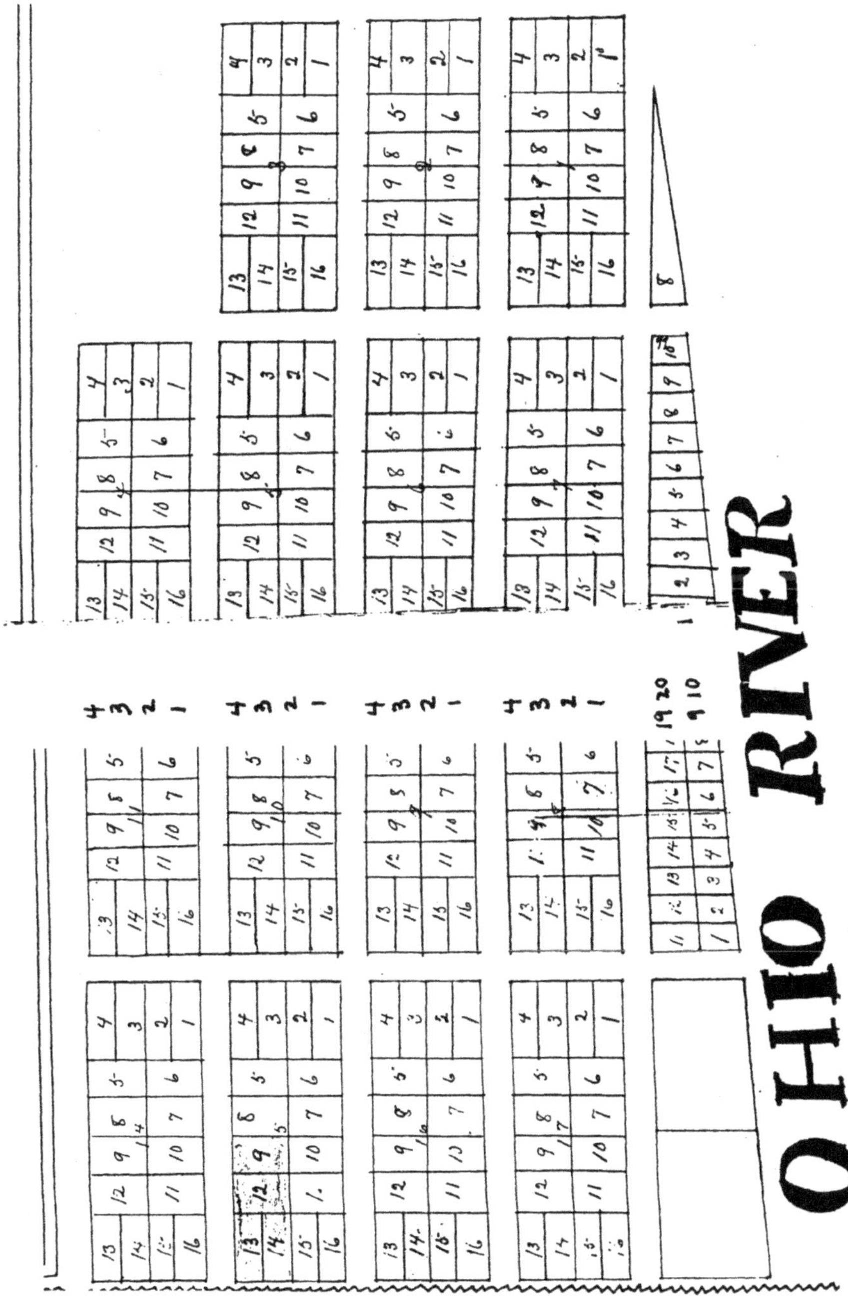

OHIO RIVER

Plat of Morristown (Vol. A, p. 51)

78 77 76 75 | 74 73 72 71 | 70 69 68 | 67 66 65 64 | 63 62 61 60

40 41 42 43 | 44 45 46 47 | 48 49 50 51 | 52 53 54 55 | 56 57 58 59

39 38 37 36 | 35 34 33 32 | 31 30 29 28 | 27 26 25 | 24 23 22 21

1 2 3 4 | 5 6 7 | 10 11 12 | 13 14 15 16 | 17 18 19 20

3 1/2 | 5 10/16 | 6 | 2 3/4

[NOTE: There was a second page to this plat; however, it did not seem to the compiler to add any essential information to the description of the city. It appeared to be an extension of the lots at the bottom of this page.]

Commons 33 feet wide S. 71½° E

Commons 33 feet wide N. 19½° E

30	29
28	27
26	25

Wooster Alley 12 feet wide

20	19
18	17

Franklin Alley 12 feet wide

12	11
10	9

Washington Alley 12 feet wide

4	3
2	1

Anne Street 60 feet wide S. 19½° W

35	36
33	34
31	32

Mercer Alley 12 feet wide

23	24
21	22

Democrat Alley 12 feet wide

15	16
13	14

Jefferson Alley 12 feet wide

7	8
5	6

Commons 33 feet wide S. 19½° W

East and West line

N

Plat of Land Adjoining St. Clairsville (Vol. A, p. 316)

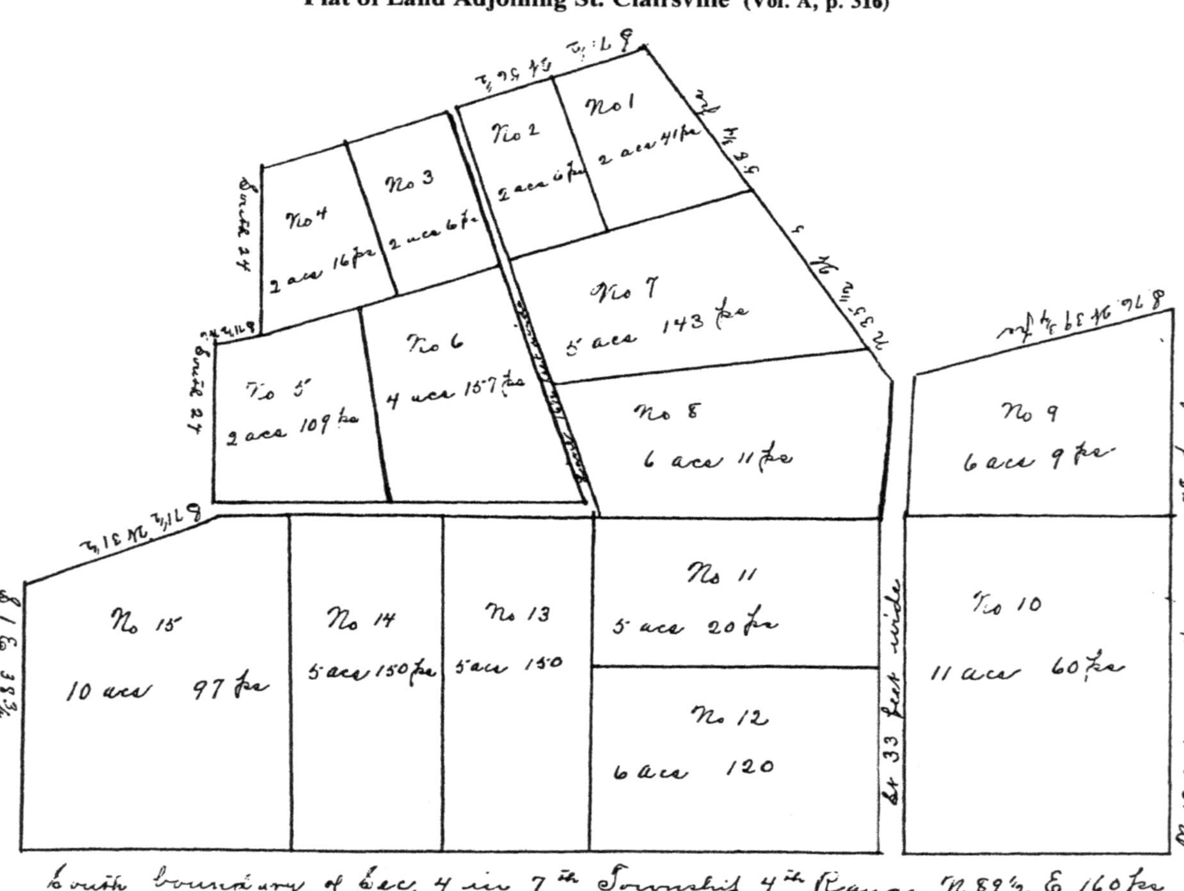

Commons 33 feet wide

3 Rood + 37 Per

14 15 16 17 18 19 20 21 22 23 24 25 26 27

1 Rod + 30 Per

37½ Per

20 feet wide

10 feet wide

3 Roods

Main Street 66 feet wide

1 Rood + 36 Per

1 Rood + 20 Per

22½ Per

2 acres + 35 Perch

13 12 11 10 9 8 7 6 5 4 3 2 1

1 Rood + 9 Per

Back Alley 10 feet

Triangle Alley

Short alley 10 feet wide

Middle alley

West Alley

Commons 10 feet wide

Commons 33 feet wide

N

Plat of Land at East End of St. Clairsville

Plat of Canton (Vol. A, p. 507)

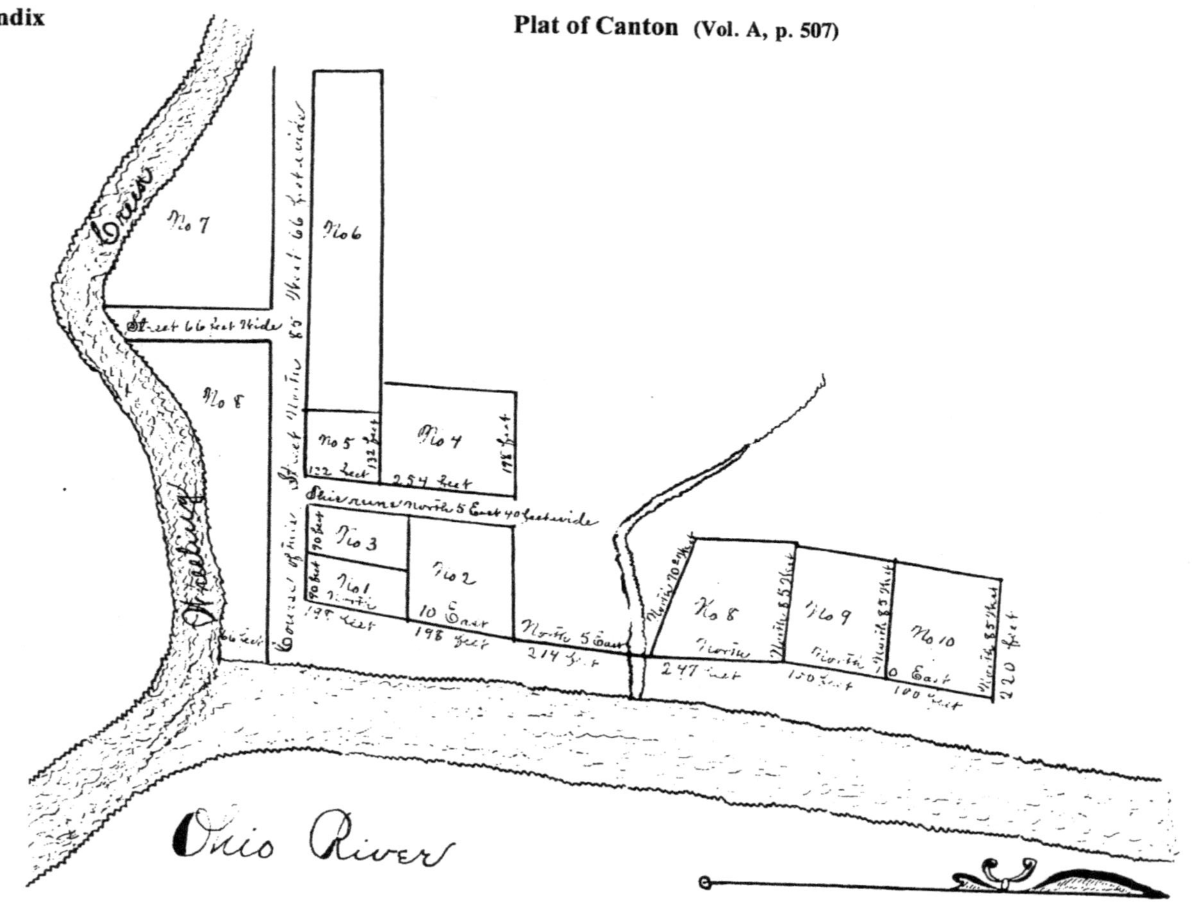

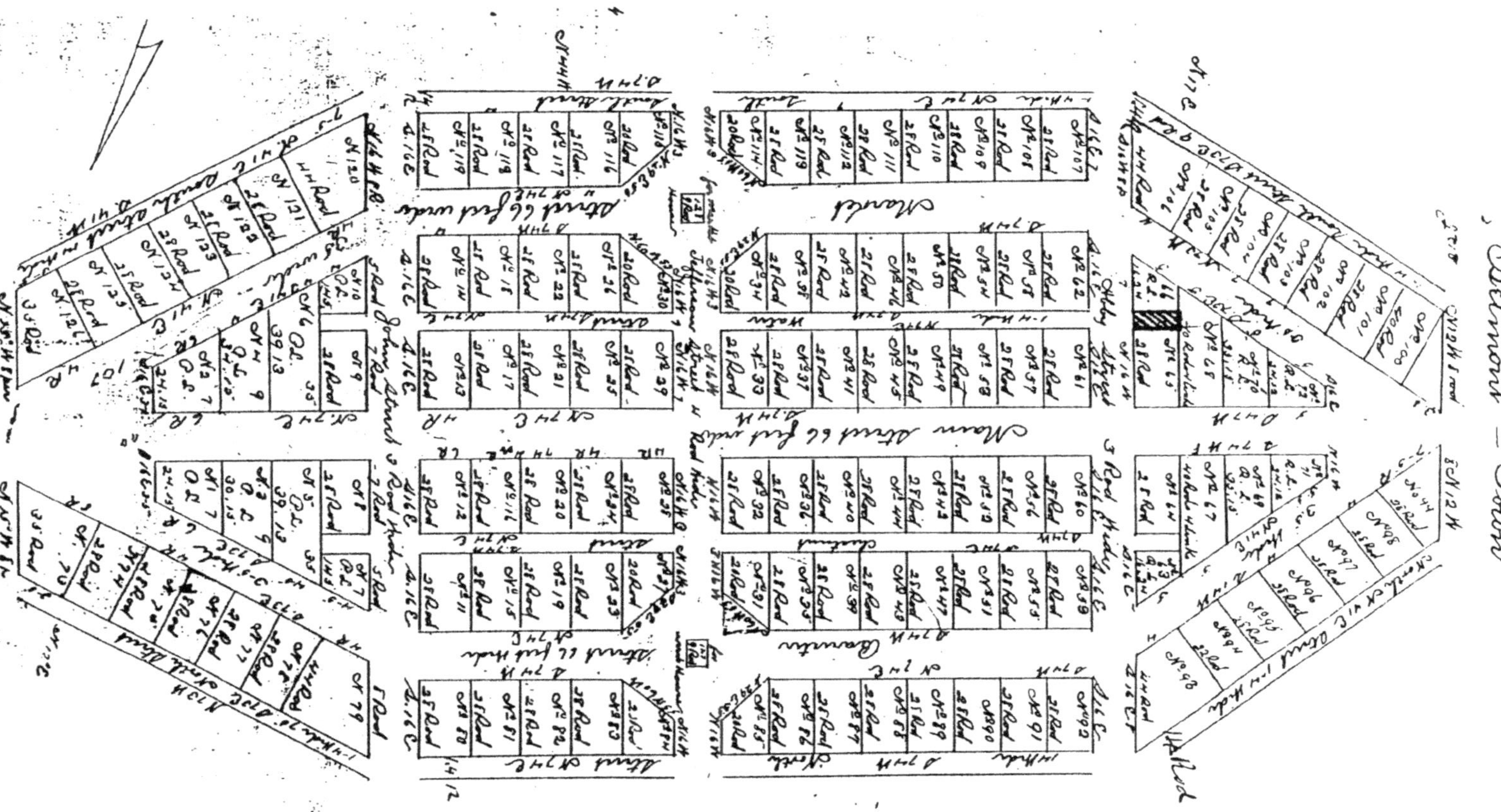

Plat of Belmont (Vol. B, p. 307)

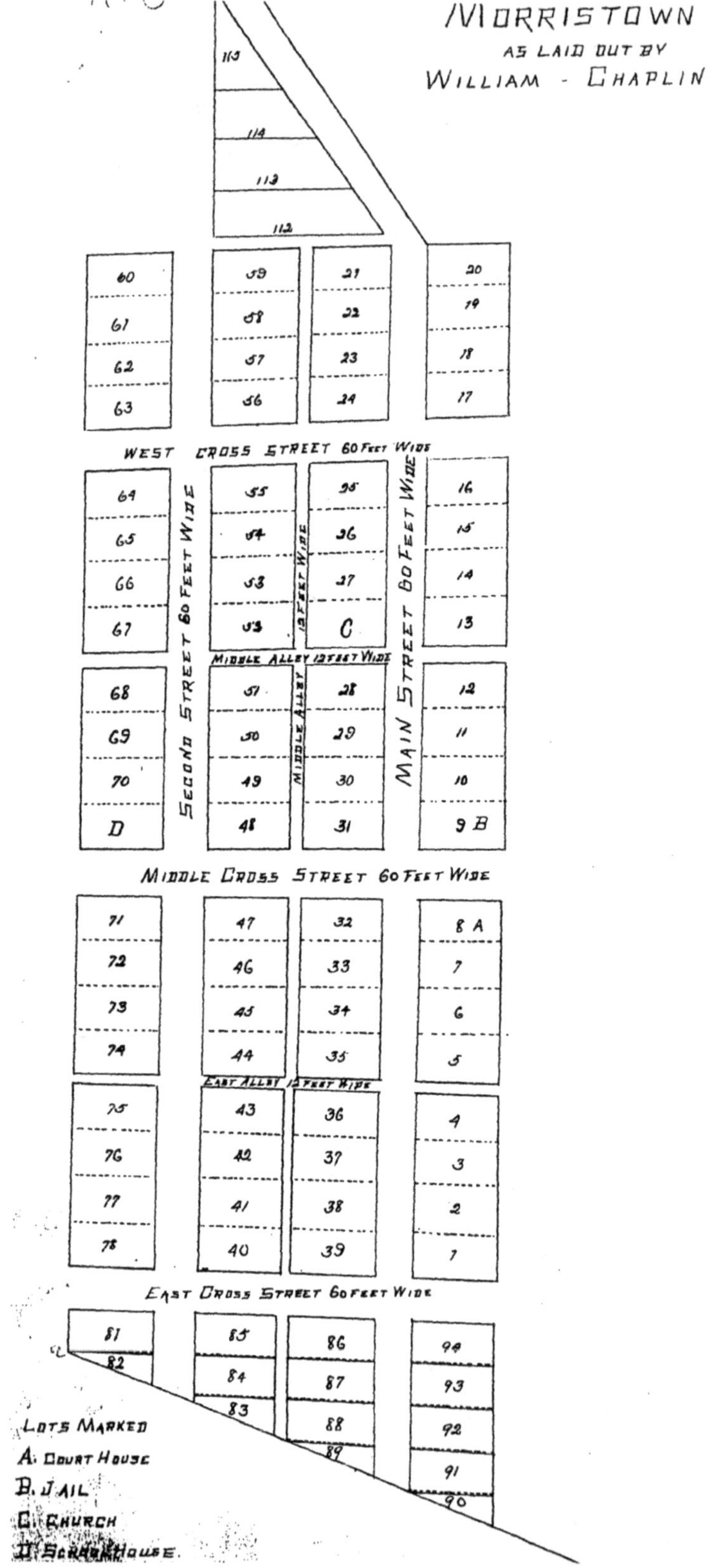

Plat of Morristown (second half) (Vol. B, p. 355)

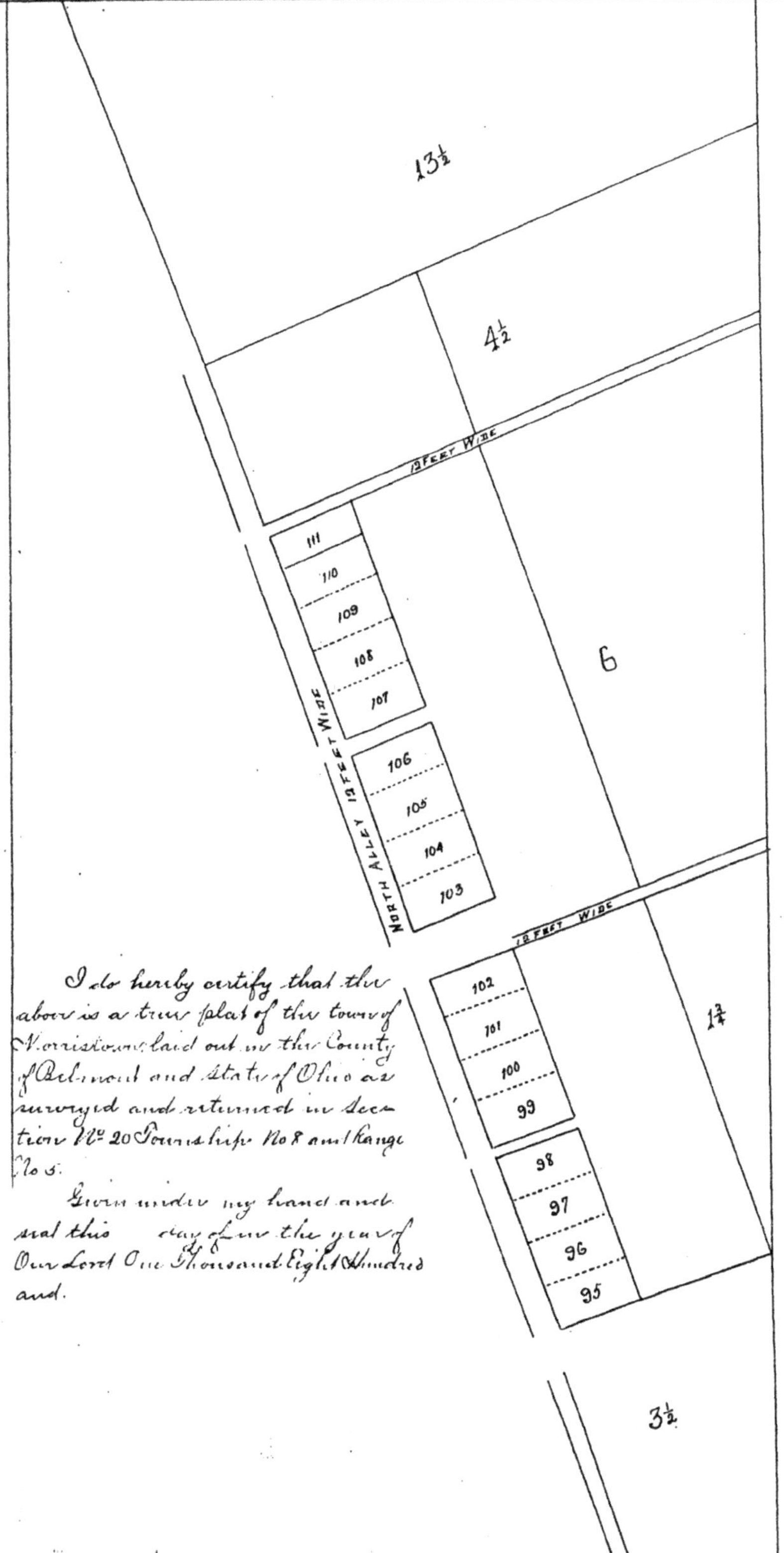

Plat of Morristown (second half) (Vol. B, p. 355)

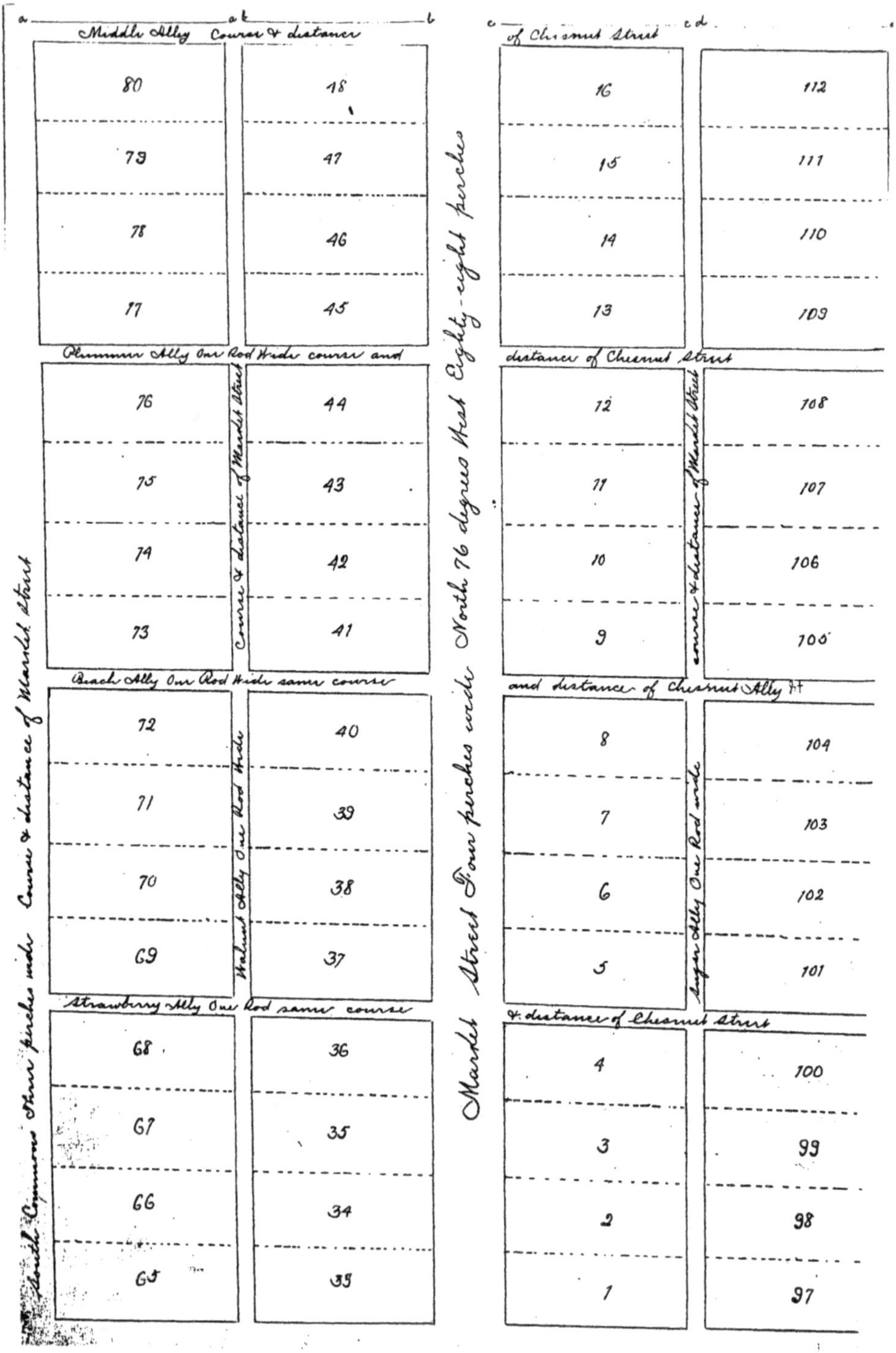

a — a k — b — c — c d

Middle Alley Course & distance of Chesnut Street

80	48	16	112
79	47	15	111
78	46	14	110
77	45	13	109

Plummer Alley One Rod Wide course and distance of Chesnut Street

76	44	12	108
75	43	11	107
74	42	10	106
73	41	9	105

Beach Alley One Rod Wide same course and distance of Chesnut Alley ft

72	40	8	104
71	39	7	103
70	38	6	102
69	37	5	101

Strawberry Alley One Rod same course & distance of Chesnut Street

68	36	4	100
67	35	3	99
66	34	2	98
65	33	1	97

Course & distance of Market Street

Walnut Alley One Rod Wide

Market Street Four perches wide North 76 degrees West Eighty-eight perches

Course & distance of Market Street

Sugar Alley One Rod wide

South Commons Four perches wide Course & distance of Market Street

96 | 64 | 32
95 | 63 | 31
94 | 62 | 30
93 | 61 | 29

Short Ally course of Chesnut Street   35 Rods Long

92 | 60 | 28
91 | 59 | 27
90 | 58 | 26
89 | 57 | 25 | 121

Strawberry Ally One Rod Wide   course & distance of Chesnut Street

88 | 56 | 24 | 120
87 | 55 | 23 | 119
86 | 54 | 22 | 118
85 | 53 | 21 | 117

Chestnut Street 4 Perches Wide   South 76 degrees 46 perches Long

84 | 52 | 20 | 116
83 | 51 | 19 | 115
82 | 50 | 18 | 114
81 | 49 | 17 | 113

[NOTE: To reconstruct these two pages, note the small letters at the bottom of this page's columns and the small letters at the top of the preceding page. Matching these should show the original form of the plat.]

NOTE

An attempt has been made in this index to group names in seeming clusters. However, the reader would be well advised to use extremely liberal rules of interpretation when looking for individuals. Scan the names, pronouncing them to see if the sound matches your name even though the spelling does not.

❦

INDEX OF NAMES